Oil and Development in Venezuela during the 20th Century

Oil and Development in Venezuela during the 20th Century

JORGE SALAZAR-CARRILLO AND
BERNADETTE WEST

PRAEGER

Westport, Connecticut
London

Library of Congress Cataloging-in-Publication Data

Salazar-Carrillo, Jorge.
  Oil and development in Venezuela during the 20th century / Jorge Salazar-
  Carrillo and Bernadette West.
    p. cm.
  Includes bibliographical references (p.) and index.
  ISBN 0–275–97262–3 (alk. paper)
    1. Petroleum industry and trade—Venezuela—History—20th century. 2.
Venezuela—Economic conditions—20th century. 3. Venezuela—Politics and
government—20th century. I. West, Bernadette, 1954–   II. Title.
  HD9574.V42S357 2004
  330.987'063—dc22   2003062252

British Library Cataloguing in Publication Data is available.

Library of Congress Catalog Card Number: 2003062252
ISBN: 0–275–97262–3

First published in 2004

Praeger Publishers, 88 Post Road West, Westport, CT 06881
An imprint of Greenwood Publishing Group, Inc.
www.praeger.com

Printed in the United States of America

Contents

Tables

Acknowledgments

This book was greatly facilitated by the help received in Venezuela from Dr. Antonio Casas González, the recent outgoing president of the Venezuelan Central Bank and former director of Petróleos de Venezuela SA. Within the Banco Central de Venezuela (BCV), Dr. Angelo Lucenti, the head of the research division, provided statistics that were an invaluable aid. Beatriz de Araujo, advisor to the president of the BCV, was also very instrumental as a liaison. At Florida International University, Erick Manuel Pérez was a helpful research assistant. The authors, of course, accept responsibility for any faults or shortcomings that may appear in this volume.

CHAPTER 1

Introduction

SCOPE OF THE STUDY

In explaining the patterns of international trade for different countries, economists have usually relied on the concepts of labor productivity and factor proportions. Such explanations have been challenged by a group of economists who, in turn, point out that labor productivity and factor proportions are themselves a function of the previous pattern of trade and production. Based on this reasoning, the latter group of economists recommended promoting patterns of trade and production that will lead to economic development and, thus, to the desirable factor proportions and labor productivity levels that are now characteristic of more advanced economies.[1] Such a trade and production mix, they believe, would deviate from the dictates of comparative advantage.

It can be argued, however, that many of today's high income per capita countries started out with patterns of trade and production that were no different from what peripheral countries had in the past and still have, in agreement with the comparative advantage rule.[2] Because diverse patterns of trade appear to have been conducive to the economic development of these high income per capita countries and their attainment of desirable levels of labor productivity and factor proportions, would this not also apply to today's developing countries? That is, can a traditional pattern of trade based on primary production for export be conducive to such economic change in peripheral countries?

To answer these questions, the sources of growth in economies characterized by a pattern of trade based on primary exports must be specified.[3] If the dynamic sector in such an economy is either total exports with heavy concentration on primary products or one of a few export-oriented, primary-producing sectors—would this help or hinder the development of the economy?

Many of today's advanced countries developed with a pattern of trade based on primary-type exports, especially after the primary-producing export sector, which constituted their main source of growth, experienced a major expansion in value terms. It could very well be presumed that their past experiences would still apply to developing countries in this century. However, according to the dissident economists mentioned above, this presumption has been proved wrong by the current experiences of the periphery.

These are important issues that are still being debated in the field of trade and development. In fact, Hla Myint referred to them when he stated the following

> The critics start with the intention of showing that the "nineteenth-century pattern" of international trade whereby the underdeveloped countries export raw materials and import manufactured goods, has been unfavorable to the economic development of these countries. But instead of trying to show this directly, they concentrate their attacks on the "classical theory," which they believe to be responsible for the unfavorable pattern of trade. The orthodox economists then come to the defense of the classical theory by reiterating the principle of comparative costs which they claim to be applicable both to the developed and underdeveloped countries. After this, the controversy shifts from the primary question of whether or not the nineteenth-century pattern of international trade, as a historical reality, has been unfavorable to the underdeveloped countries to the different question of whether or not the theoretical model assumed in the comparative costs analysis is applicable to these countries.[4]

As implied in the passage above, these issues should be illuminated by empirical verification. But the issues, as well as the different points of view taken in the debate, also need to be clarified and simplified.[5] One notable effort was Gerald Meier's *The International Economics of Development.*[6] However, even in this text, Meier did not specify the different issues involved or the facets within them; nor when covering different points of view did he appreciate that they sometimes had been formulated with varying degrees of inclusiveness in mind. In fact, Meier himself was not even explicit about the type of countries covered in his survey.

Needless to say, there has been a growing awareness of this murky problem and as a consequence, many new and important contributions have appeared in recent years to help bridge the gaps in our understanding of the relationship between economic development and international trade.

It is hoped that this book will also contribute in some way, by providing a brief but systematic review of these issues within the context of a peripheral country whose pattern of trade and leading sector is based on a primary-type export, which is its main source of growth.[7] Apart from the simplification and clarification of the theoretical issues and the elaboration of an alternative position, this study will be devoted entirely to examining the Venezuelan oil industry as a potential leading sector and main source of growth, and the degree of success it may have had in spreading economic growth to other sectors of the economy.

Venezuela was chosen for several reasons. It has a promising combination of sectoral and aggregate historical data available. Data on the petroleum sector is compiled by the Ministry of Energy and Mines (Ministerio de Energía y Minas, or MEM for short). The oil companies also provide data to the Ministry that would otherwise be unobtainable. Furthermore, the changes in the configuration of the petroleum industry, and in the petroleum policies of the Venezuelan government, can be easily followed. It is possible, therefore, to derive useful conclusions as to the effects that evolving institutional arrangements have had on petroleum's impact upon the economy.

This study does not attempt to examine other export activities or their impact on Venezuela's economic development, nor does it deal with the market structure that characterizes the oil industry.

USEFULNESS OF THE FINDINGS

An examination of these issues could result in new ideas that might possibly alter the economic policy outlook in developing countries. Until recently, many underdeveloped countries have had a bias against primary production and primary exports, due in part to the influence of the interpretation of their economic history by certain economists. As a result, these countries adopted an ill-fated *import-substitution* industrialization program as their development strategy. Import substituting industries topped their investment priority lists, were protected from foreign competition, and overall, were treated very favorably. The same cannot be said of the treatment of industries producing primary goods for export; in fact the reverse was true. Although inconsistent with most of the theoretical ideas that have nurtured the opposition to the production of primary-good exports, this bias adversely effected the production of *all* goods for export, not just primary goods.

The downfall of this strategy of favoring import substituting activities over primary export activities, as practiced in the periphery, Latin America in particular, was that it was allowed to continue for too long. Consequently, inefficient industrial sectors emerged that would never be internationally competitive, and therefore, never be fully able to exploit the promise of economies of scale that the international market offered. What limited industrialization that did take place generated high cost economies and, paradoxically, balance of payment pressures. Imports were not curtailed as expected and exports grew at a snail's pace. Insufficient foreign exchange receipts became the most serious bottleneck to growth, and in some cases forced the development process to a complete standstill. In actuality the problem was much more complicated, as it was also related to monetary, fiscal, and exchange rate policy problems, as was the case in Argentina, Chile, and Uruguay.

In light of this dismal experiment with inward looking, import substitution-led development, most economists are now of a different mind set—coming full circle in their appreciation of the role of trade in the development process. Outward looking, export-led development strategies appear to be in favor again, so the conclusions drawn from this study may well be opportune.

The economic histories of peripheral countries in the 20th century have not been widely researched, and efforts in this area are still in the nascent stage. This book makes an important contribution, as it chronicles Venezuela's economic history by quantifying the development of its petroleum sector and its impact on the rest of the economy. It is hoped that this will provide useful insight for policy makers in this country, and in other oil-producing countries as well.

NOTES

1. Terms such as "advanced" and "advancement" are used here as a convenient abbreviation for relatively high per capita income.

2. The definition of "peripheral countries" used here is that defined by Raul Prebisch in "Commercial Policy in the Underdeveloped Countries."

3. It should be understood that this pattern of trade is compatible with different sources of growth. These could stem from an industrial expansion based on an import-substitution process, an expansion of primary exports, and so forth.

4. Myint, "Classical Theory," p. 137.

5. Myint himself provides an example of the confused state of the literature in this area. In the paragraph above, he fails to distinguish between patterns of trade and sources of growth. It is really the effectiveness of primary activities as a source of growth that is central to the discussion and not the patterns of trade as Myint seems to believe.

6. Meier, *The International Economics of Development.*

7. Of course, the concept of leading sectors or main sources of growth can only be used in an a priori fashion—that is, before examining the evidence, it is only possible to determine if a sector could qualify as a leading sector. Therefore, in a strict sense, these sectors can only be "potential leading sectors." It is only after a detailed empirical inquiry that it can be said whether or not a sector has behaved like a leading sector or a main source of growth.

CHAPTER 2

A Theoretical Framework

INTRODUCTION AND OVERVIEW

The literature on trade and economic development contains a vast, rich collection of theoretical perspectives and points of view that date back to Adam Smith's *Wealth of Nations*, which provides the classic view of trade as a vent-for surplus. Twentieth century economists like Lewis, Myint, Caves, Findlay and Lundahl, and others, have looked to this insightful view to help explain differences in the growth inducing potential of exports in regions of recent settlement like Canada and Australia, and in tropical and/or lesser developed regions like the Caribbean, Asian Pacific, and Latin America.[1]

Although there has been recent interest in the classical or surplus view of trade and development, the overwhelming influence on contemporary work originated with David Ricardo's model of comparative advantage and the Heckscher-Ohlin offshoot of factor proportions that followed. This traditional or neoclassical view remains popular amongst trade and development theorists because of its mathematical sophistication. The main difference between the two views, as first suggested by Myint, is that the classical view assumes labor and other resources are in surplus before the economy opens its doors to trade, and the neoclassical view assumes that these resources are already fully employed.[2] Despite this difference, both views support the notion of positive gains from trade—the gains are presumed to be greater under the former than the latter.

In contrast, researchers like P. Baran, Gunder Frank, and Evans adopted a radical approach to trade turning to the Dependencia School for inspiration, and developing theories based on the machinations of a dominant center vis-a-vis a weak periphery.[3] According to this alternative view of trade, "surplus generated at each stage is successively drawn off toward the center."[4] The issue from this perspective is not the degree or magnitude of the gains from trade, but rather the distribution of these gains, if in fact they exist.

Many syntheses and variations on these themes have emerged in recent years. Despite these different approaches, the main thrust of this research deals with the prospects for economic growth under varying patterns of trade and varying potential leading sectors. This study also pursues this line of inquiry for a very specific case, Venezuela, where (1) the potential leading sector produces primary products, (2) the pattern of trade is based on the export of these primary products, and (3) the exporter is a peripheral country. In order to examine the possibility of economic growth under these circumstances, a testable model is needed that can explain the events of the past and will be useful in formulating present economic policy.

The spread of the industrial revolution in England and across Europe and North America helped to bring about the relatively high per capita income levels these regions now enjoy. International trade and related international factor movements played an important role in this success. In fact, international contact seems to have been an important mechanism through which economic growth was transmitted between regions. The development process that unfolded over the centuries was one that depended heavily on exports for growth, and in particular, on exports of primary goods.

Unfortunately, many of the peripheral countries today have yet to achieve similar results, even though their export sectors have expanded quite significantly.[5] Many explanations for this failure have been proposed. For example, Prebisch blamed it in on a long-run tendency toward unfavorable terms of trade for primary exports; Corden and Neary with respect to resource abundant countries—blamed it on the spending, relative price, and resource effects that accompany the Dutch Disease Syndrome; Gelb with respect to oil exporting countries—on too much domestic investment in the oil sector and insufficient accumulation of foreign assets; Duncan—on government policy failures; Rodriguez and Sachs in a study specific to Venezuela—on misguided consumption of windfall revenues; Auty—on the structure of society itself; and Lal and Myint—on the relatively higher wages in the manufacturing sectors of resource abundant countries that waited too long to industrialize.[6] This is just a small sample of the many different explanations for why peripheral countries, in general and in specific, failed to grow and develop through trade in this century. Though all have merit, the explanations that are particularly enlightening from our standpoint attribute the failure of export-led development to either (1) a failure in transmitting the export expansion to the rest of the economy a la Baldwin and/or (2) a failure to adjust to changing circumstances in international markets, despite a carry-over that did produce economic growth during these periods.[7] This study concentrates primarily on the validity of the first explanation, although its conclusions also have some bearing on the second.

DIFFERENT VIEWS ON TRADE AND DEVELOPMENT

The Classical/Neoclassical View

The essence of the classical and neoclassical view is reflected in this often quoted passage from D. H. Robertson: "The specializations of the nine-teenth century were not simply a device for using to the greatest effect the labors of a given number of human beings; they were above all an engine of growth."[8] For economists who share this vision, there is no incompati-bility between the gains from trade and the gains from growth. According to Myint, even the productivity doctrine is a concrete expression of this view because international trade is seen as a dynamic force that, by widen-ing the extent of the market and the scope of division of labor, raises the skill and dexterity of the workmen, encourages technical innovations, overcomes technical indivisibilities, and generally enables the trading countries to enjoy increasing returns and economic development.[9]

For others, like John Stuart Mill, there are also important indirect bene-fits in specialization, such as the tendency of every market extension to improve the process of production. Producing for an external market, as Mill argued, fosters a greater use of machinery and encourages technolog-ical innovation in the production process.[10]

Additionally, the expansion of trade is also seen as an aid to economic development through what Gerald Meier calls "the education effect." Classical and neoclassical economists were well aware of the importance of this effect, which includes incentives for production resulting from the desired consumption of imported goods—to the transmission of skills, knowledge, know-how, and technology.

Finally, classical and neoclassical economists maintain that trade expan-sion based on comparative advantage brings about a more efficient allo-cation of resources. This efficiency is tied to higher real incomes in the present and the potential for greater savings capacity in the future, where the contribution of greater savings to economic development can be con-siderable.

This, in essence, constitutes the classical and neoclassical view of trade and development. A corollary that follows is "if trade increases the capac-ity for development, then the greater the volume of trade, the greater should be the potential for development."[11] Or, in other words, the bigger the increments in trade, the faster the economy grows. Therefore it also follows, using the present-day terminology of leading sectors, that every country should grow as a result of an expansion in the value of one or more export lines, or in the value of exports as a whole, no matter what the pattern of trade or types of products exported.

Development Economist's View

After World War II, developed nations' interest in the economic progress of lesser developed countries mounted and a new field of economics emerged to deal specifically with the problems these countries faced. One of the main issues examined extensively was the connection between international trade and economic development. Surprisingly, the conclusions drawn by some of the prominent researchers of that day clashed sharply with the more widely held beliefs of the classical and neo-classical economists.

In particular, researchers like Singer, Prebisch, Baldwin, Myint, and more recently, Lal and Myint were finding that not all types of potential leading sectors were equally successful in spreading their expansion to the rest of the economy, at least that was the case for land and resource abundant countries in the periphery that specialized in primary exports.[12] Consequently, primary export lines were singled out as activities that *should not* be relied upon as the main potential source of growth in an economic development drive. Although other export lines were not explicitly included in the same category, the general line of reasoning implied a tighter economic policy, where any type of export would play only a secondary role.

These researchers blamed the failure of the transmission mechanism on a variety of factors related to the export of primary products. For Prebisch, it was the long-run pattern of the terms of trade in peripheral countries.[13] He and others maintained that the actual operation of the terms of trade, by sapping the purchasing power of a unit volume of traditional primary exports from these countries, was unfavorably biased toward the peripheral countries. After careful consideration, however, the force of this argument is mainly lost when the export expansion is expressed in real terms, as any deterioration in export prices would automatically deflate it. If such an expansion is accompanied by a disappointing performance in terms of value, vis-a-vis imports, what may basically be at fault is the mechanism of adjustment in the economy, and not the particular export line. That is, the economy may be failing to heed the price signals it is receiving. Furthermore, if the cost of producing the exported product is lowered at the same time—if the single factorial terms of trade do not deteriorate—then the situation cannot be considered harmful.

Others, like Corden and Neary, attributed the problem to an unfavorable inflow of factors into the periphery and to asymmetric and/or inflexible factor mobility between sectors within the periphery.[14] Because most factor inflows were supposed to have resulted from the needs of the primary export sector, the importation of labor that occurred dampened possible wage increases and the creation of labor skills, and this in turn slowed the adoption of modern techniques.[15]

Singer hypothesized that the transmission mechanism failed because the export production in the periphery was often organized like an enclave, with more external contacts than domestic ones. The skills and techniques required within this production environment were implanted, and thus, were not able to spread to the rest of the economy. Such enclaves, which were largely foreign-owned, frequently held monopsony power in factor markets, such as labor, and monopoly power in the product markets of the goods they produced and sold within the economy. Because of their powerful influence over these markets they, in effect, discouraged economic development. No incentives were provided for the accumulation of capital or for the implementation of more advanced techniques, nor were enclaves helpful in financing other sectors of the domestic economy. Foreign investment, for the most part, was earmarked toward developing "only the country's natural resources for export, to the neglect of production in the domestic sector."[16]

These enclaves created by foreign investment also gave rise to dual economies characterized by a lopsided economic structure. This duality was not only economically inefficient, but inimical to the progress and development of the backward sectors, which were disproportionately large in the periphery, mainly because the factor combinations typical of the modern sector did not generate adequate demand for the plentiful labor in the backward sector.

And finally, there were very few spillover effects emitted from these enclaves because of their limited interaction with the rest of society. Thus the stimulating income effects that would otherwise be forthcoming were lost via disproportionate leakages.

The logical conclusion was that primary production for export in peripheral countries should not be relied upon to ignite the development process in the rest of the economy.[17] If export activities are in the hands of domestic capitalists the situation may improve somewhat, but only to a small extent because many of the characteristics described above are equally applicable.

Besides the creation of enclaves, another contributing factor that is mentioned frequently in the literature is the harmful operation of the international demonstration effect that supposedly puts pressure on the balance of payments and hampers the attainment of an adequate savings ratio— through high import propensities to consume and to import. This results from the indiscriminately open character of a less developed country that is integrated in the international economy through its primary product exports and desires to imitate the consumption habits and patterns of the more advanced economies with which it comes in contact.[18]

These arguments are a condensed and unified expression of the development economist's position with respect to trade and development. Though not all economists in this field use these same arguments, or use them with the same intended slant, the doctrine of enclave or dualistic development in particular, stands on its own as an anonymous expression of the ideas of many economists from developing countries today.

As suggested above, there are alternate positions within this field that are important enough to merit attention. For example, Myrdal refers to a cumulative mechanism of causation, where international trade is just such a mechanism. By the operation of this mechanism, underdeveloped countries are led to stagnation or impoverishment and developed countries to automatic cumulative growth. The idea here is that international trade and the contacts evolving from it have favorable and unfavorable effects on developing economies. However, the favorable ones, or spread effects, are weaker than the unfavorable ones, or backwash effects. As long as the mechanism of causation continues to be weighted in this fashion, the outcome of international contacts will be cumulative impoverishment or stagnation of the poor countries. Furthermore, according to Myrdal, there is no force inherent in this mechanism that could break its ill-fated operation.[19]

The spread effects mainly consist of expanding external demand for the traditional products of the developing countries. The most important backwash effects are those arising from the adverse impact of the factor movements discussed above: (1) the perverse movements of the most efficient facts of production from the backward countries to the advanced nations; (2) the higher rates of population growth, which characterize the poorer nations after international contacts have been established; (3) the inferior capabilities of the developing nations for building an infrastructure to compensate for the lack of investment incentives resulting from their relatively unfavorable economic conditions; and (4) the weakening of the local productive structure catering to the domestic market due to the competition of cheaper imports from the advanced nations.

Another alternate viewpoint is found in Singer who suggests promoting domestic industry rather than primary production for export, because the former is more effective in promoting economic progress in the periphery due to its intrinsic characteristics, which are not shared by the latter. "Industrial endeavors are capable of being growing points for increased technical knowledge, urban education, the dynamism and resilience that goes with urban civilization, as well as the direct Marshallian external economies."[20] Singer recognizes that under different circumstances commerce, farming, and plantation agriculture have proved capable of being such "growing points." Nevertheless, he concludes that, for the underdeveloped countries, investment in these traditional lines has been incapable of generating domestic development.[21]

Singer also contends that the effects of cyclical changes in the terms of trade of primary producers discourage investment in sectors other than the export sector, and have been unfavorable to these countries. When export prices are high there are no incentives to invest in other sectors, even though funds are available. When prices are low, the incentives for the diversification of investments are there, but no funds are available.

Albert Hirschman provides yet another viewpoint. He believes that "agriculture certainly stands convicted on the count of its lack of direct stimulus to the setting up of new activities through linkage effects.... This may yet be the most important reason militating against any complete specialization of underdeveloped countries in primary production."[22]

In short, the development economists surveyed here concluded that a primary product export sector, or a particular line within that sector, could not fulfill the role of a leading sector—even if potentially qualified—if it is a peripheral country with a pattern of trade based on raw material exports.

International Trade Theorist's Views: A Reaffirmation of the Classical/Neoclassical View

The pessimistic view of trade held by development economists did not go unchallenged. Instead, it rallied many economists, particularly international trade specialists, to construct modern versions and variations of the classical/neoclassical themes that expounded the role of trade in the development process. Some early champions of the cause, Gottfried Haberler, Hla Myint, Alec Cairncross, and Peter Bauer, among others, maintained that trade can, and indeed does, promote growth in the rest of the economy. The expansion of trade in any type of product generates spillover effects that have a favorable impact on other sectors of the economy by inciting and leading their expansions.

Cairncross's statements can be considered representative of the group: "I confess to some skepticism about the supposed ineffectiveness of foreign trade in producing innovation and development. It does not strike me as entirely plausible to speak as if foreign trade could be contained within an enclave without transmitting its dynamic influences to the rest of the economy."[23]

Myint's, Haberler's, and Cairncross's arguments in favor of trade went beyond the static gains.[24] They believed there were also important indirect benefits that were dynamic in nature. For example, the educative effects of trade were viewed as the one of the most important vehicles for transmitting aspirations, skills, and technological know-how. So important were these effects, as well as other dynamic aspects of trade, that Haberler boldly concludes that international trade has made a tremendous contribution to the development of less developed countries in the 19th and 20th centuries and can be expected to make an equally big contribution in the future, if it is allowed to proceed freely.[25]

But how does trade's alleged positive influence on economic development operate? Haberler stresses first that trade provides material means (capital goods, machinery, and raw or semifinished materials) indispensable for economic development. Second, and even more important, that trade is the means and vehicle for the dissemination of know-how, skills, managerial talent, and entrepreneurship—the educative effects. Third, that trade is also the vehicle for the international movement of capital, especially from developed to underdeveloped countries. And fourth, that free international trade is the best antimonopoly policy and the best guarantee for the maintenance of a healthy degree of free competition.[26]

Bauer completes the argument with the following observation: "But is it not the case that now, as in the past, the most advanced of the underdeveloped regions and sectors are those in contact with developed countries?"[27]

As noted earlier, since these economists based their new and improved models on classical/neoclassical themes, it is not surprising that their conclusions reaffirmed the view of trade that their predecessors arrived at more than a century ago.

Staple and Export Base Theory

At the same time, a separate group of economists and economic historians (Innis, Meier, Caves and Holton, and Watkins)[28] had sought inspiration elsewhere—in the history and economic evolution of Canada. What emerged from their research has come to be known as the *staple approach* and it represents a new school of thought based on a unique interpretation of Canada's economic history. This approach has been used to examine the economic history of other countries as well, such as the United States in postcolonial times (North), Argentina in the late 19th century, and the Great Depression (Diaz-Alejandro and Cortés Condé), to name a few.[29]

The staple approach had its origins in the early work of Harold A. Innis,[30] but Chambers and Gordon are credited with being the first to formalize it.[31] The idea behind this approach, a la Watkins, is that a staple product (or products) serves as the main driving force (or leading sector) in the economic development process.[32] A staple is defined as a "product with a large natural resource content" that caters mainly to the external market.[33] Accordingly, these products, depending upon their particular characteristics, have diverse effects on the growth of an economy. This is because the combination of inputs used in the production process, the resultant income distribution, the sociological aspects of the productive organization, and the technological requirements vary from product to product. Hence, the impact of a particular line on the economy of a country will be more or less successful, depending on how effective its characteristics are for the transmission of growth to other sectors.

The staple approach concentrates on the direct contribution to the rest of the economy of the production aspects of primary goods for export. This stands in contrast to the position of the classical and neoclassical economists and their contemporary followers, which stresses the indirect benefits of trade.

Because of this concentration on the direct contribution, it has been suggested that the staple approach is a theory of induced capital formation. The purchase of local goods and services provides inducements to investment in the domestic supply activities. The same holds true for industries using the staple product as an input via the forward linking output of the staple industry. An estimate of its backward and forward linkages would then represent an approximate measure of the inducement to invest provided by the staple activity. There are also inducements to invest, operating via the income originated in the staple industry, which affect the industries catering to the domestic market.

Proponents of the staple approach provide an optimistic viewpoint on the reliability of primary products as leading sectors in the economic development of peripheral countries. In this respect, their position is in agreement with the thoughts of the classical and neoclassical economists and with the ideas expressed by their followers. They have added a word of caution, however, pointing out that primary products differ in their growth-promoting characteristics. For example, Baldwin showed that staples like sugar and cotton in the United States created linkages that were unfavorable to growth because they combined capital-intensive production with cheap labor. He believed that the characteristics of the export products determine if the carryover is successful or not.[34]

Export base theory, a similar theory to staple, has long been used by regional economists to explain differential growth potential across regions and sectors based on linkage analysis and trade multipliers.[35] This approach has also been extended to analyze the potential of export-led growth in many countries in the periphery with relatively have high foreign trade ratios.

According to this theory, the economic or *export base* of a region is defined as consisting of those industries that are principally engaged in producing products for export from that region to another region. An empirical multiplier is then estimated on the basis of an historical relationship between the export base activity and the overall economic activity of the region. On occasion, the economic or export base is taken as the whole export sector, with the multiplier redefined accordingly.

There are several minor differences between staple and export base theory. Staple theory concentrates on one or a few important export lines.

Export base theory includes all the industries mainly producing for export or, sometimes, the export sector as a whole. In cases where there is a high degree of concentration in a particular export line, the difference between the two perspectives disappears almost completely.

In this sense, the staple approach provides a more in-depth analysis of an export lines' growth-inducing potential. Not only does it go beneath the total incomes and expenditures originating from the production activity associated with the export line (or lines), but it also considers all other growth-promoting forces emanating from the staple. On the other hand, the export base concentrates on autonomous income effects and multiplier relationships, considering also nonprimary lines.

Douglas North achieved a very fruitful blend of both approaches in his analysis of the agricultural sector and the historical growth of the U.S. economy.[36] By meshing these two models, he was able to discern that the carryover from export base activities to the rest of the economy has usually been successful. However, when the export base is composed of one or a few agricultural products, and their characteristics do not favor the expansion of the domestic economy or the diversification of the export sector, this does not happen. On the other hand, if the export base is diversified, then its expansion succeeds in being transmitted to the other sectors of the economy.

In sum, staple theory economists believe that expanding primary product lines can successfully lead the economic development process in peripheral countries; however, the degree of success depends on the particular line or lines. Certain regional economists believe that an export base composed of primary products promotes growth in the rest of the economy in peripheral countries that have relatively high foreign-trade ratios. North mixes these two approaches in developing the hypothesis that only if the primary export sector is diversified or if it comprises a primary product line or lines with certain growth-promoting characteristics will its expansion successfully carry over into the other sectors of the economy.

The Views of Economic Historians

Economic historians do not have a unified position regarding the interpretation of the historical facts related to the economic growth potential of primary-based exports. Some recognize the strategic role that the expansion of primary exports have had on the economic growth of today's most advanced economies. In many cases, the contribution of primary product exports successfully acted as the main source of growth during the crucial preconditions and takeoff stages. As Cairncross has said, "whether one thinks of Britain at the outset of the industrial revolution or of the United States in the nineteenth century or of Japan in the twentieth, the expansion of exports gave a conspicuous momentum to the economy and helped it on its way to industrialization."[37]

But economic historians have also pointed out that distinctions must be drawn between different types of economies. A primary export expansion in the economies of the Old World with their centuries of evolution, and in some economies of the East with developed internal markets, is one thing; but quite another is the expansion of primary exports in the regions of recent settlement and in the peripheral countries. For the latter, there are greater facilities for external rather than for internal trade, with specialization between countries evolving before that between regions within a country. As a result, potential favorable repercussions are inhibited, and the effects of increasing exports do not spread with ease to the rest of the economy.

In contrast, there are economic historians who are of the opinion that no distinction should be made as to the type of economy under consideration. They believe that an expansion in primary export lines will lead to economic growth, irrespective of their economic history and evolution. That the impact has been favorable for the regions of recent settlement cannot be denied. These regions had as a common characteristic the "dependence on growth through primary product exports and on the private foreign investment which, directly or indirectly, was thereby induced."[38] Can the same thing be said of the countries in the periphery? According to the first group (the evolutionists), the answer is a resounding no.

The Meier Hypothesis

Gerald Meier examined the issues explored in this chapter extensively and arrived at some conclusions that differed significantly from those mentioned above.[39] His observations stem from having carefully considered the past experiences of countries in the periphery that have expanded their export sector—or one facet of it, or a few lines of it—and the impact that this has had on the rest of the economy. And though he fails to specify the types of exports to which he refers, the implication seems to be that they are of the primary variety.

In his hypothesis, he combines two main streams of thought. One that follows the line of staple theory, where the export product in question is assumed to contribute significantly to the economic development of the rest of the economy. The other considers the importance of socio-cultural factors and market imperfections as general prerequisites or preconditions to sustained growth.

Meier believes that the transmission mechanism fails to operate in peripheral countries because of "the differential effects of different exports, and ... the domestic market conditions of the poor country."[40] The extent of the carryover from the expansion in external demand varies with the characteristics of the product or products involved. As these differ not only for primary, secondary, and tertiary production but also among primary products, it follows that the success or failure in the transmission of growth varies with the particular product spearheading the export drive. Therefore, the blanket condemnation of trade via exports of primary products is not warranted. Neither is the indiscriminate position that considers all types of export production capable of promoting a successful development drive.

This could partially explain the contrasting experiences that the advanced nations and the peripheral countries have had in export-led development. There are important differences in the characteristics of the primary export products of the latter and those that were important for the development of a number of countries in the former group. For example, the production function of plantation crops in the tropics has relatively weak growth-promoting effect, and this could determine an unsuccessful carryover from expanding exports.

Up to this point, Meier's position appears akin to Baldwin's and is similar to the ideas of North. But then comes the second portion of this thesis, which is really the crucial part of the explanation. It considers why even products with characteristics amenable to a successful carryover into the other sectors will fail to get the peripheral countries moving.

Clearly, differences in the growth-promoting characteristics of the products are not the complete explanation, for countries exporting the same type of primary products have differed in the results obtained from the expected stimulation via exports. Some other factor has to determine such differences.

Meier gives a lucid description of domestic impediments as obstacles to the spillover of primary export expansions into the rest of the economy:

In connection with these domestic impediments, we can recognize that the pervasiveness of market imperfections has severely limited the carry-over from exports. The economies of poor countries are characterized by factor immobility, price rigidity, restrictive tendencies in both the factor and goods markets, ignorance of technological possibilities, limited knowledge of market conditions, and few centers of entrepreneurship.... Many of these inhibiting factors are a function of socio-cultural customs and institutions.... In terms of Rostow's scheme, the failure of the export sector to have been a primary growth sector, setting in motion expansionary forces elsewhere in the economy, may be attributed in large part to the absence of the pre-conditions necessary for the takeoff into self sustained growth.[41]

Meier constructs his hypothesis in such a way that the presence of domestic impediments end up overshadowing the effects of the export product, so that the domestic impediments become the sole explanation for this failure. This is clearly seen in the passage below:

When intersectoral relationships are many and the response to an expansion in exports is rapid and extensive in scope, then even a weak stimulus can still result in a significant carry-over. In contrast, when there are formidable domestic impediments to a transmission of the gains from exports to other sectors, then even a strong stimulus will have only slight penetrative powers.[42]

In conclusion, Meier maintains that if, as he believes happened in the past, expansion in a primary producing export sector, or in one or a few primary product lines within this sector, fails to bring about economic growth in a peripheral country, it is because of the following: (1) weak spillover effects from the external expansion, as a consequence of the characteristics of the product or products involved, and (2) domestic impediments, which inhibit the operation of the transmission mechanism. The latter he regards as the decisive factor.

A Brief Summation

Some of the hypotheses considered were formulated to cover all possible cases involving the relation of an external demand expansion with the internal growth of an economy. Others were limited to an examination of a subset of such cases. However, all these ideas are of interest, inasmuch as they apply to the case of primary production for export in peripheral countries, with patterns of trade based on primary exports.

It should be stressed that only the potentially successful expansions of primary product exports are being dealt with here. If the expanding sector could not potentially lead a growth process, then there is no point in considering the question of its success or failure in transmitting this expansion to other sectors. As noted in Chapter 1, for a primary product export sector or line to be considered as potentially leading, it must have a certain size as well as a significant rate of expansion.

The different positions examined concerning the success or failure of a transmission of an export expansion by a potentially leading primary sector or line, in peripheral countries with a pattern of trade based on primary product exports, can be summarized as follows:

1. Classical and neoclassical economists, and their present-day followers, take an affirmative position.

2. As a reaction to such views, development economists (Myrdal, Singer, and so forth) take a negative position.

3. Staple approach economists, as well as most regional economists, have a positive view overall, with the former stressing that the degree of effectiveness in the transmission mechanism depends on the characteristics of the product.

4. North, although having a generally affirmative position considers that, lacking a diversification of the export base, the characteristics of certain products

would determine the failure of the transmission mechanism. Baldwin would agree only with the latter part of this proposition.

5. Meier agrees with North and Baldwin as to the importance of product characteristics in determining the success or failure of the expansion of a potentially leading primary sector. However, he goes further, believing that even when those characteristics are favorable, a potentially leading primary export sector would not be able to lead the development of the rest of the economy if basic obstacles to growth, such as market imperfections and lack of adequate socioeconomic institutions, are present.

AN ALTERNATIVE HYPOTHESIS

Imagine a peripheral country that engages in trade. It exports primary products and imports mostly manufactures. Exports are concentrated, with one line constituting a significant percentage of the total. The value of exports in this main line shows an expanding trend over the long run. This expansion is not neutralized by contractions in other export lines or other autonomous sectors of the economy. Such main export activity is the principal potential source of growth in the economy. Which factors then, are important in determining the success or failure of the main export line in transmitting its growth to the rest of the economy and, therefore, its success or failure as a leading sector?

There are four main factors determining such performance: (1) the size of the expanding primary export line relative to the economy as a whole, (2) its rate of expansion, (3) its direct and indirect contribution to the development of the other sectors of the economy, and (4) the effectiveness with which this contribution is used. As pointed out above, only the cases of the expanding export lines that can qualify as potential leading sectors are being considered in this study—meaning those that have a rate of expansion and relative size that permit a successful carryover. Thus, under these conditions, the success or failure of a carryover will depend on the other two facts specified.

The direct contribution stems from the income and expenditures originating in the potential leading primary export line. In particular, it stems from the multiplicative and accelerative effects of its increments. These run their course through the income-product flow matrix of the economy through successive spending rounds. The direct contribution also includes: (1) the backward and forward effective linkages of the industry; (2) the external economies created; (3) the impact of its investment expenditures in the native capital goods producing sector; (4) the distribution of the income originated in the export activity, and the pattern of demand related to it; (5) the level of technology and skills, and their transfer to other sectors; and (6) the opportunities for factor substitution in the industry, to adapt to the economy's resource composition.

The indirect contribution includes the favorable forces stemming from the expanding line, which affects the rest of the economy in a more general and removed way. These include: (1) the participation of the industry in total public revenues and foreign exchange proceeds and their effects on growth, inflation, availability, mobility, flexibility, and economic efficiency; (2) the improvement in the process of production in the economy as a result of efficient specialization and trade; and (3) the greater savings made possible by the higher real income resulting from a more efficient use of resources.

The effect that these variables have on the total economy of the peripheral country depends on how they are used. In certain cases, government policy directly determines their use, as in the contribution to public revenues. In other instances, government policy measures only determine their utilization indirectly, as in the case of the foreign exchange proceeds deriving from the potential leading sector.

But the extent to which a sector contributes to growth and efficiency in the rest of the economy also depends on its negative effects. The final contribution is actually determined by the extent to which the positive contribution compensates for these negative effects. These negative elements are the following: the unfavorable demonstration effects that result from external contacts; the resulting short-run increase in population growth; external diseconomies; and the monopsony-monopoly market environment as well as other enclave characteristics that are sometimes present in primary export lines.

Many of the positive contributions are closely related to the concepts of value added, value of production, investment, and value of exports in the line. Taken collectively, they represent the broader concept of total expenditures in the particular export line. At first glance it might appear that the total expenditures of a potential leading sector could be used as an appropriate indicator of its total combined positive contribution. However, a portion of this total does not affect other domestic industries or resident factors of production. For example, the rest of the economy does not have access to all the foreign exchange earnings of the potential leading sector as some of this will be used for its own purposes. What is left, after extricating the foreign component, constitutes the portion through which the impact on the rest of the economy takes place.[43] This contribution is measured by the retained value of the sector's total expenditures and is representative of the value actually retained by the economy.

Although the total retained value can be a simple and summarized representation of the total combined positive contribution, the relationship between the two is not that straightforward, nor is it stable. In order to grasp the spread effects in their entirety, a much more detailed and complicated examination of each of the factors involved would be required. Nevertheless, variations in the retained value concept reflect quite accurately the change in some of the most important contributions of the industry, such as the domestic income and expenditures it generates, investment, and exports. Thus, as total retained value is a sufficiently close, convenient, first-hand approximation of the total combined positive contribution of a sector to the growth of the rest of the economy, the complexity of an elaborate measurement probably is not worth the improvement in precision that would be obtained.

What consequences can be expected for the peripheral economy if a potential leading primary export sector experiences a long-term expansion in its total retained value? The direct and indirect favorable influences discussed above will constitute positive forces acting for the development of the rest of the economy. Undoubtedly, however, there will be unfavorable factors working in the opposite direction. Our hypothesis is that the positive contributions will *generally* overshadow the negative effects of a primary export expansion. Thus, a potential leading export sector of the primary type will *usually* be successful in inducing growth in the rest of the economy, regardless of the type of primary product. Yet, it is believed that the characteristics of the different products will make some export lines more successful than others in the role of a leading sector. Moreover, an expansion in the total retained value of the export line should get the rest of the economy moving, no matter what the country's stage of development. No obstacles should be strong enough to neutralize the operation of the transmission mechanism from a potential leading primary export line—barring counteracting movements in other autonomous economic variables or abnormal conditions.

In some cases, expansion in the total retained value of a potential leading export sector of the primary type may not automatically spread to the other sectors of the economy. (This is why the statements above have been qualified.) This might take place if the positive contributions of a primary export line are not adequately utilized or if the negative effects are not appropriately neutralized. In these cases the automatic operation of the transmission mechanism could not by itself be expected to ensure the growth of the rest of the economy. Thus, an effective utilization of the sector's contributions and a minimization of its drawbacks through government policy might be required for a successful development process to catch on. Efficient use of the public revenues and foreign exchange earnings contributed by the sector, coordination of public investment policies with investment expenditures in the industry, effective taxation of the income it generates—these would be some of the appropriate policies that would need to be instituted to ensure a more successful transmission of the export expansion into the other sectors of the economy.

In conclusion, it is believed that expansion in a primary export line as described above can lead the rest of the economy into a process of development; in some cases, though, the transmission mechanism will not be automatic and would necessitate the implementation of appropriate government policies. This result should be obtained regardless of the type of primary product involved and the economic stage of the country in question. In fact, depending on how prolonged the export expansion is in a particular line, the country might move to the preconditions stage, grow through this period, and eventually move into the takeoff stage. Or the growth could occur during the takeoff stage and continue onward, while self-sustaining growth was being consolidated.

It is believed that, if the historical experience of peripheral countries is examined more carefully, it will be found that export expansions, while they lasted, usually led to growth in the rest of the economy, and thus, to economic development. When this did not happen, it probably was due to the absence or inappropriateness of government policies at the time (see Auty and Gelb, and Rodriguez and Sachs).[44]

The hypothesis disclosed here deals with a primary-producing export line as a potential leading sector. Nevertheless, the same proposition would hold for the case where two or more primary export lines were combined. These ideas would obviously hold a fortiori if the exports were industrial goods.

NOTES

1. See Lewis, "Economic Development"; Myint, "Classical Theory"; Caves "Vent-for-Surplus"; Findlay and Lundah, "Natural Resources." For a concise survey of "vent-for-surplus" research see Findlay and Lundah, "Natural Resources," pp. 68–70.

2. See Myint, "Classical Theory."

3. See Baran, *The Political Economy of Growth;* Gunder Frank, *Capitalism and Underdevelopment;* Evans, "Alternative Perspectives."

4. See Meier, *Classical Economics,* pp. 178–79 and fn. 14, p. 192.

5. All of this is generally presumed to be an approximation of what actually occurred. See Meier, *The International Economics of Development,* and Baldwin, *Economic Development and Growth,* as two examples.

6. See Prebisch, *Principle Problems;* Corden and Neary, "Dutch Disease Economics"; Gelb, "Adjustment to Windfall Gains"; Duncan, "Sub-Saharan Africa"; Rodriguez and Sachs, "Resource Abundant Economies"; Auty, *Patterns of Development;* Lal and Myint, *Political Economy of Poverty.*

7. See Baldwin, "Patterns of Settlement."

8. See Robertson, "The Future of International Trade," p. 501.

9. See Myint, "Classical Theory," pp. 318–19.

10. John Stuart Mill, *Principles of Political Economy,* p. 581.

11. See Meier, *The International Economics of Development,* p. 222.

12. See Singer, "Distribution of Gains"; Prebisch, *Principle Problems;* Baldwin, *Economic Development and Growth;* Baldwin, "Export Technology"; Baldwin, "Patterns of Settlement"; Myint, "Classical Theory"; Lal and Myint, *Political Economy of Poverty.*

13. See Prebisch, *Principle Problems.*

14. See Corden and Neary, "Dutch Disease Economics."

15. See Birdsall, Pinckney, and Sabot, "Natural Resources," for a model of why labor skills accumulate more slowly in resource abundant rather than labor abundant countries. This, too, helps explain the slow rate of adoption of modern production techniques.

16. See Singer, "Distribution of Gains," p. 477.

17. The empirical work of Bulmer-Thomas, *Political Economy,* and Cardosa, "Formation of the Coffee Estate," showed that coffee and bananas in Costa Rica, which are classic enclaves, did little to transform the rest of the economy.

18. See Corden and Neary, "Dutch Disease Economics."

19. Myrdal, "Trade as a Mechanism."

20. See Singer, "Distribution of Gains," p. 477.

21. Ibid., p. 476.

22. See Hirschman, *The Strategy of Economic Development,* pp. 109–10.

23. See Cairncross, "International Trade," p. 240.

24. See Myint, "Classical Theory"; Haberler, *International Trade and Economic Development;* Cairncross, "International Trade."

25. See Haberler, *International Trade and Economic Development,* p. 5.

26. Ibid., p. 11.

27. See Bauer, "International Economic Developments," p. 112.

28. See Innis, *Fur Trade;* Innis, *Cod Fisheries;* Meier, "Transfer Mechanism"; Caves and Holton, *Canadian Economy;* Watkins, "Staples Theory."

29. North, *Growth of the United States;* Diaz-Alejandro, "Argentine Economic History"; Cortés Condé, "Export Economy."

30. Innis, *Fur Trade,* and Innis, *Cod Fisheries.* Harold Innis's work has also been cited in connection to linkage analysis and export base theory. See Auty and Gelb, "Resource-Abundant States," fn. p. 8.

31. Chambers and Gordon, "Empirical Measurement." Also see Meier, *Classical Economics,* p. 69.

32. See Watkins, "Staples Theory."

33. See Caves and Holton, *Canadian Economy,* p. 31.

34. See Baldwin, "Export Technology," pp. 80–92.

35. Export base theory recognizes four categories of linkages—forward, backward, fiscal, and demand.

36. See North, "Regional Economic Growth," and North, *Growth of the United States.*

37. Cairncross, "International Trade," p. 236.

38. Nurkse, *Patterns,* p. 15.

39. See Meier, "Export-Led Development."

40. See Meier, *The International Economics of Development,* p. 240.

41. Ibid., pp. 246–47.

42. Ibid., p. 246.

43. The foreign component has only a delayed and negligible effect on the other sectors of the economy.

44. See Auty and Gelb, "Resource-Abundant States," and Rodriguez and Sachs, "Resource Abundant Economies."

CHAPTER 3

A Short Review of Methodological Problems and Data Sources

In the chapters that follow, the effects of the expansion of the oil industry on the other sectors of the Venezuelan economy and on the ultimate development of the country are explored. The analysis is divided into nine periods: 1910–1922, 1923–1929, 1930–1936, 1937–1942, 1943–1957, 1958–1973, 1974–1985, 1986–1990, and 1991–2000. The purpose of this time spacing is to separate periods in which the behavior of the industry, and of government policies (specifically those regarding oil), have been significantly different.

In each period, attention will be focused on the main contributions of petroleum to the economy of Venezuela. Four areas will be examined: foreign exchange proceeds, oil tax revenues, petroleum investment, and income expenditure generation. The combined total contribution of oil in each period, as indicated by the retained value of total expenditures, will then be examined. The total combined petroleum contribution will give an idea of the behavior of the positive contributions, which are not considered individually in this study. Finally, the relationship of the contribution of oil to investment and gross domestic product (GDP) in the nonpetroleum part of the economy will be analyzed and conclusions drawn, as to the overall effects of oil on the economy.

During the 20th century, the oil industry certainly achieved a rate of expansion and size that would qualify it as a potential leading sector. The Venezuelan economy throughout this time could be classified as a peripheral economy with a pattern of trade and production based on primary activities, which imported most of the industrial products it consumed. Thus, this empirical section can provide a partial test for the propositions stated in Chapter 2. In the remainder of this chapter, the methodological and procedural problems that were faced in this section of the study will be discussed. Most of the data that will be used in the study were developed directly in the course of research or existed in unpublished form in different sources. The figures have been calculated, for the most part, in terms of current bolívares and are referred to as such in the text. Whenever the figures appear in some other form, this will be specifically mentioned.

In every period, an examination is made of the foreign exchange contribution of the oil industry, relying on estimates of the total exports of goods and services and of the petroleum exports of goods and services. These estimates actually refer to total current account credits, including transfer payments and investment income received from abroad. Whenever data limitations do not permit such a level of detail, figures covering only the export of goods are used. All these figures are appropriately presented in current dollars, as they refer to the availability of international means of payments to the Venezuelan economy.

Figures referring to the net foreign exchange contributions of the other major sectors of the Venezuelan economy are also used. These data are also expressed in dollars and represent the actual foreign exchange originated in each of these sectors minus their own use of this foreign exchange. This sector net variable measures the contributions of a particular sector to the rest of the economy, as it excludes the foreign exchange usage of the contributing sector.

The movement of oil export prices is followed by the use of the implicit deflator of petroleum GDP with a 1957 base, and by a different price series compiled by the Ministerio de Minas de Hidrocarburos (Ministry of Mines and Hydrocarbons) in terms of current dollars. For the study of the application of funds resulting from the foreign trade contribution of oil, changes in the international monetary reserves of the country in terms of dollars, and the breakdown of the different balance of payments debits are examined. As to the last item, lack of appropriate data limited the investigation to the classification of imports by type of consumer goods, intermediate goods, and capital goods. The other debits that could have been examined to evaluate the utilization of the foreign exchange proceeds derived from oil are of minor importance when compared with goods imported.

For an examination of the public sector contribution, the total public revenues derived from oil in a direct way are compared with total public revenues. Petroleum-derived tax revenues are expressed in current bolívares and have been calculated on the basis of an unambiguous and homogeneous definition throughout the periods. In contrast, public revenues in current bolívares were compiled from different sources, with varying degrees of inconclusiveness. Up to 1950, the figures have been prepared from data appearing in the *Anuarios Estadísticos (Statistical Year-*

books) of the Minsterio de Fomento (Development Ministry). Unfortunately, these data do not include the revenues of autonomous administrative institutes and state enterprises. From 1950 until 1960, the latter are included in the figures published by the Banco Central de Venezuela (Central Bank of Venezuela). From then on the Central Bank published data for the public sector as a whole, as previously, but without the inclusion of state enterprises.

This introduces an element of lack of comprehensive comparison in the series that were constructed using these data. Total public revenues before 1950 are not comparable to those after that date. Among the latter, there are also differences between the 1950–1960 figures and the more recent ones. The same is true of the ratio of petroleum to total revenues.

The latter percentage figures could be made comparable by using the same base. Instead of using total public revenues as the base from 1950 on, the revenues of the national and regional governments could be used, as has been done for previous years. Nevertheless, this would require the use of different reporting sources in some of the periods, as the publication of the *Statistical Yearbook* has been incomplete since 1950.

The lack of revenue data corresponding to autonomous administrative institutes and state enterprises before 1950 somewhat clouds the behavior and trends in the participation of oil in total revenues during the early periods. With some of the components missing, the conclusions derived can be extended to total public revenues only by assuming that they behaved similarly to national and regional tax revenues. The same is true to a lesser extent of the 1960–1973 period, because revenues of state enterprises are missing for those years. To be more explicit, only under this assumption could it be said that the increasing share of oil-derived revenues in national plus regional tax revenues from 1936 up to 1950, is also applicable to total government revenues. According to informed sources in Venezuela, this assumption is reasonably correct, although it is impossible to document this empirically.

The appropriation of these revenues was examined in order to evaluate how effectively the public sector contribution of the oil industry was utilized. For this purpose, the determination of the surpluses or deficits in the total public budget would first be required. Again, the best that can be done here is to determine the surplus or deficit under the most inclusive public sector definition possible, given the lack of complete statistics. The surpluses or deficits to which references are made refer to different degrees of inclusiveness from 1936–1950, from 1950–1960, and from then on. Again, it is reasonable to presume that similar results will occur under these more or less inclusive definitions.

In order to appraise the effectiveness of public expenditures, the share allocated for economic development purposes should be determined. As it is impossible to estimate the latter directly, appropriate proxies are used as a replacement. Use is made of readily available estimates of social and economic expenditures in the national and regional budgets from 1936 to 1948 and of Central Bank estimates of capital expenditures for the whole public sector from then on. There is another break in the data here, then. Furthermore, during the first and second periods, we have been unable to determine the breakdown for the public sector as a whole. It can only be assumed, as previously, that the share applicable to national and regional expenditures would not be altered if the calculations would have the government sector as a whole.

The investment contribution presents even greater difficulties. Before 1950, the data available were provided by the Central Bank. The series is unpublished and does not have the same degree of reliability as more recent figures. These estimates were, in turn, adjusted by the author because of the discrepancy between the petroleum investment figures calculated directly from company data and those calculated by the Central Bank.

The figures corresponding to petroleum investment likewise present problems. In order to derive estimates for the industry as a whole from 1936 to 1942, the figures derived from our survey of the three main oil-producing company groups in Venezuela had to be adjusted. This was necessary because this period was characterized by important exploratory activities in which smaller companies were also involved, and their investment expenditures were out of proportion to their share of oil production. The adjustment was based on company reports, exploratory and development activities, and other indicators as presented in the *Memorias* (Annual Reports) of the Development Ministry (which, at the time, administered petroleum affairs).

Petroleum investment refers to gross fixed domestic investment. Estimates of changes in inventories required to present gross total domestic investment figures could not be obtained, as information on the change of raw material stocks of the industry was not reliable. Because the impact of the industry on other sectors takes place through its gross investment expenditures, it is more appropriate to use the figure of petroleum investment in such terms.

Another difficulty in estimating the investment expenditures of petroleum involves determining, out of the industry's annual purchases of goods and services, the portion that should be charged to the capital account. Due to accounting practices, some costs of the petroleum industry have been appropriately included as investment expenditures. This is especially prevalent in concession costs and exploratory activities, where certain expenses, such as taxes and intangible costs, are capitalized. It has been impossible to adjust the investment figures downward, even in an approximate manner, in order to take account of this problem, because the data are not sufficiently detailed. It is better under such conditions not to tamper with the reported figures, recognizing only that they represent slight overestimates.

Table 3.1 shows the total investment expenditures of the industry, and its concession and exploratory components, for a representative subperiod in order to give an idea of the orders of magnitude involved. Most of the concession costs represent taxes, which should not be considered a part of the industry investment. An undetermined part of exploratory costs is also improperly included in the investment expenditure estimates. The remainder in these categories can be safely considered investment.

The total investment of the Venezuelan economy is also reported in terms of gross fixed domestic investment, as the only available long-term investment series for the economy of Venezuela is in these terms. This contributed to the decision to present all investment figures in gross, fixed terms. Moreover, data on changes in stocks have been much more unreliable until very recently.

In order to analyze better the impact of the oil contributions upon the other sectors of the economy, the concept of nonpetroleum gross investment is used. By definition, it is total investment minus petroleum investment, which leaves the investment expenditures corresponding to the other sectors of the economy. This concept is expressed in the same terms as all the other investment concepts.

In examining the contribution of the petroleum industry arising from the increased expenditures and income originated in the industry, two types of variables, through which the economic activity of the industry is represented, have to be considered. Variables like the value of oil produced, the current expenditures of the petroleum industry, or the gross domestic product of oil, include components that have a relatively weak

Table 3.1.
Total Investment Expenditures of the Petroleum Industry and Its Concession and Exploratory Components as Reported by the Oil Companies, 1960–1965 (millions of bolívares)

	1960	1961	1962	1963	1964	1965
Concession Costs	7	12	0	7	1	4
Exploratory Costs	41	44	25	38	42	72
Total Investment	706	521	503	518	735	825
Concession and Exploratory Costs (as a Percent of Investment)	6.80%	10.70%	5.00%	8.70%	5.90%	9.20%

Note: These figures reflect oil company responses to quarterly inquiries and therefore differ from the adjusted yearly totals of investment expenditures in the petroleum industry reported elsewhere in this book (i.e., Chapter 9).

Source: Prepared from unpublished data provided by the Ministerio de Minas e Hidrocarburos.

effect on the rest of the economy. The opposite holds true for variables like the retained value of oil expenditures, whose components impinge very strongly on the other sectors of the economy.

Changes in the current expenditures of the oil industry or in its value of production have been derived from petroleum sales values, plus or minus any variation in the inventories of crude oil and products. The latter have been derived by pricing the changes in the physical quantities of oil held in inventory by the industry. GDP was estimated by adding the appropriate payment components of the petroleum industry. For the sake of clarity, the GDP originated by the industry in the creation of capital goods for its own use should be kept separate from that created in the production of current goods and services.

More specifically, petroleum GDP was estimated as the sum of wages and salaries, profits after taxes, interest payments, depreciation and amortization, and taxes that constitute the value added by the industry. Some of these components, as reported, were related to value of sales and, thus, had to be corrected to reflect value of production. This adjustment factor used was calculated on the basis of changes in the stocks of crude oil and other oil products.

Some of these individual components required other adjustments. Profits after taxes had to be adjusted in the 1937–1942 period to take account of the losses that the new oil companies suffered. The methodology employed of aggregating the net value added figures of the big three oil groups in Venezuela (Standard Oil of New Jersey, Shell, and Gulf), which accounted for over 99 percent of total Venezuelan production from 1937 to 1942, and adjusting for other companies in terms of their participation in total production, could not have accounted for these losses.

As for depreciation and amortization, the figures were taken as reported by the companies. No adjustments were made to try to express this capital use concept in stricter economic terms, because the information available did not allow it. Therefore, the usual obscure amortization charges of the oil sector, related to depletion, intangible costs, development, and wildcat drilling costs, were taken at face value and included in the capital use charges. A breakdown is given in Table 3.2 of the different components of depreciation and amortization, which gives an idea of the importance of each in the total capital use charges of the petroleum industry. As far as can be seen, given that it has been impossible to separate other amortization charges from depletion, the latter, as well as intangible costs, appear to be a small part of the total charges, so their inclusion does not make that much difference.

Finally, there is no information available regarding interest payments on capital borrowed from abroad by the oil industry before 1947. This fact does not seriously affect the estimates, because this item usually has represented a small part of the total interest payments. In addition, before and

Table 3.2.
Capital Use Charges of the Petroleum Industry, by Components, 1947–1962
(millions of bolívares)

Year	Depreciation Charges					Total Depreciation	Depletion and Other Amortization Charges	Intangible Costs Incurred During Other Periods
	Production	Transport	Refining	Marketing	Other			
1947	135	9	3	2	6	155	35	2
1948	188	15	3	2	2	211	36	1
1949	199	28	29	3	3	263	62	2
1950	234	32	72	3	5	346	74	0
1951	267	32	86	4	16	405	90	0
1952	310	48	83	4	11	456	74	2
1953	341	47	85	4	8	486	71	8
1954	361	50	85	5	15	516	97	20
1955	415	54	93	6	18	586	94	16
1956	461	56	95	6	20	638	93	13
1957	508	62	119	8	21	717	95	16
1958	508	68	129	8	24	738	98	13
1959	563	83	131	10	22	809	130	17
1960	545	92	128	11	25	800	148	24
1961	528	92	120	11	26	778	151	28
1962	471	76	117	12	20	696	215	32

Source: Prepared from unpublished data provided by the Ministerio de Minas e Hidrocarburos.

during World War II, outside borrowing by the industry was much smaller than in the ensuing years.

There are two principal reasons dictating the main use of GDP rather than other types of aggregate estimates for the oil industry. The only continuing figures for the Venezuelan economy, starting in 1936, are GDP estimates. It is essential that petroleum activities be expressed in equivalent terms for comparative purposes. Then, from the total value added of petroleum, other indicators of its contribution to the rest of the economy can be more exactly derived.

The concept of retained value, discussed in Chapter 2, is frequently used in the study. The retained value of total expenditures is calculated by subtracting the following elements from the total expenditures of the industry: payments to foreign factors (profits after taxes and interest), remittances abroad by foreign industry workers, imports of goods and services, and depreciation and amortization charges.

In turn, retained value of current expenditures is defined as the total value of oil produced minus profits after taxes and interest payments, remittances of foreign workers abroad, imports of current goods and services, and depreciation and amortization charges. The retained value of investment expenditures can be calculated by subtracting imports of capital goods and services from the total fixed investment expenditures of the industry.

Several variants of these concepts have been calculated in different periods. These are discussed in further detail below, but as this is done whenever the variants are introduced and because this happens at different places throughout the text, it is advisable to mention them at this point. For one thing, the retained value concept is more precise if expressed without including foreign goods purchased from domestic importers. Nevertheless, information on such purchases is available only since 1948. Correspondingly, alternative series of retained value of total expenditures figures, adjusted to exclude the value of such purchases, is presented from 1948 on.

The petroleum industry in Venezuela has paid extraordinary concession taxes on several occasions from 1936 to 1973. The concession payments in 1956 and 1957 were comparatively very large. The Ministry of Mines and Hydrocarbons does not include this payment as a part of the investment or as a part of the current expenditures of the industry in those years. However, it is clear that these payments were a substantial part of the contribution of oil to the national economy in 1956 and 1957. Therefore, the retained value of total expenditures is presented both including and excluding these tax payments.

A similar situation exists with respect to the foreign exchange taxes on the petroleum industry. For reasons given in Chapter 6, the retained value estimates presented have not generally included the proceeds from these taxes. However, if they are not taken into consideration in the 1958–1965 period, the resulting picture would be a distorted one, given that these taxes increased substantially at the end of the period.

In some of these variants of the retained value concept, it is quite difficult to separate the portion corresponding to current expenditures from that related to capital expenditures. Mostly, this is due to data problems, but in some cases, as in the one involving concession payments, even the attempt to make the distinction would not appear to be valid.

It should also be pointed out that calculation of the retained value concept is based on the assumption of negligible importation of services by the petroleum industry before 1946. Everything seems to indicate that this is a reasonable supposition. Certainly, imports of any kind were quite insignificant before then, and the petroleum industry was much more self-sufficient in its operations. Moreover, this assumption was supported through interviews held with various petroleum industry specialists in the Venezuelan government and in the oil companies, some of whom actually worked in the Venezuelan oil industry during these years. This conclusion is also partially confirmed by a declining trend in services imported as one goes back in years.

In order to analyze the influence of oil on the rest of the economy or what amounts to the same thing, the effects of petroleum in total GDP, a variable named nonpetroleum GDP is defined. This variable, which is computed as the residual GDP after the impact of petroleum on the GDP has been subtracted, is carefully examined in the chapters. As a measure of inflation in the Venezuelan economy, the implicit deflator of the GDP is mainly used between 1950 and 1973. Before then, different wholesale price indexes are utilized.

The estimates presented from 1936 to 1947 on different aspects of petroleum activity originated in the financial statements and supporting documents of the three most important company groups in Venezuela: Standard, Shell, and Gulf. These financial statements were expanded upon so as to cover the entire industry. As these groups cover over 99 percent of total production during this period, the adjustment did not endanger the accuracy of the estimates. The availability of supporting documents permitted adjustments of the figures in the main financial statements. Some of these were undertaken so that the resulting data would reflect economic rather than accounting concepts.

Finally, the different statistical series used have different sources. This introduces the problem of inconsistency, which is more acute in the early years. All work in economic history is plagued by such difficulties, and in economic history of developing nations, this even extends to the examination of relatively recent trends. Such problems were relatively mild in Venezuela, however, because of its price and exchange rate stability.

CHAPTER 4

1910–1922

In 1910 Venezuela was largely an agricultural and underdeveloped country and its economic future was highly uncertain. Yet there were strong signs that a new source of energy—oil—that was then revolutionizing the industrial world, could be found in large quantities in Venezuela. During the first part of the 1910–1922 period, concessions for the exploration of oil were issued with great success. It was not until after World War I, however, that the production of oil for exports would take place. Although the first commercial oil well became operational in 1914, the development of the oil sector in Venezuela proceeded slowly until approximately 1919, when oil exportation began.

The export of Venezuelan petroleum was fueled by a large increase in the world demand for oil. The experience of World War I left no doubt of the importance of this energy source, *black gold*, for industrial activity. Prior to 1919 oil production was very limited. Activity in this sector was concentrated mainly in exploration for oil and for the capital investments needed for extraction, storage, refining, and transportation. After 1919 both production and exports of oil increased rapidly, and the pace of capital investment in this sector accelerated as well.

By the end of 1922 Venezuela had undeniably become a significant source of supply in the world market for oil. In that year huge reserves of oil in the region of Lake Maracaibo were either confirmed or strongly suspected. In addition that year marked the government's adoption of a hydrocarbons law that favored the growth of the oil sector.

THE CONTRIBUTION OF OIL THROUGH THE
EXTERNAL SECTOR

Before the advent of oil as an export good, the vast majority of Venezuelan exports consisted of agricultural products such as coffee, cattle, and cacao. The value of these agricultural commodity exports followed a cycle determined fundamentally by world commodity prices and climatic conditions that affected agricultural yields. During the decade between 1900 and 1910 the value of these traditional exports reached its highest peak in value over the preceding 40 years. Between 1901 and 1910 the combined value of coffee, cattle, and cacao exports approximately doubled.[1]

Total exports averaged a little over 100 million bolívares per year at the time that Venezuelan oil exports began (see Table 4.1). From 1917 to 1921 the value of oil exports remained relatively small and fluctuated greatly. In 1918 oil exports reached approximately 2 million bolívares. Venezuelan oil exports virtually disappeared in 1919 and 1920, but grew dramatically in 1921 and 1922. In 1921 oil exports reached the million barrel mark, and increased to 1.8 million in 1922. By the latter year, oil exports had reached 12 million bolívares and represented nearly 9 percent of the total value of Venezuelan exports.

The pattern of oil exports (in physical terms) roughly paralleled the level of oil production. The strong increase in domestic demand between 1917 and 1920, however, kept oil exports from rising at the same rate as the

Table 4.1.
Petroleum Sector Indicators and External Sector Performance, 1917–1922

	1917	1918	1919	1920	1921	1922
Total Exports (Mill. Bs.)	118	102	256	167	129	135
Oil Exports (Mill. Bs.)	0	2	0	0	7	12
Oil as a Percent of Total	0.0%	2.0%	0.0%	0.0%	5.4%	8.9%
Total Imports (Mill. Bs.)	119	80	180	315	96	100
Net Exports (Mill. Bs.)	-1	22	76	-148	33	35
International Reserves (Mill. Bs)	36	40	52	69	69	60
Change in Reserves (Mill. Bs.)	--	4	12	17	0	-9
Oil Production (000's Barrels per day)	121	321	305	462	1,449	2,235
Oil Exports (000's Barrels per day)	57	147	14	0	1,004	1,833
Exports as Share of Production	47.1%	45.8%	4.6%	0.0%	69.3%	82.0%
Oil Export Prices (US $ per Barrel)	2.09	3.57	3.70	5.00	2.19	2.21

Note: International Reserves include only gold within the banking system, although most reserves were held in this form during the period.

Sources: Ministerio de Fomento, Dirección General de Estadísticas, *Anuario Estadístico* (Caracas, 1938 and various years); Ministerio de Minas e Hidrocarburos, *Petróleo y Otros Datos Estadísticos* (Caracas, 1964); Ministerio de Fomento, *Anuario Estadístico* (Caracas, various years); D. F. Maza Zavala, *Venezuela: Una Economía Dependiente* (Caracas, 1964).

increase in oil production.[2] In addition, the sand bars in Lake Maracaibo represented an important physical barrier to exports in this early period. The sand bars made transporting oil to the high seas terminals quite difficult, and required the use of smaller oil carriers, which either had to be constructed domestically or imported. Transport by these smaller vessels increased transportation time and costs.

Trends in international prices for oil were also favorable during the 1917–1922 period. Oil export prices more than doubled between 1917 and 1920, although they declined considerably in 1921 (see Table 4.1). This period was also one of generally favorable prices for Venezuela's traditional commodity exports and suggests that Venezuela's barter terms of trade were improving during this period.[3]

The general rise in export earnings, imported goods, and the growth of international reserves suggest that the period between 1917 and 1922 was one of increasing prosperity in the Venezuelan economy. The impact of the oil sector, at least through the foreign sector, could not have been very significant during the early part of this period because oil exports were not very great until 1921–1922. Once oil exports took off in 1921, however, the stimulative effect of oil production and export earnings on the economy was likely to have been quite appreciable.

The importance of oil export earnings in realizing Venezuela's demand for imports during this period is not very clear. At first glance there appears to be no strong relationship between imports and oil exports, although the correlation between imports and total export earnings appears to be quite strong. Fluctuations in imports during this period exceeded the fluctuation in export earnings, however. Although net exports were sometimes positive and sometimes negative, for the 1917–1922 period whole imports exceeded exports. Despite the negative trade balance, international reserves (held mainly in gold) grew steadily during this period.

Given that the Venezuelan economy seemed to have been expanding satisfactorily during these years, a policy of accumulation of reserves seemed justified. In fact, this accumulation could have financed about six months' worth of imports, which appears to be a reasonable level Also, during the final years of this period a policy toward the payoff of the public debt was initiated by President Juan Vicente Gómez, with funds produced by income generated by the oil industry. Given the high value of oil production and the high cost of servicing the debt, these measures seemed to have been appropriate, particularly in view of the general conditions of prosperity that Venezuela enjoyed at the time.

To summarize, the contribution of oil via the external sector was not important during this period, with the exception being the effects of the rapid growth of oil exports in the latter part of the period. However, the Venezuelan economy seemed to have expanded during these years. Furthermore the policy decisions regarding the use of oil exports earnings seems to have been adequate for this time. But in terms of the government policy toward petroleum, with its small contribution to the economy, there was little to depend on.

THE FISCAL CONTRIBUTION OF OIL

When Juan Vicente Gómez seized power from Cipriano Castro, Venezuela's economic situation was undoubtedly difficult. Not only was there a stagnant economy with diminishing exports, but also a large foreign debt that amounted to several times the average revenues of the fiscal budget of the country. In order to confront the crisis, Gómez would rely on the new fiscal revenues generated by the oil industry.

The concessions granted by Gómez to oil companies were based on an annual tax of one bolívar per hectare and a canon tax of 5 percent. The exploration periods consisted of two years, and the actual licenses to extract oil were awarded per 30 years. Several concessions were granted under these conditions until 1918, when special legislation regulating the oil industry was passed. From 1914 onward, production commenced under these various concessions, all controlled by the interest of Anglo-Dutch Shell.

Until 1919 the industry's development occurred at a slow pace. There existed numerous problems in recently explored areas of the country that lacked all of the needed infrastructure for production. Furthermore, the government would not even attempt to build such infrastructure or to assist the companies in any manner. T! is forced the oil companies not only to import machinery and food, but also to build roads and power plants, and to provide housing and health care for their employees.

American interests, which had so far not been granted any concessions, offered to pay up to $1,350,000 for one of the areas granted to Shell that were not currently being exploited. To further their interests, they offered a bribe to Gómez of a similar amount. Nevertheless, Shell was able to retain and guarantee all of its concessions until 1965 by paying 10 million bolívares.

All the uncertainty surrounding some of the terms of the concessions arose out of the fact that the concessions made reference to the existing mining laws, which were not entirely adequate in dealing with the conditions of the oil industry. Given that this was the fundamental cause of the delayed development of the oil industry, and of the urgency to generate oil fiscal revenues, a new law specifically directed to regulate oil concessions was passed in 1918, and at the end of the same year a decree was issued effectively enacting it. This legislation was a great leap forward and it did away with the long contracts, the large land concessions; at the same time it raised the taxes levied on the concessions according to their land allotment.

This last change brought about higher fiscal revenues. The minister of industrial planning who was involved in the preparation of this law, the famous Gumersindo Torres, was unwavering in his attempts to increase the payments to the Venezuelan government by the oil companies. His purpose was to obtain as much revenue as Mexico. From 1920 he tried to create a new law, which was opposed by the petroleum companies, particularly U.S. companies, which at the time still did not enjoy any concessions. Finally, the legislation appeared in June 1921, but no new claims on the concessions appeared, in part due to the relatively depressed conditions of the industry that year but primarily because of boycotts from the companies. A more favorable law was passed on June 13, 1922, after Torres was removed as minister. The law totally broke away from the old mining law codes and it was accepted by the oil companies as "liberal, clear, simple and efficient."[4]

The characteristics of the new law proved to be an important step in the development of the oil industry in Venezuela, because it gave the oil companies the incentives to redouble their exploration efforts in a country without scientifically certain proof of great petroleum potential. The main contents of the law were as follows:

1. The exploitation contracts with the oil companies were extended to 40 years, including refining and transportation activities.
2. Taxes per acre of land were increased, while taxes on exploration and exploitation were also raised.
3. Machinery and hospital equipment could be imported by the companies duty-free.
4. Part of the land included in the exploration concessions (which lasted for three years) had to be returned to create and enlarge the National Reserves.[5]
5. The companies had to be legally registered and established in Venezuela and come under the jurisdiction of the Venezuelan courts, and diplomatic involvement (by the home country of the firm) might result in the nullification of the contract.

The law has come under criticism by some who consider it deficient in regulating the conservation of the country's oil resources and in obtaining less fiscal revenues than it should have. But it must be recognized that, at that time, investment in oil exploration and production was still small and that large oil deposits had not been discovered. In view of the insufficient growth, it does not seem unreasonable to dictate a law that would facilitate the expansion of the oil industry. What does seem less justifiable is that certain provisions of the law remained unaltered in the following years.[6]

This is especially applicable to the fiscal aspects of the law, because just a little later it was confirmed that Venezuela's oil reserves were extensive and they could be exploited at low cost, which consequently implied that the oil companies could be taxed and would be destined to pay much higher sums for the right to exploit Venezuela's oil reserves.

Thus, fiscal revenues collected directly from oil exploration in Venezuela were determined to be relatively low in this period. There were, however, two sources of tax revenues that contributed to increase fiscal revenues: taxes on imports and other indirect taxes resulting from imports of the oil companies and its subcontractors. Both revenue sources were tied to the economic activity generated by oil. Some payments made by the oil companies for obtaining and maintaining the concessions, unfortunately, were more frequently made outside the fiscal system than within it.[7]

In Table 4.2 total fiscal revenues are shown, along with what portion was received from petroleum. With the exception of the year 1921, when there was a temporary contraction in economic activity, there was a notable upward trend in government revenues. The same trend occurred in the case of petroleum, especially with a revenue jump in 1922. As in the case of the external sector, the participation of oil in fiscal revenue became significant only in 1921, and important in 1922, the year it practically constituted 10 percent of total government revenues.

It is necessary to underline that these statistics do not include indirect sources of tax revenues that could be considered as having originated from petroleum, but were previously cited: payments for concessions, indirect taxes, and imports. This is because it is very difficult to estimate payments obtained from concessions that were made during those years

Table 4.2.
Government Sector Fiscal Indicators, 1917–1922 (millions of bolívares)

	1917	1918	1919	1920	1921	1922
Government Revenues	64	50	74	105	66	81
Public Revenues from the Oil Sector	0	1	1	1	2	8
Oil as a Percent of Government Revenues	0.0%	2.0%	1.4%	1.0%	3.0%	9.9%
Government Expenditures	55	56	63	85	92	76
Economic & Social Development Expenditures (ESD)	--	18	20	34	38	29
ESD as a Percent of Government Expenditures	--	32.1%	31.7%	40.0.5%	41.3%	38.2%
Public Treasury Reserves	34	34	33	66	45	35

Notes: Revenue and expenditure data are from the official budget and adjusted to reflect a calendar year basis. Treasury Reserves are as of end of July of each year.

Sources: Ministerio de Fomento, *Anuario Estadístico* (Caracas, 1937 and 1938); Ministerio de Minas e Hidrocarburos, *Petróleo y Otros Datos Estadísticos* (Caracas, 1965); J. J. Bracho Sierra, *Cincuenta Años de Ingresos Fiscales* (Caracas, 1963); and Charles Rollins, "Raw Materials Development and Economic Growth: A Study of the Bolivian and Venezuelan Experience," Ph.D. dissertation, Stanford University, 1956.

as well as the percentage of customs rents that could be attributed to petroleum. As for the payments for concessions, it could be perceived that they were important, at least relative to petroleum receipts included in Table 4.2, which is based on the available sources, some of which we have previously referred to.[8] The Venezuelan state was not, during those years, easily distinguishable from the clan of Juan Vicente Gómez, which dominated the country. Much of what it was paid by the oil producers in concept, the compensation for the use of the concessions, went to Gómez's favorites and possibly to him as well. This came about through the system designed by the dictator, to make the concessions on a first-term basis to his acquaintances, who at the same time would negotiate with the companies. Those who defended this system maintained that the payments to the concessions increased Venezuelan capital and possibly contributed to investment. However, it all seems to indicate that in general this was not done, and that these funds were frequently destined to buy luxury goods and real estate.[9] Therefore, even assuming that the income from concessions (or their transfer) received by Gómez and his business partners represented extensions to those officially received by the Venezuelan state, it is evident that they were not utilized, as would have been done by an eminent government. With regard to fiscal revenues obtained indirectly through the imposition of high import duties by Venezuela, we should point out that during these years Venezuela's import taxes were among the highest in the world. The import duties of Maracaibo, principally, and from La Guaira and Puerto Cabello, the major ports for importing in the country, were multiplied during these years due to the impetus of imports generated directly and indirectly by the petroleum expansion. If we take this indirect contribution into account, very possibly there would be a doubling of the petroleum participation in the total government revenues.[10] This is the case even though the import tax exemptions that were conceded to the petroleum companies for various years were only half of the sums received directly from the petroleum sector.[11]

With respect to the utilization of the fiscal contribution of Venezuela's petroleum on the rest of the economic activities, we should first concentrate on the level of public expenditures, which is shown in Table 4.2. As in the case of tax revenues, these figures refer to the expenditures of the Venezuelan government, whose structure was very simple in those years.

If we compare the expenditures with revenues, we note that during various years they represent deficits or surpluses. We should recognize, however, that this was due to the variability of tax revenues, rather than to a joint policy. We should note that during these years, the variations were principally determined by the variability of tax receipts from imports, which rose in 1919 and 1920 with the entrance of imports deferred during the war, and which declined in 1921 due to declines in the prices of export goods and economic contraction. The Treasury's deficits or surpluses were determined as a careless estimation of public revenues, based on the false expectation that public spending would automatically adjust to their growth or decline.[12] Both revenues and expenditures showed growth during this period, which was more steady than in the latter case.

As a whole, fiscal revenues grew by 26.6 percent from 1917 to 1922, the years included in the period of our analysis and when oil exports first took place. This is equivalent to a 4.8 percent increase per year in fiscal revenues. On the other hand, government expenditures increased 38.2 percent for the entire period and 6.7 percent per year. It is evident that if we take the period as a whole, the budget tended to be balanced, increasing the Treasury's reserve very little. This policy seemed reasonable during the period examined and signified the petroleum contribution, which was small except toward the end of the period.[13] The reserves of the National Treasury appear in Table 4.2.

To examine the utilization of oil tax revenues, with specific reference to the distribution of government expenditures, we should consult Table 4.2. This series is based on an estimate by Charles Rollins in his doctoral dissertation at Stanford University (published in 1955).[14]

Table 4.2 shows the percentage of total government expenditures that can be considered destined for the social and economic development of Venezuela. In the years when oil began to have a more significant impact on the Venezuelan economy, a little over one-third of public spending was directed to cover the needs of socioeconomic development. During these years this percentage had a tendency to rise, starting at 32.3 percent and ending at 38.6 percent. These statistics suggest, especially if we compare them with those of the 1940s, that the consciousness of the socioeconomic development of Venezuela was yet to appear. Nevertheless, the economic and social needs felt by the Venezuelan people were expressed clearly enough so as to assure that a continuously increasing share of the national budget would be oriented toward economic and social development.

We should consider that the utilization of public funds in general, and those coming from the oil industry in particular, was acceptable given the prevailing conditions of the times, just a few years into the 20th century.[15]

To conclude, the fiscal contribution of oil was relatively small in absolute terms during the first period of oil production in Venezuela, even if we consider the payments for concessions made within and without the national budget and the import tax revenues directly or indirectly generated by the oil industry. In relative terms when we consider total revenues, we should recognize that the contribution made by petroleum rapidly became important toward the end of the period. This contribution was not sterilized by the Venezuelan government, but in fact was spent within the limitations of the fiscal practice of balanced budgets characterized in the early part of the century. Alternatively, government expenditures for economic and social development were relatively low, but grew rapidly during the period.

If we relate these increases with the revenues coming from the oil industry, we observe that they exceeded the direct tax revenues and more or less equaled the indirect revenues, which suggests that the latter were utilized to finance the increases. Therefore the utilization of the still small fiscal contribution of petroleum was acceptable during this period, although not more than that.

THE CONTRIBUTION OF THE OIL INDUSTRY THROUGH INVESTMENT

Investment is a central variable of the economy: in advanced economies, where it develops a more important role during the economic growth cycle, and in developing economies, where it is the key element of economic growth.[16] Not only is it a reflection of the rate of capital, but it is also an important determinant of the rate of progress and technological innovation taking place.

The accumulation of capital has two aspects. On the demand side, it ensures that there will not be leakage from the circular flow of the saving component of total income, generating a multiplier effect in the economy. On the supply side, investment implies the development of the sector for the production of capital goods (including their manufacture) indispensable for economic growth. This second aspect operates on a longer term than the first, because of its impact over the total supply of goods and services that the accumulated capital determines, and because of its central participation in the production process. Meanwhile, the first aspect operates on the short run, which experiences the impact on investment spending in the economic cycle. Petroleum investments, as a part of total investment, participate in this central role and in the characteristics of the process of capital accumulation. Nevertheless, we shall recognize that during this period its relative importance, though significant, was small, especially during the first half of the period. However, given that investment was made regularly, and grew continuously (although slowly), it achieved an important participation in the spending multiplier of expenditures and revenues to which we referred above.[17] On the other hand, on the supply side, oil investment created a capacity for the considerable future expansion of the supply of oil and petroleum products, at the same time that it began to exert an influence on the development of the capital goods production sector in the country.

Table 4.3 presents the estimated investment for the years that we are examining. As can be confirmed, oil investment was maintained at constant low levels of around 8 million bolívares from 1914 to 1920. In 1920 it expanded to three times this value.[18] In 1921 petroleum investment dimin-

Table 4.3.
Gross Domestic Product and Gross Fixed Domestic Investment, Oil Sector, 1910–1922

	1910-14	1915	1916	1917	1918	1919	1920	1921	1922
Total GDP (Mill. 1957 Bs.)	--	--	--	--	--	--	2,859	2,952	3,085
Oil Sector GDP (Mill. 1957 Bs.)	0	0	0	1	2	2	3	10	16
Oil as a Percent of Total GDP	--	--	--	--	--	--	0.10%	0.34%	0.52%
Gross Fixed Domestic Investment (Mill.Bs.)									
	8	8	8	8	3	8	26	13	30

Notes: Oil sector GDP and fixed investment estimates are based on the records of the three main petroleum company groups in Venezuela: Shell Oil, Gulf Oil, and Standard Oil of New Jersey. Adjustments were then made to reflect industry totals. Gross Fixed Investment estimates may be overstated by the inclusion of exploration costs, such as concessions and capitalization costs, which are not properly fixed investment. Total GDP estimates are based on Armando Córdova, "La Estructura Económica Tradicional y el Impacto Petróleo en Venezuela," *Economía y Ciencias Sociales*, January–March, 1963, and lectures given by Bernardo Ferran on Venezuelan economic history, delivered at the Universidad Central de Venezuela, Caracas, 1963.
Sources: See Córdova (1963) and Ferran (1963).

ished substantially, recuperating during the last year of the period, when it even surpassed the 1920s record figure.

To synthesize, investment activity in the oil industry reached significant levels starting in 1914, coinciding with the first commercial oil well discovered by Shell in February of that year. From this historic peak to the end of the period, investment tripled.[19] Investment began to be directed toward nonexploratory activities starting in 1914. Shell, for example, began organizing exports from its first productive oil well with commercial possibilities in Lake Maracaibo. The construction of an oil pipeline and storage facilities by the company was directed at transporting the oil through the lake. Construction of an oil refinery began. In 1917 the first terminal for transport cargo began the exportation of Venezuelan oil by Shell through its subsidiary, the Caribbean Development Company.[20]

A period of erratic petroleum investments commenced in 1917, fluctuating from year to year according to the necessities produced by the exploration, transportation, and marketing of oil. Because there was uncertainty about the magnitude of the reserves, investment would increase markedly one year, only to be reduced drastically the next. While the companies faced enormous problems in the development of oil production in virgin zones, investment in the oil industry had not yet shown the same rising tendency that characterized it when it reached maturity in the late 1950s. To give an idea of the difficulties that the companies faced, and of the investments that they had to undertake during those years, we will mention the establishment of camps for employees and the construction of roads and sanitary and electric facilities in connection with the camps.[21] Finally, the conditions created by World War I contributed to the constrained growth of oil investment by making import and export activity more difficult.[22]

The two principal bottlenecks addressed by investment toward the end of the period were the storage and transportation of oil. Shell's subsidiary, the Caribbean Development Company, the only firm then producing commercially, towed large barges loaded with oil to its Curaçao refinery, where it processed about 80 percent of its production and to its San Lorenzo refinery, where it refined the rest. In 1922 investment began on a new means of transportation, the low-draft oil ships of which the Caribbean Company purchased a few. The company also built storage facilities in La Guaira, Puerto Cabello, and Caracas. By these measures the Caribbean Development Company became the oil company least affected by the bottlenecks of transportation and storage.[23]

There are no existing estimates of investment activity in the rest of the economy during the period 1910–1922. Thus we cannot estimate what percentage of total fixed investment the oil sector represented. It is possible, nevertheless, to make an educated guess based on the general knowledge we have of the Venezuelan economy during those years.

In the agricultural sector there should be a distinction made between production for export and production destined for the domestic market and/or the subsistence of farmers. During this period, export agriculture experienced a recuperation from the low levels of production achieved during the final decade of the previous century. This increase in production continued until 1922. The growth that was experienced in the second half of the period took the value of exports up to figures that are superior to those of the late 1880s, which was the previous production peak.[24] Undoubtedly, this brought about an increase in investment in these activities during the entire period.[25] This should have enlarged the sector's participation in total investment at least until 1920, when investment in the oil industry expanded considerably. Agricultural exports clearly represented one of the most important sources of investment, if not the most important source of investment, during this period.

Subsistence agriculture and commercial agriculture directed to the domestic market represented the other large sector of the economy before the appearance of oil. It is estimated that approximately 70 percent of Venezuela's gross national product was generated either by agricultural exports or by the rest of the agricultural sector. Thus we can conclude that the other important source of investment in the economy was the agricultural activity geared toward the supply of the needs of Venezuela's population. Given the direct impulse of the prosperity in agricultural exports, this activity must have expanded during the 12 years considered in this chapter.

It must be underlined that the Venezuelan economy had been in a state of stagnation in the decades preceding the period being covered. Therefore, we should not think that investment in agricultural activities constituted a large percentage of agricultural production, because this production was growing very slowly and the backward techniques utilized in it required little use of machinery.[26] Insofar as the industrial sector goes, it was characterized by being of the handicraft type, representing a small portion of Venezuela's gross domestic output. It had contributed little to Venezuela's growth in the past, and all indications were that it was the sector least affected by the agricultural sector's (and later the oil industry's) prosperity of those years. Its contribution to total investment, which was relatively small, showed little dynamism during the period.

The commercial sector specifically, and the rest of the country's economic activities generally, shared in the agricultural prosperity and in the investment of petroleum monies in the economic landscape of Venezuela. When combined, they constituted an important part of Venezuela's gross national product, second only to agriculture. Their focal point was export-import activity and related trade services. Although the coefficient of investment in these activities was lower than in the rest of the sectors, investment in this sector must have been important during this period, and it certainly should have been growing. Finally, the government was a significant but not very important part of the economic activity until the discovery of oil.[27]

Government revenues were exposed to the fluctuation of foreign trade, because import taxes were the largest source of tax revenues. Investments by the government were small, not yet having started the development of infrastructure that later unified the dispersed markets of the country. Nevertheless, as commercial and agricultural prosperity made its impact on the national budget, government investment must have expanded during the period that we are covering.

To give an idea of the relative importance of investment in the oil industry, let's first compare it with public expenditure and investment. We can prove that expenditures were a multiple of oil investments all through this period, to the contrary of what we will see in the following period.

With regard to the government's direct investment, although we do not have estimates of it, there exist data on expenditures on social and economic development for some of these years. In a few of the final years of this period, petroleum investment is practically of the same magnitude as that of social and economic development expenditures. If we consider that part of this spending is comprised of current expenditures, then we must conclude that at least for a couple of years (1920 and 1922), investment in the oil industry surpassed government investment. Nevertheless this does not seem to have been the case for the rest of the period.

To summarize, because investment in the oil industry was smaller than government investment, and because the latter was only a small portion of total investment, we can deduce that investment in the oil industry could not have represented much more than 10 percent of total investment, which in itself was at most 10 percent of Venezuela's GDP; therefore, even if we consider the investment that resulted from the influence of oil, like some investments in the public sector and foreign trade, the total impact of petroleum on investment was small, although significant, during this period. Because probably a great part of the machinery and equipment acquired by the oil sector was imported, the multiplier effect of its income and investment was exercised mainly through the construction activities the oil companies undertook themselves or contracted for.[28] Also through such investment spending, domestic construction companies slowly became stronger as they saw increased demand for their services for residential, infrastructure, and industrial construction. Because domestic construction companies faced competition from oil companies, or foreign contractors, the domestic construction companies were forced to improve their techniques and procedures.[29]

To conclude, the contribution of oil through investment, although not comparable to following periods, was significant during these years and certainly larger than the contributions through the foreign and fiscal sectors. The contribution of petroleum through investment began to have an important impact from 1920 to 1922.

THE DOMESTIC PRODUCT AND TOTAL
EXPENDITURES OF THE OIL INDUSTRY

The oil sector spent current funds in the payment of primary factors of production, labor, natural resources, capital, and enterprise that produced oil. It also incurred current spending dividends on the production of oil by buying the intake of goods and services concurrently produced by other sectors of activity. By adding the first type of expenses, which creates what is known as value added of petroleum, with the second type of expenses, those destined for consumption, we have the current total expenditure of petroleum. These total current expenses are equivalent to the value of oil production, which are financed by the value of physical production sales plus or minus the adjustment due to the changes in oil inventory.[30]

The current expenditures of the oil industry constitute an exogenous flow into the bulk of current expenses of the Venezuelan economy. This can be explained because almost all of the demand for oil (and the current expenditures backing this demand) originated abroad.

That is why these expenditures, by definition, have a multiplier effect in the matrix of spending relationships between sectors and factors where it is centrally considered. This is another basic contribution of oil to the Venezuelan economy. Expenditures originated abroad create income from this factor of production and in other sectors, which also create revenues for the primary factors successively. It is a multiplier mechanism frequently affecting demand for investment through the accelerator. Combining the effects of the multipliers and accelerators, each balance sheet change by oil has a multiple impact on the Venezuelan economy.

Now we know that the mechanism described above leaves some leaks as well. Part of the expenditures end up as savings, part are spent outside of the country, and so on. This signifies that there exist some limitations in the operation of these same mechanisms as multipliers, given that the leakages define a convergence of the different wheels of expenditures. Likewise it must be recognized that the first impulse generated by oil expenditures will not operate given the influence of leaks from the circular flow of the economy. In this last case we can attribute the lower limits to the multiplier effects of the current expenditures of oil, when we consider only the domestic component of oil activities. This is the retained value of current expenditures.

In the previous section we saw that investment expenditures also had a multiplier effect due to the exogenous demand for oil. Let us explicitly consider that part of these expenditures escape the circular flow of the Venezuelan economy. Instead of considering the multiplier-accelerator effect of the total expenditure of the oil sector, adjusted for the foreign component, we should instead obtain the retained earnings of total oil expenditures as an indicator of the magnitude contributed by petroleum.

Let us now observe the absolute values and the behavior of these variables during the period we are examining, which appear in Table 4.3. Concentrating first on the oil sector's value added, defined as the gross domestic product of oil at 1957 prices, we clearly see that it went rapidly from nothing in 1917 to reach 16 million bolívares in 1922.[31] The average growth in absolute terms was of 4 million bolívares annually from 1917 to 1922. If we take 1918 as a base year, oil production grew more than tenfold.

As for the retained values of total expenditures, which appear in Table 4.4, the statistics begin in 1916 and show a rapid expansion. The increases in retained value intensify from 1920 onward, with the values of this variable doubling until the end of the period. The absolute average growth of the oil sector's total expenditures retained value between 1915 and 1922 was just a little below 3 million bolívares per year, which was inferior to the rate of expansion of petroleum gross domestic product.

In Table 4.4 data are also presented on the value of oil production for those years. This variable, which is equivalent to total current expenditures of the oil sector, also experienced a rapid expansion starting with zero, like the other two previously discussed variables. The pace of expansion of this variable was less than that of the gross domestic oil product

Table 4.4.
Retained Value of Oil Sector, 1910–1922 (millions of bolívares)

	1910-15	1916	1917	1918	1919	1920	1921	1922
Retained Value of Oil Sector Expenditures	0	1	3	3	4	5	9	19
Total Value of Production	0	0	1	3	4	7	11	14
Retained Value as a Percent of Total Oil Sector Expenditures	11.1%	--	33.3%	50%	33.3%	15.2%	37.5%	43.2%

Notes: Estimates of retained value and value of production are based on adjustments to data from three main petroleum company goods. Conversion of value of sales to value of production are based on unpublished data from the Oficina Técnica de Hidrocaburos, Ministerio de Minas e Hidrocarburos. Total oil sector expenditures include the value of production and investment.

and less than that of the total retained value.[32] The value of production grew approximately 2.5 million bolívares a year from 1916 to 1922, in a consistent manner throughout those years.

As we can appreciate by examining these groups of figures, the importance of the oil sector as the generator of a multiplier-accelerator effect of expenditure and income in the Venezuelan economy was the rate of economy's expansion. In regard to the absolute value, from the domestic product to the value of retained earnings, its relative importance was still small within the context of the Venezuelan economy.[33]

The national income of Venezuela in 1914 was estimated to be about 800 million bolívares in current prices.[34] On the other hand, the GDP has been estimated at 2,859 million bolívares (in constant 1957 bolívares) for 1920 and 3,085 million bolívares for 1922, as can be seen in Table 4.3. Therefore, oil represented less than 5 percent of gross domestic product as late as 1922.[35]

The retained value of total oil expenditures not only expresses an immediate direct contribution of this sector by generating a flow of income and expenditure and multiplying it various times in the circular flow mechanism, but it also represents a reliable indicator of the net contribution of oil to the economy.[36] Thus we can conclude that the net contribution of oil expanded rapidly during this period, but that even at the end of this period, its relative importance was small for the Venezuelan economy.[37] The higher the retained value component of the oil industry's total expenditure, the greater is the industry's contribution. The percentage of total retained value over the oil sector's total expenditures (value of production plus investment) will indicate, in the case of the same increases over time, a greater preoccupation on the part of the government to extract the largest possible contribution from the oil firms.

Table 4.4 shows this indicator, and it presents erratic changes in its value from 1917 to 1922. This suggests that there was not a clear policy of increasing the domestic oil expenditures to expand the industry's contribution to the economy. In general, the government of Gómez did not seem interested in obtaining for the country any benefits from the oil business, except those that accrued to the dictator and a few privileged individuals. This became even clearer in the following periods. The behavior of the percentage appears to be determined by the low level of total expenditures until 1920, which grew rapidly in 1920 and 1921, leaving behind the local component. In 1922 the local component experienced a comeback, inspired maybe in part by measures adopted by the only *Gómecista* with a conscience, Minister of Development Gumersindo Torres, of the potential benefits that were afforded by petroleum.

The utilization of these oil contributions could not be easily evaluated directly. Indirectly, we can consider the development of the economy as the partial result of the oil activity's contribution. Collecting the scarce information available on the Venezuelan economy in this period, it would seem to indicate that the 13 years included in it were years of routine economic growth. It is possible that the growth rate during the whole period was only slightly inferior to that achieved from 1920 to 1922, which, expressed annually, is equivalent to a cumulative average yearly rate of 3.9 percent. Besides the oil activities, this can be explained fundamentally by basis of the expansion of the number of traditional products exported by Venezuela and by the general impact of the rising trend of exported goods including petroleum.[38] The result of the expansion of these exogenous forces was a bonanza for the National Treasury, and an expansion in governmental activities.

Agriculture and industry (almost entirely handicraft industry) must have expanded during those years under the influential push of the exogenous forces and the increase in government expenditure. Finally, the third-rank sectors obviously must have grown *pari passu* with the increase in the traditional exports and with petroleum, as a fundamental part of that is the export-import trade and domestic commerce. The expansion of these other sectors also contributed, along with the exogenous variables and government to the growth of the financial, transportation, and communications and service sectors related to commercial activities.

As has been pointed out previously, one of oil's contributions to the economy, as indicated by the total retained value, was realized through the services of education and healthcare performed by the oil firms. These services benefited a growing number of people through the passing of the years, because of the expansion of petroleum employment. In providing these services, the industry assumed responsibilities that really belonged to the government.[39] These services could be used by the relatives of the oil workers and once in a while by persons not related to the industry. These contributions, as well as those related to the use of roads and other construction projects and services provided and paid for by the oil industry, although not as important as the contributions previously examined, were sources of significant external savings for the Venezuelan economy.

In conclusion, the contribution of petroleum in the form of a multiplier effect on the income and expenditure of the Venezuelan economy was significant only toward the end of the period. Even during those later years, oil was still a reduced sector within the Venezuelan economy and its impact was limited in absolute terms. Nevertheless, the effect of its dynamic impact during the second half of the period under examination constituted a significant contribution by the oil industry.

If we consider the other contributions of the oil industry (external, fiscal, through investment, etc.) and especially if we take into account the impact of the area of influence of the oil sector (government, construction, commerce), the impact of oil has to be considered significant only after the end of World War I. The rapid growth experienced by these contributions starting at that time was certainly an important influence on the performance of the Venezuelan economy.

As far as the way these contributions were utilized, our only indicator is the growth of the economy itself. This appears to have been rather good during the period, which suggests that the oil revenues were used adequately by the Venezuelan economy, despite the fact that only during the period 1918–1922, the term of office of Minister Torres, did there seem to be some relevant government policy toward petroleum.[40]

NOTES

1. See R. Veloz, *Finances and the Economy of Venezuela from 1830 to 1944* (Caracas, 1945).

2. Any surplus in production was typically stored for future exports. The operations were practically all owned by Shell Oil Company, which through the Caribbean Petroleum Corporation was producing oil out of the field in Mene Grande. Shell built a small refinery in San Lorenzo and storage facilities in La Guaira, Caracas, and Puerto Cabello. With these installations Shell began to supply the principal centers of Venezuelan petroleum consumption, competing primarily in the distribution process with Standard Oil. Standard imported petroleum products because it did not extract oil in Venezuela.

3. From 1913 to just after World War I the price of Venezuelan imports is likely to have increased because these imports were primarily industrial goods that were in relatively short supply during the war. Once the conflict ended, however, import prices were likely to have fallen. A discussion and evidence of the terms of trade during this period appear in Armando Córdova, "La Estructura Económica Tradicional y el Impacto del Petróleo en Venezuela," *Economía y Sciencias Sociales,* January–March 1963.

4. See Edwin Lieuwein, *Petroleum in Venezuela* (Berkeley, 1954).

5. Supposedly for future exploitation by an agency of the Venezuelan Government.

6. This law in reality regulated the development of the industry for the following 20 years.

7. Juan Vicente Gómez and his most intimate colleagues in public and private life enriched themselves with the juicy payments of the companies, made to obtain, retain, and renew the petroleum concessions.

8. See information later in the chapter. Also see Lieuwein, *Petroleum.*

9. The exceptions were Gómez's: investments in farms, factories, and hotels. The Venezuelan courts estimated that he had benefited by approximately 20 million bolívares from the concession business.

10. For further references see Lieuwein, *Petroleum.*

11. See J.J. Bracho Sierra, *Cincuento Años de Ingressos Fiscales* (Caracas, 1963).

12. For example, the high tax revenues of 1919 and 1920, mainly a result of strong imports, seemed to have surprised the government and as a consequence produced surpluses. The opposite occurred in 1921 when a recession took place. This caused a reduction in government spending in 1922 and another surplus, although smaller than those of 1919 and 1920.

13. If we take into account not only the direct oil contribution, but payments for concessions and import tax revenues generated by the oil activities, the importance of this sector of the economy becomes much more evident.

14. See Charles Rollins, "Raw Materials Development and Economic Growth: A Study of the Bolivian and Venezuelan Experience," (Ph.D. diss., Stanford University, 1956).

15. We can write that the tax revenues were particularly well utilized because during all these years the expenditures on the social and economic development of Venezuela exceeded the tax revenues coming from oil (directly and indirectly), growing in absolute terms more than the oil revenues, which could be interpreted as their assignment to the economic and social development of the country.

16. This does not mean, on the contrary, that the role of investment is not important to the economic business cycles of developing countries or to the growth of advanced nations.

17. This was extremely important for a traditional economy like Venezuela in the decade of the 1910s, which operated in a vicious circle of low savings and low investment. Investment demand is an effective manner of breaking this cycle, and petroleum, acting as an exogenous factor, produced this effect.

18. World War I did not affect this level of investment except in 1918, the most critical year of the war, in which investment decreased to only 3 million bolívares.

19. From 1910 to 1914 investment was exclusively an exploratory activity. Few companies were actually operating in the industry and some, like the General Asphalt Company, were working in concessions that were originally granted for asphalt exploration and exploitation. The big oil companies did not appear on scene until 1914, although it is known that British interests were handling some of the more important concessions granted by Gómez, and that in 1913 Shell had purchased General Asphalt's interests. The first oil well out of which extraction was feasible in Venezuela was not commercially worthwhile. It was discovered by the New York and Bermudez Co., a subsidiary of General Asphalt, in Lake Guanoco, toward the middle of 1913. Of the three major petroleum groups, only Shell was noticeable for its activities until 1922. This has made it very difficult to estimate investment during this period, especially because starting in 1914 with the tangible discovery of oil reserves, the number of companies operating in Venezuela multiplied. We should consider our estimates to

be low given the difficulty in finding information on all the companies. However, this is compensated, at least partly, by the inclusion in our estimates of some costs that are not actually part of fixed investment in the oil industry, such as concession costs.

20. Because of the situation described previously, statistics on Venezuelan oil did not start until 1917.

21. Even foodstuffs and labor had to be imported from outside the country.

22. Another factor explaining the rapid expanding trend of the industry starting in 1919 was the relevance acquired by oil, which was made clear by the war. Therefore, although oil investment was hampered by World War I in the short run, in the long run it gave it a great impulse.

23. Investments by other companies were directed at places of exploration and extraction of crude oil with particular emphasis on the first. Already toward the end of 1922, exploratory activities had covered the major part of Lake Maracaibo. As Lieuwein put it in *Petroleum in Venezuela*, "The grand scale exploitation of oil would soon begin" (p. 70).

24. The growth in export values of the agricultural products was basically due to price increases, although export quantities also rose.

25. See Córdova, "La Estructura Económica," pp. 11, 12.

26. The population of Venezuela grew very slowly until the 1920s (less than 1 percent annually) and agriculture expanded *pari passu*, to provide a level of per capita income that was practically constant. To give an impression of the investment levels involved, there is only need to cite the estimated $3.1 million in imported machinery by Venezuela in 1913. At an exchange rate of 5.20 bolívares per dollar, these imports represented 16.3 million bolívares. See Córdova "La Estructura Económica," p. 28.

27. Although the government is usually classified in the third sector, we have preferred to treat it as separate given its strategic importance for the growth of the other sectors in the economy, which was specifically relevant in the case of Venezuela.

28. Of some importance also was the boost received by foreign trade importers of machinery and equipment.

29. Something similar, but on a smaller scale, happened in the improvement and repair of machinery and equipment for the petroleum industry.

30. That is to say, from the current expenses on primary factors and inputs, obtained a physical product is. To each of these units, a sale value is given, whether sold effectively or whether it goes on to become part of inventory.

31. Value added is gross value added, when we cannot subtract the capital used in its production—that is, capital depreciation; it is net value when we do. Because depreciation funds create replacement demand, gross domestic product offers the most adequate measure of the full impact of the total expense of the oil industry over other sectors.

32. The value of production was less than gross domestic oil product during these years because firms were spending in anticipation of future commercial petroleum production. This occurred throughout the entire period and created the discrepancy. Also an applicable number of the firms that operated in Venezuela were never able to reach their oil potential and thus suffered losses. For these firms value added was larger than value of production.

33. It should be pointed out here that the confidence levels on the estimates of the three variables presented in Table 4.4 are not equal. In the case of retained value for total expenditures, the information given by the companies and from other sources of data, about the composition of domestic and imported components, is quite precarious.

34. See Chamber of the Oil Industry, *Boletín Informativo*, no. 31.

35. If we take into account not only the direct impact of the oil sector but also the indirect effect, its significance grows by some measure. Toward the end of this era oil was already influencing commercial activity, construction, and government.

36. On this issue, and for a more detailed explanation of the concept of retained value of total expenditures, see Chapters 2 and 3. Briefly, from total expenditures we subtract all payments for imports of goods and services, those to nonresident factors of production, and the remittances of resident factors, to obtain total retained expenditures.

37. The retained value of oil, after subtracting direct taxes, was approximately three times larger than these taxes during the 1917–1922 period (see Tables 4.2 and 4.4). This signals that most of the net contribution of oil was not made through the public sector as would occur later (see Chapter 6). The small importance of the direct contribution of oil is confirmed if we compare the retained value with the government's fiscal expenditure (see Table 4.4). As an average, if we begin with 1916, the percentage that represents the retained value over public expenditures does not reach 10 percent during the period. It's a well-known fact that at the time, the government did not constitute a relevant actor in the economy of the country.

38. Oil prices, which rose rapidly until 1920, plummeted in 1921 and 1922, but were not lower than those at the beginning of oil exploration in Venezuela. On the other hand, it must be recognized that part of the increase in the prices of the traditional agricultural products of Venezuelan exports represented a rebound from the low levels that characterized the last years of the 19th century and the decade of the 1920s.

39. Because the salaries were higher than those in agriculture (5 bolívares for 12-hour workdays), the industry began to absorb labor. However, this source was not very abundant, making it necessary to import labor from the Caribbean islands. In 1921 the Caribbean Company had only 1,150 workers, four-fifths of which were unskilled Venezuelan workers (see Lieuwein, *Petroleum*). Lieuwein also informs us that around the same time, the North Venezuelan Company and the British-controlled oil fields employed 600 workers each in spite of being involved only in exploratory activities, while Venezuelan Oil Concession, another Shell subsidiary that discovered the La Rosa oil field in 1922, had 217 employees.

40. Moreover, during these years, oil policy was conceived only in terms of the bounties, especially in terms of tax revenues, that could be obtained from petroleum and not with regard to the utilization of these revenues.

CHAPTER 5

1923–1929

It was in December 1922 that the famous explosion of Pozo Barroso No. 2 occurred in La Rosa field. The quantity of oil that spewed into the air in the form of a black geyser was proof that the oil reserves in Venezuela were ready to be exploited. Just a few months before this occurrence, a law had been enacted that satisfied the oil companies. Consequently, 1923 saw the beginning of an accelerated expansion of oil production in Venezuela. This expansion occurred mainly around the rich Bolivar oil field, on the eastern coast of Lake Maracaibo.

The oil industry had uninterrupted success until 1926. During these years, the prices of traditional agricultural exports of Venezuela also rose and their production increased. The result was a correlated expansion of the other sectors of the economy, with the exception being agricultural production for the domestic market, which was much affected by labor emigration to oil-related activities. Venezuela's economic expansion occurred simultaneous to worldwide trade expansion and economic growth.

THE CONTRIBUTION OF OIL THROUGH THE EXTERNAL SECTOR

During this period, the oil sector became the most important factor in the Venezuelan economy. After 1925, oil sector exports surpassed those of the coffee industry in economic importance, which had been the mainstay of Venezuela's external sector since its independence. Oil exports exceeded all others in absolute growth, and became by far the largest contributor to total exports from 1922 onward. From 1922 to 1929, oil exports represented an average of 50.4 percent of the total exports (see Table 5.1). The share in total exports of oil grew from 8.9 to 81.1 percent.

Growth of total exports in this period was 626.7 percent, which was equivalent to a yearly increase of 32.8 percent. The above estimation yield in the case of the oil industry was 6,533.3 and 82.1 percent, respectively. It is evident that the external contribution of oil was massive, and it expanded rapidly during these years. Due to lack of statistical data we cannot assert the same about its *net* contribution (measured by exchange rates or by the net export of the oil sector), although it would be surprising if it were any different.

It should be pointed out that the volume of exports, or exports in real terms, demonstrated changes in the case of oil because in 1927 prices fell to their lowest level of the decade. A slight recuperation took place in 1929. The cause of this drop was the enormous expansion in Venezuela's oil production and in the production of the oil fields of Texas (see Table 5.1).

The volume of oil exports grew 6,450 percent during the 1923–1929 period, representing a yearly average of 81.1 percent. Obviously this rate was high partly as a result of the low initial levels of oil exports. It exaggerates the expansion in oil production that took place between 1923 and

Table 5.1.
Petroleum Sector Indicators and External Sector Performance, 1922–1929

	1922	1923	1924	1925	1926	1927	1928	1929
Total Exports (Mill. Bs.)	135	154	222	366	456	530	678	981
Oil Exports (Mill. Bs.)	12	26	74	173	307	366	535	796
Oil Exports as Share of Total	8.9%	16.9%	33.3%	47.3%	67.3%	69.1%	78.9%	81.1%
Total Imports (Mill. Bs.)	101	153	216	304	412	364	417	453
Net Exports (Mill. Bs.)	34	1	6	62	44	166	261	528
International Reserves (Mill. Bs.)	60	61	77	90	91	102	122	125
Change in Reserves (Mil. Bs.)	-9	1	16	13	1	11	20	3
Total Exports (Mil. US $)	26	29	42	70	87	101	129	187
Oil Exports (Mil. US $)	2	5	14	33	58	70	102	152
Oil Exports (Millions of Barrels)	22	3	8	18	33	57	101	131
Oil Export Prices (US $ per Barrel)	2.21	2.49	2.91	3.02	3.04	1.81	1.72	1.97

Note: International Reserves include only gold within the banking system, although most reserves were held in this form during the period.

Sources: Ministerio de Fomento, Dirección General de Estadísticas, *Anuario Estadístico* (Caracas, 1938 and various years); Ministerio de Minas e Hidrocarburos, *Petróleo y Otros Datos Estadísticos* (Caracas, 1964); Ministerio de Fomento, *Anuario Estadístico* (Caracas, various years); D. F. Maza Zavala, *Venezuela: Una Economía Dependiente* (Caracas, 1964); Banco Central de Venezuela, *Memoria* (various years).

1929. In absolute terms, production of oil grew by 128 million barrels. Among the factors that made Venezuela so successful as the second largest producer and largest exporter of oil is that the prices of oil increased favorably from 1922 to 1926.[1] Venezuela's oil and total exports in dollars are shown in Table 5.1. Because the exchange rate of the bolívar to the dollar was 5.25 with small oscillations around this rate during the 1920s, the value of exports follows the same pattern illustrated by the nominal exchange rate, a trend that did not occur in other periods.[2]

In addition to a substantial increase in the participation of oil in total exports and of the growth, in absolute terms, of oil exports, all indications are that the net contribution of oil was equally important. Although there are no data to prove this assertion (statistical data in net exports and inflows of foreign currency do not exist for the period), one could speculate about the magnitude of the net contribution of oil.

Despite the employment of foreign personnel who were paid in dollars, imports of machinery, inputs, and even consumer goods, it has been conclusively documented that employment of local labor by the oil companies grew during this period. At the same time, purchases from local businesses were made and contracts with local construction companies were granted.[3] All of this expansion was possible not only because of oil production but because of large investments in this sector. At the same rate, corporate expenses in bolívares increased to meet expenses, which implied an external contribution in expanding. Although imports in the oil industry grew, total oil exports exceeded total trade balances.

How was the exceptional contribution of oil utilized during this period? The figures in Table 5.1 in total imports of goods indicate that imports of goods quadrupled, if one takes 1922 as the starting point. If 1923 is taken as the base, they almost tripled. Imports grew at a slower pace but parallel to total exports until 1926. From 1926 on, the difference between import and export growth widened due to the very rapid expansion of the latter.[4] Toward the end of the period, repayment of foreign debt was accelerated and international reserve increased. This seems to have been the appropriate economic policy during this period, because the economy was growing at a very strong pace.

On the other hand, the utilization of contribution of foreign currency by the oil sector seems also to have been efficient, judging from the scarce statistical data on types of import goods. Table 5.2 shows the percentage composition of the value of Venezuela's imports in two years, one from the 1910–1922 period and the other from the 1923–1929 period. Assuming that these two years were representative of the import structure of their respective periods, the data show that use of foreign currency to buy capital and intermediate goods increased and imports of consumption goods decreased.[5] This implies that the Venezuelan economy was improving the distribution of currency among the different import needs. It is a known

Table 5.2.
Distribution of Imports by Type of Good, 1913 and 1926

Type of Good	1913	1926
Consumer Goods	75.7%	70.8%
Capital Goods	19.3%	20.0%
Intermediate Goods	5.0%	9.1%

Notes: Data do not include imports of gold and parcel post. Also, imports of petroleum companies are not included in the 1926 data.

Sources: Armando Córdova, "La Estructura Económica Tradicional y el Impacto Petróleo en Venezuela," *Economía y Ciencias Sociales,* January–March, 1963.

fact that as an economy accelerates the pace of development, a growing portion of its imports is made up of capital and intermediate goods.[6] The economic policies of government can help optimize the use of foreign currency in this direction. However, if an economy is developing successfully, imports will evolve as described above.

In summary, the contribution of oil to the rest of the Venezuelan economy through the external sector was very important during this period. The gross contribution of oil acquired a fundamental importance toward the second half of the period, both in relative and absolute terms.[7]

It is not difficult to conclude that the net contribution followed the same trajectory. The utilization of the contribution seems to have been very efficient during the period, insofar as the distribution of imports is concerned, and also regarding the absence of sterilization of the foreign exchange earnings generated by the oil sector.

THE FISCAL CONTRIBUTION OF OIL, 1923–1929

As we mentioned in Chapter 4, until the end of 1922 the oil industry was scarcely developed and the large reserves had not yet been discovered. The British oil companies were reluctant to start operations and the U.S. firms wanted a more liberal law before increasing their investments.[8] The Caribbean Company, a Shell subsidiary, was the only one producing at commercial scale in the Mene Grande field. Meanwhile, the other Shell subsidiaries were successfully drilling small oil wells, but were constrained by lack of adequate transportation and storage facilities. More than 80 percent of crude oil produced commercially by all Shell subsidiaries was being refined by the company's refinery in Curaçao and the rest was used for domestic consumption and refined in the San Lorenzo refinery. On the other hand, most of the Maracaibo Basin had been covered by simple exploration crews.

In the midst of this situation the oil legislation of 1922 began to be applied. Its objective was to provide incentives for the production of oil and to increase the fiscal revenues from oil. Shortly after enactment of this law the famous explosion of La Rosa in the Barroso No. 2 field occurred, approximately two kilometers away from Lake Maracaibo.

The explosion revealed the potential of the Bolivar field, which proved to be enough to produce two-thirds of Venezuela's oil. For many years the oil geyser in Barroso induced investors (particularly in the United States, which in the past had been left behind) to obtain concessions in the State of Zulia. Companies began drilling exploration fields all over the state but especially near Lake Maracaibo. Feeling themselves protected by the new oil laws, the companies expanded their investment in the areas of actual oil extraction, exploration, storage, transportation, refining, and marketing. As a result, Gulf and Standard Oil also began to export the newly discovered oil and to discover new fields. Oil production increased geometrically until 1929.[9] This brought as a consequence a large increase in tax collection of oil duties, making the dream of Venezuela's government a reality, and redefining the role of the state in the economy of the country.[10]

Gulf Oil and Standard Oil, which extracted oil from Lake Maracaibo fields, benefitted from the initial overestimation of the costs of extraction under water by obtaining a tax break from the government and better conditions in general. In reality, oil production in the lake waters turned out to be less costly than expected, owing to new technology and the advantage of the transportation the lake afforded. Furthermore, neither Gulf nor Standard Oil incurred high exploration costs. They limited themselves to drilling on the boundaries of their concessions, right next to the already drilled reserves that were also being exploited by Shell, particularly at La Rosa, where the greatest potential existed. This compensated for the disadvantage of Gulf and Standard vis-a-vis Shell, which had obtained its concessions under more favorable conditions than those made possible by the Hydrocarbons (petroleum) Law of 1922.[11] These two factors diminished the impact of this law on the fiscal revenues from oil.

Another factor that caused oil fiscal revenues to fall short of the expected levels during this period was the creation, in June 1923, by Gómez and his accomplices, of the Venezuelan Petroleum Company. This company had control of all the land that was incorporated into the national reserves—lands that were among the most important because they were part of the most productive oil concessions—which the oil companies had to give back, at least partly, to comply with the new oil laws.

Gómez began to sell concessions in these lands to the oil companies for the sole purpose of benefitting himself and his friends. He would attempt in a thousand different ways to obtain high prices, receiving from one company $250,000 for 15,000 hectares plus a 2.5 percent supplementary

property tax, and $750,000 for 75,000 hectares plus 50 percent of the sub-
sidiary company set up to exploit the concession. When the national
reserves of land were exhausted toward the end of the 1920s, the company
disappeared. It is estimated that Gómez and his comrades received
approximately 40 million bolívares in this transaction, which obviously
was a net loss in terms of fiscal revenues.[12]

On the other hand, customs revenues increased dramatically during the
period, due in part to the economic activity generated by oil. They
increased fivefold in the Maracaibo custom and doubled in La Guaira and
Puerto Cabello. This phenomenon underlines the relative importance of
oil exports, and of the imports of the State of Zulia, which revolved
around the purchases of the oil companies or their employees.

The migration to the oil-producing cities was in excess of that needed to
satisfy the oil companies. The cities that multiplied around the fields also
generated other types of employment, based on services needed by the oil
companies and their employees. The population of Cabimas, for example,
went from 2,000 at the beginning of the period to 20,000 toward the end.
Something along the same lines occurred in Lagunillas. The city of Maracaibo went from 20,000 to become the second largest city in Venezuela,
with a population in 1935 of 80,000 people.[13] In general, trade prospered
due not only to the imports of the oil companies, but also because of their
domestic purchases.

Table 5.3 shows the total tax collection, revenues, and expenditures
relating directly to oil activities. It can be noted that fiscal revenues grew
rapidly during the period, tripling from 1922 or 1923 to 1929. The direct
revenues of the oil activity expanded even more rapidly, growing seven-

Table 5.3.
Government Sector Fiscal Indicators, 1922–1929 (millions of bolívares)

	1922	1923	1924	1925	1926	1927	1928	1929
Government Revenues	81	89	112	148	179	175	204	256
Public Revenues from the Oil Sector	8	4	6	21	18	21	46	51
Oil as a Percent of Government Revenues	9.9%	4.5%	5.4%	14.2%	10.1%	12.0%	22.5%	19.9%
Government Expenditures	76	79	101	139	171	167	225	209
Economic & Social Development Expenditures (ESD)	29	29	38	60	82	93	110	107
ESD as a Percent of Government Expenditures	38.2%	36.7%	37.6%	43.2%	47.9%	55.7%	48.9%	51.2%
Public Treasury Reserves	35	51	66	71	80	83	114	100

Sources: Ministerio de Fomento, *Anuario Estadístico* (Caracas, 1937 and 1938); Ministerio de
Minas e Hidrocarburos, *Petróleo y Otros Datos Estadísticos* (Caracas, 1965); J. J. Bracho Sierra,
Cincuenta Años de Ingresos Fiscales (Caracas, 1963); and Charles Rollins, "Raw Materials
Development and Economic Growth: A Study of the Bolivian and Venezuelan Experience,"
Ph.D. dissertation, Stanford University, 1956.

fold in 1922 and thirteenfold in 1923. That of itself implies the growth of the participation of oil in tax revenues.

The participation of oil in the fiscal revenue of Venezuela went from 5 to 10 percent at the beginning of the period to 20 percent of total commencement revenues in 1929. Because government revenues tripled in this period, an increase in the participation of oil in the total fiscal revenue was hard to achieve. The oil tax revenue figures don't include taxes on import activity related to oil, which constituted the most important part of the import taxes, and in turn were the most important part of total government revenues.[14]

If we take these taxes into consideration it would be estimated that the participation of oil was about 50 percent of total government revenues in 1929. Therefore, the contribution of oil through public spending was rather important during the period under examination, especially if we take into account the indirect contribution of oil to fiscal revenues through import taxes. On the other hand, this contribution grew sufficiently to increase the general level of economic activity in Venezuela, and thus facilitated the expansion of other sectors.

Insofar as the utilization of the fiscal contribution was concerned, we should consider total government expenditures. Table 5.3 shows these fiscal spending figures for the corresponding period. This expansion was somewhat smaller than the one that occurred in fiscal revenues. As a consequence, the national reserves grew throughout the period, reaching approximately 50 percent of total fiscal spending (see Table 5.3).

This increase in the reserves of the Treasury, which represented a sterilization of the fiscal contribution of oil, could be justified in the following ways:

1. The effort being made by the Venezuelan government to pay off its external and domestic debt, which had been high in the past, and the desire to eliminate future indebtedness[15]

2. The rapid growth of the economy in these years, which caused price hikes and seemed to suggest the necessity of slowing expansion

The fiscal expenditure here can be seen as promoting the social and economic development of the country. This development is mainly achieved through more investments and expenses related to education, health, and industrial promotion efforts.

During the period in question, these types of expenditures increased more rapidly than total spending and, therefore, the proportion of development-related expenditures to total expenditures increased noticeably (see Table 5.3). At the beginning of the period this proportion represented more than a third of total fiscal expenditures, and toward the end of the period it already represented half of them. On the other hand, the proportion of expenditures corresponding to each ministry did not change appreciably as total expenditures rose, which suggests that the improved allocation took place primarily in their distribution within each ministry.

Besides the reductions of foreign and domestic debt, the other effort of the government during this period was in the area of public works. Apparently, the most important component of expenditures as a function of economic development seems to have been public works and not the development of education, health, agriculture, or industry.[16]

In conclusion, we can say that the direct contribution of oil, and even more the indirect contribution, was very important and expanded rapidly during this period. The indirect contribution was more important than the direct contribution during these years, because of the pattern established in the previous period. The extraordinary revenues obtained by the sale of concessions, which we considered an indirect source due to their special and irregular nature, were significant during this period, but much less significant than what they would have been had the concessions been granted directly to the foreign oil companies.

In reality the revenues of the Venezuelan Petroleum Company were large and represented not less than 5 percent of the average annual budget during these years. Therefore they deserve to be considered an extension of the fiscal revenues of Venezuela. Finally, due to the fiscal contribution of oil, the other sectors of the economy were relieved of fiscal pressure, which undoubtedly had a favorable effect on them.

Insofar as the utilization of the fiscal contribution of oil is concerned, we can assert that the sterilization that took place was necessary, given the pressures that existed over the productive resources during these years and the inflation that this generated. The reduction of public debt and the increase in the reserves of the treasury seem to have been the two principal mechanisms through which this partial sterilization was performed. The distribution of public expenditure improved during this period, with more attention being devoted to the promotion of social and economic development. The oil companies promoted the nations' development through their expenditures on public works, health, and education. This impulse would have been stronger if the concessions had generated revenues to the government instead of benefitting a few individuals in privileged positions. However, it must be recognized that some of these revenues would be allocated to expenditures and instruments of use, important to the development of Venezuela.

THE CONTRIBUTION OF THE OIL INDUSTRY THROUGH INVESTMENT

Oil investment contributes to the rest of the Venezuelan economy in two ways: on the one hand it is a source and a multiplier of income and expenditure, and on the other it stimulates the investment goods sector. During these years in which the Venezuelan economy was still in a traditional stage of development, the latter contribution took place solely through the construction industry, and to some extent in machinery repair activities. In these areas, the oil industry generated externalities when undertaking the activities on its own and when hiring foreign firms to undertake them: this was probably the first large-scale contract of the Venezuelan economy with modern technology.

Table 5.4 shows estimates of the magnitude of oil investment for the period 1922–1929. The oil figures toward the end of the period jumped from just a few tens of million to several hundred million bolívares in 1927. Investment dropped substantially in 1928 because of the existing oversupply of oil in the markets, recuperating partially in 1929. Most of the investments during these years took place in the western part of Venezuela, where the explosion of the Barroso well occurred in December 1922. However, investments in the eastern part of the country, which started in the middle of the period, reached appreciable levels from 1927 onward.[17] These were stimulated by the favorable conditions facing Venezuelan oil then and into the foreseeable future, and, most important, the friendliness between the government and the oil companies foreseen under the 1922 law.[18] The investments made during this period were of several types and changed Venezuela from an insignificant producer in 1922 to the largest exporter and second largest producer of oil (just behind the United States) in 1928. Invest-

Table 5.4.
Gross Domestic Product and Gross Fixed Domestic Investment, Oil Sector, 1922–1929

	1922	1923	1924	1925	1926	1927	1928	1929
Total GDP (Mill. 1957 Bs.)	3,085	3,514	3,934	4,231	4,348	4,111	4,960	4,305
Oil Sector GDP (Mill. 1957 Bs.)	16	31	65	143	255	432	758	973
As a Share of Total GDP	0.5%	0.9%	1.7%	3.4%	5.9%	10.5%	15.3%	22.6%
Gross Fixed Domestic Investment (Mill. Bs.)	30	29	90	105	234	248	171	196

Notes: Oil sector GDP and Fixed Investment estimates are based on the records of the three main petroleum company groups in Venezuela: Shell Oil, Gulf Oil, and Standard Oil of New Jersey. Adjustments were then made to reflect industry totals. Gross Fixed Investment estimates may be overstated by the inclusion of exploration costs, such as concessions and capitalization costs, which are not properly fixed investment. Total GDP estimates are based on Armando Córdova, "La Estructura Económica Tradicional y el Impacto Petróleo en Venezuela," *Economía y Ciencias Sociales*, January–March, 1963, and lectures given by Bernardo Ferran on Venezuelan economic history, delivered at the Universidad Central de Venezuela, Caracas, 1963.

Sources: See Córdova (1963) and Ferran (1963).

ments continued in exploration, development of basins, exploration of adjacent fields, production activities, transportation, storage, and refineries (expansion of the San Lorenzo refinery and construction of La Salina).[19]

As Lieuwein accurately expressed, Venezuela was like a zone of forerunners that required large initial investments in infrastructure such as highways, houses, storage facilities, repair shops, oil pipes for energy production, and transportation. Trucks and drilling equipment had to be imported from the United States and Europe. A small fleet of oil carriers was needed to take the crude oil from the lake to the loading terminals located in deeper waters.[20] This is why although many companies operated in Venezuela, most of them would sublet their concessions to the larger firms. However, it is also true that many small companies made investments but never found oil. Therefore, we must consider the investment figures of Table 5.4 as underestimating the magnitude of total investment in the sector.

The peak in oil investment that took place in this period was also backed by the technology developed by the industry in the 1920s, which was tested in the United States and applied in the basin of Lake Maracaibo.[21] This resulted in a high rate of mechanization of the industry and frequent replacement of equipment.

The oil fever in Venezuela was so intense, due to the rapid growth of output, that the drop in oil prices and the adverse market situation of the late 1920s did little to counter the enthusiasm. Investment decreased toward the end of 1927 and a good part of 1928, recovering in 1929. The fundamental cause of this phenomenon was the continued expansion of Venezuelan oil in the American and world markets. This expansion was possible because of the (relatively) lower production costs of Venezuelan oil as well as the low cost of transporting the oil to the large U.S. market. In fact, had it not been for the transportation bottleneck between the fields and the main terminals in the high seas, the expansion could have been greater.[22]

The oil companies brought or built special oil carriers to transport crude oil within the lake and to go through the sandbars that existed at its sea outlet. It was not until 1929 that a system of lights and buoys was installed to allow navigation 24 hours a day. Because of this, the demand for oil by the firms was not satisfied in a timely manner. As a matter of fact, new oil wells had to be closed temporarily while awaiting the arrival of new ships.

Another type of expenditure that contributed to the large investments of those years was in health and education. This was necessary in part to attract workers to the oil-producing areas, where locations were not very favorable for human settlements and labor. The effort to improve the hygiene and working conditions turned out to justify themselves in terms of increases in the productivity of oil workers and a reduction of exploration expenses. Firms made investments in pharmacies, hospitals, sewage, water cleaning, and general sanitation (e.g., combating the spread of mosquitoes), for the purpose of making the region of the lake habitable.[23] Something similar occurred in the area of education: the firms tried to increase the educational level of the region's population by building schools and sports areas.

One should also take note of the construction of entire settlements of office buildings (headquartered in Maracaibo with branches in Caracas), roads, and the supply of energy and water. These benefited the personnel of the oil firms in particular and, to some extent, the Venezuelan people in general. Part of this construction activity was directly undertaken by the oil firms themselves and the rest was performed by construction companies, some of which came from abroad.[24]

What was the relative importance of oil investment during this period? Because there are no estimates available of total investment in the Venezuelan economy during these years, the relative importance of oil investment can only be determined based on the general knowledge of activity in the oil-producing sectors of the economy. Because the information is unclear, we must consider our attempts to estimate the relative importance of oil investment as conjectures.

The agricultural sector must have contributed to total investment at a level consistent with supporting population growth and reproduction of its own assets. Actually export agriculture, which expanded until 1925, declined thereafter, especially in terms of value. The increases in agricultural investment that were probably made until 1925, including those in export agriculture, were probably offset by declines from 1926 to 1929. On the other hand, the rest of commercial agriculture and subsistence agriculture do not seem to have grown appreciably, and investment in turn, must not have been large. Therefore, investment in agriculture, the largest sector in the Venezuelan economy during the period, doesn't seem to have been of a large magnitude and it is even questionable whether it was more than was needed to accommodate the population growth that took place.[25]

In the industrial sector, domestic activities' competition with imports probably grew at a slower pace than agriculture, while the modern activities had a larger expansion in some areas. However, the modern activities represented an incipient sector of the Venezuelan economy. As a whole, industrial investment did not grow at a faster pace than agricultural investment and it represented, in absolute terms, a less significant impact.

The commercial sector did experience a rapid expansion during this period. The entire third-rank (tertiary) sector was second in importance to agriculture. Thus, the amount of investment in absolute terms must have been considerable. Under the direct impact of oil and the multiplier effect that occurred among the subsection of the tertiary sector and also under the secondary influence of the expansion of the public sector, tertiary investment probably grew at a faster pace than the economy as a whole.[26]

Let us now consider the public sector. One of the fundamental changes that took place with the arrival of oil to the Venezuelan economy is the considerable increase in the importance of government in the economy. In this period fiscal expenditures practically tripled (see Table 5.3) and public investment and economic and social development expenditures also increased, even relative to the total budget.[27]

Therefore, we can conclude that public investment in this period represented a rather large portion of total investment. An idea of the importance of oil investment can be obtained from a comparison of budget figures. Looking at Table 5.4, the importance of oil investments, when they became comparable to the social and economic development expenditures of the government, did not become evident until 1924. But from then on they jumped to levels comparable to total fiscal expenditure, easily surpassing public investment.

If we consider investment as a whole, it is not difficult to conclude that, given the propensity to save and invest characteristic of traditional economies, total non-oil investment was not much higher than oil investment. A rough estimate of the relative importance of oil investment placed it at around 60 percent of the total in the period 1923–1929.

Oil investment represented not only a significant portion of total investment but it influenced growth in the rest of the economy during these years. The main supports of the non-oil investment were the public and tertiary sectors, to which oil gave the strongest impulse. Furthermore, oil investment had a double positive impact: on the one hand stimulating aggregate demand through the income and expenditure multiplier, and on the other hand fueling the formation of an investment goods sector.[28]

THE DOMESTIC PRODUCT AND TOTAL OIL EXPENDITURE

In addition to its investment expenditures, the oil sector makes necessary a series of expenses for the production, refining, transporting, and marketing of crude oil and derived products. Part of these current expenses represent payment to factors of production and constitute the industry's value added. Another part consists of purchases of goods and services produced by other firms, and they correspond to the value of the inputs purchased by the industry. If we add current expenses plus investment expenditures we obtain the total expenditures of the industry, and if we consider only the portion of the latter that is spent within the country we obtain the "retained value of oil."

The current expenditures of oil have a multiplier effect on the spending and income matrix of the Venezuelan economy, just as do the investment expenditures. However, these expenditures also have an important leakage and a reduced impact because of their foreign component. The concept of retained value of total oil expenditures is a reliable indicator of the net total contribution of oil. Let us then examine the evolution of the oil industry's impact on the Venezuelan economy.

Table 5.4 shows the gross domestic product of oil at 1957 prices. This consists of the payment to the factors of production or value added without depreciating the physical capital used in oil production. From 1923 on, the GDP of oil practically doubled each year until 1927 when it continued to expand at a still very high annual rate, but less than 100 percent per year. During this period growth was approximately 60 times the actual average, which is equivalent to a cumulative rate of growth of 77 percent as an average if we go back to 1923, and 80 percent as an average if we begin in 1922.

Table 5.5 shows the retained value of current expenditures of the oil sector during the years 1922 to 1929. These expenditures are equivalent to the value of production. The behavior of this variable is rather close to that of the gross domestic product of oil, except that its rate of growth is even higher. This was because in the early years of the period the value of production was less than the value added, as the oil industry as a whole was suffering losses.[29] The impact of oil through the primary sectors of production (labor, natural resources, capital, and so on) was slightly less than its influence over all the inputs (factor of production, raw materials, and so on).

We know that the effect of the value of production, and a substantial amount of the value added of oil, leaks out of the stream of money and out of the flow of goods and services of the Venezuelan economy. This has an impact on imports and on foreign-owned factors of production. Only the retained value of the current expenditures has a direct and immediate impact on the Venezuelan economy. If the retained value of the current expenditures was the retained value of the investment expenditures, we could obtain the retained value of the total expenditures of oil. This vari-

Table 5.5.
Retained Value of Oil Sector, 1922–1929 (millions of bolívares)

	1922	1923	1924	1925	1926	1927	1928	1929
Retained Value of Oil Sector Expenditures	19	19	32	54	78	96	187	225
Total Value of Production	14	15	40	87	143	252	403	467
Retained Value as a Percent of Total Oil Sector Expenditures	48.7%	48.7%	27.8%	32.0%	21.9%	20.4%	33.8%	35.2%

Notes: Estimates of retained value and value of production are based on adjustments to data from three main petroleum company goods. Conversion of value of sales to value of production is based on unpublished data from the Oficina Técnica de Hidrocaburos, Ministerio de Minas e Hidrocarburos. Total oil sector expenditures include the value of production and investment.

able offers the best estimate—the impact of oil on income, spending, and the circulation of goods and services in the Venezuelan economy. Furthermore, the total retained value is a good proxy of the net total contribution of oil.

Of the three variables we examined above, the lowest increment is shown by the oil's total retained value. In spite of this, the total retained value of oil increased approximately twelvefold. If one considers 1922 as the reference year, then this is equivalent to a cumulative average yearly growth of 42.5 percent. If one considers 1923 as the reference year, this growth is equivalent to a rate of 51 percent. The trajectory of total retained value is similar to that of value added and that of value of production, except that instead of doubling each year until 1926 and 1927, its increments are not as pronounced. It is also worth noting that between 1927 and 1928 the retained value increased more than in the other two series.[30]

To understand the importance of the total retained value we must compare it with another oil contribution having the same character. Let us utilize for that purpose the fiscal contribution of oil, which is also characterized by having a fundamentally retained content made up of payments to the National Treasury. At the beginning of the period, the total retained value (subtracting the fiscal contribution) oscillates between one to more than three times the fiscal contribution.[31]

After determining the importance of retained value in comparison to the other contributions of oil and concluding that it represents the major impact of oil on the economy, we must evaluate the significance of the impact on the Venezuelan economy as a whole. For this purpose, a key component of the economy on which there exists plenty of information, is the public sector.

A review of the figures of total retained value and of total fiscal expenditures (see Table 5.5) indicates that at the beginning of the period the total retained value represented approximately one third of fiscal spending. Starting in 1926 its relative importance jumped to 50 percent of fiscal spending and it continued to grow until, in 1929, retained value exceeded public spending.

Given the importance of the public sector in the Venezuelan economy, we must conclude that a flow of domestic spending amounting to 51.8 percent of fiscal spending during the period constitutes a fundamental influence over the behavior and development of the Venezuelan economy. Perhaps more important is the dynamic effect that such a rapid expansion of the total retained value may have on the traditional economy.[32]

So far we have examined the relative importance and the temporal behavior of the streams of earnings and spending coming directly from oil (its domestic product, value of production, and retained value). However, we know that indirectly, as we saw in the fiscal section, oil stimulated the economic activity of a series of sectors, especially the import and domestic trade section. Also affected were construction, health and education, and the public sector, as well as domestic industries and agriculture. If we take into account the impact of these expenditures, the importance of oil in the generation of income and spending is multiplied, and its influence on the activity of the rest of the Venezuelan economy becomes evident.[33] We must also consider that the multiplier increase of spending and income generates an accelerator effect on investment, when the latter accommodates demand.

One of the problems of the oil policy toward the end of the period was that, after the potential of the country was verified, the opportunity of negotiating arrangements favorable to Venezuela was not used to full advantage. In fact, during the Gómez era it can be said that there was no oil policy per se, but a defense of the interests of the dictator and those of the oil companies, only very occasionally interrupted by attempts to implement a semi-independent policy by nationalistic ministers of development.[34] There was no understanding, not even vaguely, of the capital importance of the retained value of oil to maximize the net contribution of the oil industry to the country.

Many times, however, certain policy decisions have unintended effects on retained value. To evaluate the effectiveness of governmental policy in achieving increases in oil's retained value, we can look at Table 5.5, which shows the ratio of retained value over the industry's expenditures. It can be verified that the variation of this ratio was considerable during the period, ranging between 20.4 and 48.7 percent. A trend can be easily observed, as the ratio decreased until 1927 and increased after that year, perhaps reflecting the return of Gumersindo Torres—the oil company nemesis—to the Ministry of Development. As an average during the period, the ratio of retained value/total oil expenditure was 33.6 percent.[35]

This ratio was lower than that obtained during the contractionary period that followed.[36] The difference can be attributed to an increased awareness of the advantages that the country could obtain given the potential of its oil resources and its current position in the oil business.[37] Other factors explaining this difference were the years of Torres and Nestor Perez in the Ministry of Development, at the beginning of this period and at the end of the next, and the country's higher degree of economic development, which facilitated the hiring of domestic workers and increased domestic purchases.

Table 5.4 shows the estimates of the real GDP of the Venezuelan economy. These estimates are not very reliable, because the most recent study of reference on Venezuela's national income was done in 1936.[38] However, this series is based on the scarce information available for the period in question.[39] We can observe that the Venezuelan economy grew rapidly between 1922 and 1926 and suffered a setback in 1927, which was largely overcome by 1928, only to plummet again in 1929.

Actually, until 1926 growth was fueled by the convenience of good harvests of the traditional export goods at relatively high prices and the expansion of oil. The former factor did not operate in the second half of the period, and oil entered into a more uncertain stage, which affected oil instruments in spite of not having affected production levels directly.

Although slower growth after 1926 can be explained, the leaps and setbacks included in the estimates that we've been using seem exaggerated. On the other hand, it is hard to believe that there was no real growth in the Venezuelan economy between 1920 and 1929, though we are aware that this was a period of high prices. Thus, we have to conclude that these figures are underestimated for 1929, and that probably those presented for 1928 are the best indicator of the levels corresponding to 1929.

The rates of growth during this period are 40.9 percent from 1922 to 1926, equivalent to a cumulative yearly average growth of –0.3 percent. But if we accept that the 1928 figure really corresponds to 1929, total and yearly growth rates become 14.1 percent and 4.5 percent, respectively. These are rather high rates of growth but much lower than those at the start of the period. This is one of the periods of Venezuela's economic history in which the influence of the oil industry was strongest and most favorable. Comparable to this boom period we have only those years between 1943 and 1948, and between 1949 and 1957. Not much can be said about the performance of the different sectors of the Venezuelan economy due to lack of data. The scant information available seems to indicate that as a result of the direct and indirect effects of oil and of its total net contribution, the government, the tertiary sector, and the construction sector expanded rapidly. As agriculture increased, the export subsector expanded notably until the middle of the period, thereafter entering a stage of reduction of the volume of production. In spite of the fact that high prices continued to prevail, subsistence agriculture and agriculture for domestic consumption were given a push by oil, with export agriculture and the substantial modifications that occurred in the domestic markets contributing to their expansion.[40]

In the second half of this period there doesn't seem to be any growth in the quantities produced, although increases in the prices of agricultural goods did occur. The real value of the agricultural output domestically consumed remained constant. Industrial production, with the exception of the construction sector, must have experienced an expansion parallel to that of the rest of the economy until 1926. From then on, handicrafts seemed to have suffered a reduction in the total volume produced, owing to the expansion of the manufacturing sector and of imports of competing manufacturing goods. However, because the prices of industrial products continued to increase, it seemed unlikely that the value of industrial output would decrease.[41]

The oil sector contributed to the economy, not only with the oil activities during the period in question but through other activities that it had to develop to attain its main objectives. The construction of infrastructure was in general beneficial for the population as a whole.[42] The same can be said, although to a lesser extent, of the sanitation works and improvements in hygiene and education brought about by the oil firms, as well as of the housing and facilities of the work camps.[43] Some facilities were specifically built for the oil workers and their families/dependents, which made the oil sector an example for the training and health of its personnel.[44]

To synthesize, the generation of income and direct expenditures by the oil sector and the immediate indirect effects that the same had on the other sectors (government, commerce, construction), had a positive impact on the other sectors of the Venezuelan economy, acting through the accelerator-multiplier mechanism and in the context of the circular flows of income and spending of the economy. As a result of this contribution, the contribution through investment, the external sector, and the fiscal revenues, all of which we have summed up in the retained value of the oil sector, the Venezuelan economy experienced a rapid expansion during this period, with less intensity toward the end of it.[45] All of this happened in spite of the absence of a clear, conscious decision to extract the highest possible benefits from the oil boom and in spite of the lack of an investment policy that sought to use oil revenues in the most productive way.[46]

NOTES

1. One of the fundamental factors was the competitive extraction between the three largest oil companies operating in Venezuela (Shell, Standard Oil, and Gulf), which were exploiting the same oil field in Lake Maracaibo. Their concessions were practically next to each other and there was fierce competition on volumes of production. Shell extracted on land, but close to the lake's eastern shore, while Gulf was on shallow waters and Standard in deep waters.

2. Armando Córdova, "La Estructura Económica Tradicional y el Impacto del Petróleo en Venezuela," *Economía y Ciencias Sociales* (January–March 1963), p. 14.

3. This is what attracted labor from Zulia, Los Andes, Aragua, and from the island of Margarita to the oil fields and the cities that were built near them. Jobs were also available in commercial, construction, and services dependent on the oil sector. The result was an increase of the population in several cities in Zulia during the 1920s.

4. Excess suppliers of oil in the world market began to accumulate in 1926. However, the Venezuelan oil industry, operating with very low costs, and with exceptional transportation advantages to the southeastern United States, stopped its expansion plans only temporarily in 1927. Venezuela was the last producer to be affected by the crisis announced by the drop in world oil prices.

5. Oil firm imports, to a very large extent capital goods, are not included in the value of imports for 1926. If included, this would increase the percentage of capital goods imports in total imports.

6. In part this is because higher investment is reflected in higher imports of capital goods and increased industrial production requires an increase in the imports of intermediate goods. On the other hand, this is also explained in terms of an industrial process that generally begins by producing consumer goods domestically, reducing, as a result, the proportion of consumption goods imported.

7. Furthermore, the terms of trade seem to have favored Venezuela during most of this period, because not only did the oil prices increase toward the end of the first half of the period but also traditional exports (coffee, cocoa, leather) increased in price. Unfortunately, by the second half of the period this trend reversed itself with unfavorable repercussions on the country.

8. Edwin Lieuwein, *Petroleum in Venezuela* (Berkeley, 1954), p. 68.

9. In terms of labor force employed, the Venezuelan oil concession, a Shell subsidiary that discovered the coast field in La Rosa, expanded in terms of labor force from 217 employees in 1922 to more than 6,000 in 1929.

10. It should be noted that Mexico now lagged behind Venezuela's collection of tax revenues from the oil activity in absolute terms. In fact, Venezuela took over most of Mexico's markets. As an example, Venezuela became the largest foreign supplier to the U.S. market as early as 1928.

11. Furthermore, Standard of New Jersey, which eventually acquired the interests of Standard of Indiana in Lake Maracaibo, became during the 1930s the most powerful oil company in Venezuela. The references to Standard made up to now in this book are in connection with Standard Oil of Indiana (initially more successful) and New Jersey, because both merged in Venezuela in the beginning of the 1930s.

12. Lieuwein, in *Petroleum,* verified these estimates.

13. The increase in imports contributed to a crisis in agriculture. The result was an uneven inflation in the price of food, which in turn caused a rise in imports of these goods.

14. More than 50 percent of government revenues came from this source.

15. One must consider the previous negative experiences of Venezuela with public debt, and that the policy of a balanced budget was generally accepted in the country.

16. See Lieuwein, *Petroleum.*

17. The focal point for all these investments was the discovery of the field of Quiriquire by Standard of New Jersey on June 1, 1928. This occurred at the Maturin Basin in the State of Monagas.

18. For instance, the imports of machinery and equipment could be made duty free.

19. Part of the investment was either fruitless or had long gestation periods in which innumerable oil companies did not find oil. For example, Standard of New Jersey had invested more than 20 million bolívares in eastern Venezuela without being able to produce crude oil for commercial purposes, in spite of having discovered the Quiriquire oil field. This very company had also invested unsuccessfully in the western part of the country. For further references on this matter see Lieuwein, *Petroleum in Venezuela* (Berkeley, 1954).

20. See Lieuwein (1954).

21. We just need to mention the new techniques of oil exploration and drilling at sea.

22. As of 1929 three-quarters of Venezuelan oil production was refined near the production sites, and of these 75 percent only 4 percent was refined in Venezuela. The rest of the oil was refined in Aruba, Curaçao, and Trinidad where the large oil firms had established huge refineries. The refineries built on Venezuelan soil were, on the contrary, small.

23. The most notable during the period was the establishment of a hospital in Maracaibo by the three major oil groups to take care of their most seriously ill patients.

24. Insofar as the companies built structures, adapted machinery, and in general created or improved capital stock, they generated a value added that perhaps is not accurately expressed by the estimates of domestic product presented later.

25. This was in the neighborhood of 2.7 percent during these years. See Córdova, "La Estructura Económica," p. 21.

26. It is well known that oil had its major direct impact on both the public and the tertiary sectors. The latter, in order to expand its commercial activity, applied pressure for the expansion of financial services. It will be noted later that the economy as a whole grew at a rate of 4.9 percent per year during these years.

27. Even though we do not have estimates of the government's capital expenditure, we may suppose that they expanded parallel to the social and economic development expenditures. The latter quadrupled during the period.

28. During these years this was limited exclusively to the construction of residential housing and infrastructure, and to major machinery repairs and improvements.

29. That is, the oil firms as a whole spent more on factors of production than the income corresponding to the value of their output during the corresponding year. This was in large part determined by a series of firms failing during this period. By the same reason in certain years the difference between the value of production and value added is small.

30. We must recognize that the estimates of the total retained value of oil are not as reliable as those of the value of production. This can be explained in terms of a higher difficulty in obtaining data on the foreign component of total expenses, which includes items such as imports of goods and services, and remittances by personnel of the oil firms to their home country, on which much less information existed during that period.

31. For greater detail see Table 5.5. We must also point out that the estimate of Lieuwein on the relative importance of the contribution of oil through the net retained value on its fiscal contribution seems to have been rather accurate during the period analyzed. See page 70 of *Petroleum in Venezuela*, in which he estimates the proportion of the net retained value over the fiscal contribution at approximately three.

32. Although the expansion of domestic product and of the value of production of oil moves faster, a significant part of the impact of this flow does not affect the Venezuelan economy. Hence to evaluate the effects of oil we must concentrate on the total retained value.

33. Through its spending the oil sector generates income in the non-oil-producing sector of the economy in a first round. When these sectors in turn spend, they generate income again. In successive rounds, expenditure and income are multiplied (this is the expenditure multiplier mechanism) and frequently affect

even the original source of spending, except when, as in the case of Venezuelan oil, its demand is fundamentally exogenous to the Venezuelan economy.

34. An expression of all this was the establishment of large oil refineries that process Venezuelan oil outside of the country. Although at first sight this seems to reflect an anachronism of Gómez, it can also be explained in terms of his interest in controlling the nation and his fear that, especially in Zulia, an oil industry bonanza could add pressures that would tend to challenge his power. At any rate, Venezuela lost the opportunity of establishing other important income streams coming from oil production and refining.

35. Actually, since Torres left the ministry in 1922 we can conclude that during his absence the contribution extracted by Venezuela from the oil industry diminished considerably. However there were other factors contributing to this decrease. For instance, during the first years of the period the total expenditure did not reflect the activity of the whole industry because many firms didn't produce or suffered losses. It can also be assumed that a lower participation of retained value in total expenditure was a necessary incentive for the industry.

36. In spite of it being estimated as expressed previously, the difference between the two ratios would probably be quite impressive even if it were not.

37. Which translated into new fiscal and labor regulations being attached to the oil laws and which increased the expenses that the oil companies had to make in the country.

38. See Banco Central de Venezuela, *El Ingreso Nacional de Venezuela* (Caracas, 1949).

39. See Córdova, "La Estructura Económica."

40. This was fundamentally the result of the construction of infrastructure by the government and the oil sector, which tended to facilitate communication between the different markets within the country and the trend toward larger markets. Obviously at the base of this infrastructure were the opening of new roads.

41. We must stress the scanty information available on this subject. Some critics express much stronger positions in regard to the destruction of agriculture and handicrafts as a result of the absorption of labor force by the oil sector and the oil industry's penetration in the countryside, which disrupted the traditional activities prevailing in the earlier part of the period. Although some of these allegations are well founded, it seems that they do not complete the crossword puzzle of economic activity of Venezuela during these years. This does not seem logical in view of the shortages of labor suffered by the oil companies and of the relatively weak demand for labor created by such pressures on the traditional sector as described above. It also seems that oil activities that allegedly had the characteristics of an enclave in scarcely populated areas and that consisted mainly of exploration activities or actual concentration of extraction activities, could not have been severely affected by this disruption. Finally, even if the allegations are partly true, as seems to have been the case, we would have to consider that low productivity activities were being replaced by high productivity ones. Thus, the previous comments in the text acknowledged the criticism outlined above, but we chose to take an eclectic view of them.

42. Roads, highways, railroads, loading docks, and so on.

43. These were restricted to the oil company's personnel and their relatives and consisted of clinics, hospitals, schools, sports fields, scholarships, and the like.

44. The provision of accidental insurance, the introduction of the concept of preventive health care, and the professional training of workers had an effect over the rest of the economy. On the other hand, we must recognize that the contamination of Lake Maracaibo by the oil firms during the 1920s was an important negative aspect of the industry, showing a poor example and damaging the fishing activity in the lake.

45. It must be remembered that the retained value is a good proxy variable for the total net contribution of the oil sector to the economy.

46. However, it is necessary to recognize that the external and fiscal contribution of oil were gradually being utilized more efficiently.

CHAPTER 6

1930–1936

National income, production, and international trade decreased dramatically around the world during the years 1930 to 1936, an episode in economic history that was unparalleled in the industrial era— the Great Depression. Like many of the world's economies, Venezuela suffered the adverse effects of the Great Depression, which were most profoundly felt in its traditional export sector. Though oil exports and other general activities were also impacted, they were affected to a much lesser extent. International trade and the world's consumption of oil, which had been expanding consistently in the two previous decades, could not resist the impact of the Great Depression. This was the fundamental reason for the economic contraction suffered by Venezuela during these years. However, it must be recognized that the reduction in the level of economic activity in Venezuela was not as dramatic or protracted as that experienced by most of the countries of the world. In the following pages we will examine the contribution of oil to the other sectors of the economy during this period. We conclude that it was because of the oil sector that the Venezuelan economy was not as adversely affected by the Great Depression as other countries were.

THE CONTRIBUTION OF OIL THROUGH THE EXTERNAL SECTOR

As mentioned before, the contribution of the oil sector to the Venezuelan economy is given by the exports and other credits on the balance of payments current account and by the inflows of long-term capital and other items in the balance of payments capital account.

We must again point out that part of these credits and debits may have been utilized by the oil industry, in which case the comparison could be made between a gross and a net contribution. In the latter case debits would be subtracted from the current account and the capital account, which would correspond to the oil sector. Particularly, the concept of net contribution is ultimately linked to the foreign exchange obtained by oil, because these firms are paid in foreign currency, and they exchange into bolívares only what they need for their current and capital operations in Venezuela. Therefore, the currency exchanged by the oil industry presents the best estimate of the net retained contribution of oil through the foreign sector.

A relatively large contribution (in comparison to the inflows recorded in the balance of payments and those of foreign currency), as well as rapid growth during the period, would allow the country to maintain the level of imports necessary for a successful program of economic growth. In other words, it became feasible to import the capital goods and intermediate goods needed for investment and production, to purchase scarce factors (technology and known labor) to keep the incentives represented by the importation of some consumption goods, and to permit the existence of a competitive economy free from inflationary processes of an accelerated type. All of this contributes to maintaining the strength and dynamism of the economy, thus allowing it to become more effectively integrated into the world economy.

To measure these contributions of the oil sector to the rest of the economy, we face again the problem of having only very limited statistical data available. It is impossible to estimate the net contribution of the oil sector during the period, in order to account for the sector's utilization of resources that it brings from abroad (e.g., the oil sector's own imports). It is only possible to estimate the contribution of the oil sector in gross figures and to assume that by definition (and from our experience in measuring it in previous years) the net contribution of the sector is considerably smaller.

Table 6.1 shows the total exports of Venezuela and the country's oil exports. These figures clearly show the impact of the Great Depression on international trade. From the high figures corresponding to 1929 and 1930, both oil and total export figures plummeted to their correct level in 1933. From there on a recovery began that gained force by 1936. We must point out that the value of exports, in bolívares, shrank more due to the drop in export prices than to a reduction in the volume of exports. As we can also see in Table 6.1, oil prices, after climbing in 1930, dropped to a third of that year's level by 1933. A significant part of this reduction took place in that year. From 1934 on, export prices underwent a slow recovery.[1] On the other hand, we must consider that the value of exports (in bolívares) was also affected by the (dollar) exchange rate. This fluctuated considerably during the period, as it can be seen in Table 6.1.

Table 6.1.
Petroleum Sector Indicators and External Sector Performance, 1929–1936

	1929	1930	1931	1932	1933	1934	1935	1936
Total Exports (Mill. Bs.)	981	987	648	676	337	427	462	602
Oil Exports (Mill. Bs.)	796	859	544	579	273	363	399	517
Oil as a Percent of Total Exports	81.1%	87.0%	84.0%	85.7%	81.0%	85.0%	86.4%	85.9%
Total Imports (Mill. Bs.)	453	364	211	153	144	160	225	212
Net Exports (Mill. Bs.)	528	623	437	523	193	267	237	390
International Reserves (Mill. Bs.)	125	112	109	107	104	131	184	184
Change in Reserves (Mill. Bs.)	3	-13	-3	-2	-3	27	53	0
Total Exports (Mill. US $)	188	183	106	100	64	122	118	154
Oil Exports (Mill. US $)	152	159	89	86	52	104	102	132
Total Imports (Mill. US $)	87	62	35	23	27	46	57	54
Net Exports (Mill. US $)	101	121	71	77	37	76	61	100
Oil Exports (Millions of Barrels)	131	134	112	110	113	130	139	150
Oil Export Prices (US $ per Barrel)	$1.97	$2.07	$1.57	$1.70	$0.78	$0.90	$0.93	$1.11
Exchange Rate (Bs./ US $)	5.22	5.40	6.10	6.74	5.27	3.49	3.92	3.91

Note: International Reserves include only gold within the banking system, although most reserves were held in this form during the period. Exchange rates were calculated as a geometric average of the simple arithmetic averages of daily quotations in the free market.

Sources: Ministerio de Fomento, Dirección General de Estadísticas, *Anuario Estadístico* (Caracas, 1938 and various years); Ministerio de Minas e Hidrocarburos, *Petróleo y Otros Datos Estadísticos* (Caracas, 1969); Ministerio de Fomento, *Anuario Estadístico* (Caracas, various years); Ministerio de Fomento, *Revista de Fomento* (Caracas, various years); D. F. Maza Zavala, *Venezuela: Una Economía Dependiente* (Caracas, 1964); Banco Central de Venezuela, *Memoria* (various years).

After 1929 the value of the dollar with respect to the bolívar increased steadily until 1932, when for a few months it decreased. In 1933 the dollar fell abruptly and it continued in its downward trend during 1934. In fact, in August 1934 its value dropped below 50 percent of that reached in 1932.[2] This occurred as a result of the official devaluation of the dollar. Because the gold content of the bolívar was maintained, it appreciated in terms of the U.S. currency. In 1935 and 1936 a slight increase in the rate of exchange was stabilized, a result achieved through official intervention in the foreign currency market and by means of an agreement reached with the oil companies whereby they would sell their dollars at a fixed price.

If we take into account the exchange rate fluctuations, we notice that the decreases in exports in 1931 and 1932 were understated, whereas the decrease that took place in 1933 was exaggerated. On the other hand, the recovery that took place beginning in 1934 did not appear as significant as it should have because of the drop in the value of the dollar. The value of exports, calculated in dollars, appears in Table 6.1.

It is important during this period to take into account the dollar value of exports. The incentives to domestic production usually came from the prices expressed in bolívares because this is how the costs of the exporters are also expressed. On the other hand, some factor payments and the financing of imports must be made with foreign currency, primarily dollars. Furthermore, we are of course dealing with the operation of a simultaneous system, particularly until 1934, when the foreign exchange market operated freely. As the exports of the economy declined, the bolívar value of the dollar increased. The system continued to produce the well-known incentives to production and exports. Finally we must also consider the evolution of oil exports, already the most important export item of the country, in physical terms. An overview of Table 6.1 confirms that the volume of exports declined very little during the Great Depression. Certainly its reduction was much smaller than the reduction in its value would indicate.

It can be verified that there was a contraction in the exports of oil (in thousands of barrels) in 1931, in the vicinity of 17.5 percent. This level of exports was maintained during 1932 and 1933. Between 1934 and 1935 the export volume recuperated to predepression levels.

In 1936 the volume exported went up considerably and surpassed by over 10 percent the highest figure previously reached, corresponding to 1930. The external gross contribution of oil was not only very high during this period, representing between 81 and 86 percent of the total exports, but it allowed the Venezuelan economy, by earning foreign currency in sizable amounts, to endure a shorter, less sharp contraction in foreign trade than that suffered by more advanced countries. As we will see, the production levels and the levels of investment in the oil industry did not decrease as much as the oil exports, which prevented the foreign currency sold in the country by the oil companies from dropping considerably. We have no direct evidence of this due to the lack of statistical data, but it is easily deducted from the apparent strength of the bolívar vis-a-vis the dollar, particularly starting in 1933 (see Table 6.1).

Let's now examine the utilization of this contribution to the Venezuelan economy. Total imports appear in Table 6.1. In terms of bolívares, it can be observed that imports declined after 1929, dropping to their lowest value in 1933. Between 1933 and 1936 there was an upward trend. However, as of 1936 their level was only that of 1931, the year in which the largest decline occurred as a result of the Great Depression.

However, because the bolívar fluctuated in an irregular manner during these years, it is convenient to observe the evolution of exports in dollars. These decreased rather rapidly in 1929 and during the next few years, with a recovery beginning in 1933. In 1934 exports (in dollars) had already surpassed the 1931 levels, and in 1936 they reached figures close to those of 1929. This is a clear indication that the depression of the 1930s in Venezuela was milder and shorter than in many other countries.

The level of international reserves maintained by Venezuela during these years is evidence of the relative strength of its economy (see Table

6.1). The reserves' decline in bolívares between 1930 and 1935 was rather minor. By 1934 the reserves had already surpassed the 1929 level and by 1935–1936 they were 50 percent above the predepression level. In dollars, the decrease in the reserves seems more important until 1932, but the recovery occurring after 1933 that took them to levels much higher than those of 1929 is also more noticeable.

By comparing Venezuelan export figures, particularly oil, with import figures, we can get an idea of the utilization by the other sectors of the economy, of the export earnings of the country as a whole. Unless it was necessary to utilize exports and imports as elements of an anticyclical policy, we should expect a long-run equilibrium between these two flows. Because, in addition to exports and imports, there exist financial flows among countries, a good indicator of the utilization of foreign resources is the tendency toward the excessive accumulation of international reserves. The international reserves can generally be associated with the level of economic activity, particularly the international aspect of it, because of their liquidity. It is generally accepted that the international reserves must constitute a certain percentage of imports in such a way that the uninterrupted inflows of the latter are assured for at least a few months. As in the other types of liquid means of payments, the optimal amount of international reserves can be obtained as the solution to an inventory control problem. In the case of Venezuela, during the period under study, we note that it is only toward the end of it (1935–1936) that an excessive accumulation of international reserves was recorded. This suggests that these excess reserves could have been utilized, had a more effective program of economic recovery been implemented, to escape more rapidly in a more vigorous manner from the ongoing depression.

The difference between exports and imports is noticeable during these years. Though we must acknowledge the possibility of statistical errors, the discrepancy may have resulted, for the most part, from the payment of Venezuela's external debt, which was a goal of Juan Vicente Gómez's efforts for several years. The surplus in the trade balance made it evident that the growth of the oil industry in Venezuela had been so rapid that the rest of the economy lagged behind the oil exports, resulting in foreign currency earnings for the nation—those necessary to finance the local operations of the firms in Venezuela.[3] We must indicate that paying the foreign debt during these years was not the most appropriate policy goal. In fact economic recovery should have been a higher priority. The cancellation of foreign debt is an objective that should be pursued in years of prosperity, when the resources of the economy are being more fully utilized and it is convenient to withdraw means of payments from circulation, to reduce the pressure on the factors of production. However, we must recognize that given the situation of the world economy, there were actually not many opportunities to accelerate Venezuela's economic growth by a more rational use of foreign resources. In the absence of more information on the internal allocation of the contribution of oil by type of import, we must conclude that the utilization of that contribution by the Venezuelan economy, although not satisfactory, can be justified based on the world's economic situation.

To summarize, the contribution of the oil sector to the rest of the Venezuelan economy through the external sector continued to be very important in relative terms. However, the absolute contribution declined slightly. In spite of this contraction, the oil sector partially offset the impact of the world depression upon the Venezuelan economy. During the early 1930s the oil sector contracted in response to slack demand conditions and overproduction.[4] A recovery occurred from 1933 onward, which served to revitalize the rest of the Venezuelan economy.[5] This contribution, relatively important especially given the prevailing conditions of the world economy, was managed relatively well, although it could have been used less conservatively.

THE FISCAL CONTRIBUTION OF THE OIL INDUSTRY

In 1930 the world economy was profoundly affected by a drop in industrial production with the consequent reduction in the demand for oil. The overproduction of oil, which had affected the industry since 1927, became critical and oil prices plummeted.[6] The oil firms, which had been trying to curb production since the same year, voluntarily slowed down their operations. Oil investment in Venezuela, where output had been growing rapidly, was reduced drastically. Plans of expansion were put on hold, exploration was paralyzed, construction was reduced to a minimum, and the importation of capital goods by the industry declined considerably.

Due to the reduction of all oil companies' activities (many of the small ones even stopped altogether), local personnel were fired and even some foreign employees were sent back home. In spite of all these measures, prices continued to fall, and in April 1931 the three largest firms signed an agreement whereby production would be cut by 15 percent. A new variable came into play when the U.S. government threatened to impose a duty on Venezuelan oil for the purpose of reducing imports. With this expectation, the oil firms increased their activities to the maximum in order to export as much as possible before the duty was imposed.[7] This increased production phase lasted only a few months, since on June 6, 1932, the import tax went into effect.

Although the tax affected mainly the light varieties of oil and Venezuela's production was mainly of the heavy and intermediate types, the country lost a substantial portion of the U.S. market. However, toward the second half of 1932 the world demand for oil started to grow again, and Venezuelan oil exports replaced U.S. oil exports in Europe and South America, as U.S. producers were now supplying the former Venezuelan markets in the

United States. This reorganization of world markets allowed Venezuelan oil exports and production to be relatively unaffected by the U.S. tariff, thus beginning their slow recovery from the low levels of 1931.[8]

The layoff of personnel by the oil companies that occurred from 1930 to 1932 forced the Gómez administration to create a resettlement program for the unemployed. This policy was successful, although by 1933 the oil industry had begun to recuperate even though its investment spending still lagged.[9] The pressures applied by Minister of Production Gumersindo Torres since 1928 were such that companies found it profitable to refine their crude oil in Venezuela.[10]

By 1935 the oil industry had fully recovered. Prices had begun to rise in 1934 and this trend was maintained in the following years. In 1935 production and exports were the largest in the oil history of Venezuela in physical terms. The production of Venezuelan crude oil represented 9 percent of world output.

Investment began to recover with a lag, being concentrated in the exploratory activity and development activities in eastern Venezuela, whose Standard of New Jersey was already exploiting the resources discovered in Quiriquire in 1928. Gulf discovered the Oficina field in these years and Standard of New Jersey continued its dominance with the discovery of the Pedernales field.

Venezuelan fiscal incomes, especially oil revenues, were affected by the behavior of production and investment in the oil sector (see Table 6.2).

Table 6.2.
Government Sector Fiscal Indicators, 1929–1936 (millions of bolívares)

	1929	1930	1931	1932	1933	1934	1935	1936
Government Revenues	256	244	189	175	170	179	206	254
Public Revenues from the Oil Sector	51	47	47	45	45	52	59	64
Oil as a Percent of Government Revenues	19.9%	19.3%	24.9%	25.7%	26.5%	29.1%	28.6%	25.2%
Government Expenditures	209	325	172	168	158	168	191	281
Economic And Social Development Expenditures (ESD)	107	166	80	81	74	79	89	150
ESD as a Percent of Government Expenditures	51.2%	51.1%	46.5%	48.2%	46.8%	47.0%	46.6%	53.4%
Public Treasury Reserves	100	92	41	60	70	87	112	67

Sources: Ministerio de Fomento, *Anuario Estadístico* (Caracas, 1937, 1938, and 1939) and *Memoria* (Caracas, 1935, 1936, and 1938); Ministerio de Minas e Hidrocarburos, *Petróleo y Otros Datos Estadísticos* (Caracas, 1965); Manuel Egaña, *Tres Décadas de Producción Petrolera* (Caracas, 1947); J. J. Bracho Sierra, *Cincuenta Años de Ingresos Fiscales* (Caracas, 1963); Charles Rollins, "Raw Materials Development and Economic Growth: A Study of the Bolivian and Venezuelan Experience," Ph.D. dissertation, Stanford University, 1956.

This was in part because the fall in oil activities caused a contraction in the commercial sector that depended on the oil firms spending on their workers. The cities that had developed under the impact of the oil activity languished. Many of the import, domestic trend, and construction firms disappeared or were at the brink of bankruptcy.[11] To illustrate the crisis of the oil-producing cities at the time (practically all of them, even in the area of influence of Maracaibo), it suffices to point out that the tariff revenues in Maracaibo dropped from 55 to 19 million bolívares from 1930 to 1933.[12]

Oil taxes were specific and therefore were not affected by the reduction in the value of oil production. In particular, the surface taxes were levied in a lump sum manner. On the other hand, the sales of concessions of lands of the natural reserves produced extraordinary compensatory income. A new system of auditing and inspection of oil production, introduced by Minister Torres, brought about increases in revenue collections, because taxes were now levied in the oil fields rather than at shipping ports. Oil that was either wasted or consumed in the oil fields therefore began to be taxed.

By 1935 more than 25 percent of the fiscal reserves of the Venezuelan government came from the oil industry. We should add this to the taxes that were indirectly a result of the oil industry, especially through customs, which were due to the import activity of the oil industry and to the imports indirectly generated by the expansionary impact of it.[13] The participation of oil in the fiscal revenue increased from 19.9 percent in 1929 and 19.3 percent in 1930 to 25.2 percent in 1936. During this period total fiscal revenue remained rather stable in comparison with the extreme years.

Of course it appears that starting in 1929, and particularly since 1930, fiscal revenues as a whole decreased. However, in 1934 they began to rise and returned to their 1929 level at the end of the period. Supposedly the tax revenues from the oil industry increased more than 20 percent during the period if we take 1929 as the base year and almost 40 percent if we take 1930 as the base year.[14] In terms of compounded annual growth, the averages were very satisfactory regardless of the choice of base year, considering the deflation that the value figures underwent during these years.

Regarding oil revenues, the trajectory was somewhat similar to that of total revenues except the decline was less pronounced. The recovery of total fiscal revenues, on the other hand, was much quicker after 1933. It is undeniable that the fiscal contribution of oil was extremely important during this period, because the fiscal revenues directly generated by oil were a stabilizing force during this period of economic crisis. Not only did oil fiscal revenues support government revenues (total tax collection), they increased as a share of government revenues, as shown in Table 6.2.

Nevertheless this dynamism is in no way comparable to the growth of fiscal revenue from oil in the previous periods. One should also recognize that the contribution of oil to the rest of the economy through public spending began to expand after 1933. Through the recovery of the Venezuelan economy began after 1933, prosperity would not be achieved until 1936.

The Gómez government was succeeded by that of Eleazar López Contreras in 1936, due to Gómez's death in December 1935. López Contreras had been second in command of the Venezuelan armed forces, and yet the new administration brought with it a more democratic and liberal spirit to government. In the press and even in Congress, oil companies were passionately attacked, as their influence on the Venezuelan economy became more important than ever. Popular sentiments served to explain why the policies adopted the previous year were not only confirmed again in 1936, but also why new demands were made on the oil companies. This new set of policies can explain at least in part, the increase in the direct tax revenues from oil that accelerated toward the end of the period. Particularly, as the concessions were granted, deals were made with the companies whereby they were given nonmonetary incentives, but had to pay taxes. The 1936 oil concessions were auctioned and the taxes on exploration were raised substantially.

We must note that in 1936 these concessions had to be purchased at an overvalued exchange rate of 3.06 bolívares per dollar, instead of the official 3.90 bolívares per dollar rate. As of July 1934 the oil companies had to exchange one-third of their currency at that rate.[15] Because the official exchange rate was 3.93 bolívares per dollar when selling this currency, the government profited from the transaction. This profit constituted approximately one-third of the dollars exchanged between July 1934 and the end of 1936 plus the currency necessary to obtain the concessions in 1936, multiplied by 0.84 bolívares which was the government's fee per dollar exchanged.

The total revenue of bolívares represents an additional fiscal contribution of oil, which if we add to the direct fiscal contribution of industry (see Table 6.2) and those generated indirectly by the oil activity (especially through customs revenues) clearly shows that the Venezuelan tax revenues relied fundamentally on the oil sector during this period.[16]

How was the fiscal contribution of oil used during this period? We should first of all examine whether these funds were used to revitalize the Venezuelan economy or were sterilized. In Table 6.2 we show the reserves of the National Treasury for each year of the period in question. There seems to have existed, with the exception of 1936, a policy of maintaining an extremely high level of reserves. The low levels of 1931 seem to have been involuntary. Immediately thereafter the recovery started to reach predepression levels. This is confirmed by the effort to pay off public debt, which continued and finished during the period in question. There appeared to have been either an explicit or implicit rule to keep the reserves equal to six months of fiscal revenues. In 1935 this mark was surpassed, but already in 1936 the fiscal management was taken out by younger, development-minded individuals, which could explain the relative and absolute decline in reserves.

If we examine public expenditures in Table 6.2 we can get a firm approximation of the effective utilization of fiscal revenues, to later analyze the distribution of the same in a functional approach, and measure the developmental orientation of public spending. Except for 1930 and 1936, the rest of the period in question reflects the application of the balanced budget principle: fiscal expenditures were always below revenues. The 1930 deficit seems to have been unplanned, as we suggested before, reflecting a smaller drop in tax revenues when the forecasts were based on the upward trend of the 1920s.

The case of 1936 is different because new concepts began to be applied in what concerns fiscal management, with the purpose of utilizing fiscal policy as a tool of development policy. Under the new objective the application of a policy of surplus in times of depression and recession was anathema. Table 6.2 shows that the distribution of public spending also underwent a crisis during the period in question. The share of public spending devoted to development showed a declining tendency during the entire period, only surpassing the level of the earlier part of the period in 1936. This year, as we have seen, can be considered as the exception, because in reality it represented a change of administration and fiscal philosophy.

It is not surprising, therefore, to verify that not even a larger share than in 1929 is devoted to development-related expenditures. Actually the impression given by the Gómez government during the depression years was that of being incorrect in its evaluation of the situation and of being in the hands of foreign companies and governments. (Minister Torres, who again did an excellent job in relations with the oil firms, was placed in his post in 1931 at their request and reacted only when pressures were too strong or the path too clear.) Popular pressures and perceptions are reasons that help explain why subsidies to the agricultural sector were implemented, particularly for export products, and also why public works were continued. Still, total economic and social development spending exceeded the direct contribution of the oil sector to the National Treasury.[17] On balance, the administration appears as insecure and lacking a firm handle on the national economic activity.

In synthesis, we find a situation that weakens and reduces the fiscal contribution of oil to the Venezuelan economy during these years in spite of which oil contributes in an important way in absolute terms toward the end of the period, and in relative terms throughout the entire period. The fiscal contribution of oil is therefore remarkable within the critical situation of the Venezuelan and world economies.

Unfortunately, the utilization of oil tax revenues was not the most appropriate. Fiscal policy was the exact opposite of what was advisable during the depression, with revenues being devoted to the cancellation of public debt and the increase in international reserves. When this did not occur, the budget was managed under the principle of balancing revenues and expenditures. On the other hand, the functional distribution of these expenditures showed a decrease of development-related expenditures. For the first time it seemed that not all oil fiscal revenues were being used for expenditures that increased the future profitability of the Venezuelan economy.[18] It was only in 1936 that this tendency was altered and the fiscal contribution of oil was utilized appropriately.

THE CONTRIBUTION OF INVESTMENT

The role of investment spending in long-run economic development is perhaps even more important than its role in short-run economic performance. Investment spending in a specific sector contributes to long-run development in it's a most direct fashion when considering the sector's capital accumulation relative to total investment, and through the nature of the sectorial investment. Petroleum investment constituted an important part of total investment since the prior period; the characteristics of this same investment should be considered favorable. Not only did it create multiple sources of revenue for the nation within the macroeconomic system, already extensively described, but it was also important in the production of capital goods or in generating demand for those goods. Both of these forms of utilizing investment, on the expenditure side with the multiplier effect of revenues and expenditures, and on the production side by means of the development of the production sector in capital goods, maintained an important impact on the developing economy of Venezuela. The estimates of petroleum investment during the years that we have been examining appear in Table 6.3. In Chapter 5 we saw how investment had reached a maximum in 1927, having been propelled by the known overproduction of petroleum that impacted the world economy until 1929. However, in this year, investment still increased, appreciating in the neighborhood of 200 million bolívares. From then on the Great Depression of the 1930s affected the world economy, investment fell to an average of around 50 million bolívares annually during the worst years of this economic crisis, and rose to an annual level of 90 million bolívares during 1936.[19] It was not until 1938 that it reached the levels set before the Great Depression. There exists only one exception in regard to investment in petroleum, which happened in the year 1931, as a consequence of the level of activity in the eastern part of Venezuela. This occurred as a last effort to make ready the marketing facilities of the region, which were extremely important as sources of crude oil for Standard Oil of New Jersey.

Table 6.3.
Gross Domestic Product and Gross Fixed Domestic Investment, Oil Sector, 1929–1936

	1929	1930	1931	1932	1933	1934	1935	1936
Total GDP (Mill. 1957 Bs.)	4,305	4,357	3,416	3,399	3,313	3,954	4,350	5,166
Oil Sector GDP (Mill. 1957 Bs.)	439	421	311	329	273	237	244	351
Oil as a Percent of Total GDP	10.2%	9.7%	9.1%	9.7%	8.2%	6.0%	5.6%	6.8%
Gross Fixed Domestic Investment (Mill. Bs.)	201	69	269	52	53	72	81	88

Notes: Oil sector GDP and fixed investment estimates are based on the records of the three main petroleum company groups in Venezuela: Shell Oil, Gulf Oil, and Standard Oil of New Jersey. Adjustments were then made to reflect industry totals. Gross Fixed Investment estimates may be overstated by the inclusion of exploration costs, such as concessions and capitalization costs, which are not properly fixed investment. Total GDP estimates are based on Armando Córdova, "La Estructura Económica Tradicional y el Impacto del Petróleo en Venezuela," *Economía y Ciencias Sociales,* January–March, 1963, and lectures given by Bernardo Ferran on Venezuelan economic history, delivered at the Universidad Central de Venezuela, Caracas, 1963.
Sources: See Córdova (1963) and Ferran (1963).

There are no estimates of total investment of the Venezuelan economy during this same period, so we cannot precisely determine the percent contribution of petroleum to total investment. However, we can make a conjecture and create a rough estimate of the relative importance of petroleum investment in comparison to what is known about the Venezuelan economy during these years. It is known that other primary goods-producing sectors had certain investments during the period, as the government pursued strategies to help offset the negative employment effects that resulted from layoffs in the petroleum sector. In addition, the export subsidies provided to agriculture during this period should have led to capital accumulation in that sector. The industrial sector, moreover, demonstrated its initial growth in Venezuela during this period although it was in its early stage of development and it was probably not a major source of investment demand. Finally, the services sector suffered the combined shocks of the Great Depression and the decrease in petroleum activity, and it was also not likely to have displayed significant investment activity during this period.

The public sector, however, demonstrated appreciable investment activity in the form of public works programs, aid to the agricultural sector, and expenditures in capital for economic and social programs. If we compare the government expenditures with the investment of the oil industry (Tables 6.2 and 6.3) it can be shown that the latter constituted 53 percent of the former. Economic and social expenditures relative to total public spending during the period amounted to 49 percent. Public investment's share of this total could have been less than this percentage. We can speculate that petroleum direct investment could probably have been greater than public investment during these years.[20]

To summarize, petroleum investment being greater than public investment, and the private sector being highly affected by the depression, it would not be unreasonable to explain that the percent contribution of petroleum to total investment would lie in a range of 40 to 50 percent during this period.[21] The figures that we can use comparably in future periods—for example, those periods during the second half of the decade of the 1930s and the decade of the 1940s—demonstrated that petroleum investment represented between 30 and 40 percent of total investment. We should add that this is, *in strictu sensu,* an important component of the total investment, as it is with public investment, an important product of the impact of oil on the Venezuelan fiscal budget.

Petroleum investment, besides representing an important proportion of total investment, lessened the severity of the Great Depression on the Venezuelean economy through its revenue-expenditure effect. Even though investment did not totally recuperate as rapidly as the production of petroleum, inclusively not reaching the final levels of the 1920s, it did grow to 50 percent between 1933 and 1936. This also took place through the purchase of capital goods and services, thereby strengthening the producers of such goods and services, general commerce, and the Venezuelan economy. An important part of the demand for capital goods, in part by the petroleum sector, was satisfied internally, because the oil firms constructed settlements, schools, and ships on certain occasions, while their maintenance departments made major repairs.

In synthesis, the petroleum contribution through investment, although affected by the world depression, softened the economic impact of the crisis without having positive effects in the fiscal and external sectors.

NATIONAL REVENUES AND TOTAL OIL EXPENDITURES

Besides the expenditures in investment, the oil industry realized current expenditures in the process of producing, warehousing, transporting, and distributing the petroleum. These current expenditures are really another way of expressing the costs of the oil firms on these operations and include the depreciation and amortization of physical capital that they utilize. In all these operations, the petroleum industry originates revenues when it spends in the purchase of the factor of production—labor, capital, natural resources, and management.

The revenues originated by the economic activity in the industry, and the rest of the expenditures that we can consider as current expenditures, augment the multiplier-accelerator mechanism of the Venezuelan economy. The multiplier-accelerator process represents the basic vehicle through which the economic effects are transmitted from one sector to the other sectors in the economy. Furthermore, if we add to the current expenditures the cost of capital, these total expenditures represented an adequate indicator of the net contribution of petroleum on the economy, when we calculate that part retained in Venezuela. Besides, the rest of the total net contribution of petroleum should be more in parallel with the retained value of total petroleum expenditures.[22]

Let us examine first the revenues originated by the level of activity in petroleum or, as we shall say, the revenues or domestic product of petroleum. The gross domestic product generated by this sector is presented in Table 6.3. Net domestic product is constructed as the difference between GDP and capital consumption allowances.[23]

In the case of remittances produced by petroleum and the physical production and exports for 1936 or prior, they had already surpassed the levels of 1929. This did not happen with investment or domestic product, because the prices and of course the values related to petroleum were maintained below the levels of 1929. The bolívares of 1929 were less valuable than the bolívares of 1926 relative to dollars, due to the appreciation of bolívares that occurred in 1934.[24]

Table 6.4 presents the estimates of the value of petroleum production and of retained value in the total expenditures of the petroleum sector. The behavior of these statistics during these years of depression is not unlike that of the gross domestic product. The values of these indicators in 1936 were lower than those of 1929.[25]

We should pay greater attention to the indicator we have referred to as the retained value of total expenditures, explaining with greater detail the way it is estimated, and evaluate its importance with respect to other indicators of the relative importance of the oil sector in the Venezuelan economy. Total retained value is estimated on the basis of removing the imported component of current total expenditures and adding the investment spending of the petroleum industry. *Retained value* represents all of the expenditures in the petroleum sector that could circulate throughout the Venezuelan economy in the form of payments to domestic labor force, direct payment of taxes, purchases of national products, payment on contracts for local services, payments to individuals for concessions and use of land, and so on.

To get an idea of the importance of total retained value in the Venezuelan economy, one may compare this same value with the fiscal contribution of petroleum. Comparing Tables 6.2 and 6.4 we find that in 1929 and 1930, after reducing the direct taxes from petroleum of the total retained value, the remaining figure is much more than three times the direct fiscal contribution of petroleum. From then on, this difference fell to almost the equivalent of the fiscal contribution, and retained value net of petroleum

Table 6.4.
Retained Value of Oil Sector, 1929–1936 (millions of bolívares)

	1929	1930	1931	1932	1933	1934	1935	1936
Retained Value of Oil Sector Expenditures	225	202	159	126	102	115	138	204
Total Value of Production	458	475	371	355	275	262	302	401
Retained Value as a Percent of Total Oil Sector Expenditures	35.2%	37.5%	25.0%	31.3%	31.1%	34.4%	36.0%	41.7%

Notes: Estimates of retained value and value of production are based on adjustments to data from three main petroleum company goods. Conversion of value of sales to value of production are based on *Informes de Conservación* (Caracas, several years) and unpublished data from the Oficina Técnica de Hidrocaburos, Ministerio de Minas e Hidrocarburos. Total oil sector expenditures include the value of production and investment.

taxes in the lowest point of the depression. The difference continued to grow and the retained value minus the petroleum taxes was two times greater than the fiscal contribution in 1936. As to the importance of this total retained value in comparison to the Venezuelan economy as a whole, the most adequate would be to compare this impact with the fiscal gestation of the government expressed through the budget. If we compare Tables 6.2 and 6.4, we can prove that the retained value, although it did not reach the importance of the budgeted costs of Venezuela, was nearly approximate.[26] Therefore, the local costs of the petroleum firms were as great as the national budget, and must have had an important impact in the global economy of Venezuela, given that the public sector of 1930 had been converted in the central pivot of the Venezuelan economy, under the influence of petroleum.

The direct contribution of petroleum, expressed through its total retained value, is unquestionably a partial expression of the total impact of petroleum on the economy. If we consider what was done with the fiscal section, the level of activity generated as a consequence of the total costs of petroleum, we have to conclude that indirectly the local and import business, industry, agriculture, construction, and the sectors of health and education, were in part expressions of the activity in petroleum. Given that the direct contribution through petroleum generated indirect expenditures in the rest of the economy via the multiplier-accelerator mechanism referred to earlier, a considerable economic impact on the nonpetroleum sectors of the economy occurred.[27]

The retained value of petroleum as a percent to total of petroleum expenditures appear in Table 6.4. We note that this proportion fell during the years of the depression, recovered completely by 1935, and surpassed in 1936 the figures of 1929 and 1930, which at that time represented the highest levels registered to date. In 1928 Torres returned to the Ministry of Development and began to place greater restrictions on the activities of the oil companies. His administration, however, did not last long. The oil firms began to pressure President Gómez to remove Torres, and he acceded to their demands in 1931. It was in that year that the participation of retained value in total costs fell to their lowest levels. From then on this indicator recovered slowly when the petroleum industry started to employ part of the labor force it had previously laid off. It also started to subcontract investment and other factors. However, during all this time, except during the brief Torres period, there did not exist the notion of increasing the domestic component of the petroleum sector's expenditures. The most telling indication of the apathy and complacency of Gómez with respect to the oil sector was the frequent practice of exporting Venezuelan crude to refineries in the nearby islands of the Caribbean (Aruba, Curaçao, etc.) for reexport to the United States and other destinations.

If we consider the direct and indirect global contribution of petroleum in the economy, we should conclude that it was of great relative importance during this period. It may have been even greater than in the previous period, because the world economic crisis had its most negative effects on other economic sectors. In absolute terms, it is clear that there was no production growth of importance. Although this sector did not act as an engine of growth during these years, it did contribute to a reduction in the magnitude of the economic recession experienced by Venezuela. By 1936 this sector did give impulse to a rapid economic expansion.

This may be seen in Table 6.3, where the estimates of Venezuela's gross domestic product are presented in real terms. These estimates are based on adjustments realized over the independent series, although it is undeniable that the oldest series is less reliable. The year 1930 produced a slight expansion in the Venezuelan economy, but from then on there was a faster-than-expected decline in 1931, and it diminished slightly up until 1933. In 1934 there was considerable expansion in the economy, increasing in 1935 to a comparable 1930 level, and giving a great leap forward in 1936, so that for the first time since 1929 the economy experienced substantial growth. This growth appears so pronounced in these estimates that it represents a total growth of 20 percent for the total period, which at the same time is equivalent to an annual growth rate of 2.6 percent.[28] These estimates are in real terms and do not reflect the effect of the real appreciation in the bolivar that took place during this period.[29]

As we have pointed out before, the petroleum purchases stimulated directly and indirectly the return to growth in other sectors of the economy, particularly farming and private business. Farming benefited specifically during this period by the resettlement of the peasants, who previously had been emigrating to petroleum zones, and by the large quantity of export subsidies in the agricultural sector. In 1936 the government administration of López Contreras demonstrated that a consciousness had been created, that the riches created by petroleum should be taken advantage of and should transmit its impact to the rest of the economy. It was said for the first time "sow the oil," the concept being to take advantage of the dynamism and strength of the petroleum activity, to achieve a development of the rest of the Venezuelan economic sectors, especially agriculture, and to achieve a total balanced growth.[30] A ministry specifically devoted to agriculture was established in 1936. Subsidies were extended to other agricultural products, in addition to those for export, and programs were created for the expansion of harvesting and for improvements in cattle production.

We should recognize that even in the prior decade there had been criticism of the massive role that petroleum achieved, and of the negative impacts it had on agriculture and the overall general economy. For now we should evaluate the effects of the petroleum industry on the other industry and the agriculture of this period, considering that these were in part answers to the critical situations that were supposedly caused by the petroleum industry. It was maintained by the critics of the petroleum industry that agriculture had been affected by the use of land for exploration and extraction of oil. This diminished the use of land for farming, and also affected the transfer of labor to those activities that were directly and indirectly generated by the petroleum industry. This led to the exodus of the farmers and rural laborers, which made the production of farm products considerably more complex. The decline in agricultural production that this produced had as a consequence, a rise in imports of agricultural products and therefore a rise in their prices, which was unfavorable in the cost of living for the Venezuelan population. Agricultural exports were jeopardized by their volume being reduced. For its part, industry was also affected by the shortage of laborers, being in large measure craftsmen, supposedly reducing the production of crafts by this same motive and bringing with it a rise in prices and an increase of imports.[31]

These effects that occurred principally in the decade of 1920s are highly debatable. It can also be interpreted that, as an effect of the considerable growth in the aggregate demand, an inelastic supply curve created in part a rise in prices and in part an increase in imports. It appeared that petroleum was blamed for what occurred, something that does not seem reasonable. Unquestionably that part of the fault should be attributed also to the Venezuelan government, which during these years was acting as a true laissez faire system in regard to the nonpetroleum sectors of the economy.

One of the great contributions realized by the petroleum industry through the national component of its total costs was the infrastructure works. We have already commented that the firms received almost no help from the government in extending facilities in transportation, education, and health at the centers of petroleum activities. As a consequence, in replacing the government's role the petroleum sector provided its workers and their families these types of facilities, which were also made available to the general public with more frequency during these years, but especially in 1936.[32]

The oil companies began to give greater importance to having good relations with the government for the public at large. With the economic recovery of these years they began to make donations: for example, supplying free gas to the city of Maracaibo, building hospitals and schools in certain cities, allowing farmers to use land in which they had acquired rights to use the top layer of soil, bringing in specialists to study problems in agriculture, importing cattle from Texas in order to improve the local stock, donating materials for the construction of aqueducts, and other beneficial projects.

Another contribution of the oil firms in this period was improving the Venezuelan personnel who worked for these companies. A great number of these workers received extensive training, which made them capable of being technicians and administrators. The companies expanded the number of Venezuelan workers in positions of responsibility, or in technical or administrative positions, although in part this was due to limits imposed by petroleum legislature in respect to employing and making contracts with foreign labor for these positions. Finally, in certain cases they gave educational scholarships. All this led to improvements in the quality of petroleum labor in Venezuela.

In synthesis, the contribution made by petroleum through the turnover both direct and indirect of revenues and expenditures functioned within the macroeconomic mechanism of the multiplier-accelerator, so that the depression was neither felt as strongly nor for as long in Venezuela as it was in other countries.

The economic recovery began early in Venezuela, and by 1935 the gross national product in real terms had reached the levels set prior to the depression. In 1936 this economic indicator reached its highest historical levels for the Venezuelan economy, showing rapid growth. All of this was the combined result of the various contributions of petroleum already examined in this chapter, whose result is expressed by the absolute values and the trajectories of the retained value of total expenditures. A transfer was produced of the beneficial effects of the same sector toward the rest of the economy; it translated into an acceptable behavior of the economic activity of the country during the difficult period of the Great Depression.

NOTES

1. The price levels of 1930 were not reached again until 1948.

2. In August 1934 the dollar hit its lowest value, approximately 3.04 bolívares, below the exchange rate that had previously been fixed at 3.06.

3. The rest was used to pay for purchases made abroad, remittances, and so on.

4. The low oil prices and other raw materials whose prices dropped even further in Venezuela seem to have affected the terms of trade unfavorably to Venezuela, because the prices of industrial goods did not decrease by the same amount. See Armando Córdova, "La Estructura Económica Tradicional y el Impacto del Petróleo en Venezuela," *Economía y Ciencias Sociales* (January–March 1963).

5. As we will see later, only in 1936 did the economy reach the levels of 1929 and 1930. The recovery of the oil industry, which was a fundamental cause of the revitalization of the economy, manifested itself in an expression of investment and increased domestic spending by the oil firms. This brought about a significant increase in the currency contributed by the industry, which was undoubtedly one of the main contributions of oil through the external sector.

6. This overproduction did not affect Venezuela, due to the low costs of production prevailing in this country and its strategic geographical location, which enabled it to sell its oil in the U.S. market.

7. The tax would allow producers in the central United States to compete with Venezuelan producers on equality conditions; prior to its imposition, the delivery cost of crude oil to the eastern United States, whose oil consumption was concentrated, was for Venezuelan producers half of what it was for the U.S. producers from the central region.

8. The tariff imposed by the United States was the fundamental cause of the sale of Standard of Indiana's holdings in Venezuela to Standard of New Jersey. The first distributed oil only in the United States and the tariff endangered its markets, whereas the second had an international network of oil markets and could avoid the duty. This purchase allowed Standard of New Jersey to practically monopolize oil production in the eastern part of Venezuela, where it had discovered the first oil fields, and soon gave this company the leadership position in the oil sector. It should be noted that it was not until 1930 that the Standard of New Jersey had established a work camp and built a pipeline to export crude oil through a loading terminal in Caripito, in the central area of Venezuela, where in 1931 the construction of a refinery had begun. In 1932, with the purchase of the interests of Standard of Indiana, Standard of New Jersey became the second largest producer in Venezuela (Shell was the largest) and in 1935 started to occupy the first place.

9. Without a doubt, the decrease of oil sector production and investment affected different companies in varying ways. The smaller companies were the most affected. Such large companies as Standard of New Jersey, which expanded its share of production notably during the period, were probably only slightly impacted. In particular, activities in the eastern states of Venezuela (Monagas and Anzoategui) did not seem to suffer from the depression.

10. The prices of gasoline and other refined products were higher in Venezuela than in the United States and other Latin American countries. This was unexpected given the low costs of Venezuelan oil in comparison to others produced in the American hemisphere.

11. Although short in duration, the depression in the oil industry was serious. Toward the end of 1930, 40 percent of the oil industry work force had been fired.

12. Curiously enough the oil fiscal revenues did not diminish as much as tariff totals.

13. The customs revenues were those that most suffered during the initial years of the depression, having been reduced by 1935 to half of the 1929 levels. To better understand the significance of this return, we should point out that these revenues constituted the most important share of total fiscal revenues.

14. We should take into account the fact that the percentage changes in these figures are overstated because the base used for the calculation is small.

15. The 3.06 bolívares per dollar was the gold import point, based on the intrinsic gold values of the two currencies.

16. This reaffirmed the pattern already established in the previous period, as can be seen in Chapter 5. In spite of all this, many critics of the relations between government and the oil firms maintained that the conditions under which the oil firms operated in Venezuela were more favorable than those granted the firms elsewhere.

17. However, when both start recuperating, only half of the increases in revenues directly contributed by oil are assigned to raising economic and social development spending, the remainder goes to economic development. If we take into consideration the indirect contribution to the government, we can say that during 1932 to 1935 the economic expenses were much lower than the inflow from oil contributions.

18. We must recognize that it was in this period that the distribution of resources in the budget was tested, because given the existence of a minimum level of economic and social development spending prior to the discovery of oil, it is only when the collection of tax revenues from this sector overcome a certain level that it can be judged if they have been well utilized.

19. We are using numbers that are rounded because we are estimating certain expenditures—for example, concessions and capital taxes—that should not enter in the figures for investment. But on the flip side, because the estimates are based on the account books of the three biggest oil companies in Venezuela, it is possible to understate the investments of other much smaller companies or companies that went bankrupt, even though the intent has been made to include these latter ones.

20. The expenditures for economic development and social programs were to have been partly for current expenditures and the rest for capital expenditures. All of the capital expenditures that translate to real investments, and not only those of financial characteristics (for example, expenditures for canceling of debts), would be included in the social and economic expenditures.

21. During the decades of the 1910s to 1940s, investment represented a very small fraction of the general economic activity. This was reflected in the underdevelopment of the traditional Venezuelan economy during this period. However, the general level of investment of the economy was not much more than 10 percent of the gross national product.

22. We should explain what is meant by retained value, although this issue has been treated prior to this. Of the total expenditures of petroleum, one part is directed to the purchase of goods and services or the imported factors of production that are not domestic. The rest is the national component that we call the retained value of the total expenditures.

23. We can prove that these estimates are similar to that described before for exports, remittances, and petroleum investments. In reality the rebound that was

produced at the lowest point of the depression is more like the case of the domestic product of petroleum to that of petroleum investment.

24. If we express the gross domestic product and investment of petroleum in terms of dollars, the values of the year 1936 become greater than those of 1929 in the first series but not in the second, where the difference narrows, but it is still substantial.

25. We should recognize, however, that the estimates in total retained value do not have the same confidence level as the other estimates of petroleum presented above. To estimate the retained value, it is necessary to know the foreign component of total operations in petroleum (industry imports, foreign remittances, and interest payments in the external sector, etc.). A few of these, especially those cited, have been estimated on the basis of evidence of relative weakness, if we compare them to the components of aggregate value of petroleum appropriately said. Especially the external purchases of goods and services presented complications in that they were difficult to determine what the firms imported directly through local imports or in the form of works contracts that included imports of goods.

26. It is clear that the realized comparison of the total costs of the petroleum companies in Venezuela widely surpassed the national budget during this year.

27. The petroleum expenditures would be like the first round of stimulation, which would generate a second round by the sectors directly affected, whose expenditures would generate a third round in the sectors indirectly linked, and likewise successively. As the petroleum sector depends fundamentally on external demand, it does not receive back the effects by the expenses in the internal sectors. That is, domestic demand for products of Venezuelan petroleum is a small portion of its total demand.

28. If the growth is measured from 1930, the levels of growth are 18.6 percent for the period in total, and 2.9 percent annual accumulated average rate.

29. The year 1936 presents the possibility of comparing the gross domestic product of petroleum in nominal terms, with the total domestic product, also in nominal terms, given that the latter is expressed in 1936 bolívares. The GDP of petroleum represented, 15 years after having begun oil exploration on a grand scale, 13.9 percent of total GDP, although the prices of black oil were still probably more depressed in relative terms of the prices reached at other times than of the rest of the economy.

30. The retained value of petroleum, however, did not represent a relatively large part of the gross national product of Venezuela during these decades of petroleum exploitation. It subsequently did represent during the best years approximately 10 percent of the GDP, having grown dynamically and having a significant impact over the rest of the sectors of the Venezuelan economy.

31. The relations of cause and effect here are not too clear, in that it could very possibly be that imports that competed with domestic production had partially displaced domestic goods. The imported products began to penetrate the Venezuelan markets even more with the growing opening of the economy.

32. This included the use by non-oil businesses of the various roads constructed by the oil firms, the ease of sea travel in Lake Maracaibo, and so on.

CHAPTER 7

1937–1942

This chapter examines the contribution of oil to the other sectors of the Venezuelan economy during the 1937–1942 period. The oil contribution via the foreign sector is considered initially, followed by the public sector contribution, which is generated by oil taxes. Next, the contribution of petroleum through its investment activity is studied. Last, the contribution arising from the income and expenditures originated in the oil industry are examined. The final section also scans the behavior of the other contributions of the petroleum sector, through the performance of the retained value of total expenditures, a proxy for the total combined contribution of petroleum.

THE FOREIGN SECTOR CONTRIBUTION

The balance of payments situation determines, in many cases, the rate of inflation and the rate of growth of real income in developing economies. If the external sector constrains imports, the economy will suffer from the following:

1. Unavailability of essential goods and services
2. Inflexibility in the supply-demand relationships, with imported goods unable to alleviate bottlenecks and excess demand situations
3. The impossibility of using imports to attain efficiency in domestic production through import competition

Items 1 and 2, especially when they refer to the importation of capital or intermediate goods and services, could have an important bearing on a country's rate of growth.

The balance of payments situation may also influence the rate of inflation. Unfavorable movements in the balance of payments may lead to an increase in the rate of inflation through shortages and inefficient import substitution. Particularly if exports are affected, an ongoing process can be initiated. In turn, continuous inflation might hamper the rate of growth of real income.

The importance of these problems varies among developing countries. Even in those countries where they are not severe, just the impossibility of using the external sector in counterinflationary policy is a handicap in the appropriate management of a developing economy.

Therefore, countries that can use a favorable balance of payments situation to suppress or restrain those inflationary pressures that could prove harmful to development, as well as a direct aid to economic growth and efficiency, stand a better chance of developing at a more rapid rate.[1] This has been the case in Venezuela, as a result of the strength shown by its oil industry since the mid-1930s.

The contribution of the oil industry to the balance of payments position of Venezuela can be approximately measured in two ways. One is the gross contribution, defined as the sum of all the credits in current account and all the capital inflows by the industry. The other is the net contribution, which is the gross contribution minus the current account debits and capital outflows of the industry. Both of these measurements are important in their own right: the net measure refers to the contribution to the other sectors of the Venezuelan economy, while the gross contribution relates to the contribution of the Venezuelan economy as a whole, including the oil sector itself. In the gross concept, the foreign exchange used by the oil industry—in buying imported goods and services, for payments to nonresident factors, in transfer payments abroad, and for capital repatriation—is assumed to be necessary for its operation.

Either one or both of these measures will be presented, depending on the availability of data. Due to lack of balance of payments data on services, factor and transfer payments, and capital movements, only the gross potential balance of payments contribution of oil is presented in this period. Furthermore, because only data on the balance of trade are available for these years, the gross contribution of oil has to be computed solely in terms of the movement of goods.

Total exports of Venezuela grew by 25 percent during the 1936–1942 period, corresponding to an average annual compounded rate of 3.7 percent. This was slower than the expansion of GDP during the same period (see Table 7.1). In current terms, the share of exports in total GDP, which represented close to 25 percent in 1936, was reduced over these years.

The total exports in current bolívares declined continually from 1937 to 1939, after increasing in the former year. Afterward, they experienced an increase lasting through 1941, only to drop again in 1942. Petroleum

Table 7.1.
Petroleum Sector Indicators and External Sector Performance, 1936–1942

	1936	1937	1938	1939	1940	1941	1942
Total Exports (Mill. Bs.)	602	635	574	527	929	1003	750
Oil Exports (Mill. Bs.)	517	533	515	469	810	1001	637
Oil Exports as Share of Total Exports	85.9%	83.9%	89.7%	89.0%	87.2%	99.8%	84.9%
Exports as Share of GDP	10.0%	10.1%	9.6%	8.6%	14.1%	17.8%	12.3%
International Reserves (Mill. US $)	47	51	60	55	65	66	89
Change in Reserves (Mill. US $)	--	4	9	-5	10	1	23
Imports of Capital Goods (Mill. US $)	261.1	324.8	159.6	153.2	192.9	212.9	317.9
Ratio of Reserves to Imports	18.0	15.7	37.6	35.9	33.7	31.0	28.0

Sources: Ministerio de Fomento, *Anuario Estadístico* (Caracas, 1938); Banco Central de Venezuela, *Memoria* (Caracas, 1947); Banco Central de Venezuela, *La Economía Venezolana en los Ultimos Veinticinco Años* (Caracas, 1966), with adjustments.

exports followed the same pattern, but their overall increase was some-what lower (23 percent). Their share, which already represented 85.9 per-cent of all exports in 1936, declined to 84.9 percent in 1942 (see Table 7.1). Clearly, the gross balance of payments contribution of oil to the Venezue-lan economy was formidable throughout the period. The net contribution, although smaller, also would probably be quite important.

Although exports performed reasonably well during this period, they were not sufficient to cover the needs of the economy, which was expand-ing faster and generated a demand for imports that was even stronger. At particular times, the shortage of foreign exchange at the official rate even became acute.

In 1936 the expatriation of capital after the death of Juan Vicente Gómez, as well as a prolonged oil strike during the year, brought about a partial exchange control. Late in 1937 the establishment of an overall, but still informal, exchange control became necessary. Prime necessity imports were allowed without limitations, with the exchange remaining allocated according to previous import patterns. This situation lasted to the out-break of war in 1939, when exports expanded. In 1940, there was again need for import controls, as Venezuelan producers prepared for the war. Although the official rate was 3.19 bolívares to the dollar, the selling rate rose to 3.55 bolívares in the free unofficial market. The free market was abolished in the middle of 1940. Through the end of 1940 and the first half of 1941, the rate was stabilized at 3.19 bolívares. In July 1941 the official selling rate was changed to 3.35 bolívares per dollar. Import controls con-tinued in effect during the rest of 1941 and all through 1942.[2]

Thus, during this period, external factors constrained the growth of the Venezuelan economy. Although essential goods were still generally available, the economy lacked some of the other advantages that unrestrained imports offer. Though oil's contribution to overall foreign exchange earnings was formidable, petroleum exports simply did not expand fast enough to do away with shortages and controls during this period, even though oil prices rose over these years. Rising import prices were, to a great extent, responsible for the close to 40 percent price inflation occurring from 1936 to 1942, although import controls and deficit spending by the government also contributed to it.[3] Therefore, the Venezuelan experience in these years constitutes a good illustration of the adverse consequences that balance of payments problems bring about for growth and inflation.

THE USE OF THE FOREIGN SECTOR CONTRIBUTION

The gross balance of payments contribution of the oil industry can be utilized by the Venezuelan economy with more or less efficiency. That is, in every single period, government policies can influence the economy toward a use of the exchange proceeds derived from oil that may minimize, maximize, or affect in some way, the growth of the other sectors. This depends on how the exchange proceeds for a given period are allocated: they can either be spent or else added to the international reserves.

Adding to reserves over and above a certain level is a costly utilization of resources. This level is determined by such factors as the total value of international transactions in a country, the instability of its exports and capital inflows and their seasonal pattern, credit arrangements, currency reserve policy, and the climate of confidence that is believed necessary. This level can be expressed in terms of the coverage of the estimated normal imports for a certain number of months and can be determined by the flexible application of the technique of optimal inventory control.[4] As will be discussed in the sections to follow, an accumulation of international reserves over this level in a particular country can be justified only by a very low social marginal rate of return to investment.

On the other hand, if foreign exchange is devoted to the purchases of goods and services abroad to cover capital outflows and so forth, the effectiveness of its utilization can be determined by its allocation among different types of uses. Therefore, the general pattern of utilization of exchange proceeds is an indication of the adequacy with which the balance of payments contribution of the oil sector is employed.

The proceeds of development usually bring about a change in the composition of imports. This is a result of several forces. Consumer goods imports are substituted as development proceeds, resulting in an increase in the demand for intermediate products. Concurrently, higher levels of investment also increase the demand for capital goods. As developing countries are usually much less efficient in the production of intermediate and capital goods, these are imported. Although the demand for consumer goods also rises, this type of import does not increase as much as other types, as they are more easily substituted by domestic production. Therefore, unless a country has unusual advantages in the import substitution of intermediate or capital goods, an increase in the share of capital and intermediate goods imports would indicate that the allocation of foreign exchange earnings among competing types of goods imports is proceeding efficiently.

During the period covered by this study, the Venezuelan economy can be classified under the general case. Therefore, an increase in the share of capital and intermediate goods imports in total Venezuelan imports would indicate that the foreign exchange contribution of oil was being effectively allocated among different types of goods imports.[5]

During this period, the international reserves of Venezuela remained at approximately the same level, except for the year 1942 (see Table 7.1). The latter was the result of the upheaval created by the war economy. An excessive accumulation of international reserves did not occur over these years, especially if one considers that the determinants of increasing reserves expanded during the period. Thus, it can be said that the foreign exchange contribution of oil was effectively utilized, at least in relation to the level of international reserves.

The pattern of utilization of foreign earnings in the purchase of imported goods reveals that the share of capital goods imports rose from 18 percent in 1936 to 28 percent at the end of the period (see Table 7.1). This also suggests that the foreign sector contribution of oil was adequately utilized by the economy during these years. No other tests of the change in the effective use of foreign earnings over time can be performed, as no information is available on other types of goods.

On the whole, the effects of the foreign trade contribution of the oil sector during this period had a mixed character. An overwhelming proportion of the total exports of goods came from the oil industry, making the gross balance of payments contribution quite high. On the other hand, the increase in oil exports, albeit respectable, was not quite sufficient to cover the needs of the economy, which were expanding even faster. Such a constraint undoubtedly represented an obstacle to the achievement of a higher rate of growth of real income in Venezuela. On the other hand, the economy seems to have effectively used the contribution of oil during this period, because international reserves were not unduly incremented, and the composition of imports appears to have changed in agreement with the efficient norm.

THE FISCAL CONTRIBUTION OF OIL

Part of the value stream originating in any producing sector can be affected and appropriated by the state. In the case of a potentially leading sector, this portion can be substantial relative to the total value added by the economy. Depending on how the particular government uses these funds, the development of the country could be stimulated, stifled, or remain unaffected.

If taxes on the potentially leading sector are large, they could constitute its most important contribution to the growth of the economy. If the potential gains that this contribution can impart are to be realized, the public expenditures financed from such funds must be allocated according to sound criteria. The greater the departure from these criteria, the smaller the realized gains derived from the potentially leading sector.

The fiscal contribution of a potentially leading sector to the rest of the economy is not only exercised through the expenditures that can be financed from the taxes it pays. The revenues derived from this sector might alleviate harmful tax pressures in other parts of the economy. They also could facilitate the avoidance of budgetary deficits, when these could be harmful, thereby preventing the rise of inflationary pressures. However, excessive tax pressure on the sector might, in turn, have an adverse effect on its exports or investment.

The importance of the petroleum contribution to the Venezuelan public revenues in the 1936–1942 period is now considered. An examination of Table 7.2, showing the behavior of petroleum-derived tax revenues, provides an indication of the importance of the petroleum contribution to Venezuelan public revenues in the 1936–1942 period. During this period, the petroleum-derived tax revenues ranged from 64 million to 168 million bolívares. With respect to the participation of oil in government revenues in 1941, it reached 41.8 percent, nine percentage points over the 1936–1942 average. As can be seen from Table 7.2, the relative share of oil taxes fluctuated widely during the period, but overall it increased from 25.2 percent in 1936 to 31.8 percent in 1942. If oil revenues are expressed as a percentage of GDP to give an idea of their importance in relation to the entire economy, the average percentage for the whole period is 3.9 percent. Such magnitudes, if properly utilized, could have had a major impact on the growth of the other sectors of the Venezuelan economy.

The increase in the tax contribution of oil during these years was mostly due to increases in the tax rates applicable to petroleum operations. Almost immediately after Juan Vicente Gómez died in December 1935, his successors made clear that a revision of the government's relationship to the petroleum industry would take place. The new Hydrocarbons Law of 1936 only provided increases in the minimum royalties that could be obtained from a barrel of oil. But the concessions granted in 1936 and 1937 stipulated quite formidable increases in most petroleum taxes, and extraordinary payments were received as lump sums from the companies obtaining concessions.[6] Moreover, tighter enforcement of the tax laws was

Table 7.2.
Government Sector Fiscal Indicators, 1936–1942 (millions of bolívares)

	1936	1937	1938	1939	1940	1941	1942
Government Revenues	254	329	368	389	371	402	340
Oil Tax Revenues	64	99	153	118	107	168	108
Share of Oil Tax in Total	25.2%	30.1%	41.6%	30.3%	28.8%	41.8%	31.8%
Revenue from Exchange Differential	0	3	6	7	19	14	19
Government Expenditures	281	329	370	415	410	378	352
Economic & Social Development Expenditures	150	204	227	251	253	224	201
As a Share of Government Expenditures	53.4%	62.0%	61.4%	60.5%	61.7%	59.3%	57.1%
Public Sector Deficit	27	0	2	26	39	-24	12
Local Government Finances:							
Expenditures	24	30	29	37	41	44	49
Revenues	20	27	28	38	42	43	53

Notes: Local revenues and expenditures exclude transfers from the federal government. Data does not include the finances of state enterprises or autonomous government administrative institutions.

Sources: Ministerio de Fomento, *Memoria* (Caracas, several years); Banco Central de Venezuela, *Memoria* (Caracas, several years); Banco Central de Venezuela, *La Economía Venezolana en los Ultimos Veinticinco Años* (Caracas, 1966) and unpublished data on historical exchange rates in Venezuela; Ministerio de Minas e Hidrocarburos, *Petróleo y Otros Datos Estadisticos* (Caracas, 1965); Ministerio de Fomento, Direccíon General de Estadisticos, *Anuario Estadistico* (Caracas, 1938 and 1951); Manuel R. Egaña, *Tres Décadas de Producción Petrolera* (Caracas, 1947); Charles E. Rollins, "Raw Materials Development and Economic Growth: A Study of the Bolivian and Venezuelan Experience," Ph.D. dissertation, Stanford University, 1956.

instituted, and court claims made to the companies for back taxes were settled favorably to the government. Finally, the method of valuing petroleum for royalty payment purposes was modified.

In February 1937 the government created the Oficina de Centralización de Cambios (Exchange Centralization Office), which was to purchase and sell foreign exchange in order to stabilize the bolívar at a predetermined official rate. The Oficina proceeded to establish a system of multiple buying rates for foreign exchange. Oil companies were required to sell to the Oficina all the foreign currency that they wanted to convert in bolívares. The Oficina bought them at a rate (3.09) that was lower than the general official buying rate. The Oficina was dissolved when the Central Bank, created in 1940, took over its activities.

As a result of these operations, the petroleum companies were penalized when exchanging foreign currency into bolívares, by a penalty equal to the difference between the general official and special petroleum buying rates, multiplied by all the foreign exchange converted into bolívares. This penalty was essentially a new tax imposed on the industry.[7] On the other hand, the foreign currency coming from traditional export activities, such as coffee, cocoa, and cattle, was bought at rates higher than the general official rates and, thus, represented a subsidy to these activities. These subsidies partly offset the profits that the government reaped from the sale of petroleum foreign exchange to commercial banks.[8]

The figure reported as government revenue under the heading of profits from exchange operations is actually the net result of all profits and losses obtained in all the dealings. This, coupled with the fact that the foreign currency sold to the Central Bank was not necessarily resold by the latter to commercial banks in the same year, explains the divergence between the official figures on profits from exchange operations and the calculations of the foreign exchange tax contribution of oil, which are presented in Table 7.2. As a very high percentage of the foreign exchange profits derive from oil, the figures presented in this study are larger than the balance from the various exchange operations reported by government sources.

As can be seen from Table 7.2, during this period the tax on the foreign exchange operations of the petroleum industry did not amount to much. Nevertheless, if these taxes are added to all the other government revenues derived from the oil industry, the percentage share of petroleum revenues in total revenues increases slightly.[9]

From 1936 on, expenditure and revenue statistics of federal entities or states, as well as county or municipal governments, are available.[10] Thus, the revenue and expenditure data presented in this study embrace the national, state, and county governments. During this period, the revenues and expenditures of state and local governments were not important when compared with the total government revenues and expenditures. Table 7.2 shows that they were in the neighborhood of 10 percent of the totals for the government sector, as an average. Nonetheless, the shares of county and state revenues and expenditures expanded more rapidly than their federal counterparts. At the end of the period, they represented about 15 percent of the total government budget.

Despite fluctuations, total government revenues increased considerably during this period. If 1936 is taken as the base year (100), the index of government revenues rises to 134 by 1942, even though there was a sharp drop in that year. This represents an annual average compounded rate of growth of 5 percent a year, most of which resulted from an expansion in the revenues of state and local governments. If only the national budget is considered, the index rises only to 123 in 1942, which is equivalent to a 3.5 percent compounded average rate of growth per year.

The course of oil revenues shows a greater variation, but a more dramatic increase. At the end of the period, the 1936-based index stood at 169. In terms of compounded annual growth, this corresponds to a 9.1 percent rate of increase. This means that the tax contribution of petroleum expanded in relation to the Venezuelan GDP, which only expanded at a compounded annual average rate of 6.2 percent in current terms.

THE UTILIZATION OF TAX REVENUES FROM OIL

All this shows that petroleum taxes, if properly used, could have had a significant impact on the growth of the rest of the Venezuelan economy. How effectively were they utilized? The most satisfactory procedure to measure such effectiveness in a simple, straightforward manner is to estimate the portion of government expenditures devoted to fostering the economic development of the country. The percentage of capital expenditures in total government expenditures would also appear to be an adequate indication of effectiveness in the use of government funds; but this is not so, because it does not include current expenditures promoting economic growth.

Because there are no estimates of economic development expenditures of the public sector during the period examined, it is necessary to rely on estimates of expenditures of a social or economic nature.[11] These estimates are available only with respect to expenditures of the national government. It will, therefore, be assumed that the pattern of expenditures at state and county levels is close enough to that of the federal or national government. This is not an unreasonable assumption and, in any case, it cannot introduce significant inaccuracies, because county and state expenditures are a small part of total government expenditures.

Government expenditures of a social and economic type represent an outer bound for public expenditures of an economic development nature. But if it happens that these variables move roughly together, it is still possible to use the former as a proxy for the latter. This is the contention made here, based on the evidence given by Charles Rollins in his study of public expenditures in Venezuela.[12]

From Table 7.2 it can be seen that the share of social and economic expenditures increased from 53.4 percent in 1936 to 57.1 percent in 1942. In fact, during the in-between years, the share was always higher than in 1942, the peak year being 1937, with 62.0 percent. As an average over the whole period, the percentage share was 59.6 percent.

Since 1936, one of the most important principles of government policy in Venezuela has been the use of oil funds for the long-run development of the economy. This objective has been summarily expressed in the "sow the oil" motto. This concept implies that oil revenues are earmarked for long-run development projects. Thus, instead of merely considering how overall expenditures have been allocated, it might be better to work under the supposition that the entire oil revenues are devoted to economic development expenditures. Therefore, by examining the composition of total expenditures, and attributing the same breakdown to expenditures financed from oil revenues, we can inquire if the economic and social expenditures have been at least as large as oil revenues. Furthermore, the increments in both can be compared to see how marginal oil revenues have been utilized.

This test shows that social and economic expenditures were larger than oil revenues during this period and that increments in oil revenues were more than fully utilized for social and economic expenditures. The tendency to run a surplus on the national government account, which was prevalent previously, was reversed. In fact, during most of these years, public expenditures were in excess of public revenues (see Table 7.2). These deficits were financed in two ways: (1) by a dwindling of Treasury reserves, to the accumulation of which oil revenues had contributed in the past; and (2) through debt financing, to which the oil companies contributed directly by purchase or indirectly through the strength of their deposits and other assets supplied to the financial institutions operating in Venezuela.

In summary, during the 1937–1942 period, the contribution of the oil sector to the rest of the economy via the fiscal system was substantial, in terms of its share of the total tax burden and its increasing tax contribution. The government's utilization of these revenues also improved considerably during the period. The surplus budgets of the past were abandoned, and expenditures that could potentially contribute to the economic development of Venezuela increased in relation to total government expenses. Finally, this type of expenditure seemed to have been related to oil revenues throughout the period. All this indicates an increasing positive influence of oil on other sectors of the economy, through its fiscal contribution. This strong showing by petroleum also helped to alleviate tax pressures on the rest of the economy and helped to expand government services, without incurring large deficits.

Finally, the petroleum companies have provided health, education, communication, transportation, and other facilities in the communities where they were located, easing the pressures on government to do so. On the other hand, the hydrocarbon department of the government has participated only slightly in the total public budget. Although it is impossible to obtain exact data on the period examined, as hydrocarbon activities were then included in the Development Ministry, it is clear that it must have been quite small, since the ministry was allotted only 2.4 percent of the total expenditures of the national government in 1940.[13]

TOTAL INVESTMENT AND THE CONTRIBUTION OF OIL INVESTMENT

After examining both cross-sectional and historical data, Simon Kuznets concluded: "In the study of economic growth, wide interest attaches to the proportion that capital formation constitutes of national product. The larger it is (i.e., the larger the part of current product retained for use in further production), other conditions being equal, the higher the rate of growth of national product that can be generated."[14]

In developing economies, the processes of capital widening, capital deepening, and technical modernization are in their initial stages. In some economies, and Venezuela is certainly one of them, inflows of factors and resources can remedy the deficiencies that limit absorptive capacity. In these countries, the social marginal rates of return on investment are probably substantially higher than the opportunity cost of capital. Assuming this is correct, and barring other complications, these economies should be expected to allocate a substantial portion of their resources to investment in order to maximize the rate of growth of output over the long run.

The investment rate in the Venezuelan economy seems to have been quite respectable during the period examined. The percentage share of gross fixed domestic investment over GDP in constant 1957 prices (see Table 7.3) was 10.7 percent in 1936. By the end of the period, the accumulation of capital in the Venezuelan economy was at a much higher level (15.1 percent in 1941 and 13.9 percent in 1942). In the interim, the rate had soared in 1938, 1939, and 1940, probably as a result of the recovery from the depression and the preparation for World War II.

In absolute terms, the allocation of income to real gross fixed capital formation increased up to 1939. From then on, it declined. For the whole period, investment increased to a figure of 130, on an index scale based on 1936 equal 100. This corresponds to a 4.5 percent yearly rate of compounded increase. It was much greater in current prices, as the latter rose approximately 40 percent during the period.

Table 7.3.
Gross Domestic Product and Gross Fixed Domestic Investment, Oil Sector, 1936–1942

	1936	1937	1938	1939	1940	1941	1942
Total GDP (Mill. 1957 Bs.)	5,166	5,291	5,392	5,468	5,748	5,752	5,193
Oil Sector GDP (Mill. 1957 Bs.)	1,106	1,328	1,344	1,462	1,314	1,621	1,059
Other Sector GDP (Mill. 1957 Bs.)	3,668	3,458	3,342	3,316	3,924	3,624	3,780
Oil as a Percent of Total GDP	21.4%	25.1%	24.9%	26.7%	22.9%	28.2%	20.4%
Gross Fixed Domestic Investment (GFDI, Mill. Bs.)	555	746	1056	1313	1290	866	721
Oil Sector (Mill. Bs.)	180	252	452	410	260	198	155
Other Sectors (Mill. Bs.)	375	494	604	903	1030	668	566
Oil Investment as a Percent of GFDI	32.4%	33.8%	42.8%	31.2%	20.2%	22.9%	21.5%
GFDI as a Percent of GDP	10.7%	14.1%	19.6%	24.0%	22.4%	15.1%	13.9%

Note: Other Sector GDP is calculated here as Total GDP minus Oil Sector GDP minus Fixed Investment in the Oil Sector.

Sources: Banco Central de Venezuela, unpublished statistics; financial statements and supporting documents from the three main oil company groups in Venezuela, extrapolated to obtain industry-wide estimates; Bernardo Ferran, unpublished estimates presented in lectures on the economic development of Venezuela, delivered at the Universidad Central de Venezuela, Caracas, 1963.

Gross fixed domestic investment in petroleum represented an important part of total gross fixed domestic investment during this period. It rose from 32.4 percent in 1936 (see Table 7.3) to a peak 42.8 percent in 1938. From then on, it declined. If the public investment derived from petroleum taxes is added, the oil sector accounts for a much larger portion of total investment.

Petroleum investment, which started recuperating from the depression in 1934, was spurred during the 1936–1938 period by concessions taking place in 1936 and 1937 and by the prospects of increasing demand for oil in Europe, as a result of the conflagration. By 1939 the first factor was wearing off, and the European war was resulting in diminishing sales in Europe. From then on, investment contracted, the spreading war proving to be an obstacle to the expansion of the oil industry, because of transportation difficulties and shortages of skilled personnel and capital goods. In constant 1957 prices, petroleum investment was lower in 1942 than in 1936. In current prices, it was only 18 percent greater than in 1936.

If petroleum investment is subtracted from total investment, the residual obtained indicates the accumulation of capital taking place in the other sectors of the economy. It is important to examine the investment activity there for further evaluation of the impact of the autonomous forces of petroleum on the economy. Nonpetroleum investment, expressed in 1957 bolívares, is shown in Table 7.3. This variable increased continually and considerably up to 1940, and decreased from 1940 to 1942. During the whole period, it moved consistently with petroleum investment, with a one-year lag. By 1942, nonpetroleum gross investment in constant 1957 bolívares had increased by 51 percent throughout the period, equivalent to a compounded annual average rate of growth of 7.1 percent, which was much greater than that of overall gross investment.

NONPETROLEUM INVESTMENT AND RETAINED VALUE

The most important contributions of the oil sector are undoubtedly exercised through the current expenditures it generates in yearly production. These expenditures consist of payments to productive factors and to the government and other producers and are financed from exports and other sales of current production. However, not all of these expenditures affect the economy of Venezuela directly. Only those going to native factors or firms or to the Venezuelan government can be considered as a direct contribution to other economic sectors.[15] These expenditures constitute the portion retained by Venezuela of the current expenditures of the industry.

Looking at petroleum investment expenditures in terms of their contribution to the strength of the domestic capital goods-producing sector, a corresponding parallel is found. It is only the local purchase of capital goods and their construction by native factors that represents a direct contribution to other sectors in the economy. This portion of the total investment of the industry constitutes the retained value of its investment expenditures.

In fact, it has been argued above that the total combined contribution that a sector can make to an economy is somewhat related to the retained parts of total industry expenditures (current plus investment expenditures). As retained value of total expenditures changes, similar variations take place in the total combined contribution of the industry to other sectors of the economy. For example, as retained value increases, the overall contributions of the industry to the economy also rise. However, it should be understood that each particular contribution may not have the same relationship to total retained value as the overall contribution.

As pointed out above, nonpetroleum gross investment expenditures have moved with a one-year lag with respect to gross petroleum investment. Nevertheless, it was found that petroleum investment was much more affected by the war than the other components of investment. Would nonpetroleum gross investment be more closely related to retained value of total petroleum expenditures during this period?

Retained value of total expenditures in current prices experienced only two setbacks in its increase during the period examined. These were in 1940 and 1942, as can be seen in Table 7.4. For the period as a whole, it increased 21 percent, which corresponds to a 3.2 percent compounded annual average. This increase resulted from rising prices of crude and

Table 7.4.
Retained Value of Oil Sector Expenditures, 1936–1942

	1936	1937	1938	1939	1940	1941	1942
Retained Value of Total Expenditures (Mill. Bs.)	204	244	313	318	271	289	246
As a Percent of Total Expenditures	41.7%	39.8%	47.3%	47.6%	46.7%	39.4%	48.5%
Retained Value of Current Expenditures (Mill. Bs.)	142	162	144	163	181	215	177
As a Percent of Current Expenditures	35.4%	34.0%	33.8%	35.8%	40.7%	34.7%	43.9%
Retained Value of Current Expenditures per Barrel of Oil (Bs.)	0.92	0.87	0.77	0.79	0.98	0.94	1.20
Retained Value of Total Expenditures per Barrel of Oil (Bs.)	1.32	1.31	1.66	1.54	1.47	1.27	1.66
Total Value of Production (Mill. Bs.)	401	476	426	455	445	619	403
Oil Sector GDP (Mill. Bs.)	351	425	415	428	419	580	393

Notes: Estimates of retained value and value of production based on adjustments to data from three main petroleum company groups. Conversion of value of sales (or current expenditures) to value of production based on *Informes de Conservacion* (Caracas, several years) and unpublished data from the Oficina Técnica of the Ministerio de Minas e Hidrocarburos.

products, as, in real terms, retained value was in 1942 at the same level it had been in 1936.

As noted above, petroleum was among the sectors to first recuperate from the depression, not having been affected by it as much as the other sectors. Although oil prices increased up to 1936, from then until 1940 a decreasing trend set in once more. On the other hand, production increased up to 1939. In terms of current value, the industry expanded in 1937, decreased in 1938, and rose again in 1939. Nevertheless, if the period is taken as a whole, the value of petroleum production was 13 percent higher in 1939 than in 1936 (see Table 7.4). As a result of government policy, the share of the value of oil production remaining in Venezuela increased slightly faster, with the retained value of current expenditures, in current bolívares, rising 15 percent above the 1936 level.[16]

However, as shown earlier, petroleum investment increased considerably from 1936 to 1938, diminishing only slightly in 1939. This was partly the result of a recovery from the depression; more significantly, however, it resulted from the 1936–1937 concessions and the positive expectations deriving from the early stages of what was to become World War II. As a result, even during this period there was an increase in the retained value of *total* expenditures. In response, investment expenditures in the rest of the Venezuelan economy expanded. Part of the increased investment in the nonpetroleum sectors resulted from a rising share of government expenditures devoted to investment, a favorable outlook for future years, and the expectation of spreading war.

Nonpetroleum investment in real terms increased in 1940, but from then on it moved downward. Petroleum indicators moved in the same direction, as the war affected the petroleum industry, except that the highest point was reached in 1939. The fact that nonpetroleum investment was still growing, even though petroleum activity had begun its downturn, is explained by three factors: lags in the adjustment process, the three-year development plan started by President López Contreras in 1938, and the anticipation of expanding hostilities.

INVESTMENT EFFECTIVENESS

It is interesting that nonpetroleum investment expenditures in some years exceeded the portion of the total expenditures of the petroleum industry that were retained in Venezuela during this period (see Table 7.3). For the period as a whole, the rest of the economy invested an amount about as great as the payments received from the oil industry by native factors of production, local firms, and the Venezuelan government. This would suggest that the nonpetroleum part of the economy devoted a quite satisfactory amount of these resources to investment during these years.

Although capital formation proportions are a crucial factor for economic growth, the productivity of the resources devoted to capital accumulation is almost as important. Thus it would be appropriate to inquire about the social productivity and efficiency of investment resources in the Venezuelan economy. But appraisals of the efficiency in the use of investment funds are scant, as well as being limited to the public sector. The only seemingly objective evaluation found during this period concludes that significant resources were wasted by devoting them to unproductive uses. Misallocation also ruled in the shares of government investment going to the different productive sectors, as well as in the division between capital expenditures for directly productive activities and for social overhead. This is driven home with force by the fact that agricultural production declined during this period, despite increased government attention.[17]

In sum, gross fixed domestic investment in real terms increased respectably during this period, although negatively affected by war conditions in 1941 and 1942. Nonpetroleum gross fixed domestic investment in real terms did even better. Although gross investment in the petroleum industry in equivalent terms failed to rise during the period, it increased considerably up to 1939. The increase in petroleum investment, coupled with an expansion in the retained value of total expenditures in the oil industry, a promising outlook, and war expectations, seem to have been the forces promoting the investment performance of the nonpetroleum sector up to 1940. It has been impossible to separate nonpetroleum investment in its public and private component in this analysis.

Overall, the nonpetroleum part of the economy succeeded in devoting to investment an amount comparable to the retained value of the total expenditures originating in the petroleum industry. This is consistent with an extension to the whole economy of the "sow the oil" concept. Nevertheless, there are reasons to believe that the social profitability of investment left much to be desired.

Finally, petroleum investment constituted a prominent portion of total investment in this period: over one-third as an average from 1936 to 1939. Although the contribution of oil constituted a growth-promoting force up to 1939, from then on its impact became disappointingly small.

TOTAL DOMESTIC PRODUCT AND THE EXPENDITURES OF THE OIL INDUSTRY

As a potentially leading sector expands, its income-expenditure effects spread throughout the economy. Additional factor employment in the industry usually results, and average factor earnings rise. Government revenues deriving from the industry increase, and purchases from other business firms are raised. Finally, the expansion probably would enlarge the industry's investment spending. The effects of this expansion are woven through the oft-described multiplier-accelerator mechanism and reverberate throughout the economy.

Paying strict attention to the impact on other domestic economic sectors, and barring repercussions from imports or factor payments abroad, only a portion of these expenditures can be said to have a direct and immediate leverage. These portions have been called the retained values of current and capital expenditures. Retained value of total expenditures is the sum of the current and investment-retained value components.

As pointed out in previous chapters, it is unnecessary to go through the lengthy and still-imprecise process of evaluating and weighing each of the contributions of a potentially leading sector, and its impact, in order to appraise with sufficient accuracy how successful the sector has been in transmitting growth to the rest of the economy. It is sufficient to examine some of the potentially leading sector's main contributions and their influence on the other sectors of the economy. However, this must be accompanied by a similar analysis of the sector's total combined contribution, as represented by the behavior of the retained value of its total expenditures.

The income-expenditure contribution originating in the petroleum industry throughout this period should be examined at this point. In 1936 petroleum activity in Venezuela, while recuperating from the depression, was still quite off its previous highs. The value of oil output and the gross value added of petroleum spurted in 1937 and then moved erratically under the contradictory influences of World War II. Nevertheless, their trend was upward, and in 1941, spurred by war demand, they attained the highest level of the period. In 1942 the industry slumped, as a result of war scarcities and transportation difficulties in the Caribbean. In that year, the value of petroleum production and its GDP stood barely above 1936 levels in current terms (see Table 7.3).

In 1936 the contribution of the oil sector to the GDP of Venezuela (in constant 1957 bolívares) was already a shade above 20 percent (see Table 7.3). It hovered above that percentage during the next 10 years, reaching a high of 28.2 in 1941. In 1942 the participation of oil in total production declined to 20.4 percent, lower than in 1936. These figures clearly show the importance of petroleum in the economy of Venezuela. In this period, from one-fifth to over one-quarter of all economic activity in the country was derived from petroleum.[18]

The effects of gross fixed petroleum investment on the Venezuelan economy were examined in a previous section. Reference has been made to the behavior of the current expenditures of the petroleum industry, which generate gross multiplier-accelerator effects throughout the economy. Both the value of production and GDP of petroleum experienced an upward *trend* up to 1941, with a big increase in that year (see Table 7.4). Because the oil industry exports an overwhelming fraction of its total production, these income-expenditure injections were basically exogenous in character.

From 1936 to 1940, the value of petroleum production in current terms increased 11 percent, a compounded annual average rate of 2.7 percent. The GDP, in current bolívares, rose 19 percent, for a 4.4 percent annual average. Although a tremendous increment took place in both these variables in 1941, its consequences were short-lived because a severe contraction occurred in 1942. Only the retained portion of the expenditures of the industry actually directly influenced the economy of Venezuela.

The behavior over time of retained value of current expenditures appears in Table 7.4. In current bolívares, the retained value of current expenditures increased in 1937 but returned to the 1936 level the next year. From then on, it advanced continually up to the 1942 decline. At the end of the period, it had increased 24 percent, for a 3.8 compounded annual average rate of growth. Such an increase was greater than that experienced by either the value of production or GDP of the industry. This means that the fraction of current expenditures retained in Venezuela expanded more rapidly than total current expenditures. Both government policies and more enthusiastic industry compliance with them brought this about.

Expressed as a percentage of total current expenditures (value of production), retained value increased throughout the period from 35.4 percent to 43.9 percent. Although this increase was not smooth, it undoubtedly indicates that a greater portion of the current expenditures of the industry affected the Venezuelan economy directly. Similarly, Table 7.4 shows that retained value of current expenditures per barrel was much higher at the end of the period. This is partially attributable to the increase in oil prices that took place during the war. The remainder results from an increase in the portion of current expenditures retained in Venezuela.

The figures for retained value of investment expenditures do not have the same degree of precision as the estimates of retained value of current expenditures. If these two estimates are combined, retained value of total expenditures results. This variable had an upward course during these years, except for 1940 and 1942, with an overall growth of 21 percent throughout the period, good for a 3.2 percent average annual compounded growth (see Table 7.4).

The percentage share of total retained value in the total expenditures of the industry grew considerably, too (from 41.7 percent to 48.5 percent), although in an uneven fashion. Again, this can be attributed to government policy and industry collaboration. If this variable is expressed in a per barrel basis, an increase is also evident. At the beginning of the period, the retained value of total expenditures per barrel stood at 1.27 bolívares. By the end of the period, it had climbed to 1.66 bolívares per barrel, again in an uneven way, for the same reasons given above.

In terms of output, the oil industry had recovered from the depression by 1934. But as a result of lower prices, the value of production was even smaller than in the pre-depression era. The industry expected to be favorably affected by the rumbles of war in Europe. Events fell quite short of expectations, as the spurt of prices from the 1933 low ended in 1936. From then until 1940, prices declined, increasing from that year to 1942.

As an outcome of favorable expectations, production increased in 1937. But shattered dreams, resulting from disappointing European demand, affected it on and off in succeeding years. The year 1941 saw an expansion in production, again due to the geographical extension of the war, its greater intensity, and its effects upon other supply sources. However, a severe setback occurred the next year, as the conflagration reached the waters of the Caribbean and war scarcities imposed heavy pressures upon the industry.

On the other hand, the oil sector was confronted from the beginning of the period by a more aggressive Venezuelan government. Since the death of Gómez, airs of reform had filled the Venezuelan atmosphere. These reforms were advocated by old Gómez followers and turned out to be moderate in nature. The government received special payments from the companies for the privilege of obtaining concessions, even though higher taxes accompanied them.[19] Even more, the companies were urged in other ways to increase their expenditures in Venezuela.

The rule of duty-free importation of those goods needed by the industry to conduct their operations, which had been included as a *matter of course* clause in past concessions contracts, was questioned. The dispute between the executive branch of the government and the oil companies was taken before Venezuelan courts. The government maintained that the clause was meant to apply only when such goods were not available from Venezuelan producers. The matter was not settled during this period. But in the meantime, the companies were forced to submit lists of their planned imports to the Development Ministry for approval. This resulted in the companies turning to local firms for procurement in order to avoid the haggling involved, even though their rightful obligation was still undetermined.

Other government actions also affected the industry. The 1936 labor law increased the required minimum representation of Venezuelans in the labor employed by the industry. Then, the minimum wage was raised from about 7 bolívares a day to 9.77 bolívares, and fringe benefits for petroleum workers were considerably increased. Also, the law stipulated that companies would have to use more Venezuelans in skilled, technical, administrative, managerial, and executive capacities and begin training them for such purposes.

Finally, the government made an about-face in the refining question. Gómez had not encouraged refining in Venezuela, and the companies,

wary about what would happen if he disappeared, had set up big refineries in Aruba and Curaçao. The only clause in the Venezuelan petroleum
legislation promoting oil refinement in Venezuela permitted the locally
refined products to pay only 50 percent of the taxes that the imported
refined products had to pay. As the Venezuelan market was quite small,
this did not prove to be a good incentive. Government incentives to local
refining became more attractive when preference in the granting of concessions was given to those companies that agreed to establish or expand
their refineries in Venezuela. This brought along a considerable increase in
the production of refined oil products in the country.

These measures, coupled with some labor unrest, political agitation
against the companies, and litigation with the government in other fronts
had helped, by 1938, to bridle the industry's enthusiasm. Yet, the situation
had improved somewhat by 1941, and from then on, the situation was ripe
for large gains, whenever world demand would act as the spark plug.

EFFECTS OF POPULATION SHIFTS

Although this period was not one of significant expansion for the industry, the higher level of its retained value did have some beneficial effects
on the Venezuelan economy. In the geographic areas where oil was produced, a moderate expansion took place. Yet the sharp contraction of 1942
resulted in so much unemployment that an organized back-to-farm movement had to be instituted with the collaboration of the petroleum industry
and the government.

Between 1926 and 1936, the population in the petroleum states
increased 23.9 percent, while the increase in total population was 15.3 percent. During the same period, the population in the federal district (part of
the Caracas Metropolitan Area) increased by 45 percent.[20] Comparable figures for the 1936–1942 period show a 25 percent increase in the population
of the petroleum states at the same time that total population increased
14.5 percent. The population in the federal district grew 34.3 percent during the latter period.

Thus, petroleum was pulling population to the areas where its activity
took place, at a similar pace, over these two periods. The oil industry also
contributed significantly to the movement of population to the federal district: directly, by establishing administrative offices and making purchases
in the area and, indirectly, through government expenditures, which were
very heavily concentrated in Caracas.

The concentration of population in the federal district apparently slackened during the 1936–1942 period. However, the population increase in
the federal district did not abate as much as it might appear, and perhaps
not at all. This is because a comparison of the population in the federal district for the years 1926 and 1936 would tend to exaggerate its expansion. In

1936, conditions in the rural areas were influenced by the depression, and agricultural workers had flocked to urban areas, while 1926 had been a good year for Venezuelan agriculture, which would have tended to keep the labor force in the rural areas.

IMPACT ON NONPETROLEUM GROSS DOMESTIC PRODUCT

Venezuela's GDP in constant 1957 prices grew 11 percent from 1936 to 1941. This is equivalent to a 2.2 percent compounded annual average rate of growth. Although this might seem small, it was sufficient to maintain previous levels of income per capita, as the rate of population growth in Venezuela by that time was also approximately 2.2 percent. The oil crisis and mounting war difficulties crippled the economy of Venezuela in 1942. The GDP, in 1957 prices, fell almost as much as it had grown in the previous five years (see Table 7.3).

The GDP, in figures that exclude the petroleum component, shows just how the nonpetroleum sector of the Venezuelan economy behaves. The influence of the oil sector was eliminated in the calculation of nonpetroleum GDP in constant 1957 bolívares, which appear in Table 7.3. Both the value of oil production and gross fixed investment in the industry were subtracted, because they are taken into account in the calculation of total GDP and because they influence the gross value added in other sectors.

Nonpetroleum GDP, in 1957 prices, seems to have grown very little from 1936 to 1942, its expansion amounting to only 3 percent during this period. Still, this is larger than the growth of the total GDP (less than 1 percent) and of petroleum GDP (which declined somewhat). Interestingly, it was only toward the end of the period that the influence of petroleum's expansion up to 1939 was felt by the other sectors. Thus, the effect was delayed and unusually protracted. This can probably be explained by the political and economic uncertainty prevalent during the initial years of the López Contreras regime and the normal gestation period of investments. The lag does seem to have worked on a more reasonable one-year basis in the latter part of the period.

Although the retained value of total expenditures expanded up to 1939, the nonpetroleum GDP, in 1957 bolívares, declined during this period and jumped upward in 1940. As petroleum's retained value sagged in 1940, its effects on the rest of the economy were felt the following year. The same thing occurred, in the opposite direction, with the 1941 expansion in the retained value.

The total retained value of the petroleum industry expanded throughout the period at a 3.2 percent average compounded rate of growth per year, while nonpetroleum GDP in 1957 prices rose only 3 percent in the six years. Even though the nonpetroleum part of the Venezuelan economy did better in its expansion up to 1940, it only rose at a 1.7 percent compounded annual average, which is much lower than the average increase in petroleum's retained value for the whole period. Moreover, from 1936 to 1940, retained value expanded at a 7.4 percent compounded yearly average.

It is easier to understand all this if the 1936–1942 period is divided into two parts and each is examined in detail. From 1936 to 1939, the petroleum sector augmented its contribution to the other sectors and spread exogenous injections to the rest of the economy. The nonpetroleum part of the economy did not seem to be affected by such autonomous forces, with production only beginning to react in 1940, although investment had been affected much sooner.

The main explanation of what took place during those years must lie in the uncertain political atmosphere following the passing away of Gómez. It took some time before López Contreras emerged, apparently in full control of the situation. It was even longer before Venezuelans felt confident that his regime was stable.

Being one of the old dictator's strong generals, López Contreras nevertheless admitted most of the groups that had opposed Gómez into the political arena. Some of these were quite liberal; others had radical ideas that they could now express rather freely. Other groups were moderate, but either sided with the liberals in the condemnation of the oil industry and in other economic matters or had unorthodox ideas of their own. Many of these sat in Congress, and some, like Nestor Perez, the development minister, were even in López Contreras' cabinet. Moreover, much agitation occurred during the government of López Contreras, especially in the early years, when unrest among petroleum workers was at its peak and spreading to other sectors. All this frightened the business community, and it took some years for the confidence of the economic classes to return. The economic development program of López Contreras, which started rolling in 1938, and which included measures for the promotion of domestic production, helped considerably in changing business attitudes.

The unfavorable performance of Venezuelan exports was another factor that contributed to the stagnation of the nonpetroleum part of the economy. Nonpetroleum exports declined from 1937 to 1942, and this coincided with a considerable expansion in imports in anticipation of the spread of war, as well as rising import prices.

Just at the time the business community was reacting favorably to the expansion in oil, the latter began losing momentum and became a depressing force in the economy. Thus, during the second part of the period, the performance of the economy as a whole was quite disappointing and GDP declined from its high in 1940.

THE IMPACT OF OIL ON OTHER SECTORS: A DISAGGREGATED ANALYSIS

How the various Venezuelan industries have fared over time will now be examined. This will be accomplished by using output indexes, as no discriminated time series in terms of values exist for this period. The petroleum industry has been examined and will not be included in the tables presented later.

Most of the national income originated in the Venezuelan economy in 1936, if petroleum and government are excluded, corresponded to tertiary activities (45.6 percent). As Table 7.5 shows, commerce constituted the larger part of the tertiary sector. The industrial sector, including extractive activities, represented 26.2 percent of the economy, after petroleum and government have been taken out. Manufacturing accounted for most of this (24.7 percent). Agriculture constituted 28.1 percent, with livestock representing a sizable part of it (7.2 percent).

Discriminating a bit further within each of these sectors, it is found that textiles and clothing were estimated to be about one-half of the income originated in industry (see Table 7.6). The food industry also seems to have accounted for an important part of industrial value added (18.3 percent). Most of the industries listed can be classified as consumer goods industries.

If a similar level of detail is presented for the agricultural sector, it is found that coffee, sugar, and corn were the major crops in 1936, represent-

Table 7.5.
Income Originated by Type of Activity, 1936

Activity	Income (Mill. Bs.)	Share
Industry	**322**	**25.8%**
Manufacturing	303	24.3%
Extractive	9	0.7%
Construction	10	0.8%
Agriculture	**369**	**29.6%**
Crops	285	22.9%
Dairy & Livestock	84	6.7%
Commerce	**223**	**17.9%**
Real Estate	**173**	**13.9%**
Private Services	**160**	**12.8%**
Transport	64	5.1%
Domestic Service	52	4.2%
Public and Personal Services	44	3.5%
Total	**1247**	**100.0%**

Note: Does not include petroleum or government.
Source: Banco Central de Venezuela, El Ingreso Nacional de Venezuela (Caracas, 1949).

Table 7.6.
Income Originating in Industry by Type of Activity, 1936

Activity	Income (Mill. Bs.)	Share (%)	Cumulative Share (%)
Textiles and Clothing	162	50.3	50.3
Food	59	18.3	68.6
Hides and By-Products	21	6.4	75.0
Wood	20	6.2	81.2
Construction	10	3.1	84.3
Extractive	9	2.8	87.1
Power	8	2.5	89.6
Printing	6	1.9	91.5
Chemical	6	1.9	93.4
Cement, Tile, Ceramics, and Kindred	6	1.9	95.3
Tobacco	6	1.9	97.2
Metals	4	1.2	98.4
Other	5	1.6	100.0
Total	322	100.0	

Source: Banco Central de Venezuela, *El Ingreso Nacional de Venezuela* (Caracas, 1949).

ing altogether 45 percent of the total value of agricultural production. Meat, dairy products, cocoa, cassava, and bananas were also important. Many other products were grown, as can be seen in Table 7.7.

An examination of the commercial activities in 1936 shows that food held the largest market share, while clothing and cosmetics also accounted for a large share of commerce (see Table 7.8). Transportation and domestic services (see Table 7.9) accounted for over 70 percent of income originated in the other services category.

Actual volume figures are available only in agriculture. In Table 7.10, the breakdown of agricultural production is shown for 1936; corresponding figures for 1945 are presented whenever possible in order to give an indication of how the different agricultural activities have fared over time. In Table 7.10, the years 1936 and 1945 are compared by means of an index. It is found that most categories and certain important products declined.

In particular, farm food crops appear to have declined. This is true for each of its subcategories except fruits and vegetables, on which no figures are available. The production of industrial crops, as well as coffee and cocoa, also diminished. The animal products category expanded, mainly due to fish production, because most other products contracted. Finally, timber production expanded considerably, but from a slim base.

Hence, it appears that there was a contraction in agriculture during the period. Although the government demonstrated its worry about agriculture (in the "sow the oil" motto), it was not successful in this sector. Overall, government policy was mainly directed toward self-sufficiency and diversification and, together with aid to local industry, tried to stimulate

Table 7.7.
Value of Agricultural Production by Type of Product, 1936

Product	Value (Mill. Bs.)	Share (%)	Cumulative Share (%)
Coffee	62	16.8	16.8
Sugarcane	58	15.7	32.5
Corn	47	12.7	45.3
Steers	29	7.9	53.1
Cheese	23	6.2	59.3
Milk	21	5.7	65.0
Cocoa	16	4.3	69.4
Cassava	15	4.1	73.4
Plantain	13	3.5	77.0
Bananas	11	3.0	79.9
Beans	13	3.5	83.5
Pigeon Peas	8	2.2	85.6
Tobacco	4	1.1	86.7
Coconuts	4	1.1	87.8
Yautia	3	0.8	88.6
Goats	3	0.8	89.4
Rice	3	0.8	90.2
Potatoes	3	0.8	91.1
Fruits	3	0.8	91.9
Cotton	3	0.8	92.7
Feed	3	0.8	93.5
Vegetables	3	0.8	94.3
Wheat	2	0.5	94.8
Butter	2	0.5	95.4
Yams	2	0.5	95.9
Horses	2	0.5	96.5
Cream	1	0.3	96.7
Onions	1	0.3	97.0
Mares	1	0.3	97.3
Donkeys	1	0.3	97.6
Other Roots	1	0.3	97.8
Celery	1	0.3	98.1
Lard	1	0.3	98.4
Garlic	1	0.3	98.6
Other Products	5	1.4	100.0
Total	369	100.0	

Source: Banco Central de Venezuela, *El Ingreso Nacional de Venezuela* (Caracas, 1949), p. 102.

agricultural production. But though a considerable share of public investments of a directly productive type have been devoted to agricultural development, in general, urban development has been emphasized at the expense of providing basic facilities in the rural areas. Some of the investments specifically designed for agricultural development have not been well conceived, so that the capital created has not been fully utilized.[21]

A general index for manufacturing and extractive activities is presented in Table 7.11, together with indexes for particular industrial and manufac-

Table 7.8.
Income Originating in Commerce by Type of Activity, 1936

Activity	Income (Mill. Bs.)	Share (%)	Cumulative Share (%)
Food	62	27.8	27.8
Clothing, cosmetics, etc.	23	10.3	38.1
Advertising, Radio, etc.	14	6.3	44.4
Banks and Insurance	11	4.9	49.3
Motor Vehicles and Gasoline	8	3.6	52.9
Pharmaceuticals and Similar Products	7	3.1	56.1
Other	98	43.9	100.0
Total	223	100.0	

Source: Banco Central de Venezuela, *El Ingreso Nacional de Venezuela* (Caracas, 1949).

turing lines. They show expansion, especially for manufacturing in general, and for textiles, energy, cement, beer, and crackers in particular.

The figures exaggerate the growth that actually took place. First, some of the indexes refer to consumption rather than output, and, when referring to particular lines, they represent growth from quite slim bases. Second, the growth in manufacturing is to 1945, which undoubtedly was much more than the expansion to 1942, as other indexes and all evidence indicate.

Different policies were instrumental in bringing this industrial growth about: tariffs were raised, quotas were established, and exchange controls were enforced at different times during the period. Toward the end, the

Table 7.9.
Income Originating in Service Sector by Type of Activity, 1936

Activity	Income (Mill. Bs.)	Share (%)	Cumulative Share (%)
Domestic Services	52	32.5	32.5
Land Transport	33	20.6	53.1
Water Transport	19	11.9	65.0
Other Transport (excl. Air Transport)	11	6.9	71.9
Repair Shops	10	6.3	78.1
Diverse Services (incl. Private Hospitals)	10	6.3	84.4
Realtors and Employment Agencies	7	4.4	88.8
Restaurants and Hotels	7	4.4	93.1
Barber Shops and Community Swimming	6	3.8	96.9
Entertainment	2	1.3	98.1
Air Transport	1	0.6	98.8
Photographic Services	1	0.6	99.4
Laundry and Cleaners	1	0.6	100.0
Total	160	100.0	--

Source: Banco Central de Venezuela, *El Ingreso Nacional de Venezuela* (Caracas, 1949).

Table 7.10.
Agricultural Production by Commodity, 1936 and 1945 (thousands of metric tons)

Commodity	1936	1945	Commodity	1936	1945
Farm Food Crops:	**1129.7**	**497.4**	**Industrial Crops:**	**440.3**	**163**
Cereal:	380.5	290.3	Fibers and Oils:	179.1	12.6
Corn	*361.3*	*253.8*	*Sesame*	*0.7*	*2.0*
Shelled Rice	*12.7*	*29.6*	*Peanuts*	*0.3*	*0.3*
Wheat	*6.5*	*6.9*	*Copra*	*7.0*	*N.A.*
Legumes:	56.8	43.1	*Raw Cotton*	*8.5*	*10.3*
Beans	*30.8*	*22.1*	*Sisal Fiber*	*0.1*	*N.A.*
Pigeon Peas	*4.3*	*5.0*	*Others*	*162.5*	*N.A.*
Kidney Beans	*14.3*	*8.0*	Sugar	21.0	27.2
Peas	*7.4*	*8.0*	Unrefined Sugar	136.6	50.0
Roots and Tubers (a):	181.7	164	Tobacco	4.9	N.A.
Cassava	*115.4*	*N.A.*	Coffee	74.6	58.1
Yautia	*35.1*	*N.A.*	Cacao	24.1	15.1
Yams	*14.7*	*150.0*	**Animal Products:**	**252.5**	**277.8**
Celery	*5.9*	*N.A.*	Meat	72.5	70.1
Potatoes	*10.6*	*14.0*	Poultry	2.0	2.0
Fruits and Vegetables:	510.7	N.A.	Fish	16.0	54.7
Bananas	*281.9*	*N.A.*	Eggs	1.0	1.5
Plantains	*159.2*	*N.A.*	Dairy Products:	161	149.5
Other Fruits	*56.8*	*N.A.*	*Milk*	*74.5*	*62.0*
Vegetables	*12.8*	*N.A.*	*Cheese*	*86.5*	*87.5*
			Forestry (b) :	**24.7**	**98.5**
			TOTAL	**1847.2**	**1036.7**

Notes: Roots and tubers, except for potatoes, are estimates. Forestry output is measured in cubic meters.

Source: Derived from Juan P. Perez Castillo, "Some Aspects of Venezuela's Economic Development: 1945–1960," Ph.D. dissertation, Tulane University, 1963.

cessation of hostilities became a central factor in the expansion of industry. The scarcities it brought about facilitated the substitution of imports by Venezuelan producers. This analysis shows that the small growth in non-petroleum activities during this period concentrated on the industrial sector (extractive activities included). Tertiary activities may have grown somewhat, as was shown for government.

Table 7.11.
Index of Industrial Production, 1936–1948

	1936	1937	1938	1939	1940	1941	1942	1943	1944	1945	1946	1947	1948
Products:													
Rayon	N.A.	N.A.	100	N.A.	600	2,233	3,600	3,766	4,100	5,566	N.A.	N.A.	N.A.
Cotton	N.A.	N.A.	100	140	170	227	680	797	733	713	N.A.	N.A.	N.A.
Sugar	N.A.	N.A.	N.A.	N.A.	N.A.	N.A.	100	116	108	90	N.A.	N.A.	N.A.
Butter	N.A.	N.A.	N.A.	N.A.	N.A.	N.A.	100	126	116	133	N.A.	N.A.	N.A.
Meat	N.A.	N.A.	N.A.	N.A.	N.A.	N.A.	100	95	103	111	N.A.	N.A.	N.A.
Beer	N.A.	N.A.	N.A.	N.A.	N.A.	N.A.	100	112	146	185	N.A.	N.A.	N.A.
Milk (Pasturized)	N.A.	N.A.	N.A.	N.A.	N.A.	N.A.	100	109	111	102	N.A.	N.A.	N.A.
Crackers	N.A.	N.A.	N.A.	N.A.	N.A.	N.A.	100	118	124	219	N.A.	N.A.	N.A.
Textiles	N.A.	N.A.	100	119	142	181	131	151	141	176	N.A.	N.A.	N.A.
Electricity	N.A.	N.A.	100	107	129	155	162	167	181	207	242	284	344
Tires	N.A.	N.A.	N.A.	N.A.	N.A.	100	85	172	265	246	298	283	285
Energy	N.A.	N.A.	100	112	98	142	142	150	195	211	261	400	484
Cement	86	71	100	98	200	237	303	283	289	289	325	353	502
Industry Group:													
Extractive	100	104	102	96	150	166	149	128	135	127	182	175	248
Manufacturing	N.A.	N.A.	100	N.A.	N.A.	N.A.	N.A.	N.A.	N.A.	245	255	234	350

Notes: Textiles, energy, and cement represent consumption. N.A. means not available.

Source: Evelyn M. Baran, "The Economic Development of Venezuela," Ph.D. dissertation, Radcliffe College, 1959.

It is difficult to pinpoint which lines have felt a stronger impact from petroleum, as the breakdown available is not sufficiently detailed. Still, the expansion in the consumption of cement and energy are clearly an outcome of petroleum activity and its indirect effects. The per capita consumption of energy in Venezuela expanded substantially from 1937 to 1952. In the terminal year, it was the highest in South America.[22] Cement and timber consumption were tied to construction in the petroleum industry and to the expansion in government expenditures and the increased urbanization it fostered. The trend in other consumer product lines is tied in a more roundabout fashion to the expansion of oil.

SUMMARY

In conclusion, during the first part of this period, all the contributions examined—with the exception of petroleum exports—and the total combined contribution of petroleum to the rest of the economy expanded considerably. Because of an unfavorable political and economic climate, the other sectors of the Venezuelan economy failed to expand *pari passu* in real terms. Though some of the contributions examined continued to expand in the second part of the period, the total combined contribution of oil declined from 1939. The rest of the economy followed suit. In *real per capita terms,* the Venezuelan economy, as a whole, did not grow from 1936 to 1941. Surprisingly, all this took place while the investment rate—gross fixed investment over GDP—constituted a respectably high figure. This was particularly true at the beginning of the period, during which investment expanded.

This seeming contradiction can be explained by an increasingly higher investment component in the public sector, by capital spending in anticipation of the war, and by the lag existing between the particular investment expenditure and the time when it actually became productive. Moreover, public investment was heavily weighted in favor of social overhead projects. This assumes no excess capacity in the economy, which is a realistic supposition for this period, as the economy had recuperated from the depression by 1936. By the end of 1942, the structure of the Venezuelan economy had changed only slightly from what it had been in 1936. Industrial production was in its infancy, and the economy was completely dependent upon oil.

NOTES

1. This is especially true, if such beneficial conditions in their external sectors have not resulted from large devaluations or entailed adverse movement in the terms of trade. This would ensure that the national currencies involved would maintain their purchasing power in terms of other currencies and that no decline in the standard of living has occurred.

2. On all this, see United States Tariff Commission, *Economic Controls and Commercial Policy in Venezuela* (Washington, D.C.: U.S. Government Printing Office, 1945).

3. In economics with a high average propensity to import, the overall price level tends to be greatly influenced by the behavior of the prices of imported goods. On this see Henry Wallich, "Monetary Problems of an Export Economy," *Harvard EC Studies,* vol. 88 (Cambridge, Mass.: Harvard University Press, 1950).

4. For a survey of different views on reserve levels, see Herbert Grubel, "The Demand for International Reserves: A Critical Review of the Literature," *Journal of Economic Literature* (December 1971).

5. For some evidence on all these points, see Nassau A. Adams, "Import Structure and Economic Growth: A Comparison of Cross-Section and Time-Series Data," *Economic Development and Cultural Change* (January 1967).

6. The Hydrocarbons Law of 1938 raised all petroleum taxes considerably. But it was applicable only to new concessions. As the companies, in opposition to the law, did not apply for them, and because they decided against converting or adapting the old concession to this law, the rate increases embodied in the law had little practical effect.

7. The Venezuelan Ministry of Finance includes it among its tax revenues as profits from exchange operations. The latter is slightly different from the concept previously discussed, as will be shown, being also extended to other industries covered under the same regulations.

8. These proceeds were also partly used for covering the expenses incurred in the administration of the foreign exchange program.

9. If foreign exchange tax revenues from the oil sector are included in oil revenues and compared to total government revenues, the participation of oil in the latter becomes exaggerated. But as has been seen, if they are not included, the share of oil in total tax revenue is underestimated. As the exact percentage share cannot be determined, these two different measures are used and determine a range that includes the exact share.

10. The same cannot be said for state enterprises and autonomous government administrative institutes.

11. See Charles Rollins, "Raw Materials Development and Economic Growth: A Study of the Bolivian and Venezuelan Experience" (Ph.D. diss., Stanford University, 1956).

12. Ibid., ch. 2.

13. On this point, see Banco Central de Venezuela, *La Economía Venezolana en los Ultimos Veinticinco Años* (Caracas, 1966), Sección Finanzas Públicas.

14. Simon Kuznets, *Six Lectures on Economic Growth* (Glencoe, Ill.: Free Press, 1959), p. 70.

15. Even in this case some of the local purchases are actually imported goods. Strictly speaking, these purchases should not be classified together with those directly affecting the domestic economy. These purchases could only be considered different from direct imports by the companies on the basis that they might help to strengthen the native commercial sector.

16. This increase would have been somewhat greater if the foreign exchange tax had been included in retained value.

17. See Evelyn M. Baran, "The Economic Development of Venezuela" (Ph.D. diss., Radcliffe College, 1959). The author also finds some indication that the same characteristics were present in the investment activities of the private sector.

18. The estimates of petroleum GDP referred to above comprise only the value added by the petroleum sector in the production of oil. But the petroleum sector also engages in the production of capital goods for its own use. The factor payments and taxes related to such activity are capitalized by the companies and do not appear as part of the value of petroleum's current output. If the income originated in the capital goods section of the petroleum industry is added to the estimates presented above, the petroleum share of GDP would be even larger.

19. The procedure was that different companies bid for the concessions, with the highest bidders usually receiving them.

20. Economic Commission for Latin America, United Nations, *Recent Facts and Trends in The Venezuelan Economy* (Mexico, D.F., 1951), p. 54.

21. Baran, "Economic Development of Venezuela."

22. See United Nations, *Statistical Yearbook* (New York, 1954), p. 277.

CHAPTER 8

1943–1957

This chapter examines the impact over the decade and a half in which oil's potential contribution to the Venezuelan economy appeared to attain its peak. As will be seen, this appeared to coincide with a period of unparalleled growth in other sectors of Venezuela's economy.

In order to best examine the impact of petroleum's contribution, and how effectively it was utilized, as well as to evaluate the extent to which oil acted as a leading sector, it is important to separate these 15 years into two quite distinct subperiods. The first subperiod begins with the abatement of World War II and the conversion and granting of oil concessions that took place in 1943, and continues through the end of the war and the early postwar years. The second subperiod starts with the downfall of the Acción Democrática regime, which ruled in Venezuela from 1945 to 1948 and introduced many reforms, especially with respect to government relations with the oil industry. It ends with the oil concessions of the late 1950s and the overthrow of the Perez Jimenez military dictatorship. The approach introduced in Chapter 4 will be followed in each of the subperiods.

THE 1943–1948 SUBPERIOD: THE FOREIGN SECTOR CONTRIBUTION

Total exports of goods increased almost fivefold from 1942 to 1948 (see Table 8.1). This expansion was continuous, with the exception of 1945, and was much faster than that of the GDP. The share of exports in the GDP was enlarged from 20 to 30 percent, reversing the pattern of the preceding period.

Table 8.1.
Petroleum Sector Indicators and External Sector Performance, 1942–1948

	1942	1943	1944	1945	1946	1947	1948
Total Exports (Mill. US$)	226	275	356	351	512	691	1,102
Oil Exports (Mill. US$)	206	254	342	332	485	664	1,069
as a percent of Total	91.2%	92.4%	96.1%	94.6%	94.7%	96.1%	97.0%
International Reserves (Mill. US$)	89	115	142	208	232	234	362
Change in Reserves	23	26	27	66	24	2	128
Share of Capital Goods/Total Imports	0.28	0.108	0.198	0.379	0.228	0.36	46.1%
Import Capacity Index (1959=100)	25.4	28.8	33.6	31	43.2	53.2	68.2
Net Barter Terms of Trade Index	172.9	160.2	131.2	95.8	111.9	123.4	141.8

Sources: Ministerio de Fomento, *Anuario Estadístico* (Caracas, 1938); Banco Central de Venezuela, *Memoria* (Caracas, 1947) and *La Economía Venezolana en los Ultimos Veinticinco Años* (Caracas, 1966), with adjustments.

Petroleum exports expanded even faster. The share of oil in total goods exported rose from 91.2 percent in 1942 to 97.0 percent in 1948 (see Table 8.1). Thus, the gross balance of payments contribution of oil was very considerable, as well as expanding. Undoubtedly, oil was the basic force, ensuring the strong foreign payments position attained by Venezuela toward the end of the period, in spite of the high import levels sustained during these years. As in the previous period, no data are available for calculating the net balance of payments contribution of oil.

The strong showing of oil exports ended the need for import controls in 1944. The Import Control Commission was then replaced by the National Supply Commission, a body to control the demand and supply of certain goods that were scarce because of the war. After the war, normal trading conditions were slowly reestablished, and totally unrestrained imports became the rule once more, for the first time since the late 1920s.

Although the rate of inflation was somewhat high during this period— over a 7 percent compounded annual average—it resulted from abnormal conditions prevailing in the second half of World War II and in the initial postwar years. There is no connection between Venezuela's rate of inflation and its balance of payments in this period. Price hikes in Venezuela followed those of its trading partners, whose prices rose as a result of postwar conditions such as rationing and scarcity of nonmilitary goods. The inflation, moreover, had no adverse effect on the economy's development.

The import capacity of Venezuela broadened during this period. However, the net barter terms of trade evolved unfavorably from 1942 to 1945 and started to move in favor of Venezuela in 1946, although never regaining the 1942 or 1943 levels (see Table 8.1).

The effectiveness with which the foreign exchange proceeds contributed by oil were actually used during this period can be evaluated by looking at the composition of the total Venezuelan goods imports. Although this constitutes a partial measurement, as it does not refer to other kinds of foreign exchange uses such as imports of services and capital outflows, it is the only one possible in this period.

Table 8.1 reveals that the percentage of imported goods devoted to capital formation during this period rose from 28.0 percent in 1942 to 46.1 percent in 1948. This is a general indication that the allocation of foreign exchange proceeds among different types of import goods was efficient. Such a shift must be interpreted with caution, because in 1942 there were import controls, and capital goods were in scant supply. On the other hand, in 1948 there were no import restrictions, and the scarcity of capital goods was more benign. Thus, most of this shift can best be explained in terms of changing circumstances.

Venezuela accumulated international reserves throughout this period (see Table 8.1). However, this accumulation was small in almost all of these years, as world commerce and international availability of goods were still affected by war conditions.

In summary, over these years an overwhelming and growing portion of the foreign exchange earnings of Venezuela was derived from the oil industry. Petroleum exports expanded quite rapidly, assuring the Venezuelan economy of a strong balance of payments position. This meant that the external sector served as an aid to growth. On the other hand, the terms at which Venezuela traded in foreign markets deteriorated somewhat throughout the period. Finally, the economy utilized this increasing oil contribution more effectively, as an apparently larger share of the total import of goods was used for capital formation, while no excessive accumulation of international reserves took place. Therefore, the foreign sector contribution of oil was an important force working for development during this period, and the economy took advantage of it. This represented a great improvement over the previous period.

The Fiscal Contribution of Oil

Petroleum's impact upon the government sector—and, through the latter, upon the rest of the economy—was examined for the years 1936–1942 in Chapter 7. In the subsequent period, the contribution of oil to government revenues increased considerably; concurrently, use of these funds by the government improved significantly. An examination of Table 8.2 shows how petroleum-derived tax revenues behaved during 1942–1948.

The same forces that caused the increase in the percentage share of oil revenues in the previous period were again instrumental in eliciting a

Table 8.2.
Public Sector Fiscal Indicators, 1942–1948

	1942	1943	1944	1945	1946	1947	1948
Total Public Sector Revenues (Mill. Bs.)	340	375	599	734	943	1,417	1,939
Tax Revenue from Petroleum	108	161	290	369	497	695	1,163
As a Percent of Total Public Sector Revenues	31.8%	42.9%	48.4%	50.3%	52.7%	49.0%	60.0%
Tax Revenue from Exchange Differential	--	53	129	79	128	198	468
Government Expenditures (Mill. Bs.)	353	395	480	652	1,054	1,297	1,846
Economic & Social Development Expenditures	201	216	285	411	583	887	1,187
As a Percent of Government Expenditure	57.0%	0.5%	59.4%	63.0%	55.3%	68.4%	64.3%
Public Sector Deficit (Mill. Bs.)	13	20	-119	-82	111	-120	-93
Local Government Finances:							
Expenditures (Mill. Bs.)	49	58	70	71	102	123	137
Revenues	53	56	65	74	94	136	163

Notes: Local revenues and expenditures exclude transfers from the federal government. Data not include finances of state enterprises or autonomous government administrative institutions.

Sources: Ministerio de Fomento, *Memoria* (Caracas, several years); Banco Central de Venezuela, *Memoria* (Caracas, several years), *La Economía Venezolana en los Ultimos Veinticinco Años* (Caracas, 1966), and unpublished data on the historical exchange rates in Venezuela; Ministerio de Minas e Hidrocarburos, *Petróleo y Otros Datos Estadísticos* (Caracas, 1965); Ministerio de Fomento, Dirección General de Estadísticos, *Anuario Estadístico* (Caracas, 1938 and 1951); Manuel R. Egana, *Tres Décadas de Producción Petrolera* (Caracas, 1947); Charles E, Rollins, "Raw Materials Development and Economic Growth: A Study of the Bolivian and Venezuelan Experience," Ph.D. dissertation, Stanford University, 1956.

higher level of oil participation. Petroleum GDP became a larger proportion of total GDP, and petroleum taxes were raised radically at this time.

Most petroleum taxes were raised by the Hydrocarbons Law of 1943, to which practically all petroleum companies converted their concessions, and which, therefore, became applicable to the industry as a whole. Moreover, petroleum operations were further affected by the establishment of an income tax, applicable almost exclusively to the petroleum companies.[1]

Then, during 1944 and 1945, the government granted new concessions, which resulted in special concession payments and increased exploration tax revenues. In addition, when the Acción Democrática Party came to power in 1945, it instituted the famous "fifty-fifty" provision, ensuring that total oil profits would be divided equally between the companies and the government.

In 1943 the participation of oil in government revenues jumped to 42.9 percent, 10 percentage points over the 1936–1942 average. Table 8.2 shows that the percentage share increased from 1943, with the exception of 1947, until it reached 60 percent in 1948. The average for the whole period was 52.9 percent—19.6 percentage points higher than the average for the preceding period.

If the taxes of oil companies were compared to GDP during this period, they would amount to 7.5 percent as an average for the whole period. Thus, it is clear that the potential contribution of oil to the economy via the government sector was quite sizable during these years, even in terms of the total economic activity of Venezuela.

If the exchange tax is taken into consideration, then oil's contribution looms still larger. In July 1941 the bolívar was devalued. The buying rate for foreign exchange of commercial banks was raised to 3.32 bolívares to a dollar; but the devaluation did not affect the special buying rate for the petroleum sector. As a result, the contribution of the foreign exchange tax on oil to government funds was computed on the basis of a higher tax rate throughout the 1943–1948 period. Oil revenues from this source also rose due to an increase in the amount of foreign currency exchanged into bolívares by the oil companies (see Table 8.2).

Both total revenues and oil revenues increased continually during this period. The former expanded to almost six times its 1942 level. Oil revenues expanded faster, registering a tenfold increase from 1942. The index of government revenues increased from 100 in 1943 to 517 in 1948, a compounded average growth of 31.5 percent per year. Oil revenues increased to 722 from the base value of 100 in 1943, for a compounded yearly average rate of 39 percent.

Oil-derived revenues contributed substantially to the financing of the government sector. As a result, the other sectors had to bear a much lighter burden in government financing, which undoubtedly helped to strengthen them.

Effectiveness in the Use of the Fiscal Contribution

In order to judge the Venezuelan government's effectiveness in the use of these funds, it is necessary to estimate the portion of total government expenditures devoted to furthering economic development. Total social and economic expenditures were utilized for this purpose in the previous period. Lacking a better alternative, the same variable will be used once more.

In the 1943–1948 period, a slightly higher proportion of the government budget was devoted to social and economic expenditures when compared to the previous period: 60.8 percent, as compared to 59.6 percent. This resulted from the more soundly based appropriations of the Acción Democrática Party, which came to power in 1945.

In 1943 the share of expenditures for social and economic objectives continued the downward trend begun in 1941, reaching its lowest level since 1936 (see Table 8.2). But it rebounded in 1944, and at the end of the period it stood at 64.3 percent. In absolute terms, social and economic expenditures increased throughout the period. In another test of the effectiveness in the utilization of oil revenues, it was found that during this period the social and economic expenditures of the government were larger than the revenues derived from oil in absolute terms (see Table 8.2).[2]

Furthermore, the growing oil revenues appear to have been devoted to expenditures of a social and economic character during this period, as their increase was more than matched by an increase in this type of expenditures (Table 8.2). The "sow the oil" policy was evidently taken seriously over these years.

Budgets showed alternating deficits and surpluses in this period, as Table 8.2 shows. No Treasury reserve accumulation policies were followed. Therefore, taking the period as a whole, those impulses originating in petroleum and directed to the government sector were not neutralized, being used for increased spending. At the same time, the plentiful tax revenues derived from oil allowed the Venezuelan government to expand needed public services, while relatively few tax pressures were imposed on other economic sectors—and without any resort to chronic deficit spending. The latter has been isolated as perhaps the major proximate cause of inflation in Latin American countries. If deficit spending had been utilized to a greater extent, it probably would have aggravated the inflationary process that, mostly as a result of war and postwar scarcities Venezuela was experiencing.

In sum, petroleum's contribution to government revenues increased tremendously during this period. The share of oil in total revenues rose. Oil-derived revenues expanded very fast, facilitating a high level of public expenditures, with no undue pressure on the rest of the economy and without recourse to public indebtedness. Effective use of the oil contribution to public revenues even improved during this period.

The Contribution of Oil Investment

As a proportion of GDP, gross fixed investment dropped to 12.3 percent in 1943, the lowest it had been since 1936.[3] From then on, investment surged until this percentage reached 38.3 in 1948 (see Table 8.3). The increase was even more phenomenal in absolute terms. Gross investment in real terms rose continually from 1942, except for a mild decline in 1943. From 1943 to 1948, gross investment in real terms increased over sixfold (see Table 8.3), representing a 45 percent average annual compounded increase. In current prices, the increase was even greater.

The investment rate—gross fixed domestic investment over GDP—was much higher in this period than in the preceding one. As will be seen, this reflected itself in comparatively higher growth rates, which is in agreement with Simon Kuznets's findings.[4]

During this period, gross petroleum investment in current terms also increased continually. In 1943 the industry invested 161 million bolívares, an increase from 1942. By 1948 the amount devoted to investment expenditures climbed to 1,630 million bolívares, which meant a little over a tenfold

Table 8.3.
Gross Domestic Product and Gross Fixed Domestic Investment, Oil Sector, 1942–1948

	1942	1943	1944	1945	1946	1947	1948
Total GDP (Mill. 1957 Bs.)	5,193	5,478	6,515	7,592	8,707	9,911	11,225
GDP, Oil Sector (Mill. 1957 Bs.)	1,059	1,283	1,838	2,312	3,778	3,109	3,503
GDP, Other Sectors (Mill. 1957 Bs.)	3,780	3,736	3,981	4,283	4,566	4,976	5,462
Oil as a Percent of GDP	20.4%	23.4%	28.2%	30.5%	43.4%	31.4%	31.2%
Gross Fixed Domestic Investment (GFDI, Mill. Bs.)	721	675	1,061	1,717	2,228	3,478	4,304
Oil Sector (Mill. Bs.)	155	220	350	563	843	1,238	1,598
Other Sectors (Mill. Bs.)	566	455	711	1,154	1,385	2,240	2,760
Oil Investment as a Percent of GFDI	21.5%	32.6%	33.0%	32.8%	0.4%	0.4%	37.1%
GFDI as a Percent of GDP	13.9%	12.3%	16.3%	22.6%	25.6%	35.1%	38.3%

Notes: Oil and non-oil GDP do not add to total. See text for explanation of methodology and adjustments to data.

Sources: Banco Central de Venezuela, unpublished statistics; financial statements and supporting documents from the three main oil company groups in Venezuela, extrapolated to obtain industry wide estimates; Bernardo Ferran, unpublished estimates presented.

increase since 1943. Petroleum investment expressed in real terms also increased considerably throughout the years. In constant bolívares of 1957 (see Table 8.3), gross investment increased over sixfold from the 1943 base, after making a healthy advance in 1943. This increment was equivalent to approximately a 36 percent average compounded rate of growth per year.

The share of gross petroleum investment in total gross investment shifted upward in 1943, going from 21.5 percent to 32.6 percent (see Table 8.3). It was even higher at the end of the period (37.1 percent in 1948), so that the contribution of petroleum to total Venezuelan investment rose impressively, and the capital goods sector was considerably strengthened under its impact. (The contributions of oil would loom much larger if account were taken of the oil-derived revenues used for public investment.) From 1939 to 1949, net investment by the government represented over 34 percent of total net investment as an average, according to the Central Bank.[5]

In 1948, investments in petroleum refineries represented 21 percent of total petroleum investment, while investments in production amounted to 56 percent, an important part of the latter being devoted to roads, camps, houses, schools, and hospitals.[6]

As to nonpetroleum investment, after suffering a setback in 1943, it rose continually until 1948. In real terms, the growth was nearly 500 percent from the 1943 base, for approximately a 43 percent average annual compounded rate of advance (see Table 8.3).

Throughout the period, nonpetroleum gross fixed domestic investment did not exceed the retained value of petroleum expenditures—that is, the payments made to local factors of production and producing firms—as well as the government. This means that at least the rest of the economy did not invest an amount greater than the immediate domestic expenditures originated in the oil sector during this period. As to the social productivity of the investment resources, at least with respect to public investment, the allocation of investment funds seems to have improved relative to the previous period, especially under the Acción Democrática administration, during the years 1945 to 1948.

The impressive expansion in external sales, tax proceeds, and investment expenditures in the oil sector occurred when the transportation difficulties, capital and technical shortages, and war scarcities began clearing up in 1943 and, especially, in 1944. Venezuelan oil began to flow unrestrictedly once again to meet increasing demand. The worldwide conflagration proved that access to oil was essential for military power. After the war, the pent-up demand and the reconstruction effort assured increased needs for *black gold*. Demand increased, and prices moved upward. This proved to be a boon for oil producers, particularly for Venezuela, which still produced very large quantities of oil at a very low relative cost.

On the national front, as a result of several reforms—the most important being the new tax legislation—the retained portion of the petroleum expenditures increased even more than the other petroleum variables. This, combined with a better use of the contribution of petroleum in the foreign trade and public sectors, spearheaded the expansion in investment activity in the rest of the Venezuelan economy.

To recapitulate, petroleum investment expanded sharply during this period, contributing significantly to the high level of capital accumulation sustained by the economy and promoting some local production in its wake. However, the investment rate of the country was not high enough to ensure that the amount of nonpetroleum income invested was greater than the retained value in the oil industry.

Both petroleum investment and the overall contribution of the oil industry to the economy, expressed in terms of the retained value of its total expenditures, were the exogenous elements inducing an expansion in investment into the nonpetroleum part of the economy. It was found that the retained value explained 95.3 percent of the lagged variation in nonpetroleum investment. Certainly, another important factor in the investment surge was a more effective utilization of oil's public sector and foreign sector contributions by the economy, resulting to a great extent from more enlightened government policies.

Total Domestic Product and the Expenditures of the Oil Industry

In examining some of the important variables determining the contribution of oil to the other sectors of the Venezuelan economy, it has been seen that during this period they were characterized by a sharp upward trend. Understandably, the same can be said about oil's output and its value of production. As a consequence of an increase in the price of oil, the latter rose eightfold from 1942 to 1948. This represented a corresponding annual average compounded rate of approximately 44 percent from 1942 (38 percent from 1943). A similar increase took place in the GDP of petroleum in current prices. In constant 1957 prices, the trend is identical, but with smaller increases (see Table 8.4).

Petroleum became even more important to the Venezuelan economy in terms of its share in GDP in real terms (1957 prices) during this period. Petroleum accounted for participation of 20.4 percent in 1942 and of 31.2 percent in 1948. The enhanced participation of petroleum is not so great, however, if compared with the year 1941, when petroleum represented 28.2 percent of total GDP. Yet, these two years (1941 and 1942) cannot be considered representative of petroleum's contribution to the total production of the Venezuelan economy. In 1941 petroleum was at a peak, while the rest of the economy was still in a lull; in 1942 just the opposite took place. It would be more reasonable to compare the 1948 percentage share of petroleum in total GDP, with the average for the previous period. Such a comparison indicates that the participation of oil in the economy increased significantly over a short spell, as the previous period average was 24.3 percent, while the 1943–1948 average was 30.0 percent.[7]

Table 8.4.
Retained Value of Oil Sector Expenditures, 1942–1948

	1942	1943	1944	1945	1946	1947	1948
Retained Value of Total Expenditures (Mill. Bs.)	246	439	607	862	1280	2077	3167
as a percent of Total	48.5%	57.6%	55.2%	57.5%	59.3%	59.0%	60.9%
Retained Value of Current Expenditures (Mill. Bs.)	177	303	437	616	821	1399	2103
As Percent of Total Expenditures	43.9%	50.5%	52.5%	58.2%	55.7%	58.6%	59.0%
Retained Value of Current Expenditures per Barrel of Oil Produced (Bs.)	1.2	1.69	1.7	1.91	2.42	3.22	4.21
Retained Value of Total Expenditures per Barrel of Oil Produced (Bs.)	1.66	2.45	2.36	2.67	3.3	4.77	6.46
Total Value of Production (Mill. Bs.)	403	600	832	1,059	1,473	2,389	3,564
GDP Oil Sector (Mill. Bs.)	393	474	738	912	1,292	2,028	2,920

Notes: Estimates of retained value and value of production based on adjustments to data from three main petroleum company groups. Conversion of value of sales to value of production based on *Informes de Conservación* (Caracas, several years), and unpublished data from the Oficina Técnica, Ministerio de Minas e Hidrocarburos. Total oil sector expenditures include value of production and investment.

Thus, the petroleum industry generated exogenous injections into the Venezuelan economy during this period. As the multiplicand enlarged, the multiplier-accelerator mechanism acted in a continuous and reinforcing fashion. The value of production and the formation of capital in the oil industry constitute what can be called the gross income-expenditure generating base of the industry, which expanded considerably. But only the retained part of the gross expenditures of the industry has direct and immediate impact on the Venezuelan economy. The retained value of current expenditures expanded continually throughout the period, increasing over elevenfold from 1942 to 1948, for an average increase of over 50 percent a year compounded (43 percent from 1943), which is higher than that of any other petroleum indicator examined (see Table 8.4).

The share of retained value of current expenditures in the total current expenditures of the petroleum industry reached 43.9 percent in 1942. By 1943 it had jumped to 50.5 percent. Except for 1946, it continued to increase until 1948, when it reached 59.0 percent. This increase was due, to an important degree, to increasing tax rates for the petroleum industry. Other contributing factors included the following: (1) a change in the procedures for determining the oil prices to be used in calculating the income and royalty taxes to be paid by the industry; (2) a more efficacious administration of the tax laws; (3) a substantial expansion in refining capacity; (4) increased wages and more liberal fringe benefits for petroleum workers; (5) the limitation of tariff exemption to goods not produced in Venezuela; and (6) special payments made to the Venezuelan government for new concessions granted in 1944 and 1945.[8] Retained value of current expenditures per barrel of oil produced jumped from 1.20 bolívares per barrel in 1942 to 4.21 bolívares in 1948, an almost fourfold increase, resulting from the expanding share of retained value of current expenditures in the value of output and from increasing oil prices.

In Chapter 7, it was explained that the estimates of retained value of investment expenditures were not considered as reliable as the other retained value estimates. These suggest a meteoric ascension in the retained value of investment expenditures, in keeping with the growth of petroleum investment during the period.

Retained value of total expenditures also had an astounding increase. At the end of the period, it had risen more than twelvefold, which is even greater than the increase experienced by the retained value of current expenditures (see Table 8.4). If retained value of total expenditures were taken as a share of value of production plus investment expenditures in the petroleum industry, it would represent an estimate of the degree of participation by domestic factors, producers, and government in the total activity of the sector. This percentage stood at 48.5 percent in 1942, rose to 57.6 percent in 1943, and stood at 60.9 percent in 1948. As can be seen in Table 8.4, it did not increase smoothly throughout the period, having mild setbacks in 1944 and 1947.

The same forces causing the increase in retained value of current expenditures determined the expansion of the retained value of investment expenditures. With rising demand and increasing sales of Venezuelan oil, favorable prospects for the future, and new concessions to work on, investment in the Venezuelan petroleum industry expanded considerably from 1943 on. With the spurt of investment and an increasing proportion of capital expenditures being directed to local producers and native factors, the retained value of investment expenditures was the petroleum indicator rising the fastest during this period. As retained value of investment expenditures is a component of total retained value, its increase greatly contributed to the expansion of the latter and explains why it was greater than the expansion in retained value of current expenditures.

The expansion of all these concepts was much less in terms of constant 1957 prices, but nonetheless impressive. Again, the growth rate for the period is smaller if an average for the previous period is used, instead of taking the 1942 low as the base year, but results are not appreciably changed.

The Impact of Oil on the Rest of the Economy

What overall effects did the oil sector's contributions from 1943 to 1948 have upon the overall behavior of the other sectors of the Venezuelan economy? Were the positive effects of sufficient strength to offset the negative influences of the oil sector? Were the net effects important enough to draw the conclusion that oil acted as a leading sector during this period?

The impact was quite substantial in those geographic areas where petroleum activity took place. But most of retained value consisted of tax payments, and government expenditures arising from the latter were not concentrated in the petroleum areas. Moreover, a substantial part of the industry procurement within Venezuela involved nonpetroleum regions. Therefore, the influence of petroleum and the economic growth it caused were spread among various other regions.[9]

Population statistics give an idea of the economic expansion that occurred in those places where oil activities were concentrated. Statistics show that population in the petroleum states increased 46.8 percent between 1936 and 1947. The federal district experienced a 42.5 percent increase in population during the same period, while all of Venezuela had a population growth of only 20.2 percent from 1936 to 1947.[10]

From 1936 to 1941, the population in petroleum states grew 25.0 percent; that in the federal district expanded 34.3 percent and in the overall population, 14.5 percent. If these rates are compared with those just cited, it is immediately apparent that the growth of population in the petroleum states during the second half of the 1936–1947 period was quite impressive, surpassing the population expansion in the federal district. This was to be expected, as the rise in oil activity from 1941 to 1947 was much greater than the expansion from 1936 to 1941. Such population data give an approximate indication of the remarkable economic expansion—in terms of income and product—that took place in the petroleum districts during this period. The rates of growth of regional GDP in these areas must have been much higher than those for the country as a whole. It appears then that a major part of the economic expansion in Venezuela from 1936 to 1947 was centered in the petroleum states and in the federal district.

The GDP of Venezuela in real terms more than doubled from 1942 to 1948 (see Table 8.4). To be exact, this aggregate grew about 114 percent in that time span, equivalent to a compounded annual average growth rate of 13.5 percent (15.4 percent per year from 1943). As a rise in prices occurred during the period, the increase in GDP in current prices was still greater.

However, what is of greater interest is the effect of the oil expansion on the other sectors of the economy, as indicated by the nonpetroleum GDP. With the exception of 1943, this indicator grew continually during the period. In real terms, it expanded at a 6.3 percent compounded average rate per year, with the overall growth between 1942 and 1948 being 44.5 (see Table 8.4). From 1943 to 1948, the yearly average rate of growth was 7.9 percent. The increase in current prices was much greater.

A more disaggregative examination of how these different sectors have fared over time would be fruitful at this point. The agricultural sector appears to have rebounded from the low production levels of 1942. As was noted in Chapter 7, there is a statistical gap between 1936 and 1945 in the agricultural output series, but there are indications that production was lower in 1942 than in 1945. The actual extent of the increase in production between these two years remains a conjecture, but the data on agricultural output presented in Table 8.5 evidence a substantial increase from 1945 to 1948.

An index of agricultural output is presented in Table 8.5. From 1945 on, agricultural production decreased each year to 1947, probably as a result of greater competition from imports just after the war. Then it surged in 1948, when postwar readjustments were complete and more sound economic policies, attaining a better balance between the promotion of directly productive activities and social overhead investment in rural areas, began having effects. Forestry production increased considerably from 1945 on. If forestry were included with agriculture, production in the year 1946, and maybe 1947, would have been larger than in 1945. Lack of detailed information does not allow a more definite statement.

Agriculture and forestry production are shown as disaggregated as possible in Table 8.5. The table is partly incomplete before 1948, and that explains the absence of subtotals for those years. From 1945 to 1948, the greatest increases were in cereals (82.7 percent), unrefined sugar (77 per-

Table 8.5.
Agricultural Output, 1942–1948

	1942	1943	1944	1945	1946	1947	1948
Retained Value of Total Expenditures (Mill. Bs.)	246	439	607	862	1280	2077	3167
as a percent of Total	48.5%	57.6%	55.2%	57.5%	59.3%	59.0%	60.9%
Retained Value of Current Expenditures (Mill. Bs.)	177	303	437	616	821	1399	2103
As Percent of Total Expenditures	43.9%	50.5%	52.5%	58.2%	55.7%	58.6%	59.0%
Retained Value of Current Expenditures per Barrel of Oil Produced (Bs.)	1.2	1.69	1.7	1.91	2.42	3.22	4.21
Retained Value of Total Expenditures per Barrel of Oil Produced (Bs.)	1.66	2.45	2.36	2.67	3.3	4.77	6.46
Total Value of Production (Mill. Bs.)	403	600	832	1,059	1,473	2,389	3,564
GDP Oil Sector (Mill. Bs.)	393	474	738	912	1,292	2,028	2,920

Note: N.A. means not available.

Sources: Evelyn M. Baran, "The Economic Development of Venezuela," Ph.D. dissertation Radcliffe College, 1959; Juan P. Perez Castillo, "Some Aspects of Venezuela's Economic Development: 1945–1960," Ph.D. dissertation, Tulane University, 1963.

cent), and eggs (106.7 percent, but from a low base). Corn was mostly responsible for the rise in cereal production in 1948. Much of this increase can be attributed to climatological conditions. Venezuela waited for 14 years before having a large crop of cereals.

Fibers and oils, although not as important as cereals or sugar, expanded consistently. They increased 61.1 percent between 1945 and 1948, but from low levels. As to the traditional export products, although cocoa output increased 57.9 percent, coffee declined. Animal products expanded modestly from 1945 to 1948. Fish, eggs, and milk led the expansion, which amounted to 42.3 percent overall. Forestry products increased 54.3 percent during this time span.

Total agricultural output, excluding forestry, expanded at a 2.7 percent compounded annual average from 1945 to 1948 (see Table 8.5). Forestry expanded at a 15.6 percent average yearly percentage increase. From 1942 to 1945, the increases were smaller. Hence, during these years the growth in population outstripped the growth of agriculture production. Imports were needed to close the gap, especially because, in contrast with the previous period, per capita income rose. There are data on agricultural imports showing that their value and volume stood at 78,000 metric tons and 31 million bolívares in 1936, and at 340, 200 metric tons and 349 million bolívares in 1948.[11]

Industrial and extractive production expanded at a very fast pace from 1942 on. Table 7.11, an output index for extractive activities—petroleum not included—showed an increase of 8.9 percent per year from 1942 to 1948. Yet the expansion took place in the second half of the period and represented increases from a thin base.

No information on the trend of manufacturing production from 1942 to 1945 is available. Still, indexes for particular manufactured products presented in Table 7.11 depict a sizable expansion. As was pointed out in Chapter 7, the industrialization process picked up momentum in these years, so a similar expansion probably held for manufacturing as a whole.

Acute shortages resulting from World War II were the main forces behind the expansion in manufacturing production. Over and above the general policies of manufacturing promotion, these sorts of natural obstacles greatly facilitated the import-substitution process. Increases in demand were mostly translated into expanding domestic production.

From 1945 on, the information is more complete. The index of manufacturing output presented in Table 7.11 rose 42.9 percent up to 1948, representing a 12.6 percent average yearly compounded increase. The increase in the second part of the period was probably not as great as in the initial years. The expansion was almost totally concentrated in 1948, with the preceding two years being a period of readjustment to increasingly normal trade relations, with imported manufactures regaining lost markets.

At a more disaggregative level (see Table 8.6), it can be seen that most industries expanded between 1945 and 1948. Expanding at the swiftest pace were the beverage and timber industries, which more than doubled production, and the cement industry, which almost doubled it. The leather and chemical industries grew by more than 50 percent. The rubber industry increased 22 percent and the food processing industry somewhat over 30 percent, their growth being in turn slower than the overall growth of manufacturing.

The increase in the output of the utilities component of the industrial sector is suggested by trends in the production of electricity and in energy consumption presented in Table 7.11. In this sector, consumption is a precise indicator of domestic production due to the nontradable and nonstorable nature of these products. Energy consumption more than tripled between 1942 and 1948. In terms of average compounded yearly increases, the expansion came to approximately 23 percent per year. Hence, the utilities sector appeared to expand more rapidly than manufacturing over these years.

The construction industry also expanded very rapidly. The rapid expansion of the timber and cement industries is an indication of this. (As in the utilities field, construction activities are mostly of a domestic nature. The consumption of cement can suggest the trend in consumption activities.) From 1942 to 1948, cement consumption expanded about 66 percent, for a yearly average compounded rate of growth of 8.8 percent. In contrast with the utilities sector, which grew in a continuous and regular fashion, the

Table 8.6.
Manufacturing Production, by Industry and Commodity, 1945 and 1948

Industry	1945 Volume	1945 Index	1948 Volume	1948 Index
Food processing (tho. metric tons):	**N.A.**	**100**	**N.A.**	**132**
Pasteurized milk (tho. liters)	N.A.	N.A.	15.7	100
Milk for butter	N.A.	N.A.	34.4	100
Powdered Milk	1.5	100	1.7	113
Vegetable oils	3.6	100	10.1	281
Peanut Oil	0.7	100	0.5	71
Sesame Oil	0.7	100	1.3	186
Coconut Oil	0.9	100	1.3	144
Cotton Oil	0.5	100	0.2	40
Canned fish	6	100	9.3	155
Chocolate	N.A.	N.A.	1.2	100
Cookies	2.5	100	6.3	252
Pastries	3.1	100	6.7	216
Sugar	27.2	100	26.6	98
Rice	12.4	100	5	41
Salt	57.5	100	35.5	62
Beverage Industries (Mill. liters):	**69.2**	**100**	**161.9**	**234**
Beer	40.1	100	57.8	144
Liquor (other than rum)	3.9	100	5.6	144
Rum	3.1	100	4.6	148
Gaseous drinks	22.1	100	93.9	425
Textile Industries (tho. metric tons):	**N.A.**	**100**	**N.A.**	**100**
Cotton suits	7.6	100	7.2	95
Linen and canvas	4.3	100	3.7	86
Cotton cloth	9.4	100	9.8	104
Cotton knits	0.2	100	0.3	150
Cotton bedspreads (Millions each)	0	100	0.1	253
Cotton blankets (Millions each)	0.4	100	0.6	150
Cotton towels (Millions each)	0.4	100	0.2	50
Cotton underwear (Millions each)	1.1	100	1.3	118
Cotton footwear (Millions each)	0.9	100	1.6	178
Rayon cloth	1.7	100	3.3	194
Rayon knits	0	100	0.3	750
Rayon footwear (Million pairs)	0.3	100	0.2	67
Rayon/cotton footwear (Million pairs)	0.7	100	0.6	86
Nylon footwear (Million pairs)	N.A.	N.A.	0.1	100
Wool suits	0.1	100	0.1	90
Wool knits	N.A.	N.A.	0.1	100
Linen cloth	0.1	100	0	30
Rope	0.7	100	0.9	129

(Continued)

Note: N.A. means not available.

Source: Juan P. Perez Castillo, "Some Aspects of Venezuela's Economic Development: 1945–1960," Ph.D. dissertation, Tulane University, 1963, corrected for certain errors in the 1948 index.

Table 8.6.
(Continued)

Industry	1945 Volume	Index	1948 Volume	Index
Leather Industries:	N.A.	N.A.	N.A.	N.A.
Leather soles (meters)	N.A.	100	N.A.	164
Leather linings (tho. square feet)	18	100	30.3	168
Other products (tho. cubic meters)	0.3	100	0.5	167
Paper and cardboard (meters)	6.1	100	8.7	143
Rubber Industries:	59	100	72	122
Tires (tho. each)	34	100	39	115
Inner tubes (tho. each)	25	100	33	132
Tobacco Industry (Mill. each):	2.1	100	1.9	90
Timber Industry (Thou. cubic meters):	21	100	58	276
Chemical Industries:	N.A.	100	N.A.	157
Paint (tho. metric tons)	1	100	1.4	140
Distilled alcohol (tho. liters)	2.4	100	3	125
Soap (tho. metric tons)	15.3	100	20	131
Candles (tho. metric tons)	N.A.	N.A.	2.6	100
Industrial gas (Mill. cubic meters)	N.A.	N.A.	0.7	100
Animal feed (Mill. kilograms)	5.7	100	10.3	181
Construction Materials: Portland cement (Mill. metric tons)	115	100	215	187

construction industry was adversely affected by the war and actually contracted from 1942 to 1945, because of unavailability of imported materials.

There is very little information available on the growth of tertiary activities during this period. Government expenditures, for one, showed the highest sector growth rates. If expressed in real terms, to make them as comparable as possible with the output indexes presented above, it is found that they quadrupled from 1942 to 1948.

If the growth of the Venezuelan economy in this period is expressed in per capita terms, a substantial rise is still found. In per capita terms, real GDP amounted to 1,472 bolívares in 1941, when a population census was taken. In 1950, when another census was conducted, the same aggregate in per capita terms had increased to 2,518 bolívares. This amounts to a 70.7 percent increase over that period and is equivalent to a 6.1 percent average compounded increase per year. The Venezuelan economy put on quite a performance during this period, contrasting favorably with what had taken place in any previous period.

Petroleum was the strongest force in the promotion of growth throughout these years. To a certain extent, this was attributed to rising petroleum prices—an externally determined variable that boosted the value of production and income from petroleum in Venezuela. Most of the growth, however, was the result of increasing output.

The retained value of total oil expenditures experienced a very substantial increase, and the particular contributions from oil, which have been examined, were also substantially enlarged. This coincided with a more effective use of petroleum's contributions by the Venezuelan economy and was the main force behind the quite satisfactory expansion of many other sectors of the economy. The basic conditions for economic progress that were slowly cultivated since the initial oil spurt in the 1920s now were starting to bear fruit. The Venezuelan economy had demonstrated it was ready to establish the preconditions for takeoff, and the year 1943 would be its starting point, thanks largely to the leadership exercised in the petroleum sector and the increase in nonpetroleum GDP that it helped generate.

Which activities were particularly affected by the petroleum industry? It appears that, as in the previous period, construction and utilities were most directly and importantly influenced by the expansion in petroleum.[12] Petroleum investment had a high construction component in this period. Refineries and transportation facilities were built; houses, schools, hospitals, and roads were constructed; and storage and distributive facilities were provided. This required increasing production and importation of cement, timber, and other construction materials and services. Government expenditures in public works, education, and health increased six or seven times in current bolívares from 1942 to 1948, mainly as a result of the oil industry's tax contribution.[13] This also required a strong expansion of construction activities.

The operations of the oil industry have high-energy requirements in almost all its stages. This explains the high and increasing per capita consumption of energy in Venezuela. Heavy investment in social overhead facilities by the government was also instrumental in the expansion of the utilities sector.

The production of refined oil more than doubled from 1942 to 1948, but still represented only about 10 percent of the total output of oil.[14] The utilization of petroleum by-products in other uses had not begun in this period.

THE 1949–1957 SUBPERIOD: THE FOREIGN SECTOR CONTRIBUTION

Oil exports continued their strong performance during the 1949–1957 period. Expressed in terms of current dollars, they came to almost two and one-half times the 1948 level by the end of this period, enough for a 10.2 percent compounded average annual increase. Though this was not so strong a showing as in the foregoing period, it was quite impressive (see Table 8.7).

As verified by Table 8.7, total exports expanded just a shade faster. The participation of oil in total exports thus declined from 97 percent in 1948 to 93.4 percent in 1957. But this diminution still does not detract from the gross balance of payments contribution of the oil sector during this period.[15]

Since 1953, it is possible to obtain balance of payments data in a more disaggregative fashion. The gross balance of payments contribution of oil can then also be computed in terms of the current account credits generated by the industry. In Table 8.7, the current account credits of the oil industry and of the Venezuelan economy are shown for the latter part of the period. Their trend is similar to that in exports of goods, with the share of oil being slightly smaller in terms of current account credits.

Table 8.7 also shows all foreign exchange proceeds of the Venezuelan economy from 1950 to 1957, with the petroleum share shown separately. These are the exchange proceeds contributed by the different sectors net of their own needs. Although the foreign exchange proceeds contributed by oil rose substantially from 1950 to 1957, their share in the total proceeds was reduced from 84.7 percent in 1950 to 71.5 percent in 1957. Altogether, it is clear that the net balance of payments contribution of oil, though smaller than the gross contribution, was nevertheless quite significant.

During this period, data on net capital inflows by the oil industry also became available. Although prima facie this might appear as an important source of foreign means of payment, this was not so during these years. The inflow of foreign capital to the Venezuelan petroleum industry was

Table 8.7.
Petroleum Sector Indicators and External Sector Performance, 1948–1957

	1948	1949	1950	1951	1952	1953	1954	1955	1956	1957
International Reserves (Mill. US$)	362	424	342	379	448	494	492	539	927	1,396
Change in Reserves	128	62	-82	37	69	46	-2	47	388	469
Gold as a Share of Reserve	94.6%	84.2%	100.0%	100.0%	86.1%	77.9%	84.3%	0.8%	62.7%	47.4%
Composition of Imports:										
Share of Capital Goods	--	--	25.6%	28.9%	32.4%	30.7%	33.5%	33.6%	32.7%	42.5%
Share of Intermediate Goods	--	--	0.4%	0.4%	0.4%	42.9%	0.4%	44.1%	43.1%	39.9%
Share of Consumer Goods	--	--	0.3%	0.3%	0.2%	0.3%	0.2%	0.2%	0.2%	17.6%
Import Capacity Index (1959=100)	68.2	61.6	78	80.9	87.4	91.8	96.8	111.7	120.9	137.5
Net Barter Terms of Trade Index	141.8	132.5	148.9	136.5	136.8	146.4	142.4	144.5	136	137.9
Total Exports (Mill. US$)	1,102	990	1,155	1,370	1,446	1,498	1,648	1,891	2,211	2,751
Oil Exports (Mill. US$)	1,069	966	1,124	1,297	1,384	1,428	1,564	1,791	2,086	2,570
Oil Exports/Share of Total	97.0%	97.6%	97.3%	94.7%	95.7%	95.3%	94.9%	94.7%	94.3%	93.4%
Foreign Exchange Earnings (Mill. US $)										
Total	--	--	658	775	917	1,013	1,094	1,291	1,849	2,464
From Oil	--	--	557	657	758	809	828	916	1,363	1,761
Oil as Share of Total	--	--	84.7%	84.8%	82.7%	0.8%	75.7%	71.0%	0.7%	71.5%
Currents Account Credits:										
Total	--	--	--	--	--	1,557	1,705	1,906	2,303	2,871
From Oil	--	--	--	--	--	1,441	1,572	1,805	2,115	2,595
Oil as Share of Total	--	--	--	--	--	92.5%	92.2%	94.7%	91.8%	90.4%

Note: Current account credits include exports of goods and services, transfer payments, investments and investment income.

Sources: Ministerio de Fomento, *Anuario Estadístico* (Caracas, 1938); Banco Central de Venezuela, *Informe Económico* (1959), *Memoria* (several years), and *La Economía Venezolana en los Ultimos Veinticinco Años* (Caracas, 1966), with adjustments.

concentrated in the years 1948–1949 and 1956–1957 (see Table 8.7). All other years were characterized by declining or stagnant net capital inflows, with no foreign funds being brought into the country by the oil companies.

Exports advanced every year except 1949, the same being true for petroleum exports. Such expansion took place at improved external prices. Yet, import prices rose throughout the period, and the net barter terms of trade moved slightly against Venezuela (see Table 8.7). As a result of the increase in exports and foreign exchange proceeds, coming to a substantial degree from the oil industry, the foreign trade sector was able to play its role as growth promoter and inflation suppressant during this period. No controls were placed on imports, and a free flow of productive factors and technical knowledge took place.

Foreign exchange proceeds derived from Venezuelan exports, capital inflows, and so forth are resources that can be used to import required goods and services, or, alternatively, they can be added to the international reserves of the country, to be utilized at some future date, or not at all. During this period, the total reserve holdings of Venezuela increased considerably, doubling between 1947 and 1953, and almost tripling from then until 1957, as can be seen in Table 8.7. This occurred in the face of increased unemployment toward the end of the period. With a fair degree of unemployed and underemployed resources and the possibility of bringing about an inflow of those in scarce supply, as well as improvements in techniques and capital usage (still a realistic possibility), more expansive economic policies, which could have utilized foreign exchange more fully, could have brought about increased growth and employment.

This is even more strongly so because of the traditionally heavy gold content of the Venezuelan international reserves, from which practically no earnings were derived (see Table 8.7). Furthermore, only part of the reserves not in gold provided some yields. Throughout the years, about one-half of the non-gold assets were kept in the form of deposits that could be withdrawn at sight. This was especially true during the period being examined.[16]

However, even if the reserves had been kept in income-earning assets, it is doubtful that their return would have been higher than the social marginal return to investment in Venezuela. Although there are no careful studies on the rate of return to investment in Venezuela, it is difficult to imagine that the government could not have loaned (or invested) its capital in a more profitable fashion. Recent empirical evidence has found that the rate of return on investment in developing economies is at least as high as in the United States.

Furthermore, in recent applications of Cobb-Douglas functions to Venezuelan data, the product-factor partial elasticities of capital were above 0.30.[17] Finally, the impression obtained in conversations with

Venezuelan economists, businessmen, and bankers was that the marginal rates of return to capital were without doubt above 20 percent, with an abundance of projects in which such returns could be realized.

Idle resources in the form of excessive international reserves indicate that the contribution of oil during this period was not that effectively utilized. A part was neutralized by the accumulation of reserves beyond the level dictated by the nature of international flows of Venezuela. In fact, in this respect, it appears that the use of foreign exchange funds in the previous period was comparatively superior.

A portion of the foreign exchange proceeds earned by the Venezuelan economy was utilized in the purchase of goods and services or left the country as transfer payments, capital outflows, or other payments abroad. An examination of the composition of the goods imported into the country suggests how well these funds were used. The composition shown in Table 8.7 indicates that these funds were not used inefficiently. Imports of capital goods expanded greatly, and intermediate goods also increased their share somewhat, except for the year 1957.

In summary, oil contributed most of the foreign exchange proceeds of the Venezuelan economy over these years, albeit a contracting portion. At the same time, the value of oil exports expanded considerably, providing the economy with the resources required for adequate growth and stability. Yet, the economy did not utilize this contribution as effectively as in the previous period. Even though the allocation of foreign exchange proceeds, as indicated by the breakdown in goods imports, was not inefficient, excessive international reserves were maintained.

The Fiscal Contribution of Oil

More complete public finance statistics are available for this period, so it is possible to use figures of revenues and expenditures of the public sector as a whole from 1950 on, including autonomous administrative institutes and state enterprises. So defined, public revenues expanded greatly from 1950 to 1957. By 1957, public revenues had doubled (214), based on an index scale with 1950 equal to 100. This is equivalent to an annual average compounded increase of 11.5 percent (see Table 8.8). Between 1948 and 1949, public revenues, not including enterprises and autonomous administrative institutes, increased by 5.9 percent. From 1949 to 1950, they declined a little. Although such rate of expansion fell short of that corresponding to the previous period, it was nonetheless outstanding.

Oil revenues expanded at a faster rate due to the increase in the value of petroleum output and the payments for the 1956 and 1957 concessions. The 1949 base index rose to 331 in 1957, representing an annual average compounded rate of growth of 16.1 percent. Between 1948 and 1949, oil revenues experienced an increase of 9.8 percent (see Table 8.8).

Table 8.8.
Government Sector Fiscal Indicators, 1948–1957

	1948	1949	1950	1951	1952	1953	1954	1955	1956	1957
Government Revenues (Mill. Bs.)	1,939	2,169	2,796	3,235	3,385	3,616	4,022	4,469	6,087	7,283
Oil Revenues	1,163	1,277	901	1,332	1,508	1,606	1,515	1,734	3,058	3,846
Share of Oil in Total	0.6	0.589	0.322	0.412	0.445	0.444	0.377	0.388	0.502	0.528
Change in Oil Revenues	--	114	-376	431	176	98	-91	219	1324	788
Foreign Exchange Tax on Oil	155	153	120	140	171	173	176	196	301	403
As a Percent of All Foreign Exchange Taxes	68.0%	65.9%	36.5%	45.5%	49.6%	49.2%	42.0%	43.2%	0.6%	58.3%

Notes: For 1948 and 1949, autonomous administrative institutes and state enterprises are not included in total revenues of the public sector. After 1949, total revenues are defined as current revenues *(ingresos ordinarios),* including those of autonomous institutes in their own right. Petroleum taxes do not include foreign exchange taxes. Local revenues and expenditures exclude transfers from the federal government. Government revenues include profits from foreign exchange transactions.

Sources: Ministerio de Fomento, *Anuario Estadístico* (Caracas, 1951); Banco Central de Venezuela, *Memoria* (Caracas, several years), and *La Economía Venezolana en los Ultimos Veinticinco Años* (Caracas, 1966); Ministerio de Minas e Hidrocarburos, *Petróleo y otros Datos Estadísticos* (Caracas, 1965); Charles E. Rollins, "Raw Materials Development and Economic Growth: A Study of the Bolivian and Venezuelan Experience," Ph.D. dissertation, Stanford University, 1956; J.J. Bracho Sierra, *Cincuenta Años de Ingresos Fiscales* (Caracas, 1963).

If compared to total GDP, oil-derived revenues represent an average of 11.6 percent of GDP for the period—an increase from the previous average of 7.5 percent. The participation of oil revenues in total government revenues increased from 1950 to 1953, diminished in 1954 and 1955, and rose again in 1956 and 1957.[18] At the end of the period, they had increased 20 percentage points from 1950. However, that year was sort of a low base, as petroleum revenues had diminished sharply between 1949 and 1950. As an average, from 1950 to 1957 petroleum revenues represented 46.0 percent of total public revenues.

As shown above, oil's contribution to the public sector was significant in terms of the total activity of the Venezuelan economy over these years. Moreover, a substantial portion of government revenues was derived from the petroleum industry. Petroleum-derived tax receipts expanded considerably, permitting the government to use funds that otherwise probably would have been sent abroad. Oil revenues also permitted the government to spend a substantial amount of funds, without having recourse to deficit financing and with very little tax pressure on other sectors. If the proceeds from the foreign exchange levy were added, then the percentage share of oil in total revenue would be even larger, because substantial revenues were derived from this source (see Table 8.8).

Have petroleum taxes been appropriated according to adequate criteria? Because this study aims at determining if and how effectively the oil sector has been leading economic development in the other sectors, the appropriate indicator should be the proportion of public expenditures devoted to the furthering of economic development. However, it has been impossible to classify expenditures according to this criterion. Instead, the portion of public expenditures devoted to capital formation will be used. Although not as inclusive as the concept of economic development expenditures, which includes public investment as well as other types of expenditures, it is the best replacement available.

It is our belief that public capital expenditures are at least as close as social and economic expenditures (which are too comprehensive) to the concept of economic development expenditures. In any event, it is impossible to continue using the latter concept, as no estimates are available for most of the recent years. On the other hand, statistics on public investment are available only since 1950. As a result of this conceptual change, and also because a different public expenditures definition was used previously, it is also impossible to compare the utilization of oil revenues in this period with preceding ones.

From 1950 on, public expenditures charged to capital accounts increased in a continuous way, with a single setback occurring in 1952. By 1957 these expenditures had increased by 233 percent, for an average annual compounded rate of growth of 18.8 percent (see Table 8.8). As a share of total public expenditures—including state enterprises and autonomous institutions—capital expenditures rose from 37.1 percent in 1950 to 57.8 percent in 1957. This increase took place mostly at the end of the period, since the share was quite stable up to 1953.

Another test of the effectiveness in the use of the funds contributed by petroleum is the ratio of public capital expenditures over oil revenues. If the "sow the oil" policy was taken seriously, public capital formation should have exceeded the revenues derived from oil. In this period, the ratio was both above and below unity, mostly below. As an average, it was 96.8 percent, a respectable figure (Table 8.8), suggesting again that, in terms of basic apportionment, the potential contribution of oil had been put to good use.

Finally, although at the beginning of the period the marginal increments in oil revenues were not accompanied by marginal increases in public investment, the situation did change at the end of the period. In fact, by then, the marginal increments in the latter were greater than those in the former. Full use of petroleum tax revenues was partly circumvented by a recurrent preoccupation with balancing the budget that was reminiscent of the Gómez era. In some years, huge amounts were added to Treasury reserves, neutralizing somewhat the potential effects of oil on other sectors of the Venezuelan economy.

In conclusion, the petroleum sector was an even stronger mainstay of government finances during this period. Its revenue expansion permitted the government to greatly expand its own activities without recourse to debt financing, while only light tax pressures were put on the other sectors of the economy. This helps explain how the GDP deflator, despite more than doubling of government expenditures, rose less than 10 percent from 1950 to 1957.

Still the contribution of petroleum was not utilized as effectively as in previous periods. Budgetary surpluses became more frequent and larger, thereby neutralizing the potential expansionary effects of oil revenues. This was especially damaging at the end of the period, when unemployment mounted. Stability was not a problem during these years, so that appropriate policies should have exploited the favorable balance of payments situation and the budgetary surpluses in order to foster further the country's economic growth and to solve the unemployment problem.

It is apparent that an increasing share of public expenditures was devoted to capital formation throughout the period, with much of the rise in oil revenues apparently being allotted to this purpose. On the other hand, the evidence seems to indicate that all this was accompanied by increasing waste and lower productivity in the use of capital funds by the government.

The Contribution of Oil Investment

Capital formation in the Venezuelan economy increased at a fast pace during this period. By 1957, gross domestic investment in constant prices was 49.4 percent above the 1948 level, equivalent to a compounded annual average rate of growth of 4.6 percent. Growth was not continuous, however, and slumps occurred in 1950 and 1955 (see Table 8.9).

However, GDP outpaced capital formation during these years. In 1957, gross fixed domestic investment represented 26.5 percent of GDP, as compared to 38.3 percent in 1948 (see Table 8.9). But the gross investment rate was at its peak during 1948. As an average, the economy devoted more resources to capital formation from 1949 to 1957 than in the previous period, in which investment was very low at the beginning. In all, the investment rate must be considered highly satisfactory during the period, since it was never below 25 percent.

Investment in the petroleum industry was a substantial share of total investment (see Table 8.9). Nevertheless, as an average, its participation was the lowest ever during any period, partly as a result of a relatively slow (11.8 percent) increase in petroleum investment from 1948 to 1957 in real terms (equivalent to a 1.2 percent average compounded rate per year). Still, it represented well over 20 percent of total investment. The strengthening of the other sectors of the economy during this period also contributed to the lessening of petroleum's participation in total investment. Despite this, the average of petroleum investment in absolute terms was much greater during this period than in previous ones.

Table 8.9.

Gross Domestic Product and Gross Fixed Domestic Investment, Oil Sector, 1948–1957 (millions of 1957 bolívares)

	1948	1949	1950	1951	1952	1953	1954	1955	1956	1957
Total GDP:	11,225	11,726	12,593	14,270	15,202	16,257	18,222	19,645	21,281	24,295
GDP, Oil Sector	3,503	3,448	3,851	4,469	4,730	4,780	5,192	5,909	6,543	7,249
GDP, Other Sectors	5,462	6,443	7,249	8,185	8,541	9,776	11,205	11,869	12,228	13,854
Oil as a Percent of GDP	31.2%	29.4%	30.6%	31.3%	31.1%	29.4%	28.5%	30.1%	30.7%	29.8%
Gross Fixed Domestic Investment:	4,304	4,458	3,234	3,573	4,379	4,797	5,822	5,363	5,584	6,429
Petroleum Sector	1,598	1,186	664	798	1,051	1,007	1,135	1,086	1,352	1,822
Other Sectors	2,706	3,272	2,570	2,775	3,328	3,790	4,587	4,277	4,232	4,607
Petroleum as a Percent of Total Fixed Investment	37.1%	26.6%	20.5%	22.3%	24.0%	21.0%	19.5%	20.3%	24.2%	28.3%
Fixed Investment as a Percent of GDP	38.3%	38.0%	25.7%	25.0%	28.8%	29.5%	32.0%	27.3%	26.2%	26.5%

Notes: Oil and non-oil GDP do not add to total. See text for explanation of methodology and adjustments to data. Total investment data from the Banco Central were adjusted to take into account the difference between Banco Central estimates and Ministerio de Minas e Hidrocarburos estimates.

Sources: Banco Central de Venezuela, unpublished statistics and *Memoria* (Caracas, several years); Ministerio de Minas e Hidrocarburos, *Petróleo y Otros Datos Estadísticos* (Caracas, 1965); Evelyn Baran, "The Economics of Development in Venezuela," Ph.D. dissertation, Radcliffe College, 1959.

The share of investment related strictly to the production of oil grew during these years, as is shown in Table 8.10. This took place, even though it suddenly shrank in 1956 and 1957. Actually, the participation of investment in purely productive activities changed abruptly as a result of bursts of capital expenditures in refining and transport (see Table 8.10). In Venezuela, spells in refining investment have been usually determined by government influence and generally follow concession periods. This results from the selective concession policy utilized by the Venezuelan government since 1936, in which an expansion in domestic refining is one of the requisites for obtaining (sometimes favorable) concessions. Investment in transport facilities is tied to the exploration, development, and exploitation of new concessions.

The share of transport investment increased during this period from 10 to 15 percent, while that of refining investment decreased somewhat, although picking up substantially in 1956 and 1957. Investment in marketing was more or less stable throughout, and all other types of investment expenditures declined considerably.

As could be surmised, nonpetroleum investment expanded much faster than total investment during this period. It grew 70.3 percent from 1948 to 1957 in real terms, equivalent to a 6.1 percent average compounded yearly

Table 8.10.
Gross Fixed Investment in the Petroleum Sector by Type of Investment,
1948–1957 (millions of 1957 bolívares)

	1948	1949	1950	1951	1952	1953	1954	1955	1956	1957
Total Investment in Petroleum	1,630	1,127	561	727	967	901	933	928	1,232	1,822
Total Investment in Production	921	563	340	508	725	709	689	790	779	1,204
as a percent of total	56.50%	50.00%	60.60%	69.90%	75.00%	78.70%	73.80%	85.10%	63.20%	66.10%
Total Investment in Transportation	163	101	36	107	129	70	67	40	121	274
as a percent of total	10.00%	9.00%	6.40%	14.70%	13.30%	7.80%	7.20%	4.30%	9.80%	15.00%
Total Investment in Refining	347	401	122	54	56	63	104	65	233	268
as a percent of total	21.32%	35.60%	21.70%	7.40%	5.80%	7.00%	11.10%	7.00%	18.90%	14.70%
Total Investment in Marketing	14	12	11	4	7	14	14	12	14	18
as a percent of total	0.90%	1.10%	2.00%	0.60%	0.70%	1.60%	1.50%	1.30%	1.10%	1.00%
Total Investment in Other Sectors	185	50	52	54	50	45	59	21	85	58
as a percent of total	11.30%	4.40%	9.30%	7.40%	5.20%	5.00%	6.30%	0.02%	6.90%	3.20%

Source: Ministerio de Minas e Hidrocarburos, *Petróleo y Otros Datos Estadísticos* (Caracas, 1965).

rate of growth. Nonpetroleum investment grew every year with the exception of 1950 and 1955 (see Table 8.9).

Nonpetroleum investment was almost as high as the retained value amounts in some of these years. On the basis of this crude test, Venezuela seemed to be devoting, for investment purposes, an amount almost equivalent to the local payments originating in the petroleum industry. This was an improvement over the previous period.

In summary, the economy's rate of capital formation was most satisfactory, although it was a notch down from the unusually high investment activity of the postwar years.[19] The petroleum industry constituted a declining but significant part of total investment in this period. Investment expenditures in the industry, although expanding at a disappointing rate, still remained quite high as an average during the period, being larger than in any previous period. The oil sector provided a stimulus to the local construction and capital goods industries through these huge investment expenditures.

Finally, investment in the nonpetroleum sectors moved rather consistently with petroleum investment and even more closely with the retained value of total petroleum expenditures. After a one-year lag, changes in the latter were followed by equivalent changes in nonpetroleum gross fixed investment. Thus there are indications that the behavior of nonpetroleum investment can be explained by the changes in total retained value of oil.

Total Domestic Product and the Expenditures of the Oil Industry

The value of oil production during this period continued its uninterrupted expansion, although it declined in 1949. To be exact, the expansion from 1948 to 1957 was 141.4 percent, corresponding to a compounded annual average growth rate of 10.3 percent (see Table 8.11). This expansion was smaller than that experienced in the previous period, but nonetheless quite remarkable, especially if the fact that it took place from a higher base value is taken into account.

The participation of petroleum in total GDP (in real terms) hovered between 28.5 and 31.3 percent in this period. The share had an erratic movement within this narrow range, experiencing a mild overall decline from the 1948 level, as can be seen in Table 8.9.[20] The strong showing by the petroleum sector resulted from favorable demand conditions for most of the period. After a mild slump in 1949, demand picked up, spurred mostly by the Korean War. After the latter ceased, another moderate lull affected the market, lasting until 1956, when the situation improved somewhat. During the Suez Canal crisis that took place in 1957, the demand for Venezuelan oil and its derivatives skyrocketed and prices soared. These conditions prompted increased levels of activity from the oil industry in Venezuela,

Table 8.11.
Retained Value of Oil Sector Expenditures, 1948–1957 (millions of bolívares)

	1948	1949	1950	1951	1952	1953	1954	1955	1956	1957
Retained Value of Total Expenditures	3,167	2,385	2,451	2,809	2,990	3,329	3,542	3,542	3,806	4,840
as a percent of total	60.9%	55.8%	57.3%	54.5%	52.6%	52.6%	56.3%	51.9%	47.1%	46.4%
Except locally purchased Imported goods	3,100	2,343	2,421	2,766	2,934	3,274	3,485	3,469	3,705	4,684
Retained Value of Current Expenditures	2,103	1,891	2,221	2,570	2,721	3,015	3,138	3,261	3,686	4,677
as a percent of total	59.0%	60.2%	59.8%	58.1%	58.1%	60.1%	58.7%	55.4%	53.9%	54.4%
Retained Value of Current Expenditures per barrel of Oil Produced (Bs.)	4.21	3.92	4.06	4.13	4.12	4.68	4.54	4.14	4.1	4.61
Retained Value of Total Expenditures of Oil Produced (Bs.)	6.46	4.95	4.48	4.51	4.51	5.17	5.12	4.5	4.23	4.77
Total Value of Production	3,564	3,141	3,716	4,420	4,681	5,020	5,348	5,885	6,840	8,604
GDP Oil Sector	2,920	2,505	2,973	3,584	3,803	3,896	4,335	4,940	5,784	7,249

Notes: Estimates of retained value and value of production based on adjustments to data from three main petroleum companies. Conversion of value of sales to value of production based on *Informes de Conservación* (Caracas, several years) and unpublished data from the Oficina Técnica, Ministerio de Minas e Hidrocarburos. Total oil sector expenditures include value of production and investment. Retained value estimates exclude foreign exchange taxes on oil.

Sources: Ministerio de Minas e Hidrocarburos, *Petróleo y Otros Datos Estadísticos* (Caracas, 1965) and unpublished statistics.

even though, altogether, the market for oil was not as firm as in the previous period. As has been seen in the previous section, investment expenditures were much less affected by all this. However, it is through the portion retained in Venezuela that the increments in the expenditures of the oil industry exert its direct and most important impact. Therefore, the evolution of retained value during the period will now be examined.

In current bolívares, the retained value of current expenditures more than doubled between 1948 and 1957, but still failed for the first time to grow faster than petroleum GDP. Petroleum GDP increased 148 percent, while retained value of current expenditures only increased 122 percent, both in current bolívares (see Table 8.11). The fact that no new tax increases were imposed on petroleum in this period, coupled with a curtailment in industry employment, determined a lower expansion in the retained value components of value added than in other components. Except for a mild setback in 1949, the retained value of current expenditures increased every year, although its overall expansion cannot be compared to that of the previous period. As petroleum prices rose throughout the years, the rise in retained value of current expenditures in constant 1957 prices was smaller than in current prices.

Retained value of current expenditures per barrel of oil produced increased from 1948 to 1957, attaining unequaled highs during this period (see Table 8.11). However, this path was highly erratic over time, and abrupt changes took place quite frequently. Interestingly, the retained value of current expenditures per barrel declined in real terms in the last three years of the period, being much lower in 1957 than in 1948. However, compared with previous ones, the average for this period was nonetheless higher.

The proportion of total value of production that retained value of current expenditures represented decreased sharply at the end of the period. Table 8.11 shows how it hovered at a relatively high level up to 1954 only to fall from 1955 onward. Nevertheless, the average proportion for the period was still higher than that of the previous period.

The retained value of investment expenditures in current bolívares declined from the peak levels of the 1947–1949 period, especially if imports of services, which were very low during and before the war, are taken into consideration. If the retained value of both current and investment expenditures are put together in terms of current bolívares, a decline is apparent from the peak 1948 level up to 1952. It then picks up, surpassing the 1948 level. Nevertheless, this variable's growth (see Table 8.11) is disappointing, compared to the other petroleum indicators already examined in this section. Retained value of total expenditures grew 52.8 percent during the period, equivalent to a compounded annual average of 4.8 percent a year.

In this section, the performance of the oil industry has so far been treated without taking into account the special tax payment for concessions in 1956 and 1957. The performance by the oil industry would certainly look much better if these were added. As pointed out in Chapter 3, these payments are capitalized by the companies and do not affect current expenditures or value added. But they cannot very well be considered as part of gross domestic investment in the industry and are, therefore, excluded from both the investment and retained value of investment figures for the industry. Nevertheless, these payments are part of the contribution of oil to the Venezuelan economy and have been dealt with accordingly in the section on the industry's fiscal contribution.

If these payments were added to retained value of total expenditures, the results would be quite different. Instead of 3,806 million and 4,840 million bolívares in 1956 and 1957, respectively, the figures would be 4,780 and 5,982. The expansion throughout the period would become 88.9 percent, for a compounded yearly average of 7.4 percent. Such a performance is still much less impressive than that of the other indicators reviewed above, which is to a great extent due to the lack of expansion in the gross investment of the oil industry throughout the period.[21]

Retained value of total expenditures per barrel shows a decline from the peak 1948 level, even if concession payments are added (see Table 8.11). A comparison with the previous period average shows a gain, though, which would be larger if concessions payments were taken into account. The retained value of total expenditures as a percentage of the value of all petroleum expenditures—value of production plus gross domestic investment—decreased almost continually from 60.9 percent in 1948. In some years the proportions rose, as in 1950, 1953, and 1954, but these were the exception. Even if concessions payments were added in 1956 and 1957, the share of retained value in total petroleum expenditures would be lower as an average during this period than during the 1943–1948 period.

During this period, oil prices increased. Therefore, the increase in retained value of total expenditures expressed in constant 1957 dollars was even lower. The average retained value of total expenditures per barrel during the 1949–1957 period, if expressed in constant 1957 prices, drops below the mean for the 1943–1948 period. Even if concessions payments are taken into consideration, retained value of total expenditures per barrel, in constant terms, is lower, as an average, and for the year 1957, than the average for the previous period.

Part of the local procurement undertaken by the oil companies does not end in the purchase of goods produced in Venezuela. Whenever foreign goods are purchased from local importers, the gains to the Venezuelan economy are obviously relatively small. Strictly speaking, only those expenditures destined to pay for local factors, to buy locally produced goods, and to pay taxes to the Venezuelan government should be considered part of retained value. Previous estimates have included these purchases because lack of data made it impossible to take this factor into account in the estimation of retained value. From 1948 the Oficina Técnica de Hidrocarburos began publishing data on local purchases of foreign goods. On the basis of these data, it has been possible to derive a more precise estimate of the retained value of total expenditures, which is presented in Table 8.10. These estimates of retained value of total expenditures do not depart significantly in their trend from the estimates of retained value presented previously in this section, although their growth since 1948 is small.[22]

Although much smaller than in the previous period, the rate of growth in the different indicators of oil activity, such as value of production and retained value, was respectable from 1948 to 1957, especially if concessions payments are taken into account. The only exception was the retained value of investment expenditures, which grew disappointingly. Therefore, the exogenous income-expenditures injections originating in the petroleum industry in this period were substantial, and the total positive contributions of the oil industry to the rest of the Venezuelan economy also appear to have experienced a substantial expansion.

What effects did all this have on the rest of the Venezuelan economy? Were the contributions sufficient to compensate for any unfavorable effects to which the industry might have given rise? And if so, were the net positive effects strong enough to lead to growth in the other sectors?

The Impact of Oil on the Rest of the Economy

The effects of oil in the economy of producing states were not in parallel with population growth. Total labor requirements of the industry actually diminished in absolute terms. A look at population statistics for the different regional entities or states, compiled in 1950 and 1961, indicate the changes throughout this interval. The average annual rates of growth for the petroleum states expanding their production during the period (Zulia, Anzoategui, and Barinas) are higher than those for the whole country (see Table 8.12). However, they are smaller than the rate for other areas, notably Caracas.[23] Of course, the petroleum industry also aided the growth in Caracas and in other areas where fast population growth occurred, indirectly through purchases and tax contributions. This was especially true of Caracas, where the industry expanded its central administrative headquarters considerably.

As for the Venezuelan economy as a whole, its performance was quite satisfactory. Total GDP doubled in constant prices, doing better than retained value of total expenditures in current terms. It grew 116.4 percent from 1948 to 1957, which corresponds to an almost 9 percent compound average rate of increase per year. The higher average investment rate in this period did not bring about a faster rate of growth. This must be interpreted with care; however, as the periods examined are rather short and the differences in rates are quite small.

Table 8.12.
Average Annual Rates of Growth of Population for Different States, 1950 and 1961

Region	Percent
Petroleum States	
Zulia	4.95
Anzoategui	4.55
Barinas	5.56
Other States	
Federal District	5.74
Aragua	5.01
Carabobo	4.51
Miranda	5.80
Portuguesa	5.12
Gurico	3.96
Bolivar	5.16
Venezuela	3.99

Source: Ministerio de Fomento, Censo de Población (Caracas, 1950 and 1961).

The average investment rate in this period was 28.3 percent, higher than the 27.2 percent average for the previous period. The Venezuelan economy grew at an annual compounded rate of growth of 9 percent from 1948 to 1957 and 13.5 percent from 1942 to 1948. At first glance, this might appear contrary to Kuznets's findings. However, this evidence must be interpreted with care. The periods examined are rather short, and the difference in rates might not be that large (if any) if the lower 1942 base is taken into account.

In order to better appraise the performance of the other sectors of the Venezuelan economy, the nonpetroleum GDP should be looked at. It appears that these sectors grew faster than petroleum during this period. Nonpetroleum GDP, in constant 1957 bolívares, increased 153.6 percent, equivalent to a 10.9 percent annual average compounded rate of growth, from 1948 to 1957 (see Table 8.9).

The behavior of these different sectors during the period is now considered. The agricultural sector, including forestry, continued its disappointing growth in this period. Production increased 29.3 percent from 1948 to 1957, for a 2.9 percent annual rate of growth. All product groups, except cereals and the traditional products—coffee and cocoa—had rates of growth higher than those of the sector as a whole. Sugar, fibers and oils, and roots and tubers grew fastest, increasing over 100 percent from 1948. Among roots and tubers, the growth in potato output was extraordinary. In the cereals group, the production of rice and wheat was especially disappointing. Then, the doubling in the production of industrial crops gives evidence of the increasing importance of manufacturing in the economic life of Venezuela. In toto, the agricultural sector failed to cover the needs of the Venezuelan population, which expanded at approximately 4 percent per year during this period.[24]

In contrast, the production of manufactures expanded 313.1 percent from 1948 to 1957 (see Table 8.13), a 17.1 percent average yearly percentage increase. The leather, rubber, and construction materials industries were the fastest growing. The paper and cardboard, printing, metal, and vehicle assembly industries also registered high rates of growth, with the growth in the last two taking place from a particularly slim base.

The figures that are presented in Table 8.14 indicate how the structure of manufacturing was changing. Intermediate and capital goods industries experienced the fastest growth for the first time, indicating that the industrial process in Venezuela had achieved a certain level of sophistication. The consumption of energy—an indicator of production in the utilities sector—expanded 39.4 percent between 1948 and 1950, an 18.1 percent

Table 8.13.
Growth of Output in Manufacturing, 1948–1957

Year	Index (1938 = 100)
1948	350
1949	413
1950	538
1951	650
1952	760
1953	880
1954	1000
1955	1165
1956	1273
1957	1446

Sources: Evelyn M. Baran, "The Economic Development of Venezuela," Ph.D. dissertation, Radcliffe College, 1959; Banco Central de Venezuela, *Memoria* (Caracas, 1959).

average rate per year.[25] From 1950 on, there are only estimates of value added for this sector. Expressed in terms of 1957 bolívares the GDP of this sector grew 244.9 percent from 1950 to 1957, corresponding to a 19.3 percent average yearly percentage increase (see Table 8.15). This represents a remarkable growth although from a small base.

The construction activities, and the remaining industrial sector, expanded quite rapidly also. The index of cement consumption, an indicator of production in this sector, increased 140 percent between 1948 and 1950, which represented an annual average rate of growth of over 50 percent. From 1950 on, GDP estimates for this sector are also available. As can be seen in Table 8.14, the construction industry did not expand as fast as the other components of industrial product from 1950 to 1957, although there are indications that the growth of this sector was underestimated in the national accounts. Its rate of increase, in terms of constant 1957 bolívares, was 191.1 percent overall during the period, for an average of 9.7 percent per year.

Extractive activities—oil excluded—expanded over 20 times from the 1948 base, the highest rate of growth of all (see Table 8.15). A very substantial expansion in the mining of iron ore was responsible for such extraordinary growth. The expansion, which corresponded to an annual average compounded rate of growth of approximately 42 percent, can be largely explained in terms of the relative unimportance of mining in the total product of Venezuela at the beginning of the period. In 1950, the share of GDP, in constant bolívares, corresponding to mining was a little over *one-tenth of 1 percent.*

Data on tertiary production are available for the first time in this period. The GDP of this sector, in constant 1957 bolívares, is presented in Table 8.15. Total tertiary activities—public services included—expanded 78.8 percent from 1950 to 1957, for an 8.7 percent annual average rate of growth. Commercial activities experienced the fastest expansion within the sector, growing over 100 percent from 1950 to 1957.

Basic to the growth in manufacturing output occurring during this period was the expansion in aggregate demand resulting from increasing petroleum activity, high levels of public expenditures, and rising exports. Venezuela's market enlarged to the extent that domestic production of certain manufactured goods became economically feasible. At the same time, the government continued its promotion of these activities by restraining import competition, facilitating loans, and other similar promotion measures. Finally, the strong balance of payments position was instrumental in completely fulfilling the requirements of intermediate and capital goods of the sector at relatively low cost.

The rest of the industrial sector was influenced to an even greater extent by the expansion of public expenditures. Between 75 and 80 percent of total construction was financed by public institutions in this period, and the utilities sector was dominated by government enterprises.[26]

Table 8.14.
Manufacturing Production by Industry, 1948 and 1957

Industry	1948	1957	Percent Change
Food Processing Industries (Thou. metric tons):	--	--	2.477
Pasteurized milk (Thou. liters)	15.7	127.1	7.096
Milk for butter	37.4	50	0.453
Powdered milk	1.7	4.5	1.647
Vegetable oils	10.1	29.5	1.921
Peanut oil	0.5	N.A.	N.A.
Sesame oil	1.3	12.3	8.462
Coconut oil	1.3	1.6	0.231
Cotton oil	0.2	1.2	5
Canned fish	N.A.	N.A.	2.28
Ground coffee	6	12	1
Chocolate	1.2	2.2	0.833
Cookies	6.3	6.1	-0.032
Pastries	6.7	38.2	4.701
Sugar	26.6	192.8	6.248
Rice	´5.1	27.1	4.314
Salt	35.5	85.7	1.414
Fruit juices (Thou. liters: 1950, 1957)	2.9	17.6	5.069
Beverage Industries (Mill. liters):	161.9	408.9	1.526
Beer	57.8	153.9	1.663
Liquor	5.6	10.1	0.804
Rum	4.5	0.9	-0.8
Gaseous drinks	93.9	244	1.599
Textile Industries (Thou. metric tons):	--	--	1.7
Cotton suits	7.2	N.A.	N.A.
Linen canvas	3.7	3.6	-0.027
Cotton cloth	9.8	6	-0.388
Rayon and cotton cloth	N.A.	4.5	N.A.
Cotton knits (Mill. kilograms)	0.3	0.6	1
Cotton bedspreads (Mill. units)	0.1	0.5	4
Cotton blankets (Mill. units)	0.6	0.9	0.5
Cotton towels (Mill. units)	0.2	1.2	5
Cotton underwear (Mill. units)	1.3	1.5	0.154
Cotton footwear (Mill. units)	1.6	1.4	-0.125
Rayon cloth	3.3	25.1	6.606

(Continued)

Note: N.A. means value added.

Source: Juan P. Castillo, "Some Aspects of Venezuela's Economic Development: 1945–1960," Ph.D. dissertation, Tulane University, 1963, corrected for certain inaccuracies in the computation of the index numbers.

Table 8.14.
(Continued)

Industry	1948	1957	Percent Change
Textile Industries (continued):			
Rayon knits (Mill. kilograms)	0.3	0.5	0.667
Rayon footwear (Mill. pairs)	0.2	0.1	-0.5
Rayon/cotton footwear (Mill. units)	0.6	0	-1
Nylon footwear (Mill. units)	0.1	13.2	131
Wool suits (Mill. units)	0.1	0.8	7
Wool knits (Mill. units)	0.1	1.2	11
Linen cloth	0	0.8	25.667
Rope	0.9	3.1	2.444
Sisal bags (Mill. units; 1950, 1957)	0.5	5.3	9.6
Leather and Hides Industries:	--	--	4.518
Leather soles (meters)	4	5	0.25
Leather linings (Thou. square feet)	30.3	2.952.8	96.452
Other products (Thou. cubic meters)	0.5	10.2	19.4
Paper and Cardboard Industries:	--	--	0.563
Rubber Industries (Thou. units)	72	1048	13.556
Tires	39	576	13.769
Inner tubes	33	472	13.303
Tobacco Industry (Thou. metric tons):	1	3.5	2.5
Timber Industry (Thou. metric tons):	58	206	2.552
Chemical Industries:	--	--	2.471
Paint (Thou. metric tons)	1.4	18.1	11.929
Distilled alcohol (Mill. liters)	3	5.5	0.833
Soap (Mill. metric tons)	20	18.2	-0.09
Candles (Thou. metric tons)	2.6	5.4	1.077
Matches (Mill. units)	N.A.	8.1	N.A.
Industrial gas (Mill. cubic meters)	0.7	3	3.286
Animal feed (Mill. kilograms)	10.3	84.9	7.243
Metal Industries (Mill. metric tons):	--	--	4.62
Nails (1950, 1957)	2.4	7.5	2.125
Tin cans (1950, 1957)	N.A.	17.8	N.A.
Vehicle Assembly Industries (Thou. units):	--	--	3.93
Passenger (1950, 1957)	0.1	8.9	88
Commercial (1950, 1957)	2.9	5.9	1.034

(Continued)

Table 8.14.
(Continued)

Industry	1948	1957	Percent Change
Construction Material Industries (Mill. metric tons):			
Portland cement	215	1747	7.126
Lime (1950, 1957)	49.1	57	0.161
Cement blocks (Thou; 1950, 1957)	209.5	220	0.05
Cement tubes (Thou.)	N.A.	0.9	N.A.
Mosaic, and so forth	466.7	616	0.32
Bricks and tiles	116.5	134	0.15
Value Added in Selected Industries:			
Furniture	--	--	0.81
Paintings	--	--	3.83
Machine construction and repair	--	--	0.75

Some of the factors that created a favorable climate for the rising industrial production were also conducive to higher levels of agricultural production. The meager growth in this sector—in spite of these incentives—is explained by a lack of appropriate promotion policies. Even though the need for infrastructure investment was heeded, no efforts were devoted to the solution of basic institutional problems. The land tenure system, unavailability of credit and extension services, lack of agricultural research and the implementation of its findings, and a background production and marketing organization impeded satisfactory progress in agriculture.

The oil industry, particularly through its fiscal sector balance of payments and income-expenditure contributions, was of central importance

Table 8.15.
Gross Domestic Product in Selected Economic Sectors, 1948–1957 (millions of 1957 bolívares)

Year	Utilities	Construction	Extractive Index 1936 = 100	Transport and Comm.	Commerce	Other Services
1948	--	--	248	--	--	--
1949	--	--	293	--	--	--
1950	69	827	293	699	1726	3301
1951	83	1032	558	706	1983	3528
1952	97	1144	977	675	2085	3760
1953	119	1220	1058	842	2291	4086
1954	135	1376	--	876	2678	4383
1955	159	1363	--	951	2862	4636
1956	187	1605	--	945	3156	4963
1957	238	1581	--	940	3933	5365

Sources: Banco Central de Venezuela, *La Economía Venezolana en los Ultimos Veinticinco Años* (Caracas, 1966), and *Memoria* (Caracas, 1959); and Evelyn Baran, "The Economic Development of Venezuela," Ph.D. dissertation, Radcliffe College, 1959.

in bringing about an expansion in the industrial sectors and in the rest of the economy. The retained value of total expenditures—the summary indicator of all combined contributions of oil—expanded at a satisfactory pace during the period, appearing to have sparked the expansion of other sectors of the economy. In fact, almost 70 percent of the changes in the latter can be explained by the variation of total retained value. Thus, the petroleum sector appears to have behaved like a leading sector during these years. Given that petroleum activities led the growth of the Venezuelan economy in the 1949–1957 period, any unfavorable effects on the other sectors must have been neutralized by policy decisions or compensated by part of the contributions or favorable effects of the industry.

The industrial statistics available are not fine enough for pinpointing which were the main industries directly affected by the expansion in petroleum activities. However, it seems reasonable to venture that through the backward linkages of the industry, and of the government expenditures it supports, a strong demand for metal products, energy, construction activities, and services was created. On the other hand, forward-linking industries experienced considerable growth. The output of petroleum products increased seven times during this period. Finally, the use of natural gas for domestic consumption, and of natural gas and heavy oil for the production of electricity, materialized and expanded during these years.

The process of import-substitution became a more important force in the economy during this period. It advanced the furthest in industry, aided by multi-pronged promotion devices. This constituted the first inkling of the possibility of future economic growth with a certain degree of independence from petroleum. Although a somewhat less important but similar expansion had occurred in the previous period, it was spurred by the artificiality of war conditions.

Government policy was less successful in extracting from oil its *potential* contribution during this period. Therefore, the expansion in retained value resulted, to a great extent, from the automatic growth in the economic activities of the industry, working within a policy framework mostly engineered in the previous period. Furthermore, previous sections indicate that the use of the oil contribution by the economy was somewhat less effective in these years, as a result of a less enlightened government policy.

The total combined contribution of oil to the other sectors of the economy expanded at a much lower rate during this period, relative to the foregoing one. Yet, the size of the petroleum sector should be taken into consideration when comparing the contributions in each period. Due to the smaller size of the oil industry in the 1943–1948 period, the average absolute yearly increase in its total combined contribution was smaller than the corresponding rise in the contributions in the 1948–1957 period. In fact, if the overall absolute contributions are compared to the size of nonpetroleum activity at the beginning of the respective periods, which is a more appropriate way of evaluating them, the difference in the increase in the contributions is not so great. During the 1943–1948 period, the increase represented 77.3 percent of the value of nonpetroleum GDP in 1942, while for the 1949–1957 period the figure was 71.5 percent. However, the latter period is longer, which raises its corresponding percentage.

Thus, it appears that the actual increase in the total combined contribution of the petroleum sector to the rest of the Venezuelan economy was greater in the earlier period. If the effectiveness in the use of this contribution were considered, the comparison would even be more favorable to the 1943–1948 period.

Venezuela grew satisfactorily, even in terms of GDP per inhabitant, from 2,518 bolívares in 1950 to 3,661 in 1957 (in real bolívares), which amounted to a 5.5 percent compounded annual rate. But, more important, this period witnessed what apparently were the initial steps in the transformation of the Venezuelan economy into an economy less dependent on oil, and with the basic conditions and productive structure necessary for self-sustained growth.

NOTES

1. The Hydrocarbons Law of 1943 put an end to the haggling over exemptions to imports by petroleum companies. These were to be restricted to the cases in which there was no domestic production of the goods in question. Although the Venezuelan government had objected to a blind application of the exemption provisions in 1938—and from then on it did not grant the exemptions unquestioningly—this was still a controversial and unresolved issue.

2. In order to make this comparison for the government sector as a whole, as the latter has been defined before, it was necessary to assume that the percentage of social and economic expenditures in the federal budget was equally applicable to state and municipal expenditures. No actual data on the composition of the latter are available. Note, however, that they constitute only a very small part of total government expenditures, as is shown in Table 8.2.

3. Both in 1957 bolívares.

4. See Simon Kuznets, *Six Lectures on Economic Growth* (Glencoe, Ill.: Free Press, 1959), for a comparison of investment rates and rates of economic growth for particular countries for long periods of time.

5. See Banco Central de Venezuela, *Memoria* (Caracas, 1949), p. 81.

6. The industry had to provide its workers with certain facilities according to legislation enacted in 1922. This requirement was further strengthened by new legislation in 1928 and, then, by the 1936 labor law and the post–World War II collective agreements.

7. Reference has been made only to those portions of value added in the petroleum industry that are connected with the production of petroleum. Some of the industry's factor and tax payments are capitalized, deriving from the production of capital goods undertaken by the industry for its own use. If these are added to the estimates presented above, the importance of oil in the economy would be greater.

8. Moreover, as a result of shortages of certain goods during the war and post-war periods and of increased domestic production of industrial goods, the petroleum industry found it increasingly convenient to turn to native sources for its requirements of goods and services.

9. Because the geographic pattern of production and government expenditures converged in Caracas, it turned out that most of the growth taking place outside the petroleum states occurred there.

10. See Economic Commission for Latin America, United Nations, *Recent Facts and Trends in the Venezuelan Economy* (Mexico, D.F., 1951), p. 54.

11. See Juan P. Pérez Castillo, "Some Aspects of Venezuela's Economic Development: 1945–1960" (Ph.D. diss., Tulane University, 1963).

12. See United Nations, *Statistical Yearbook* (New York, 1954), p. 277.

13. Prices increased much less, close to 50 percent in this period, so the increase in real terms was still formidable.

14. See Banco Central de Venezuela, *La Economía Venezolana en los Ultimos Veinticinco Años* (Caracas, 1966), Sector Petróleo.

15. As a percentage of total GDP in current bolívares, exports climbed from 32 percent at the end of the previous period to 38 percent in 1957.

16. On this, see Ministerio de Fomento, *Anuario Estadístico* 1957–1963 (Caracas, 1964).

17. See Banco Interamericano de Desarrollo, *Datos Básicos y Parámetros Socio-Económicos de Venezuela, 1950–1965* (Washington, D.C., 1967), Table 2.

18. Only from 1950 on are revenue data presented for the public sector as a whole. Percentage shares from previous years are not directly comparable.

19. Those high rates were actually rather abnormal, as they were mainly caused by the pent-up demand built during the war. Moreover, quite extraordinary investment expenditures took place in the petroleum industry during these years. A continuation of such high investment rates was not to be expected.

20. If the income originated in the oil industry through the production of capital goods for its own use is added, the participation of oil becomes even greater.

21. This partly resulted from the fact that investment in the industry outstripped the growth of production in the previous period, as capacity expanded, based on the expectation of rising demand, and postponed wartime investment requirements were satisfied. Furthermore, the 1947–1949 level of investment was undoubtedly affected by a combination of intensive exploration of new concessions, enormous increase in refining capacity, and expansion of the oleoduct-gas-duct-storage-terminal transportation system for the industry.

22. It is impossible to determine if the local purchases of foreign goods are for investment purposes or not. Therefore, this adjustment can only be made for retained value of total expenditures as a whole and not for its current and investment components.

23. The Caracas area continued to be favored in the geographical distribution of government expenditures, as was the State of Bolívar starting at the end of the period.

24. Heavy immigration took place over these years.

25. See Baran, "The Economic Development of Venezuela" (Ph.D. diss., Radcliffe College, 1959).

26. See Banco Central de Venezuela, *Memoria,* pp. 154 ff.

CHAPTER 9

1958–1973

The next decade and a half in the evolution of the Venezuelan economy, and the influence that oil has had on the country's development, will be explored in this chapter. After the climax reached at the end of the 1943–1957 period, the potential contribution of oil appeared to experience a relative decline. However, in 1973, with an excess demand situation in the world market for oil, which seemingly would keep oil prices at high levels for at least five more years, a reversal of this trend appeared probable.

Again, in order to best examine petroleum's contribution to the economic development of Venezuela and to see how effectively it was used—and thus evaluate the role of oil as a potentially leading sector—two subperiods will be considered. The first begins in 1958, with the revolutionary and democratic regimes that supplanted the military rule of Perez Jimenez, which brought about a policy of no new oil concessions and tougher petroleum tax laws. It ends in 1965, just after Romulo Betancourt had finished his term as the first democratically elected Venezuelan president in 15 years. During the second subperiod, the democratic process is consolidated in Venezuela, and an increasingly tougher stance toward the oil industry takes shape. Not only are oil income taxes raised, so that over 80 percent of profits accrue to the state, but new exploration and development of petroleum takes place only through service contracts rather than concessions. By 1973 steps related to the eventual nationalization of the oil concessions, which was supposed to take place in 1983, were taken. However, with the rise of oil prices, there was increasing talk about the possibility of accelerating nationalization, so that it would take place sooner than had been planned.

THE 1958–1965 SUBPERIOD: THE FOREIGN SECTOR CONTRIBUTION

More detailed balance of payments calculations since 1953 have made possible the measurement of the gross balance of payments contributions of the oil sector in terms of the current account credits it generates. In current dollars, these credits experienced an overall decline from the peak year of 1957. Its behavior over time was erratic, decreasing from 1957 to 1960 and then increasing in 1965 (see Table 9.1). Oil current account credits also declined in current dollars. Their behavior throughout these years was more erratic than that of total current account credits, with their decline being more pronounced in relative terms. Therefore, the share of oil in the total came down from 90.4 percent in 1957 to 89.1 percent in 1965.

Oil still represented the salient source of export earnings at the end of the period. Thus, its gross balance of payments contribution was substantial. On the other hand, the current account credits of the petroleum industry failed to provide an expanding base, which the economy could use to cover increasing needs for payments abroad. As total GDP increased throughout these years, the proportion that exports represented of the total product of Venezuela contracted significantly.

The net balance of payments contribution of oil is measured by the foreign currency turned in by the industry as a percentage of all foreign exchange proceeds. This contribution is net in the sense that the oil industry does not use these exchange proceeds at all. They are entirely at the disposal of the rest of the economy. The foreign exchange proceeds derived from oil also contracted during this period, as can be seen in Table 9.1. However, even then their share in total foreign exchange proceeds increased from 71.5 percent in 1957 to 72.2 percent in 1965.

Table 9.1.
Petroleum Sector Indicators and External Sector Performance, 1957–1965

	1957	1958	1959	1960	1961	1962	1963	1964	1965
Total Exports (Mill. US$)	2,871	2,590	2,487	2,478	2,492	2,592	2,594	2,611	2,616
Oil Exports (Mill. US$)	2,595	2,324	2,169	2,183	2,264	2,366	2,360	2,362	2,330
As a Percent of Total	90.4%	89.7%	87.2%	88.1%	90.9%	91.3%	91.0%	90.5%	89.1%
Foreign Exchange Earnings From All Sources (Mill. US$)	2,464	1,971	2,167	2,521	1,741	1,603	1,669	1,850	1,899
Oil (Mill. US$)	1,761	1,340	1,611	1,406	1,350	1,255	1,351	1,398	1,371
Oil as a Percent of Foreign Exch. Earnings	0.7147	0.6799	0.7434	0.5577	0.7754	0.7829	0.8095	0.7557	0.722
International Reserves (Mill. US$)	1,396	1,011	709	605	585	583	740	835	853
Import Capacity Index	136	127.8	100	99	99.7	99.9	108.9	114.7	106.1
Net Barter Terms of Trade Index	136	127.8	100	94.1	93.7	86.7	93.1	93.1	84.7
Composition of Merchandise Imports (Current Bs.) Capital Goods	0.425	0.355	0.324	0.246	0.172	0.197	0.213	0.256	0.266
Intermediate Goods	0.399	0.421	0.403	0.454	0.513	0.537	0.561	0.546	0.555

Sources: Banco Central de Venezuela, *Memoria* (Caracas, several years), *Informe Económico* (Caracas, several years), and *La Economía en los Ultimos Treinta Años* (Caracas, 1971).

Only in 1958 and 1959 did the oil industry need to rely on capital inflows for the financing of its operations, particularly its investment program. Since then, the industry has been repatriating its capital.[1]

Doubtless, the Venezuelan economy did not experience an export-oriented development from 1957 on. Although oil bounced back about the middle of the period, this was only a recovery. Inflationary forces were held in check during these years though, and the growth of the economy continued. In order to come up with these results despite stagnating exports, selective exchange controls had to be imposed at the end of 1960, and Venezuela had to dig into its international reserves and negotiate diverse loans. The controls were not harsh, but a divergence between the official and free market foreign exchange selling rates ensued in 1961, culminating in the official devaluation of the bolívar in 1964.

In the end, all this seems to have provoked a shift in Venezuela's import ratios, and from 1963 on, reserves began piling up again.[2] Finally, both the net barter terms of trade and the import capacity terms of trade of Venezuela deteriorated during this period, with export prices declining sharply and import prices increasing substantially (see Table 9.1).

The expansion in GDP in real terms amounted to a 6 percent compounded average per year, with unemployment spreading throughout the period. Unemployment conceivably could have been reduced if international reserves would have been used more fully. However, maintaining such a high level of international reserves—close to $600 million at the lowest point—might have been totally justified under the conditions of lack of confidence and uncertainty characterizing this period. Nonetheless, it appears that this policy was too cautious at the end, when reserve accumulation started again. The level of international reserves is shown in Table 9.1.

The effective utilization of international means of payment provided by balance of payments credits can be measured by the composition of some of the corresponding debits. Concentrating on the composition of imported goods, for the reasons given above, a decreasing trend in the share of investment goods in total imports is found (see Table 9.1). Both the participation of intermediate and consumer goods in total imports rose, especially the former. Therefore, the evolution of the import pattern of the Venezuelan economy up to 1961 indicates a somewhat ineffective utilization of foreign exchange proceeds, reflecting, to an important degree, a decline in aggregate investment. Nevertheless, the pattern of imports turned for the better from 1962 on.[3]

The importance of oil as a generator of foreign exchange was still large during this period. Nevertheless, oil exports and foreign exchange proceeds failed to expand at a satisfactory pace. If other factors, like the depletion of international reserves, increased foreign lending, and, later, the devaluation of the bolívar, had not compensated for this, the economy would have been more seriously affected.[4] Overall, the utilization of the international reserves of Venezuela improved in comparison with the previous period. In contrast, the allocation of balance of payments credits by Venezuela appears to have deviated from an efficient norm during part of the period, which had not been the case previously.

The Fiscal Contribution of Oil

Although public revenues experienced a sharp setback in 1958, this was almost totally made up in 1959. It is impossible to make a comparison between 1959 and 1960, because of a change in the manner of presentation of the public sector accounts. From 1960 on, public revenues are defined as the total revenues of the national government, states, and municipalities, in addition to the revenues received by autonomous administrative institutes in their own right (state enterprises are not included). These revenues increased every year from 1960 on (see Table 9.2), and if 1960 is taken as the base (equals 100), 1965 would represent 148. This is approximately equal to an 8.1 percent rate of growth per year as an average,

Table 9.2.
Public Sector Fiscal Indicators, 1957–1965 (millions of bolívares)

	1957	1958	1959	1960	1961	1962	1963	1964	1965
Total Public Sector Revenues	$7,283	$5,870	$7,023	$5,548	$6,366	$6,539	$7,340	$8,036	$8,202
Tax Revenues from Petroleum, excl. Foreign Exchange Taxes	$3,846	$2,740	$3,253	$3,036	$3,289	$3,280	$3,659	$4,803	$4,863
As a Percent of Total Public Sector Revenues	52.8%	46.7%	46.3%	54.7%	51.7%	50.2%	49.9%	59.8%	59.3%
Foreign Exchange Tax Revenues on Petroleum	403	310	356	307	1,958	1,821	1,966	98	117
Tax Revenues from Petroleum, incl. Foreign Exchange Taxes	4,249	3,050	3,609	3,343	5,247	5,101	5,625	4,901	4,980
As a Percent of Total Public Sector Revenues	58.3%	52.0%	51.4%	60.3%	82.4%	78.0%	76.6%	61.0%	60.7%
Total Public Expenditures	6,390	7,261	7,669	7,396	8,540	7,954	8,678	9,050	9,601
Public Investment Expenditures	3,693	3,190	2,692	3,881	3,925	3,376	3,129	3,118	2,842
As a Percent of Total Public Expenditures	57.8%	43.9%	35.1%	52.5%	46.0%	42.4%	36.1%	34.5%	29.6%
Changes in Oil Revenues	--	-1,199	559	-266	1,904	-146	524	-724	79
Changes in Public Investment	--	-503	-498	1,189	44	-549	-247	-11	-276
Cumulative Oil Revenues	--	7,299	10,908	14,251	19,498	24,599	30,224	35,125	40,105
Cumulative Public Investment Expenditures	--	6,883	9,575	13,456	17,381	20,757	23,886	27,004	29,846

Notes: "Revenues" refer to current revenues (ingresos ordinarios). From 1957 to 1959 total revenues include the revenues of state enterprises, but after 1959 they do not. The 1957 revenue data do not reflect the sizable concession payments or the foreign exchange taxes collected on those payments. Public expenditure data includes expenditures of state enterprises.

Sources: Banco Central de Venezuela, *Memoria* (Caracas, several years), *Informe Económico* (Caracas, several years), and unpublished statistics; Ministerio de Minas e Hidrocarburos, *Petróleo y Otros Datos Estadísticos* (Caracas, 1965); J. J. Bracho-Sierra, *Cincuenta Años de Ingresos Fiscales* (Caracas, 1963).

meaning that during this entire period, public revenues expanded more rapidly than GDP in current bolívares.

Oil revenues increased considerably, after having suffered a decrease in 1958. From then on their increase was quite rapid (see Table 9.2), which can be attributed to the following: (1) the tax reform of 1958, which introduced the 60–40 sharing of oil benefits in place of the 50–50 formula; (2) the establishment of the pay-as-you-go system, which made tax payments due every month of the current year, rather than payable the year after; and (3) the devaluation in the exchange rate of 1964, which augmented petroleum tax receipts in terms of bolívares.

If the foreign exchange tax is also taken into account, a completely different picture of the oil contribution to government revenues is obtained. Considered as a loss of income to the oil sector and as a source of revenue to the government, the proceeds from this tax had increased slowly over time.[5] They jumped to a higher level in 1956 and hovered around it until 1960, as a result of increased investment activity related to the mid-1950 concessions (see Table 9.2). Because the partial devaluation of 1961 did not apply to the petroleum rate, the revenues lost by the petroleum industry as a result of the foreign exchange regulations soared. A dollar sold by the companies to the Central Bank for 3.09 bolívares ultimately could be bought by the purchasers of dollars at 4.50 bolívares or more. However, in 1964, when the government brought the petroleum rate closer into line with the general official rate, these taxes went down abruptly.[6]

Until now, it has been possible to talk about petroleum taxes with and without the inclusion of the foreign exchange tax. This manner of presentation does not present any problems, as long as the foreign exchange tax follows closely the movement of all the other petroleum taxes. But a computation of petroleum taxes without the inclusion of the exchange tax during this period shows that the contribution of oil to the public sector increased in 1964 and 1965; if the exchange tax is included, the opposite conclusion is reached.[7] A similar problem occurs with respect to the 1961 statistics. Although in this case the alternative ways of expressing the contribution of oil coincide in the direction of the change, they differ substantially as to the amount. The increase in oil revenues, not including the foreign exchange tax, is over 200 million bolívares. If the latter is considered, the figure jumps to about 1.9 million bolívares.

Unequivocally, the figures that should be used to indicate the contribution of oil are the ones including the foreign exchange tax. Oil revenues, when defined in this fashion, experienced a decrease in 1958 (see Table 9.2) and from then on the year-to-year variations were mixed, with increases in 1959, 1961, and 1963.[8] In 1963, oil revenues were the highest they had ever been, experiencing the above-referred cutbacks in 1964 and 1965. Overall, petroleum tax revenues increased 17.2 percent from 1957 to 1965. Over the 1958–1965 period, the increase amounted to 63.3 percent.

The 1957–1965 expansion rate was equal to a compounded annual average of 2 percent; in the 1958–1965 period, expansion represented approximately a 7.2 percent compounded average rate growth per year.

The share of oil in public revenues decreased in 1958 and 1959, although it still was much greater than the average share during the 1950–1955 period. Total revenues decreased 3.5 percent from 1957 to 1959; oil revenues declined 15 percent during the same time span.

Public revenues before and after 1960 are not comparable. However, from 1960 to 1965 total revenues increased at an average compounded rate of 8.1 percent yearly. Overall, oil revenues increased a little bit faster (8.3 percent annually). Therefore, the share of oil in total government receipts increased slightly from 1960 to 1965.

If the 1958–1965 period is taken as a whole, it seems that total public revenues fared slightly better than oil revenues. This had not occurred before, which could be taken as a sign of diversification in the Venezuelan economy.

Table 9.2 shows that the contribution of oil to public revenues has been quite important, either with or without the foreign exchange tax. The average for the years 1958 and 1959 is 46.5 percent without the foreign exchange tax and 51.6 percent with it. For the 1960–1965 interval, these percentages are 54.6 and 69.5 percent, respectively. Expressed as a part of GDP, the contribution of oil through tax funds was 15.3 percent of GDP with the foreign exchange tax and 12.4 percent without it during the 1958–1965 spell. This is a substantial contribution in terms of the public sector and the economy as a whole.

The Utilization of Oil's Fiscal Contribution

How well were the contributions of oil to government revenues utilized? One thing is evident from the start: there were no accumulations of Treasury reserves during this period. If anything, the pattern seems to have changed. Balanced budgets are not to be found until 1963.

Contrary to public revenue data, which present a break in the middle of the period because of a definitional change, there is continuity in the public expenditure series. It shows that total expenditures increased at a very fast pace during these years. Between 1957 and 1965, an overall increase of 50.2 percent was experienced, for a yearly rise of 5.2 percent. From 1958 to 1965, the increase came to 32.2 percent, which represents a 4.1 percent rate of growth per year (see Table 9.2). When compared with the trajectory of public revenues, it is seen that public expenditures behaved differently. They increased substantially until 1960, when public revenues were slightly declining. From then on, they rose at a slower pace than public revenues did.

Thus a good portion of public expenditures had to be debt financed. Though the participation of oil in public finances has been examined just in relation to tax revenues, the importance of petroleum in all government revenues is as great or maybe greater. The petroleum sector had an important share in financing the government deficit, specifically by purchasing a substantial number of Treasury bills and other credit documents. In fact, the oil sector has contributed more in this respect than any other sector. Clearly, however, petroleum tax revenues did not increase fast enough to obviate the need for deficit financing or to spare the other sectors from higher tax pressures.

As to the basic allocation of public expenditures between capital and current expenditures, reference is made to Table 9.2. Capital expenditures, which are the best available indication of economic development expenditures, contracted from 1958 to 1965 by 11 percent. There was also a decline from 1957 to 1958. The share of public investment in total investment, which stood at 57.8 percent in 1957, shrank to 29.6 percent in 1965. The process, nevertheless, was not a smooth one, with sharp increases in capital expenditures in 1960 and 1961, after decreases in 1958 and 1959. From 1962 on, capital expenditures declined again. The same pattern is exhibited by capital expenditures expressed as a share of total expenditures.

The average share of capital expenditures was somewhat smaller during this period when compared with the previous one. From 1950 to 1957, the average share of capital expenditures in the public sector was 45.4 percent, while from 1958 to 1965 it was 39.5 percent. Nevertheless, if 1956 and 1957 are excluded, the comparison is not so much in favor of the former.

On the other hand, during this period the allocation of investment funds seems to have improved considerably. Waste was greatly eliminated. The apportionment of investment funds among different sectors was more closely in agreement with sound investment criteria, and the breakdown between investments in directly productive activities and social overhead capital seems to have improved also.

Finally, how do capital expenditures in the public sector compare with oil revenues during this period? At the beginning, public investments, including those in state enterprises, were usually larger than oil revenues, with foreign exchange taxes not included. From 1963 on, however, the pattern was inverted, with capital expenditures usually being much smaller than petroleum taxes. If proceeds from the foreign exchange tax are included, then the revenues derived from the oil sector were higher than public investments in every year. However, for the whole period it is evident that the increments in oil revenues were not devoted to increased public investment, whether oil taxes are included or not. Yet, up to 1960 (see Table 9.2), oil revenues and government investment are closely tied.

The government used oil revenues for current expenditures to a greater extent during this period than in the past, which certainly jibes with the lower rate of capital accumulation found. The "sow the oil" policy, which asserted that oil funds were to be devoted to economic development expenditures, appears not to have been followed.

Summary

To review, oil revenues failed to expand at an appropriate pace during this period, and, as a result, other sectors of the economy had to bear an increasing tax burden. Nevertheless, two different stages must be distinguished: 1958 to 1960, in which petroleum taxes experienced a declining trend from 1957 levels; and from 1961 on, in which an opposite trend set in, with the peak attained in 1963 but with sharp decreases in 1964 and 1965.

On the other hand, it is difficult to determine if the contribution of oil was used more effectively than in the previous period. Oil funds devoted to capital formation were disappointingly low, and the share of capital expenditures in the total activities of the public sector decreased. But these things were compensated for by a fuller use of revenues—since the government did not indulge in the accumulation of treasury reserves—and a more efficacious allocation of investment funds.

Overall, the impact of the oil sector on the rest of the economy through the government was disappointing during this period, if compared with the previous one, because of a less-important petroleum revenue contribution, which was not utilized more effectively. This was especially true in the first part of the period, with all of the increases in oil-derived tax revenues from the 1957 base taking place only after 1961.

The behavior of the gross fixed domestic investment of Venezuela was also disappointing during this period. Investment decreased in absolute terms, expressed in constant 1957 bolívares, from 1957 to 1961. It rebounded from then on but never attained the 1957 level.

As a percentage of GDP in 1957 prices, investment declined up to 1963, then enlarged its participation in 1964 and 1965. In Table 9.3 it can be seen that the Venezuelan economy reduced its investment rate from 26.5 percent in 1957 to 13.1 percent in 1963. By 1965 the investment rate had shown a slight recuperation, up to 14.4 percent.[9]

Petroleum investment experienced a similar declining trend, which started in 1959 instead of 1958. In 1963 there was a reversal in the trend, but even then, the gross fixed domestic investment in the industry in 1965 was just a shade over one-third of petroleum investment in 1957 (see Table 9.3). This decline was much greater than that experienced by total investment.

The composition of petroleum investment changed radically during this period. Investment in refining and transport experienced a sharply declining trend. On the other hand, investment in the production of crude oil, even though decreasing in absolute terms, increased its share from

Table 9.3.

Gross Domestic Product and Gross Fixed Domestic Investment, Oil Sector, 1957–1965 (millions of 1957 bolívares)

	1957	1958	1959	1960	1961	1962	1963	1964	1965
Total GDP:	24,295	24,078	25,799	27,038	28,488	29,841	32,947	36,345	38,612
GDP, Oil Sector	7,249	6,710	7,307	7,697	8,003	8,491	8,574	9,100	9,444
GDP, Other Sectors	13,854	14,167	16,143	17,458	18,939	19,491	22,426	25,166	27,193
Oil as a Percent of GDP	29.8%	27.9%	28.3%	28.5%	28.1%	28.5%	26.0%	25.0%	24.5%
Gross Fixed Domestic Investment (GFDI):	6,429	6,180	6,054	4,725	4,019	4,196	4,307	5,178	5,558
Oil Sector	1,822	1,828	1,263	723	488	422	440	622	641
Other Sectors	4,607	4,352	4,791	4,002	3,531	3,774	3,867	4,556	4,917
Oil Investment as a Percent of GFDI	28.3%	29.6%	20.9%	15.3%	12.1%	10.1%	10.2%	12.0%	11.5%
GFDI as a Percent of GDP	26.5%	25.7%	23.5%	17.5%	14.1%	14.1%	13.1%	14.2%	14.4%

Notes: Oil and non-oil GDP do not add to total. See text for explanation of methodology and adjustments to data.

Sources: Banco Central de Venezuela, unpublished statistics; financial statements and supporting documents are from the three main oil company groups in Venezuela, extrapolated to obtain industry-wide estimates.

66.1 percent of the total in 1957 to 87.0 percent in 1965. The share devoted to marketing also expanded greatly up to 1964—even experiencing an absolute increase up to that year—but contracted in 1965 to wind up with a moderate increase (see Table 9.4).

Investment in the petroleum industry was a diminishing portion of total investment from 1958 on, although it recuperated slightly at the end of the period. In Table 9.3, the time path of this percentage is shown. Investment, in turn, represented a smaller share of GDP. In fact, from 1958

Table 9.4.

Gross Fixed Investment in the Petroleum Sector by Type of Investment, 1957–1965

	1957	1958	1959	1960	1961	1962	1963	1964	1965
Total GDP:	24,295	24,078	25,799	27,038	28,488	29,841	32,947	36,345	38,612
GDP, Oil Sector	7,249	6,710	7,307	7,697	8,003	8,491	8,574	9,100	9,444
GDP, Other Sectors	13,854	14,167	16,143	17,458	18,939	19,491	22,426	25,166	27,193
Oil as a Percent of GDP	29.8%	27.9%	28.3%	28.5%	28.1%	28.5%	26.0%	25.0%	24.5%
Gross Fixed Domestic Investment (GFDI):	6,429	6,180	6,054	4,725	4,019	4,196	4,307	5,178	5,558
Oil Sector	1,822	1,828	1,263	723	488	422	440	622	641
Other Sectors	4,607	4,352	4,791	4,002	3,531	3,774	3,867	4,556	4,917
Oil Investment as a Percent of GFDI	28.3%	29.6%	20.9%	15.3%	12.1%	10.1%	10.2%	12.0%	11.5%
GFDI as a Percent of GDP	26.5%	25.7%	23.5%	17.5%	14.1%	14.1%	13.1%	14.2%	14.4%

Source: Ministerio de Minas e Hidrocarburos, *Petróleo y Otros Datos Estadísticos* (Caracas, several years).

to 1965, the investment rate was only slightly higher than in the 1936–1942 period, while in the interim years it had been significantly above that rate. As to the share of petroleum investment, it was even lower during these years than in the 1936–1942 period. The average of petroleum investment in constant terms was lower during the 1958–1965 period than in the 1948–1957 period.

Nonpetroleum gross fixed investment, in constant 1957 prices, experienced a decline up to 1961 and then reversed its trend (see Table 9.5). By the end of the period, it had risen 6.7 percent from the 1957 level, for a 0.8 percent yearly compounded average growth. Although this is not a satisfactory rate, it is much better than the performance of petroleum investment.

The disappointing performance of total investment during the early part of the period resulted from the following forces:

1. After the Suez Canal crisis, which increased Venezuelan oil prices substantially, the world market for crude oil and products was characterized by excess supply. By then, Venezuelan oil was at a disadvantage because of relatively high costs, and its export volume was rising very slowly.[10] Such a situation, coupled with no new concessions, political uncertainty, and lack of confidence in the Venezuelan economy, led the oil companies to follow restrictive policies with regard to investment.

2. The other sectors of the economy were affected by the gloomy outlook for petroleum and by the lull in its activity. But because government policy partly

Table 9.5.
Retained Value of Oil Sector Expenditures, 1957–1965 (millions of bolívares)

	1957	1958	1959	1960	1961	1962	1963	1964	1965
Retained Value of Total Expenditures	5,087	5,691	5,474	5,388	6,885	6,880	7,140	7,457	7,610
As a Percent of Total Expenditures	48.7%	60.3%	63.6%	64.9%	86.1%	81.6%	84.7%	63.5%	63.3%
Retained Value of Expenditures Per Barrel of Current Oil Produced (Bs.)	5.02	5.98	5.41	5.18	6.46	5.89	6.02	6.00	6.00
Total Value of Production	8,604	7,644	7,343	7,302	7,475	7,958	7,910	10,948	11,216
GDP Oil Sector	7,249	6,301	5,977	5,911	6,274	6,759	6,748	9,328	9,680

Notes: Estimates of retained value and value of production based on adjustments to data from three main petroleum company groups. Conversion of value of sales to value of production based on *Informes de Conservación* (Caracas, several years), and unpublished data from the Oficina Técnica, Ministerio de Minas e Hidrocarburos. Total oil sector expenditures include value of production and investment. Total retained value includes foreign exchange taxes on oil, but excludes concession payments of 1957.

Sources: Banco Central de Venezuela, *La Economía Venezolana en los Ultimos Veinticinco Años* (Caracas, several years), *Informe Económico* (Caracas, several years), and unpublished statistics; Ministerio de Minas e Hidrocarburos, *Petróleo y Otros Datos Estadisticos* (Caracas, 1965).

neutralized such contraction, effective demand never actually weakened very much. In fact, the capital goods sector, still very small in Venezuela, was severely hit, with only moderate curtailments taking place in the consumer goods sectors. Therefore, in the end, nonpetroleum investment expenditures did not diminish as much as could have been expected, with a 25 percent reduction from 1957 to 1961, the trough year in the recession. Thus, the contraction was relatively mild, when compared with the 75 percent reduction experienced by oil investment over the same years.

The relationship of petroleum investment and nonpetroleum investment weakened throughout these years, as the economy became much more independent of oil. Short-term counter-cyclical policies had much to do with this, with investment in oil and in the rest of the economy moving in opposite directions in certain years. The relationship of nonpetroleum gross fixed investment (lagged one year) with the retained value of total oil expenditures is somewhat closer, but the correlation between them is still quite low.

During this period, nonpetroleum investment was a substantial share of the total retained value of oil, although a much lower one than in previous periods. On the other hand, the average productivity of public investment appears to have increased. There was a cut in waste, and more thought appears to have been given to investment decisions. As the Venezuelan economy improved its institutions, it became more mobile, flexible, and informed, with the profit-conscious class of entrepreneurs becoming more numerous and sophisticated. As a result, a better allocation of investment resources probably occurred in the private sector also.

In short, both petroleum and nonpetroleum investment moved disappointingly from 1958 to 1965. This was especially so in the early part of the period. The behavior of petroleum investment was particularly distressing, with its level dropping as much as 75 percent in the through year. The signs of some independence from oil, which came to the fore in the last period, were stronger during these years. Nonpetroleum investment experienced an overall expansion during the period, in the face of a contraction in petroleum investment.[11] A very weak connection was found between the former and the retained value of total oil expenditures.

TOTAL DOMESTIC PRODUCT AND THE EXPENDITURES OF THE OIL INDUSTRY, 1966–1973

Increments in the total income and expenditures originating in an exogenous sector constitute injections into the economic flows of a country. An income-expenditure effect is derived from these injections, as they run their course through the producing and consuming sectors of an economy. Have such repercussions arisen from the petroleum industry in this period?

In a previous section, the behavior of petroleum investment expenditures was examined. Similar attention should now be given to the variables related to value of production. The latter declined from the 1957 level up to 1960 and then started moving up again. A big jump in 1964 resulted from the extension of the devaluation to the oil sector (and, thus, covers the whole Venezuelan economy). A similar trend was followed by the GDP of petroleum in current bolívares (see Table 9.5).

In constant terms, petroleum's GDP grew at a 3.4 percent compounded annual average per year in this period. As a percentage of total GDP in constant 1957 prices, the petroleum sector hovered between 28 and 30 percent. This means that petroleum had become a less-important part of total GDP. The average share in the previous period was 30.1 percent, as compared to 27.4 percent from 1958 to 1965. In 1965 the share was 24.5 percent, as against 29.8 percent in 1957 (see Table 9.5).[12]

The total expenditures of an exogenous sector constitute the leverage on which its income-expenditure effects are based. But actually, only a part of such total expenditures has an immediate and significant influence over the other sectors of the economy. This is the retained value portion of total expenditures, as defined in preceding chapters. The concept of retained value is also an approximate summary indicator of the total combined contribution of a sector to an economy. Therefore, the movements of the retained value of oil expenditures over the period, as well as its impact on the rest of the economy, must also be examined.

In this period, the manner in which the retained value of total expenditures is calculated must be altered, so as to incorporate the contribution of oil to government revenues through the exchange rate tax. In the past, the trend in such tax revenues was substantially the same as that for all petroleum tax revenues. This, plus the awkwardness of the levy—which makes its classification difficult—and the fact that these taxes had to be estimated in an imprecise manner, prompted us to exclude such taxes from the previous retained value figures.

However, the exchange rates for the economy and for the petroleum sector altered drastically during this period, with the differential in these two rates abruptly becoming very wide in certain years. In turn, this caused exceptional variations in the petroleum foreign exchange tax receipts. As a result, if the foreign exchange tax receipts are included, the whole picture of the industry's retained value of expenditures is changed, and a more accurate representation of the actual changes in retained value is obtained.[13]

It is not possible to determine accurately which portion of the foreign exchange tax contribution of oil is attributable to current expenditures and which to capital expenditures during these years. Thus, only total retained value figures are used in this section, with no separate calculation presented of the retained values of current and capital expenditures of the oil industry.

Retained value of total expenditures, defined in this fashion, increased in 1958 and then declined up to 1960. It subsequently increased up to 1965, mainly as a result of the increased exchange rate tax in 1961, 1962, and 1963, and also because of increased income and royalty taxes in 1964 and 1965. Overall, it increased 50 percent, which is equivalent to a compounded annual average increment of 5.2 percent from 1957 to 1965 (see Table 9.5). The increase would be less in constant 1957 bolívares, as the implicit deflator for petroleum GDP increased in 1964 and 1965.

However, if the extraordinary payments for oil concessions taking place in 1956 and 1957 are included in the retained value figures for those years, then the 1957–1965 increment drops to 22.2 percent overall, which corresponds to a 2.5 percent annual average compounded rate of growth. The increase in real terms is, again, something less than that.

The retained value of total petroleum expenditures per barrel of oil produced, including exchange taxes, also increased during the period in both current and constant prices. Not only was an overall increase registered, but the average for this period was greater than the average for the previous one—all this in the face of decreasing oil prices.

Retained value of total expenditures represented a higher average share of the value of production plus investment expenditures in the petroleum industry during the 1958–1965 period than in the preceding one. This is so even considering the concession payments in 1957. The percentage share was much higher in 1965 than in 1957.

During this period, the government was able to increase retained value from the 1957 levels in the face of declining investment. This was made possible through higher income tax rates for petroleum, a rise in the petroleum foreign exchange tax rate, increased tax revenues resulting from the 1964 devaluation, and more effective tax enforcement. Another contributing factor of lesser importance was increasing local procurement by the oil companies.

However, in absolute terms, the total combined growth-promoting contributions of the oil industry to the economy expanded at a slow and unsatisfactory pace during this period. Such a performance stands in contrast with those in the previous periods. It is possible, but by no means certain, that excessive tax pressures affected the investment decisions—and, perhaps, the export potential—of the oil industry in these years.

Notwithstanding the weak contribution of petroleum, Venezuela's GDP grew 59 percent in real terms from 1957 to 1965. This is equivalent to a compounded average rate of increase of 6 percent a year (see Table 9.5).[14] This is quite an impressive gain in light of unsatisfactory growth in the oil industry, the reduction in total investment, and the uncertain conditions referred to in the investment section. The growth appears even more remarkable if we take into account that 1957 was a boom year for oil and a record year for the Venezuelan economy. Yet, on the whole, the rate of economic growth was lower than in the previous period, in consonance with the lower investment rate from 1958 to 1965. This certainly agrees with the findings of Simon Kuznets, which have been discussed in Chapters 7 and 8.

Moreover, the increment in nonpetroleum GDP was even greater, as can be seen from Table 9.3. From 1957 to 1965, this aggregate increased 96.3 percent, representing an annual average compounded rate of growth of 8.8 percent.[15] Government policy was quite effective in neutralizing the adverse effects taking place in the first part of the period. Although the petroleum sector expanded more slowly than the economy as a whole, it rebounded in the second part of the period, to ease the burden of the government sector. However, it seems that both the government sector and the import-substituting industries were the most important leading sectors in the economy during this period, with petroleum providing added support in the second half. The nonpetroleum part of the Venezuelan economy continued the trend initiated at the end of the war, gaining considerably in strength and independence. In fact, the takeoff of the Venezuelan economy probably began in the 1958–1965 period.

The agricultural sector, forestry included, grew satisfactorily from 1957 to 1965, in contrast with previous periods. In fact, it expanded at a compounded annual average growth rate of 6.1 percent. Cereals, fibers and oils, sugar, animal products, and forestry products had the highest rates of growth. The production of fibers and oils and cereals about doubled in this span, and animal products nearly accomplished it. Among cereals, the production of rice expanded close to 10 times, although from a low base. Sesame and cotton were the main cause of the expansion in fibers and oils. Dairy products, eggs, and poultry were the most rapidly expanding categories among animal products.

The governments that succeeded the military regime of Marcos Perez Jimenez implanted basic institutional reforms in the rural areas and devoted a larger share of public resources to agricultural investment and agricultural credit. Measures such as land redistribution, more extensive production and investment credits, sound and far-reaching extension services, and well-thought-out overhead facilities were responsible for the performance of this sector.

Manufacturing activities had big gains in this period. The index of manufacturing production grew 104 percent, including petroleum refining, for a 9.3 percent compounded average yearly increase. As petroleum refining—which represented over 10 percent of manufacturing production throughout this period—had a slower growth, if it is excluded the rate of growth of manufacturing would be even greater.[16]

In Tables 9.6 and 9.7, manufacturing output is presented in a disaggregate fashion. Up to 1963, the paper and cardboard industry and the tobacco industry (see Table 9.6) had the fastest expansion. Table 9.7 is expressed in terms of the product originated in each industry in constant

Table 9.6.
Manufacturing Products by Industry, 1957 and 1963

Industry	1,957.00	1,963.00	Percent Change
Food processing (Thou. metric tons):	--	--	0.383
Pasteurized milk (Thou. liters)	127.10	178.90	0.408
Milk for butter	50.00	45.00	-0.1
Powdered milk	4.50	20.90	3.644
Vegetable oils	29.50	35.40	0.2
Peanut oil	N.A.	N.A.	N.A.
Sesame oil	12.30	22.70	0.846
Coconut oil	1.60	0.50	-0.688
Cotton oil	1.20	3.50	1.917
Canned fish	N.A.	17.40	0.27
Ground coffee	12.00	17.60	0.467
Chocolate	2.20	2.00	-0.091
Cookies	6.10	9.30	0.525
Pastries	38.20	46.90	0.228
Sugar	192.80	275.60	0.429
Rice	27.10	26.70	-0.015
Salt	85.70	76.40	-0.109
Fruit juices (Thou. liters; 1950, 1957)	17.60	30.70	74.4
Beverage Industries (Mill. liters):	408.90	665.70	62.8
Beer	153.90	248.80	0.617
Liquor	10.10	11.30	0.119
Rum	0.90	0.20	-0.778
Gaseous drinks	244.00	405.40	0.661
Textile Industries (Thou. metric tons):	--	--	0.778
Cotton suits	7.00	12.70	0.814
Linen canvas	3.60	5.90	0.639
Cotton cloth	6.00	38.40	5.4
Rayon and cotton cloth	4.50	7.50	0.007
Cotton knits (Mill. kilograms)	0.60	0.80	0.333
Cotton bedspreads (Mill. units)	0.50	0.30	-0.4
Cotton blankets (Mill. units)	0.90	1.50	0.667
Cotton towels (Mill. units)	1.20	2.30	0.917
Cotton underwear (Mill. units)	1.50	N.A.	N.A.
Cotton footwear (Mill. units)	1.40	1.70	0.214

(Continued)

Note: N.A. means not available.

Source: Juan P. Perez Castillo, "Some Aspects of Venezuela's Economic Development: 1945–1960," Ph.D. dissertation, Tulane University, 1963, corrected for certain errors in the 1948 index.

Table 9.6.
(Continued)

Industry	1,957.00	1,963.00	Percent change
Textile Industries (continued):			
Rayon cloth	25.10	34.00	0.355
Rayon knits (Mill. kilograms)	0.50	0.40	-0.2
Rayon footwear (Mill. pairs)	0.10	N.A.	N.A.
Rayon/cotton footwear (Mill. units)	0.00	N.A.	N.A.
Nylon footwear (Mill. units)	13.20	18.30	0.386
Wool suits (Mill. units)	0.80	0.80	0
Wool knits (Mill. units)	1.20	1.70	0.417
Linen cloth	0.80	N.A.	N.A.
Rope	3.10	2.70	-0.129
Sisal bags (Mill. units; 1950, 1957)	5.30	5.80	0.094
Leather and Hides Industries:	--	--	0.183
Leather soles (meters)	5.00	4.90	-0.02
Leather linings (Thou. square feet)	2,952.80	3,485.40	0.18
Other products (Thou. cubic meters)	10.20	21.60	1.118
Paper and Cardboard Industries:	13.60	40.00	1.941
Rubber Industries (Thou. units):	1,048.00	1,567.00	0.495
Tires	576.00	978.00	0.698
Inner tubes	472.00	589.00	0.248
Tobacco Industry (Thou. metric tons):	3.50	8.30	1.371
Timber Industry (Thou. metric tons):	206.00	171.00	-0.17
Chemical Industries:	--	--	1.872
Paint (Thou. metric tons)	18.10	19.40	0.072
Distilled alcohol (Mill. liters)	5.50	9.60	0.745
Soap (Mill. metric tons)	18.20	25.50	-0.86
Candles (Thou. metric tons)	5.40	6.00	0.111
Matches (Mill. units)	8.10	12.80	0.58
Industrial gas (Mill. cubic meters)	3.00	3.50	0.167
Animal feed (Mill. kilograms)	84.90	305.00	2.592
Metal Industries (Mill. metric tons):	--	--	0.518
Nails (1950, 1957)	7.50	4.00	-0.467
Tin cans (1950, 1957)	17.80	34.40	0.933

(Continued)

Table 9.6.
(Continued)

Industry	1,957.00	1,963.00	Percent change
Vehicle Assembly Industries (Thou. units):	--	--	0.501
Passenger (1950, 1957)	8.90	16.50	0.854
Commercial (1950, 1957)	5.90	5.70	-0.034
Construction Material Industries (Mill. metric tons):	--	--	-0.14
Portland cement	1,747.00	1,570.00	-0.101
Lime (1950, 1957)	57.00	48.00	-0.158
Cement blocks (Thou; 1950, 1957)	220.00	28.00	0.273
Cement tubes (thou.)	0.90	1.00	0.111
Mosaic, and so forth	616.00	401.00	-0.349
Bricks and tiles	134.00	107.00	0.201

1957 bolívares, with the year 1953 as the base. Table 9.7, in contrast with the previous table, presents a more comprehensive coverage of the manufacturing sector (petroleum refining excluded).

Several industries grew faster than the manufacturing sector as a whole from 1957 to 1965. They mostly were capital goods industries; rubber; vehicle construction, assembly, and repair; machinery construction, assembly, and repair; and metals. These represented about 12 to 13 percent of total manufacturing over these years. Some intermediate industries— namely, the chemical and paper and cardboard industries—also expanded

Table 9.7.
Index of Production in Manufacturing by Commodity, 1957–1965 (1953 = 100)

	1957	1958	1959	1960	1961	1962	1963	1964	1965
Food Processing	161	161	185	203	224	244	257	295	322
Beverage	133	166	191	204	200	203	207	216	230
Tobacco	126	137	154	239	260	279	297	312	346
Textile	201	216	257	258	294	339	375	437	440
Clothing and Apparel	208	205	220	191	200	185	178	233	199
Paper and Cardboard	320	348	537	627	737	770	928	1,186	1,269
Printing	180	217	222	217	204	217	280	237	262
Leather	187	204	247	313	301	267	246	314	262
Chemical	194	204	238	220	249	277	299	371	410
Timber	185	178	247	139	142	144	159	192	207
Furniture	206	184	202	169	180	208	223	243	329
Rubber	224	260	289	299	313	362	374	420	476
Construction Materials	175	159	187	153	152	152	156	190	220
Construction Assembly and Machinery Repair	149	167	176	179	190	269	298	399	554
Construction Assembly and Vehicle Repair	151	161	172	158	169	168	205	281	353
Metal Work	371	487	580	620	657	765	722	893	924
Basic Metals	402	309	486	379	510	1,703	2,975	3,531	4,389
Jewelry	152	217	218	303	257	182	217	307	314

Sources: Banco Central de Venezuela, La Economía Venezolana en los Ultimos Treinta Años (Caracas, 1971), and Informe Económico (Caracas, 1969).

Table 9.8.
Gross Domestic Product in Selected Economic Sectors, 1957–1965 (millions of 1957 bolívares)

	1957	1958	1959	1960	1961	1962	1963	1964	1965
Utilities	238	281	336	371	422	501	590	663	738
Construction	1,581	1,618	1,707	1,647	1,471	1,420	1,340	1,496	1,545
Extractive, Excluding Petroleum	383	379	420	463	358	333	282	390	425
Transport and Communication	940	1,002	1,090	1,011	996	996	1,045	1,181	1,267
Commerce	3,933	3,803	4,003	3,976	3,811	4,051	4,315	4,932	5,455
Other Services	5,365	5,825	6,296	6,989	8,381	9,595	10,946	11,987	12,665
Total	10,238	10,630	11,389	11,976	13,188	14,642	16,306	18,100	19,387

Sources: Banco Central de Venezuela, *La Economía Venezuela en los Ultimos Veinticinco Años* (Caracas, 1966), *La Economía Venezolana en los Ultimos Treinta Años* (Caracas, 1971), and *Informe Económico* (Caracas, 1965 and 1969).

faster than total manufacturing, and also from a slim base. Of the consumer goods industries, only tobacco and textiles expanded significantly faster than the overall manufacturing sector. Among these, the fastest growing from 1957 to 1965 were the machine construction and repair industry, the paper and cardboard industry, and the basic metals group.

The performance of the rest of the industrial sector was mixed in character, as Table 9.8 shows. The utilities sector expanded close to 210 percent from 1957 to 1965. This represents an annual average compounded rate of growth of approximately 15.2 percent. On the other hand, construction activities contracted slightly over these years. As in the previous period, the performance of these sectors is measured in terms of GDP in constant 1957 bolívares.

The key to the growth in the manufacturing sector was the import-substitution drive, which attained prominence as the most dynamic force in Venezuelan economic growth during this period. The process of import substitution began to affect intermediate goods, and even some capital goods lines, but basically fed on consumer goods industries. Other important factors in the expansion of manufactures were the fostering policies of the government, especially credit facilities and tax and tariff rebates.

The tremendous expansion in the utilities sector resulted to a great extent from the growth of industry and agriculture and the urbanization process they helped generate. However, the fulfillment of previously unsatisfied needs for these services (utilities) was also an important factor.[17] The contraction in the construction sector is explained in terms of the reduction in investment expenditures that took place in this period. This affected the capital goods industries through its major component: the construction industry.

Extractive activities, petroleum excluded, rose slightly, as Table 9.8 shows. This can again be explained in terms of the factors affecting the iron industry, which represents close to 90 percent of the product originated in this sector. As iron faced an unfavorable situation in the international markets from 1960 to 1963, the product originated in mining contracted, *pari passu* with the reduction in the production of iron. Together with iron, it rebounded strongly in 1964 and 1965, surpassing the 1957 level.

Tertiary activities expanded greatly from 1957 to 1965—even faster than that of industry. As shown in Table 9.8, this expansion amounted to about 90 percent overall, for an annual average rate of growth of 8.3 percent. Services experienced the strongest expansion, with an overall increase of 136 percent. Commerce and transport and communications activities expanded at a much slower pace—about 35 percent—from 1957 to 1965 (see Table 9.8).

Although the oil industry did not lead the economic growth of Venezuela in this period, the importance of its contributions to the industrial strength of the country cannot be overlooked. The backward linkages of the industry were partly responsible for the growth in the metal (especially basic metals) and machinery industries, while the forward linkages were basic in the expansion of fertilizers, the petrochemical industry, and several uses of natural gas.

The decline in external petroleum prices constituted the big difference in the contribution of oil to the rest of the Venezuelan economy during this period. Since 1936 the general trend has been one of rising prices. This meant externally determined increases in petroleum and total GDP. The opposite was true in this period. The total contribution of petroleum over these years was constrained by a declining value for each barrel of oil produced.

Although encouraging progress was experienced in the nonpetroleum part of the economy, overall the Venezuelan economy did not gain that much in per capita terms. The very high rate of growth of population in Venezuela partly explains this. Total GDP per inhabitant enlarged from 3,661 to 4,427, in constant 1957 bolívares, for a 20.9 percent increase overall. This represents a compounded annual average of 2.4 percent.

However, a most important phenomenon was occurring. As the economy of Venezuela grew, a new pattern of production and trade emerged. This change had started back in the late war years and had ripened sufficiently to pass its first test respectably. Such factors were considerably aided during the 1957–1965 period by a substantial reduction in excess capacity.[18] However, it became evident that the Venezuelan economy had become sufficiently diversified to be adequately prepared for short-cycle slumps in the oil sector.

The secondary and tertiary sectors increased their importance considerably during this period. Agriculture, with its share still decreasing over time, grew relatively faster over these years, in consonance with the country's rapid population growth. Exports of manufacturing goods expanded greatly, and the prospects for continued expansion seemed encouraging.

However, the improvement occurred toward the end of the period, with a large expansion in petroleum exports and a favorable and considerable rise in Venezuela's foreign trade being experienced in 1973. As the outlook for Venezuelan oil became more attractive, a future could be foreseen in which petroleum's contribution to the economy through the external sector could be compared in its relative importance to the prosperous times of the 1950s.

The current account credits of Venezuela's balance of payments appear in Table 9.9, with petroleum's share also indicated. The same table shows the amount of foreign exchange received by Venezuela due to these and other balance of payments credits. Just a quick glance is sufficient to conclude that the year 1973 constitutes a jump in the time series.

Oil foreign exchange earnings, for example, increased roughly 60 percent during the years 1965 to 1972; nevertheless, this figure doubles if one considers the year 1973 as the final one in the period. This means a very quick increase in the cumulative yearly growth rate, which reaches 10.5 percent if 1973 is taken as the end of the period. (The yearly growth rate increases to 12.1 percent if we consider 1966 as the base year.) It should be pointed out that oil's current account credits did not increase as fast. Even though it was not possible to obtain the corresponding estimate for 1973 in the Central Bank's statistics, an estimate could be made, based on the data

Table 9.9.
Petroleum Sector Indicators and External Sector Performance, 1965–1973

	1965	1966	1967	1968	1969	1970	1971	1972	1973
Total Exports (Mill. US$)	2,616	2,539	2,695	2,738	2,761	2,894	3,396	3,432	--
Oil Exports (Mill. US$)	2,330	2,239	2,361	2,398	2,360	2,436	2,935	2,910	--
As a Percent of Total	89.1%	88.2%	87.6%	87.6%	85.5%	84.2%	86.4%	84.8%	--
Foreign Exchange Earnings from all Sources (Mill. US$)	1,899	2,050	2,259	2,304	2,382	2,640	3,421	4,081	5,587
Oil (Mill. US$)	1,371	1,369	1,536	1,587	1,595	1,686	1,686	2,190	3,045
Oil as a Percent of Foreign Exch. Earnings	1	1	1	1	1	1	1	1	1
International Reserves (Mill. US$)	853	772	874	928	939	1,023	1,479	1,747	2,389
1959 = 100 (at realized prices)									
Import Capacity Index	106.1	99.9	106.2	106.8	102.4	99	111	101.3	126.3
Net Barter Terms of Trade Index	84.7	81.4	82.5	83.1	77.9	73.5	86.7	85	100.9
1968 = 100 (at reference prices)									
Import Capacity Index	--	--	--	100	102.8	95.5	113.3	119.7	147.7
Net Barter Terms of Trade Index	--	--	--	100	100.4	95.4	110.1	111.7	142.5
Composition of Merchandise Imports (Current Bs.): Capital Goods	0.266	0.275	0.258	0.275	0.3	0.27	0.391	0.305	0.306
Intermediate Goods	0.555	0.555	0.569	0.552	0.534	0.574	0.56	0.536	0.545
Consumer Goods	0.179	0.17	0.174	0.172	0.166	0.156	0.149	0.159	0.149

Notes: All figures at realized or sale prices, unless noted otherwise. Composition of imports for 1973 refer to first semester.

Sources: Banco Central de Venezuela, *La Economía Venezolana en los Ultimos Treinta Años* (Caracas, 1971), and *Informe Economico* (Caracas, 1973).

provided by the Ministry of Mines and Hydrocarbons. By relating exports at realized or sale prices with those at reference or fiscal prices, obtained from the Ministry of Mines, oil's credits are estimated at realized or sale prices as $4,416 million. Therefore, the increase in these credits was 89.5 percent as a whole, equivalent to an annual compounded growth rate of 8.5 percent, with respect to 1965, and of 97.2 percent, in relation to 1966, corresponding to a yearly compounded rate of 10.2 percent.

The fact that the increment in petroleum's foreign exchange earnings was superior to the increase in its current account credits denotes the pressure that the Venezuelan government has been exerting to enlarge the obligations that the petroleum companies must settle in bolívares in Venezuela. This is also reflected in total foreign exchange earnings, which grow faster than total credits, even though this is also due to the behavior of the capital account transactions in Venezuela's balance of payments.

In general, we may conclude that the expansion in Venezuela's current account credits, and, in particular, petroleum's contribution through the external sector, were satisfactory during the period 1966–1973. However, it should again be underlined that this was so mainly because of the jump that occurred in 1973. On the other hand, the contribution in terms of exchange earnings is even more positive. Partly because of these favorable conditions, Venezuela's GDP was able to expand, and the percentage that balance of payments current account credits represented of GDP (at current prices) declined from 30.9 to 27.8 percent.

Before considering the utilization of oil's contribution through the external sector, it is necessary to emphasize two relatively important points related with the considerations made above. First, it is evident that oil's share in Venezuela's external sector decreased slightly during the period 1966–1973 (see Table 9.9). Second, as Table 9.9 shows, it was the rise in the price of oil that fundamentally determined the satisfactoriness of its contribution during the period. The series appearing in Table 9.9 shows that the net terms of trade index rose quickly beginning in 1971, surpassing, in 1973, the 1959 base. If this index is computed based on reference or fiscal prices, the same trend is found with a sharper increase, however (see Table 9.9).

It has been seen that gross (in terms of current account credits) and net (in terms of foreign exchange earnings) contributions were satisfactory in the period examined. How were these contributions utilized? In the first place, it is seen that Venezuela's international reserves increased continually throughout these years, reaching levels comparable to those in developed countries toward the end of the period. The reserves, in dollars, as can be seen in Table 9.9, tripled during this period, after experiencing a shortfall in 1966. The annual compounded rates of increase were 17.5 percent for the period in question and 13.7 percent if 1965 is taken as the base year. Therefore, excessive reserves were again accumulated, while the economy grew at a rate (4.8 percent a year, compounded) that, although satisfactory, seemed insufficient, given the underemployment of the Venezuelan labor force. Yet it is possible that Venezuela's absorptive capacity of investment was limited by certain bottlenecks during these years. On the other hand, the high level of reserves, and, thus, the strong import capacity of the Venezuelan economy, continued to allow the maintenance of very low inflation rates. Nevertheless, toward the end of the period, the scarcity of a series of basic foodstuffs, the generalization of price hikes throughout the world, and Venezuela's tariff reforms led to rates of price increases that had not been felt for many years in Venezuela.

How were the foreign exchange earnings put to use—that is, those that did not end up enlarging Venezuela's international reserves? An important contribution of oil's exchange earnings was to allow the processes of capital accumulation, production, and spending to take place unimpeded by any important constraint. This has prevented the appearance of bottlenecks in terms of availability of goods and services and seems to have been one of the main reasons for Venezuela's growth.

However, the effective use of these external resources requires that the importation of goods and services maintain a certain path throughout time. This is determined by the importance that capital formation holds in the process of economic development and by the stages generally traced by a country's industrial growth. An effective use is indicated by a relative increase in capital goods imports and a decrease of consumption goods imports. The evolution of the import components, according to type of goods, appears in Table 9.9, and it is seen that, during this period, imports of capital goods increased to about 30 percent of total imports, while the imports of consumption goods decreased to less than 15 percent. This implies that the net resources contributed by the petroleum sector for import financing were well employed during the period 1966–1973.

Altogether, oil's contribution through the external sector was still considerable during this period. In relative terms, oil was the most important factor in the enormous increase in the Venezuelan economy's current account credits (especially occurring in its exports of goods and services). It also had a very high participation in its total foreign exchange earnings. Thus, its relative contribution was similar to that made in the previous period (1957–1965). However, its contribution was much more satisfactory during the most recent period, when the *absolute* growth in current account credits and foreign exchange earnings is considered. On the other hand, the use of the contribution was much more effective during the years 1966–1973. The pattern of imports and its evolution throughout the period fitted the development and industrial growth norm mentioned above, and the price increases in the period were reasonably contained considering the circumstances. The only negative aspect in the utilization of petroleum's contribution was the accumulation of international reserves to a degree that could be considered excessive. Given the problems facing the Venezuelan society, to have vast capital reserves yielding very low returns is difficult to justify. It should be recognized that this is a very debatable point; it should also be made clear that, in 1973, the Venezuelan authorities became quite preoccupied about the allocation of international reserves. In fact, this happened exactly when foreign reserve flows grew to such an extent that it became evident that some sterilization was required, given the danger of upsetting the country's internal monetary flows.

The Fiscal Contribution of Oil

The government's overall fiscal revenues, excluding those of government firms, increased twofold during the period being examined. Again, the jump experienced by petroleum revenues in 1973 was the principal cause of this extraordinary increase. Whether 1965 or 1966 is taken as base, the result is very similar when the increase is expressed in terms of annual compounded growth rates. These turn out to be between 10 and 11 percent as an average.

The petroleum sector contributed to this expansion by more than doubling the revenues it paid the Venezuelan government. However, it should be pointed out that, in 1969 and 1970, the relative share of petroleum's fiscal revenues decreased to less than 60 percent of the total (roughly 55 percent). The following years it experienced a recovery culminating in 1973, when petroleum-derived revenues represented 64 percent of total fiscal revenues. The average yearly compounded growth rate of revenues from petroleum fluctuated between 11 and 12 percent, respectively, whether the last year of the preceding period or the first year of this period is taken as base.

These fiscal revenue growth rates, which are a bit larger than those of GDP at current prices, are due, in great part, to the fiscal pressures applied to the petroleum sector during the period. The government forced the petroleum companies to apportion 80 percent of their profits to the state and 20 percent to themselves, basically through use of the income tax. At the same time, they were made to pay using reference or fiscal prices and not-realized or sale prices as base, although the latter are the ones the companies declared they had received.

The growth rates of both oil and total fiscal revenues are smaller if 1965 is used as a base year and larger if 1966 is used. The basic data for these calculations appear in Table 9.10. Finally, oil revenues also increased toward the end of the period, mostly as a result of the rapid rise in oil prices, even though the volume of oil sold also expanded significantly.

If the revenues resulting from the exchange rate differential applied to the oil sector are added, the contribution of oil would still be greater. The tax revenues derived from foreign exchange petroleum transactions rose at the same rate as the rest of its fiscal contribution, reaching the sum of 259 million bolívares in 1973. Table 9.10 shows the magnitude of the

Table 9.10.
Public Sector Fiscal Indicators, 1965–1973 (millions of bolívares)

	1965	1966	1967	1968	1969	1970	1971	1972	1973
Total Public Sector Revenues	8,202	8,430	9,600	9,865	9,804	10,854	13,172	13,979	17,867
Tax Revenues from Petroleum, excl. Foreign Exchange Taxes	4,863	5,143	5,866	6,075	5,597	5,885	7,860	8,138	11,440
As a Percent of Total Public Sector Revenues	59.3%	61.0%	61.1%	61.6%	57.1%	54.2%	59.7%	58.2%	64.0%
Foreign Exchange Tax Revenues on Petroleum	117	117	131	135	136	143	184	186	259
Tax Revenues from Petroleum, incl. Foreign Exchange Taxes	4980	5260	5997	6210	5733	6028	8044	8324	11,699
As a Percent of Total Public Sector Revenues	60.7%	62.4%	62.5%	63.0%	58.5%	55.5%	61.1%	59.5%	65.5%
Total Public Expenditures	8,251	8,809	9,668	10,615	11,516	12,137	13,971	15,102	17,386
Public Investment Expenditures	1,964	3,072	3,576	3,774	4,234	3,814	4,591	4,687	5,351
As a Percent of Total Public Expenditures	23.8%	34.9%	37.0%	35.6%	36.8%	31.4%	32.9%	31.0%	30.8%
Changes in Oil Revenues	--	280	737	213	-477	295	2016	280	3375
Changes in Public Investment	--	1,108	504	198	460	(420)	777	96	664
Cumulative Oil Revenues	--	10,240	16,237	22,447	28,180	34,208	42,252	50,576	62,275
Cumulative Public Investment	--	5,036	8,612	12,386	16,620	20,434	25,025	29,712	35,063

Notes: "Revenues" refer to current revenues (ingresos ordinarios), excluding the revenues of state enterprises and concession or service contract payments. Expenditure data excludes public enterprises.

Sources: Banco Central de Venezuela, *Memoria* (Caracas, several years), *Informe Económico* (Caracas, several years), and unpublished statistics; Ministerio de Minas e Hidrocarburos, *Petróleo y Otros Datos Estadísticos* (Caracas, 1972)

exchange rate differential contribution, which, when added to the rest of oil's fiscal contribution, increased its share in total government revenues to more than 65 percent in 1973.

It should be kept in mind that reference is being made to ordinary fiscal revenues only. Therefore, payments resulting from service contracts signed with petroleum companies are not included. However, these payments were much less than those resulting from the concessions awarded in 1957.

It is evident that oil's contribution to public finances is extremely important in Venezuela. Moreover, during this period its importance grew, contradicting the trend toward diversification, which became clear in the preceding period. Petroleum's participation in fiscal revenues during the 1966–1973 period represented 59.6 percent of the total, as an average. If the foreign exchange tax is included, this expands to 61.0 percent. In terms of GDP at current prices, oil's contribution amounted to 18.2 and 18.8 percent, respectively. All of this is a clear indication of the importance of petroleum's fiscal contribution and that it had become more relevant in this period.

The Utilization of Oil's Fiscal Contribution

One characteristic of these last years, as in the preceding period, was to have deficits in the government budgets. Only in 1973 was there a surplus.

This could easily be attributed to the fact that fiscal revenues in this year were greater than expected. The two years registering the greatest deficits were 1970 and 1972. This points to the fact that oil revenues were used in their entirety during the period and were even complemented by an increase in the public debt. Contrasting with the 1950s, when the Venezuelan Treasury accumulated reserves, the government did not sterilize petroleum's fiscal revenues and continued to increase the public debt and the influence of the public sector in the nation's economy.

In Table 9.10 it is clearly seen that the deficits have not been very large. It is also evident that the share of capital expenditures in total expenditures, after having increased during the years 1967, 1968, and 1969 to more than 36 percent as an average, decreased to roughly 30 percent toward the end of the period. Now, if the entire period were averaged out, the share of public investment would be 33 percent. Thus, one-third of public expenditures were channeled to capital formation.

As can be deduced from the above statements, public expenditures expanded considerably in this period. Just like public revenues, these expenditures doubled, growing at an average compounded growth rate of 10.2 percent per annum. Government capital spending did not increase as fast, but it did grow at 8.2 percent, as an average, from 1966 to 1973 (see Table 9.10). If the growth in public expenditures is compared to that experienced in the preceding period, it must be concluded that government activities were quite dynamic during the more recent period, and, looked at from this angle, it seems that oil's contribution was used much more efficiently. Also, the trajectory of government expenditures during these years was similar to that of government revenues, with no undue accumulation of Treasury reserves. As for government capital expenditures, their evolution has not been as favorable, when contrasted with that in the period 1957–1965. During the previous period, 40 percent of government spending was allocated to what was called, in a broad sense, development expenditures. As has been seen, during the years 1966 to 1973, only one-third of government expenditures were devoted to development expenditures. In this sense, oil's contribution was not employed as effectively.[19]

However, it should be pointed out that the 1957–1965 series and the most recent one are not strictly comparable. The last one excludes government enterprises, while the first one includes them. It has been impossible to homogenize the series, because the Central Bank does not have data on the capital and total spending of public firms for most of the recent years. Given that the expenditures of public firms were small relative to total government expenditures, and because their nature should not be that different from the rest of public spending, the rate of growth of total expenditures and its share of capital spending should not differ significantly, whether public firms are included or not. Moreover, given that the differences in the *rates* of development expenditures (capital spending) between both periods are noteworthy, it is difficult to imagine that the conclusions reached could be altered by the inclusion or not of public firms.

As to the effectiveness in the use of funds devoted to public investment, even though not comparable to the waste that characterized the 1950s, its allocation seems to have been less rational and efficient than in the preceding period. The continuous increase in petroleum revenues seemed to bring about a relaxation in the management of the fiscal funds, which contrasted with the care shown in the preceding period. This was particularly the case in the allocation of investments to agriculture, which were again hurt by sharing insufficiently in public finances. However, a very successful effort was undertaken in the industrial field. Because of the latter, an acceptable balance was maintained between investments in infrastructure and direct investments in productive activities.

Another indication of the effectiveness in the utilization of the funds generated by petroleum can be seen when comparing the change in oil-derived revenues with those of government investment during these years. Table 9.10 shows that annual changes in these variables have almost always been positive, which again contrasts with the preceding period. It is easy to see that the yearly increases have been much greater in the fiscal revenues generated by petroleum. Looking at the period as a whole, it is even clearer that the increase in petroleum's fiscal contribution was not utilized for investment or developmental purposes, as it should have been to be consonant with the broad interpretation of the "sow the oil" motto.

Approximately one-half of the increments in oil's fiscal revenues seem to have been devoted to public investment, even though it should be pointed out that the gaps between oil revenues and public investments began to appear in 1970, when oil revenues started to expand rapidly. It should be recognized, however, that government investment has been defined as excluding state enterprises, and, as such, it appears in Table 9.10; on the other hand, petroleum's foreign exchange tax revenues have not been included among the oil revenues. Considering all these factors, it should be concluded that, continuing the preceding period's trend, petroleum's fiscal contribution was not well utilized to promote Venezuela's economic development during this period.[20]

Summary

Petroleum's fiscal contribution was very important during this period, even more so than in the anteceding one. Oil's fiscal revenues grew rapidly due to a favorable world market situation, government pressure to increase petroleum taxes, and the prices charged for Venezuelan oil. Through this rapid expansion, the petroleum sector gave the necessary support for an expansion in the rest of the economy, given its high share in total fiscal revenues and the fast pace at which these revenues grew, helped to a great extent by those contributed by oil.

Nevertheless, the utilization of the fiscal contribution in many ways left a lot to be desired. Although the petroleum funds were used almost in their entirety, because there was no accumulation of Treasury reserves, the share of capital outlays decreased and the yearly increases in petroleum funds were not channeled into investment during the period. On the other hand, the allocation and application of the government investment funds seems not to have been well planned during these years. Therefore, even though oil's fiscal contributions increased during the period, in great part due to policies of the Venezuelan government, the authorities did not use this contribution as effectively as in the preceding period.

Venezuela's gross fixed investment increased rapidly during the 1966–1973 period, especially from 1968 on. In 1973, investment at 1957 prices almost doubled if compared to 1965, the last year of the previous period. This represented a complete turnabout, as real investment, although underestimated, appeared to decrease in the preceding period. This can be explained in terms of a more effective rate of capital utilization during 1958–1965, a smaller savings rate, and a restraint of investment in the petroleum sector. The first two aspects appear not to have operated during the years 1966 to 1973, seeming to imply that a point was reached when it was necessary to expand productive capacity, given the decrease in slack from the late 1950 levels.

Table 9.11 shows that the investment rate—that is, gross fixed investment divided by GDP, both at 1957 prices—increased during the period

Table 9.11.
Gross Domestic Product and Gross Fixed Domestic Investment, Oil Sector, 1965–1973 (millions of 1957 bolívares)

	1965	1966	1967	1968	1969	1970	1971	1972	1973
Total GDP	38,612	39,287	41,104	43,223	45,077	49,437	50,120	51,615	54,502
GDP, Oil Sector	9,444	8,990	9,625	9,794	10,058	10,874	9,842	8,404	8,646
GDP, Other Sectors	27,193	28,598	29,891	31,316	33,164	37,157	38,325	42,300	44,862
Oil as a Percent of GDP	24.5%	22.9%	23.4%	22.7%	22.3%	22.0%	19.6%	16.3%	15.9%
Gross Fixed Domestic Investment (GDFI)	5,558	5,920	6,118	7,164	7,496	7,635	8,532	9,499	11,068
Oil Sector	641	637	639	1,141	1,505	1,207	1,118	815	800
Other Sectors	4,917	5,283	5,479	6,023	5,991	6,428	7,414	8,684	10,268
Oil Investment as a Percent of GFDI	11.5%	10.8%	10.4%	15.9%	20.1%	15.8%	13.1%	8.6%	7.2%
GFDI as a Percent of GDP	14.4%	15.1%	14.9%	16.6%	16.6%	15.4%	17.0%	18.4%	20.3%

Notes: Oil and non-oil GDP do not add to total. See text for explanation of methodology and adjustments to data.

Sources: Banco Central de Venezuela, *Informe Económico* (Caracas, 1969 and 1972); Ministerio de Minas e Hidrocarburos, *Petróleo y Otros Datos Estadísticos* (Caracas, 1972); unpublished statistics from the Banco Central and the Ministerio de Minas e Hidrocarburos.

being considered. In 1973 the investment rate appeared just to be on the verge of returning to the greater than 20 percent levels that had character-ized the Venezuelan growth process, which was based on a fast rate of capital accumulation from the end of World War II up to the early 1960s.

Petroleum investment revived in the years 1968 to 1971, driven by the new service contracts between the government and the oil companies, by investments on petroleum desulfurizing, by new explorations, and by the push to increase known reserves. Nevertheless, it decreased abruptly dur-ing the last two years of the period, declining to figures that were lower than 10 percent of total Venezuelan investment, which had not occurred for over 30 years. The petroleum sector's investment, as a percentage of total investment, followed the course set by the former, surpassing the 20 percent level during the middle of the period and declining toward the end. After all, even though investment in the petroleum sector grew since the beginning of the period, its annual compounded rate of growth was 2.8 percent, while that of total investment was roughly around 9.0 percent.

As for the composition of petroleum investment, significant changes occurred. Investment in petroleum production per se greatly declined, contrary to what had occurred in the previous period. With respect to investment in transport capacity, its percentage in terms of total petroleum investment increased substantially, contradicting the previous period trend. Investment in refining facilities increased somewhat, again contra-dicting the tendency of the preceding period, in which it had considerably decreased proportionally.[21] All these investment data appear in Table 9.12.

The lack of dynamism of investment in the petroleum sector during the 1966–1973 period is noteworthy. Petroleum's investment average share of

Table 9.12.
Gross Fixed Investment in the Petroleum Sector by Type of Investment, 1965–1973 (millions of bolívares)

	1965	1966	1967	1968	1969	1970	1971	1972	1973
Total Investment in Petroleum	825	638	647	1,182	1,574	1,294	1,287	1,000	1,121
Production	718	502	514	870	855	943	945	758	829
As a Percent of Total	87.0%	78.7%	79.4%	73.6%	54.3%	72.9%	73.4%	75.8%	74.0%
Transportation	41	65	39	58	178	107	134	67	201
As a Percent of Total	5.0%	10.2%	6.0%	4.9%	11.3%	8.3%	10.4%	6.7%	17.9%
Refining	29	38	52	185	387	216	170	131	47
As a Percent of Total	3.5%	6.0%	8.0%	15.7%	24.6%	16.7%	13.2%	13.1%	4.2%
Marketing	12	13	21	8	17	20	11	7	5
As a Percent of Total	1.5%	2.0%	3.2%	0.7%	1.1%	1.5%	0.9%	0.7%	0.4%
Other	25	20	21	61	137	8	27	37	39
As a Percent of Total	3.0%	3.1%	3.2%	5.2%	8.7%	0.6%	2.1%	3.7%	3.5%

Source: Ministerio de Minas e Hidrocarburos, *Petróleo y Otros Datos Estadísticos* (Caracas, 1972), and unpublished data.

total investment had never been so low in previous periods, not even during the years 1936–1942, when oil was just becoming a prime mover in the Venezuelan economy. It is evident that oil's contribution, from the point of view of investment expenditures, even though significant, cannot be considered important during the recent period. In fact, this confirms a tendency set in the preceding period, which will probably continue indefinitely, because Venezuelan oil production will, at most, be maintained at the present absolute levels over the next years.

The weakness of investment in the petroleum sector in this period makes the dynamism of investment in the nonpetroleum sectors stand out even more. In real terms (at constant 1957 prices), gross fixed investment in the nonpetroleum part of the economy grew at a higher rate than total gross fixed investment, as can be seen in Table 9.11. The average annual compounded nonpetroleum investment growth rate was 9.6 percent.

The recuperation of the economy's investment outlays occurring during this period should be noted. As to the relationship that had existed between investment in the petroleum sector and that in the rest of the economy, which had become weaker during the previous period, it totally disappeared during these last years. This constitutes another proof of the increasing coming of age of the Venezuelan economy.

Investment in the petroleum sector was revived somewhat at the beginning of the period by service contract concessions and by some investments at the refining stage (mainly in oil desulfurizing); toward the end, petroleum was affected by the policy of conservation of oil resources and by the excess capacity existing in the industry. Contrastingly, investment in the rest of the economy expanded, as excess capacity in many sectors and aggregate demand grew as a result of the expansion of the public sector and of petroleum sector export values, the latter toward the end of the period.

As for the relationship between total gross fixed investment and the retained value of total petroleum expenditures, it seems to have been rather close during these years. The last variable is an expression of short-run activity in the oil sector, being expressed in current terms and, thus, reflecting changes in oil prices. Furthermore, it also reflects the increasing pressure applied by the Venezuelan government in order to increase the proportion of the industry's total expenditures retained by Venezuela. Thus, the evolution of total retained value of petroleum does not have to coincide with that of real investment in the petroleum sector, which responds to longer-run forecasts, reacts more sluggishly to current events, and is deflated to reflect real values. This explains why nonpetroleum investment accompanied the evolution of one (total retained value) and not the other (petroleum investment).

During this period, investment in the nonpetroleum part of the economy still represented a substantial part of oil's total value, even though a somewhat smaller one than in the previous period and, therefore, even smaller than in preceding subperiods. Even though it is still a point of controversy, it would seem that the productivity of Venezuelan investment, especially in the case of public investment, seemed at best to have been equivalent to that of the previous period. As a whole, the petroleum sector's direct and immediate contribution, through the retained value of its total expenditures, was not employed as well as in the previous period, in terms of an increase in quantity or quality of the country's productive capacity through capital formation.

In summary, the contribution of petroleum investment to the Venezuelan economy during this period is the smallest amount of investment made of all the time periods that have been examined. Furthermore, the use of this contribution apparently was not more fruitful than in earlier periods. Even though the relationship between investments in the petroleum and nonpetroleum sectors was weak, the latter increased substantially during the years 1966–1970. It is important to stress that nonpetroleum investment followed closely the trajectory of the total retained value of petroleum's expenditures, indicating that, although the impact of oil on total investment through its investment expenditures had not been significant, its total impact was.

TOTAL GROSS DOMESTIC PRODUCT AND THE EXPENDITURES OF THE OIL INDUSTRY

In order to study the impact of the current expenditures of the oil sector on the rest of the economy, the value of oil production will be examined more closely. In current terms, the value of oil production increased very slightly up to 1971, when it experienced a considerable increment. There was an even heartier increase in 1973. Actually, the latter part of the period represents a violent turnabout from the trend that Venezuelan oil had been observing ever since the mid-1960s. This was due to an increase in the demand for oil in the world markets, which was faster than foreseen, and to the increasing influence of the main oil-producing nations, which banded together in the Organization of Petroleum Exporting Countries (OPEC), to dictate oil prices. As for oil's GDP, in current bolívares, after declining in 1966 it experienced a continuous growth, with higher increments toward the end of the period. The compounded yearly rate of growth in the value of oil production was 7.2 percent, equivalent to an overall increase of 74.8 percent (see Table 9.13) during the period.

As for oil's GDP in current terms, it grew at an average compounded rate of 8.9 percent per annum during the period examined, faster than the value of production (see Table 9.13). Adjusting these figures for price inflation, and expressing them in 1957 bolívares, one finds that the GDP of the petroleum sector declined roughly 34 percent during the period as a

Table 9.13.
Retained Value of Oil Sector Expenditures, 1965–1972 (millions of bolívares)

	1965	1966	1967	1968	1969	1970	1971	1972
Retained Value of Total Expenditures	7,610	7,099	6,636	7,940	7,678	8,149	10,511	9,801
As Percent of Total Expenditures	63.3%	64.2%	66.1%	64.1%	61.9%	63.9%	69.4%	68.9%
Retained Value of Expenditures Per Barrel of Current Oil Produced (Bs.)	6.00	5.77	5.91	6.02	5.85	6.02	8.12	8.32
Total Value of Production	11,216	10,415	10,923	11,197	10,824	11,449	13,859	13,234
GDP Oil Sector	9,680	9,269	9,970	10,186	10,460	11,244	12,775	13,085

Note: Total retained value includes foreign exchange taxes on petroleum.

Source: Banco Central de Venezuela, *La Economía Venezolana en los Ultimos Treinta Años*
(Caracas, 1971), *Informe Económico* (Caracas, several years), and unpublished statistics;
Ministerio de Minas e Hidrocarburos, *Petróleo y Otros Datos Estadísticos* (Caracas, 1972).

whole, which represents a compounded yearly rate of decline of 0.4 percent as an average. Throughout the period, the share of petroleum's GDP in total GDP, in real terms, decreased substantially. This meant a continuation of the trend that was apparent in the previous period—a decrease in the relative importance of oil in economy. By 1973 the share of oil in total GDP had been reduced to 15.9 percent. During the interval examined, the share of oil in total GDP decreased to less than 20 percent for the first time, beginning in 1971. The average share for the period as a whole was 20.7 percent, comparable only to that found in the initial period, covering the years 1936–1942.[22]

After decreasing in 1966, oil's total retained value grew almost continuously during the following years, with slight reductions in 1969 and 1972 (see Table 9.13). These increases were basically caused by the rise in oil prices, through their effect in the value of oil production, by stronger tax pressures, and by the government tending to augment the share of the total expenditures of the industry retained in Venezuela. From 1965 to 1973, the total retained value of oil expenditures grew 98.5 percent, representing a yearly compounded growth rate of 8.9 percent. Using 1966 as the base year, the overall expansion of the total retained value during the period would have been 112.8 percent, equivalent to a yearly compounded rate of increase of 11.4 percent. At 1957 prices, this increment would be much less.

Petroleum's total retained value per barrel of oil produced, including petroleum foreign exchange taxes, doubled during the period, expanding at the same yearly rate of total retained value. If total retained value per barrel of oil is expressed 1957 prices, there still is an increase, but of much smaller importance.

As for retained value's share in total expenditures (value of production plus investment in the oil sector), it remained at about 65 percent until the final part of the period, when it rose to about 70 percent. Even though the share was increasing over the period, going from 63.3 percent in 1965 to 72.9 percent in 1973, the overall average was slightly lower than that of the preceding period. Actually, this was due to very high participation shares in the years 1961, 1962, and 1963, which were principally determined by the wide differential that existed between the foreign exchange rates applicable to oil and to the rest of the economy, which resulted in very sizable foreign exchange taxes on oil.

Contrary to the previous period, oil's total combined contribution to the economy grew very fast during the recent years. However, this high growth rate cannot be considered comparable to that experienced in the earlier periods, because it was not smooth, occurring mainly from 1971 on. Impelled in part by the growth in petroleum's contributions, expressed through the retained value of total petroleum expenditures, the GDP of Venezuela increased by 41.2 percent in real terms from 1965 to 1973. This is equivalent to a 3.5 percent yearly compounded growth rate, which is not very satisfactory (see Table 9.11).

It is important to make clear that these rates of change are calculated from our GDP estimates at 1957 prices. This series, which differed very little from those estimates presented by Venezuela's Central Bank in earlier periods, represents toward the end of the period examined an attempt to link two different series. This had to be done because for the last years of the period the Central Bank has only published estimates of real GDP in terms of 1968 prices. The linkage was made on the basis of Central Bank estimates at both 1957 and 1968 prices for the years 1968 and 1969. It should be pointed out that if the two series are kept separate instead of linking them, GDP growth estimates for the period would not be affected by much.[23] Moreover, considering that growth estimates toward the end of the period are calculated in constant 1968 bolívares, which have a smaller purchasing power than those of 1957, it is not surprising to find that growth is somewhat smaller in terms of the latter.

On the other hand, it is not difficult to explain the apparently small repercussion of the petroleum sector over the economy as a whole. It has been already noted that the effects of petroleum operate with a lag on Venezuela's overall economic activity and that petroleum expansion really took place in the last couple of years of the period considered. Moreover, when the expansion is expressed in real terms, then the effects of the terms of trade in total income are not noticeable. Given that the terms-of-trade effect was unquestionably favorable, especially in the last year of the period under examination, the conversion of petroleum income into real terms tends to underestimate the impact of petroleum on the economy.

The total GDP growth between 1966 and 1973 amounts to 38.7 percent, corresponding to a yearly compounded growth rate of 4.8 percent. It should be pointed out that the estimated growth was smaller in the period considered, even though it had a higher investment rate than in the previous one. It appears that in the present period it was necessary to undertake a faster increase in the process of capital accumulation, after having reduced excess capacity in the 1958–1965 period. Once again, this appears to show the dangers of relating the investment rate with the rate of growth of gross product during relatively short periods, since contradictions may appear with the direct relationship, found by Kuznets when longer historical periods are examined.

Examining now the behavior of the GDP of the nonpetroleum part of the economy (see Table 9.11), it is found that its total increase was 57.1 percent from 1966 to 1973. An increase of 65 percent is found, if the last year of the preceding period (1965) is taken as the base. Although these figures are greater than those corresponding to growth of total GDP, they represent annual compounded average changes of 6.5 and 6.7 percent, respectively, which are significantly smaller than those experienced by the nonpetroleum GDP in the previous period.[24]

The expansion of the petroleum sector's contributions to the Venezuelan economy was important only toward the end of the period and, in real terms, oil's GDP decreased. Therefore, it is not surprising that petroleum's impact during this period was much weaker than in the preceding one. The indication that, even toward the end of the period, the carryover of the oil sector's impulse to the rest of the economy seems to have been weak appears to be partly explained by the apparent loss of dynamism of the industrial import-substitution process and to the slackening of the agricultural sector's growth rate.

The Venezuelan economy, which had taken off in the previous subperiod, showed that it was not yet sufficiently independent of oil so that its nonpetroleum sector would not become affected by the adverse conditions encountered by Venezuelan oil up to the end of the 1966–1973 period. The signs that the process of import substitution was reaching a point of maturity and that the agricultural sector's growth process was being hindered by adverse policies and conditions appear to have been important factors also.

Although the agricultural production series, which had helped to interpret the sector's economic evolution, was recently discontinued, the estimates of GDP at 1957 prices in agriculture point out that the sectoral growth was less than 4.0 percent yearly, compounded, as an average, during these years (see Table 9.14). The unavailability of volume indexes, as well as the change in the base of the GDP series, renders different the detailing of those products that grew faster during this interval. The substantial decrease in the agricultural growth rate, when compared with the previous period, seems to have been due, to a great extent, to the fact that the priority given to agriculture was not so high in this period. The enthusiasm for agrarian

Table 9.14.
Gross Domestic Product in Selected Economic Sectors, 1965–1973 (millions of 1957 bolívares)

	1965	1966	1967	1968	1969	1970	1971	1972	1973
Agriculture	2,546	2,653	2,798	2,938	3,030	3,246	3,219	3,282	3,471
Construction	1,545	1,648	1,682	2,040	1,975	1,959	2,289	2,867	3,176
Utilities	738	808	894	1,041	1,147	1,287	1,422	1,517	1,682
Extractive, Excluding Petroleum	425	427	411	366	454	484	454	412	512
Transport and Communication	1,267	1,306	1,310	1,460	1,466	1,739	1,870	2,047	2,154
Commerce	5,455	5,695	5,907	6,344	6,501	7,139	7,431	7,809	8,199
Other Services	12,665	13,202	13,550	14,119	15,075	15,924	16,642	17,845	18,838
Total	19,387	20,203	20,832	21,293	23,402	24,802	25,943	27,701	29,191

Sources: Banco Central de Venezuela, *La Economía Venezolana en los Ultimos Veinticinco Años* (Caracas, 1966), *La Economía Venezolana en los Ultimos Treinta Años* (Caracas, 1972), and *Informe Económico* (Caracas, 1969 and 1972).

reform policies, which greatly stimulated agrarian production, began declining as the years passed, and, at the end of the period, the lack of dynamism in this sector constituted a general preoccupation in Venezuela.

Manufacturing production indexes and the detailed estimates of physical volumes presented in the first part of this chapter were also discontinued during the present term. However, the value added at 1957 prices by industrial category was estimated until 1972, and the manufacturing industry's GDP for the entire period was also available. By concentrating on the latter, and linking those series in 1957 prices with those in 1968 prices, both published by the Central Bank, the overall performance of the manufacturing sector can be evaluated. The cumulative growth in real GDP of manufacturing was above 6 percent per year as an average in this period.[25] These series include oil refining in the manufacturing sector. Evidently, the growth in manufacturing was much slower during this period, when compared with previous periods, and particularly with the pace of growth during the years 1958–1965.

Data on the value added, by type of manufacturing industry, are shown in Table 9.15. Those industries experiencing fastest growth were of the capital goods type: metallurgy and construction, assembly, and repair of machinery. The lumber and printing industries, producing in great part intermediate and capital goods, also grew very fast. These industries expanded at a faster pace than the manufacturing sector as a whole. It should be noted that no consumer goods-type industry grew faster than manufacturing as a whole, confirming the previously noted tendency of concentrated expansion in the capital and intermediate goods industries, although at more moderate absolute rates than in the preceding period.

As for the rest of the secondary activities, the production of water and electrical services more than doubled, as can be seen in Table 9.14. This

Table 9.15.
Index of Value Added in Manufacturing, 1965–1972 (1953 = 100)

	1965	1966	1967	1968	1969	1970	1971	1972	1972/65	1972/66
Food Processing	322.0	312.9	335.2	336.6	345.0	363.6	396.0	428.9	33.2%	37.1%
Beverage	229.9	238.7	257.9	263.7	291.4	308.9	326.8	357.2	55.4%	49.6%
Tobacco	346.1	349.4	376.2	400.5	411.3	432.4	460.0	526.7	52.2%	50.7%
Textile	440.2	441.4	459.1	487.3	515.6	531.6	572.5	644.1	46.3%	45.9%
Clothing and Apparel	199.1	206.6	213.0	214.5	231.4	245.3	271.8	289.5	45.4%	40.1%
Paper and Cardboard	1,269.2	1,283.3	1,336.6	1,485.0	1,498.4	1,597.3	1,677.3	1,851.6	45.9%	44.3%
Printing	262.1	282.3	331.3	372.0	403.4	430.4	466.6	506.3	93.2%	79.3%
Leather	262.0	295.6	279.1	263.0	257.5	276.3	289.0	305.8	16.7%	3.5%
Chemical	409.9	412.8	452.4	489.5	526.2	555.7	597.9	642.7	56.8%	55.7%
Timber	206.7	194.4	203.2	239.5	236.1	270.6	294.4	338.0	63.5%	73.9%
Furniture	329.0	356.5	377.1	389.5	426.1	449.1	473.8	498.9	51.6%	39.9%
Rubber	475.7	504.5	472.5	543.0	557.1	590.5	638.3	688.7	44.8%	36.5%
Construction Materials	220.0	217.0	236.2	244.4	228.8	237.0	270.9	312.1	41.9%	43.8%
Construction Assembly and Machinery Repair	554.1	605.9	692.9	769.8	890.7	925.4	948.5	1,149.6	107.5%	89.7%
Construction Assembly and Vehicle Repair	353.0	371.0	356.6	275.7	416.3	371.8	397.8	446.7	26.5%	20.4%
Metal Work	923.5	905.6	980.6	1,030.6	1,265.6	1,471.9	1,675.0	1,933.0	109.3%	113.4%
Basic Metals	4,389.0	4,096.0	4,878.1	5,823.0	5,165.0	5,934.6	6,124.5	6,332.7	47.6%	54.6%
Jewelry	313.8	307.4	321.6	337.7	349.9	372.6	391.2	435.8	38.9%	41.8%

Sources: Banco Central de Venezuela, *La Economía Venezolana en los Ultimos Treinta Años* (Caracas, 1971), and *Informe Económico* (Caracas, 1969).

expansion was of the order of 10.8 percent, when expressed in compounded annual average rates. However, these services represented a very small part of total GDP. The construction sector's growth was a shade lower than that of electricity and water, since they slightly more than doubled, attaining a compounded annual average growth rate of 9.4 percent during this time period. However, it must be recognized that construction has a greater weight on total GDP (see Table 9.14).

As pointed out before, the process of import substitution of manufactures, concentrated on intermediate and capital goods, was the main agent in the development of this sector. However, everything seems to indicate that the existence of a limited market and other production difficulties, together with the lack of an effort oriented to support the more efficient manufacturing lines, especially those with an export potential, were the key factors determining a smaller vitality in this sector.

The rapid growth of the utilities sector (electricity and water) was based not so much on the expansion of manufacturing and agriculture, but on the dynamism of the construction sector. In this respect, what occurred in this period differs again from the experience in the previous one, when manufacturing and agriculture grew more rapidly. It should also be considered that, even though the pace of expansion in electricity and water slowed down during this period, it still maintained a high growth rate, which can be partially attributed to the fact that those services were not yet sufficient to fill the needs of the entire Venezuelan society. At the same time, the expansion in the construction sector was mostly determined by the recovery of gross fixed investment that took place in the 1966–1973 period, as well as the high level of government expenditures taking place during those years.

The growth of the mining sector during these years, after petroleum is excluded, was as slow as it was in the preceding period. Mining activities expanded 20 percent overall, tantamount to a compounded annual rate of approximately 2.5 percent. This sector's GDP at 1957 prices moved somewhat erratically, with a considerable jump in 1973. If it had not been for this large increase, the sector's value added would have decreased during the years examined.

Finally, the rate of growth of tertiary activities also declined during these years. There generally exists a close relationship between the rate of growth of manufacturing and that of the tertiary sector, and this has been found to be applicable to Venezuela also. In this period, the expansion of tertiary activities in real terms was also smaller than the one in manufacturing. However, it was still larger than the expansion in primary activities, including oil. As may be seen in Table 9.14, tertiary activities increased more than 50 percent overall, which represents a compounded annual growth rate of approximately 5.3 percent as an average. Of all tertiary activities, transportation and communication, having grown by 70 percent, experienced the largest expansion in the period. Commercial and service activities grew at a smaller but still respectable rate of about 49 percent during these years. Given that commerce and services constitute most of the tertiary sector, the growth in transportation and communication did not have a significant effect on the magnitude of the expansion in tertiary production.

It was only toward the end of the period that oil began again to contribute substantially to the growth of the rest of the Venezuelan economy, through the increase in the retained value of its total expenditures. Although there has generally been a lag between the growth in petroleum's contributions and the growth of the economy's nonpetroleum sectors, the response to the substantial expansion of the oil sector from 1971 on appears to have been exceptionally delayed. This may have been due to the irregularity in the growth of total retained value of oil expenditures, which jumped ahead in 1971, contracted in 1972, and advanced even more in 1973. But it could have also been that the mechanism of transmission of the oil sector's expansion to the rest of the economy might not have been operating so effectively during the 1970s given the structural change experienced by the economy of Venezuela. On the other hand, the effectiveness in the use of petroleum's contributions (especially the fiscal one) left a lot to be desired during this period, and this may also help explain the slower and weaker reaction.

By some combination of these reasons, the impact of petroleum in 1971 and the following years does not seem to have brought about a corresponding increase in the real product of the nonpetroleum part of the economy. Yet, it did bring about a considerable increase in the Venezuelan investment rate.[26] Also, the favorable terms-of-trade effects, resulting from the rapid rise in petroleum prices, substantially raised the total income of the Venezuelan society, in current terms, through its international exchange.

All of this demonstrates the need to carefully analyze the effects that the expansion of retained value of total petroleum expenditures had on the nonpetroleum GDP during this period. This will probably shed further light on the operation of the mechanism of transmission of an oil expansion to the rest of the economy, under the conditions given by the change in Venezuela's economic structure. It is also possible that what appears to be a time lag in the reaction of the nonpetroleum sectors to a considerable increase in petroleum contributions is actually a sample of the increasing independence of the rest of the economy since the end of the 1950s.

The per capita growth of the Venezuelan economy in real terms was rather small during these years, because of its high population growth rate. Per capita GDP grew from 4,427 to 4,810 bolívares (constant 1957 bolívares), representing an overall increase of 8.6 percent from 1965 to 1973. When expressed as an average yearly compounded rate, this figure amounts to roughly 1 percent. However, the nonpetroleum sector expanded at a rate that, if not comparable to that of the previous period, at least could be considered satisfactory. At the same time, these sectors continued to bolster their independence from oil, which began to constitute a smaller part of Venezuela's GDP in real or constant terms.

What seems to demand greater attention is finding ways to improve, through economic policy measures, the transmission of the positive benefits that the petroleum sector might be able to generate in the future, given that the means of ensuring that its adverse conditions, which seem to have been developed during the 1960s, are not carried over to the rest of the economy. Equally important is the thinking through of new strategies for expanding the nonpetroleum sectors, since the process of import substitution of manufactured products appears to have lost its dynamism in Venezuela.[27]

NOTES

1. Ministerio de Minas e Hidrocarburos, *Petróleo y Otros Datos Estadísticos* (Caracas, 1965), p. 131.

2. Reserves were still relatively high when the exchange controls were established in 1960, but they had halved between 1957 and 1960.

3. Note that in this period these calculations were made in terms of current bolívares.

4. However, it must be recognized that Venezuela had been able to put these reserves aside as a result of a strong showing by the petroleum industry in previous periods.

5. The foreign exchange tax proceeds calculated in this fashion differ from the foreign exchange profits reported by the government because of the following: (1) during a given year, the amount of foreign currency turned in by the petroleum companies is not necessarily equal to the amount sold by the Central Bank, and on which profits are made; and (2) the government reports the combined net profits in the Central Bank's operations, and usually there have been losses as a result of subsidies to other sectors, as well as profits derived from other industries, and also the expenses incurred in the operation of the program are deducted. Moreover, the figures presented in this study are an approximation obtained by multiplying the foreign exchange sold by the oil companies to the Central Bank during a year by the difference between the petroleum buying rate and the official rate (called "controlled official rate" since 1960) up to 1960, and the petroleum buying rate and the controlled free buying rate from 1961 to 1964. From 1964 on, the difference again reverted to the pre-1961 system. This is an approximation, because the actual profits derived from oil result from complicated operations, with different types of buying and selling rates by the Central Bank and the commercial banks and changes in these rates over time. Moreover, not all petroleum-supplied foreign exchange has been bought by the Central Bank at the established rates. Whenever the supply of foreign exchange from petroleum companies exceeds the demand for foreign exchange by the Venezuelan economy, a lower buying rate can apply, corresponding to the gold import point. On certain occasions, this rule has been put into effect.

6. In January 1964 the petroleum rate was devalued to 4.40 bolívares per dollar.

7. If the exchange tax is not included, oil revenues amounted to 4,803 million bolívares in 1964 and 4,863 million bolívares in 1965, a rise from the tax level of 3,659 million bolívares in 1963. With the exchange tax included, the 1963 figure was 5,625 million bolívares, with 4,901 million and 4,980 million bolívares, respectively, in 1964 and 1965.

8. Keep in mind that, in 1956 and 1957, the oil industry made concession payments of 974 million and 1,142 million bolívares, respectively, to the Venezuelan government.

9. As shall be seen later, the GDP series has been revised by the Central Bank, while the investment figures were not. As the GDP estimates were corrected upward, there is reason to believe that gross fixed investment has been underestimated in turn. This would particularly affect the investment rate, which is the relation between those two variables.

10. From 1957 to 1965, production rose at a compounded annual average rate of 2.9 percent.

11. This does not mean that the Venezuelan economy could continue to achieve long-run growth in per capita terms without at least some moderate expansion in the oil sector at this moment. However, the rest of the economy was beginning to move on its own to a greater extent. A continuation of this trend would eventually lead to a situation in which the rest of the economy would not be much affected by the oil sector in the determination of its level of activity, except in the short run.

12. All of these estimates would have been larger if they had included the income originated in the production of capital goods for the petroleum industry's own use.

13. These receipts are defined as the loss of income to the petroleum sector of a less-favorable conversion of foreign currency into bolívares.

14. This figure may be exaggerated, as the national account figures were revised in 1970 by the Central Bank. The revisions of the GDP were generally upward, but were only covered back to 1960. Thus, it might be inferred that the 1957–1959 figures shown in Table 9.5 are underestimated.

15. The growth rate in nonpetroleum GDP is probably overestimated, because the revisions undertaken by the Central Bank in the GDP figures largely affected the nonpetroleum sectors.

16. It was not possible to present accurate estimates of the overall increase in manufacturing production without petroleum refining for the whole period. See Banco Central de Venezuela, *La Economía Venezolana en los Ultimos Treinta Años* (Caracas, 1971), Sector Secundario.

17. Note that the base from which this growth took place is comparatively small. Thus, the relative rate of increase is exaggerated.

18. Witness the slow growth of investment vis-a-vis the total GDP.

19. Curiously, investment outlays expanded year after year (see Table 9.10), with the exception of 1970. However, its share of total expenditures declined significantly during the interval, although erratically, since it practically increased until 1969, declining from then on.

20. Toward the end of the period, government investment, excluding state enterprises, accounted for less than one-half of oil's total revenues.

21. It is interesting to note that, toward the end of the period, investment in petroleum refining had increased until it represented 25 percent of overall investment in the petroleum sector.

22. As in preceding periods, the product originated by the petroleum sector in the production of capital goods for its own use has not been included.

23. See GDP estimates at constant prices in Banco Central de Venezuela, *Informe Económico* (Caracas, 1969, 1972, and 1973).

24. This conclusion would still hold, even after taking into account the possible overestimation of the growth in nonpetroleum GDP during the 1958–1965 interval.

25. See the manufacturing industry's GDP in *Informe Económico* (Caracas, 1969, 1972, and 1973).

26. It is possible that the increase in investment might have been tied to the slow reaction of the rest of the economy. The economy appears to have been affected by restrictions in capacity and even bottlenecks in certain sectors, which require a special effort in the investment sector.

27. Economic policies to ensure the sustained and fast growth of the agricultural sector should be considered here. This would allow Venezuela to continue and conclude a take-off period in the 1970s and to foresee the possibility of self-sustaining growth from the 1980s on.

CHAPTER 10

1974–1985

In this chapter we will examine in detail the distinct types of contributions that the oil industry made to other sectors in the Venezuelan economy during the oil boom that lasted from the mid-1970s to the mid-1980s. This provided Venezuela with a fresh and unique opportunity to "sow its oil."

THE IMPORTANCE OF OIL IN THE FOREIGN SECTOR

During the period from 1974 to 1985, the contribution of the oil industry in Venezuela's external commerce was greater than at any other time in its history and even surpassed, in relative importance, its performance in the prosperous years of the 1950s.

The world shortage of petroleum—resulting from the Arab-Israeli Yom Kippur War and the Middle East tensions that continued thereafter, and from the growth of worldwide demand for oil—caused prices of crude oil to more than triple in 1974 (from $3.42 to $10.35 per barrel). At the same time, after growing at an annual rate of 5.4 percent from 1974 to 1978, the average price of crude oil increased rapidly in 1979, and ultimately reached a level of $19.88 per barrel. The increase in oil prices of the later 1970s led to increases in non-OPEC sources of supply as well as declines in world demand. The mid-1980s were therefore characterized by significant declines in the world market price of crude oil. The volume of petroleum exports declined during the 1974–1985 period, and as world prices fell during the latter part of this period so did the value of petroleum exports.

Venezuela's current account revenues on a gross basis for the petroleum sector appear in Table 10.1. This table also indicates the contribution of

Table 10.1.
Petroleum Sector Indicators and External Sector Performance, 1973–1985

	1973	1974	1975	1976	1977	1978	1979	1980	1981	1982	1983	1984	1985
Total Exports (Mill. US$)	5,201	11,973	10,094	10,378	10,948	10,856	16,306	22,232	24,519	20,122	17,341	18,067	16,901
Oil Exports (Mill. US$)	4,618	10,875	8,739	8,864	9,383	8,962	14,132	19,279	20,413	16,410	14,000	15,100	13,054
As a Percent of Total	88.8%	90.8%	86.6%	85.4%	85.7%	82.6%	86.7%	86.7%	83.3%	81.6%	80.7%	83.6%	77.2%
Foreign Exchange Earnings From All Sources (Mill. US$)	--	13,217	13,261	13,914	16,821	24,010	39,138	39,469	50,129	80,246	37,813	20,728	17,078
Oil (Mill. US$)	--	9,377	8,549	6,735	7,576	6,920	9,098	12,641	18,961	18,984	13,335	14,212	12,386
Oil as a Percent of Foreign Exch. Earnings	--	70.9%	64.5%	48.4%	45.0%	28.8%	23.2%	32.0%	37.8%	23.7%	35.3%	68.6%	72.5%
International Reserves	--	6,581	9,243	9,285	9,129	7,599	8,819	8,885	11,409	11,624	12,181	14,303	15,478
Import Capacity	--	248.8	349.5	445	641.8	696.6	674.9	729.3	775.9	842.6	--	--	--
Terms of Trade	--	424.5	353.5	357	366.9	352.9	543.9	738	773.1	634.3	--	--	--

Note: Index value 1968 = 100.

Sources: Banco Central de Venezuela, *Anuario de Cuentas Nacionales* (various issues); Ministerio de Minas e Hidrocarburos, *Petróleo y Otros Datos Estadísticos* (various issues).

petroleum exports to foreign exchange inflows corresponding to each year within the period being considered. These data show that petroleum revenues in the current account grew by 20 percent between 1974 and 1985, representing an annual average growth rate of 1.9 percent. If, however, one compares 1985 with 1973, then one finds that revenues have tripled since 1973. Foreign exchange inflows from 1983 to 1985, however, fell rather sharply owing to the steep declines in oil export revenues. The decline in oil revenues was large enough to result in a drop in the relative share of this industry's exports in total current account exports. By 1985 this share had fallen to its lowest level during the period. The nationalization of the petroleum industry, however, fostered a large increase in foreign borrowing, and the inflow of foreign exchange grew at an annual average rate of 2.85 and 3.08 percent, respectively, for the petroleum sector and for all other sectors between 1973 and 1985. It is evident that the contribution of the petroleum industry to inflows of foreign exchange reached very high levels during this period, despite periodic fluctuations in the average export price of crude oil and the OPEC-required reductions in the volume of exports. Despite continuing efforts by Venezuela's government to increase nontraditional exports, the country was still dependent on petroleum revenues as its primary source of foreign exchange earnings. This dependence grew toward the end of the period as a result of the drastic declines in foreign lending to Venezuela, and foreign direct investment in the country.

The data appearing in Table 10.1 illustrate the results achieved by the rapid rise in the price of crude oil. The index of terms of trade was drastically affected by rising world oil prices to the point of reaching a level of 424.5 in 1974 after having been placed only at 142.5 during 1973. The terms of trade index reached a peak value of 773.1 in 1981, culminating a strong ascent that began anew in 1979.

Table 10.1 reveals that international reserves have increased rather steadily over the period being considered. The increase in reserves is even more pronounced if one takes 1973 as the year of comparison. It is also important to note that in 1982 two things occurred that did not allow the level of international reserves to diminish appreciably, despite the decline in oil export earnings. In the first place, nonoperating reserves grew due to the revaluation of gold reserves of the Central Bank of Venezuela. This represented an increase of nearly $2.7 billion. In the second place, the Central Bank of Venezuela began reporting the external assets of Petróleo de Venezuela, the national petroleum firm.

The considerable growth in inflows of foreign exchange by Venezuela permitted the process of capital formation, public expenditures, and production to continue without impediment, and in many cases achieving extraordinary growth. The inflow of foreign exchange also permitted significant increases in domestic demand while maintaining low levels of inflation. The growth of domestic demand that could not be satisfied by domestic production was satisfied by increases in imports. Toward the end of the period being considered, however, the government saw the need for limiting the use of foreign exchange, as a consequence of the large burden of interest payments on the external debt and the expected lower price of exported crude oil.

To determine if the resources originated by the external sector of the petroleum industry were utilized efficiently during this period, one may examine Table 10.2, which reveals the evolution of total import composition. We can observe that during the first five years of the period, imports of capital goods grew progressively in relative and absolute terms, and the relative share of imports in real terms of consumer goods and intermediate goods fell gradually. This implies, overall, that foreign exchange resources were utilized largely to increase productive capacity during the early part of this period. Beginning in 1979, however, we observe a

Table 10.2.
Imports F.O.B. by Use of Commodity, 1974–1985 (millions of bolívares)

	1974	1975	1976	1977	1978	1979	1980	1981	1982	1983	1984	1985
Capital Goods	3,629	5,985	8,677	13,574	14,842	11,118	10,961	11,949	11,816	6,926	8,254	12,176
As Percent of Total	22.3%	26.2%	29.8%	32.4%	32.6%	27.0%	24.0%	23.6%	23.6%	20.5%	17.4%	22.0%
Intermediate Goods	10,765	14,511	17,326	23,827	24,735	24,401	27,876	31,187	30,858	23,057	33,506	36,440
As Percent of Total	66.2%	63.6%	59.5%	56.8%	54.4%	59.1%	61.0%	61.5%	61.7%	68.4%	70.5%	66.0%
Consumer Goods	1,859	2,331	3,116	4,520	5,924	5,742	6,898	7,546	7,382	3,736	5,789	6,640
As Percent of Total	11.4%	10.2%	10.7%	10.8%	13.0%	13.9%	15.1%	14.9%	14.8%	11.1%	12.2%	12.0%

Source: Banco Central de Venezuela, *Anuario de Cuentas Nacionales* (various issues).

marked decline in the relative share of capital goods in total imports, even reaching a low point of 17.4 percent in 1984. The beginning of the 1980s was also marked by private capital flight, which represented a nonproductive use of the economy's foreign exchange resources.

In general, the 1974–1985 period was characterized by an economic expansion fueled by petroleum exports. This economic expansion elevated foreign exchange flows and average living standards to unprecedented levels. The rapid growth in foreign exchange, together with certain errors in fiscal, financial, and commercial policies, led to radical changes in the structure of the economy and delayed the import substitution program that had begun at the beginning of the democracy. Nevertheless, the growth of Venezuela's exports and OPEC exports in general served as an incentive for the international banking community to provide foreign savings to countries like Venezuela, which at that time were in a period of intermediate industrialization.

On balance, the contribution made by petroleum exports to the long-term economic growth prospects of Venezuela were rather modest in comparison to what would have been possible had foreign exchange resources been more heavily channeled into private investment spending and the process of import substitution had continued.

THE OIL INDUSTRY'S CONTRIBUTION TO GOVERNMENT REVENUES

Ordinary revenues of the general government were strongly influenced by the changes that occurred in the international oil market over the 1974–1985 period. After the rapid rise in revenues coming from petroleum during 1974, these revenues stabilized and then fell appreciably as oil's revenues declined in following years. Significantly, the share of petroleum revenues fell gradually to 56.5 percent of total revenues in 1978. As a consequence of the rise in petroleum prices in the 1979–1981 period, the fiscal contribution of the petroleum sector grew again, in both relative and absolute terms (see Table 10.3). In the years following 1981, excess supply conditions in the world oil market brought as a consequence a drastic reduction in government revenues generated by the petroleum output. The decline in oil revenues together with increasing reliance on alternative revenue sources resulted in a decline in petroleum's share of government revenues.

It is important to note that if we add to these ordinary revenues the implicit taxes generated through exchange rate differentials, the fiscal contribution of the oil sector would be more pronounced. Due to the existence of multiple exchange rates during this period, these implicit revenues fluctuated without a discernable trend. These implicit taxes ranged from a minimum of 138 million bolívares in 1978 to a maximum of 20,901 million in 1985. The implicit revenues from this concept appear in Table 10.3.

Table 10.3.
Public Sector Fiscal Indicators, 1974–1985 (millions of bolívares)

	1974	1975	1976	1977	1978	1979	1980	1981	1982	1983	1984	1985
Total Public Sector Revenues	45600	46000	43700	47200	45710	53896	71092	100826	87624	88501	117812	125234
Tax Revenues from Petroleum, excl. Foreign Exchange Taxes	36445	31648	28012	29407	25810	33308	45331	70885	49223	40546	60561	62103
As a Percent of Total Public Sector Revenues	79.9%	68.8%	64.1%	62.3%	56.5%	61.8%	63.8%	70.3%	56.2%	45.8%	51.4%	49.6%
Foreign Exchange Tax Revenues on Petroleum	938	855	674	152	138	182	253	379	380	13302	11192	20901
Tax Revenues from Petroleum, incl. Foreign Exchange Taxes	37383	32503	28686	29559	25948	33490	45584	71264	49603	53848	71753	83004
As a Percent of Total Public Sector Revenues	82.0%	70.7%	65.6%	62.6%	56.8%	62.1%	64.1%	70.7%	56.6%	60.8%	60.9%	66.3%

Sources: Banco Central de Venezuela, *Anuario de Cuentas Nacionales* (various issues); Ministerio de Minas e Hidrocarburos, *Petróleo y Otros Datos Estadísticos* (various issues).

Regarding the utilization of the fiscal contribution of the petroleum sector, one should note that not only did fiscal receipts grow substantially, but also expenditures rose more proportionally as well. This translated into chronic fiscal deficits during the years in question.

The data in Table 10.4 reveal that while total government outlays rose substantially, the share of outlays dedicated to investment declined radically, even after having achieved unprecedented values in the beginning of the period. One must point out that the component of investment outlays most affected was the one devoted to "financial" investment, which was reduced approximately by one-third between 1974 and 1985.

Public investment outlays were reduced not only in relative terms, but also in absolute terms. Although this situation worsened toward the end of the period due to economic recession and the fall in petroleum export prices, we may conclude that the fiscal contribution of the retained value

Table 10.4.
Public Investment, Public Outlays, and Changes in Petroleum Revenues, 1974–1985 (millions of bolívares)

	1974	1975	1976	1977	1978	1979	1980	1981	1982	1983	1984	1985
Public Outlays	43,487	42,214	45,038	57,238	57,267	54,020	76,480	98,155	98,658	85,746	93,678	104,051
Public Investment	26,213	21,377	19,842	26,445	24,258	13,714	25,668	34,040	28,520	21,495	19,115	20,834
Investment as a Percent of Outlays	60.3%	50.6%	44.1%	46.2%	42.4%	25.4%	33.6%	34.7%	28.9%	25.1%	20.4%	20.0%
Change in Public Investment	20,862	-4,836	-1,535	603	-1,987	-10,744	11,954	8,372	-5,520	-7,025	-2,380	1,719
Oil Revenues	25,005	-4,797	-3,636	1,395	-3,597	7,498	12,023	25,554	-21,662	-8,677	20,015	1,542
Change in Public Investment as a Percent of Oil Revenues	83.4%	100.8%	42.2%	43.2%	55.2%	-143.3%	99.4%	32.8%	25.5%	81.0%	-11.9%	111.5%

Notes: Public investment includes financial investments. Oil revenues do not include revenues from exchange differential.

Source: Banco Central de Venezuela, *Anuario de Cuentas Nacionales* (Caracas, various issues).

of petroleum expenditures was not effectively employed. This may have been the result of redirecting fiscal resources to noninvestment expenditures due to the substantial growth in revenues, or perhaps because of the lack of a coherent fiscal policy.

In summary, the fiscal revenues from petroleum were, in absolute terms, the most pronounced to date in the history of the industry. The fiscal revenues derived from petroleum grew substantially due to the existence of a favorable situation in the petroleum world market and the culmination of the nationalization process of the industry. Throughout the period, the petroleum sector generated extraordinary support to the growth of the rest of the economy as is evident by the growth of total fiscal revenues, especially if the exchange differential is included. However, this elevated contribution, which could have facilitated the redirection of public expenditures, was not well utilized as is evidenced by the sharp decline in public investment outlays.

THE CONTRIBUTION OF OIL INVESTMENT

During the first five years of the period studied, fixed total investment grew at an accelerated pace, reaching a peak level in 1978. However, this important variable was adversely affected toward the end of the 1974–1985 period. By 1985, total investment expenditures had actually fallen below the 1974 levels.

Table 10.5 illustrates that during the late 1970s and early 1980s, investment as a share of GDP rose to very high levels. After 1982, however, this ratio declined virtually as rapidly as it had risen in the earlier period. The decline in the investment ratio is even more impressive when one considers that GDP was also declining. The pattern of investment spending witnessed from 1974 to 1985 can be explained by the changing economic environment of the time. In the early part of the decade the growth of internal demand was very strong and growth of domestic capital was required to alleviate capacity constraints. As the decade progressed, private capital flight, scarcity of qualified resources, potential devaluations, and lack of demand could be listed as the principal reasons for the drastic fall in the investment rate.

The changes in investment in the petroleum sector resulted largely from the nationalization of the industry. It was not until this process was completed by the beginning of the 1980s that the contribution of the industry to total investment was back in line with previous (normal) levels. While nonpetroleum sector investment was declining in early 1980, petroleum sector investment was increasing. Over the entire decade petroleum investment grew at an average annual rate of 5.18 percent while total investment fell, thereby increasing the relative importance of this industry in total fixed capital formation.

Table 10.5.
Gross Fixed Domestic Investment, Oil Sector, 1974–1985 (millions of 1957 bolívares)

	1974	1975	1976	1977	1978	1979	1980	1981	1982	1983	1984	1985
Total GDP	53,293	56,523	61,487	65,622	67,023	67,922	66,583	66,367	66,817	63,077	62,222	62,378
Gross Fixed Domestic Investment (GFDI):	13,222	16,612	21,342	27,522	28,619	22,883	19,562	20,149	19,397	14,287	11,592	12,432
Oil Sector	1,235	657	556	943	1,524	2,053	2,707	3,567	4,317	3,061	2,224	2,090
Other Sectors	11,987	15,955	20,787	26,580	27,095	20,830	16,854	16,582	15,080	11,226	9,368	10,343
Oil Investment as a Percent of GFDI	9.3%	4.0%	2.6%	3.4%	5.3%	9.0%	13.8%	17.7%	22.3%	21.4%	19.2%	16.8%
GFDI as a Percent of GDP	24.8%	29.4%	34.7%	41.9%	42.7%	33.7%	29.4%	30.4%	29.0%	22.7%	18.6%	19.9%
Distribution of Oil Investment:												
Production	76.8%	54.6%	91.3%	83.0%	66.1%	65.9%	62.0%	65.3%	76.9%	81.7%	84.4%	80.2%
Transport	8.3%	16.4%	0.0%	0.6%	6.1%	0.0%	0.4%	9.3%	1.8%	4.9%	0.4%	0.5%
Refining	5.8%	11.9%	2.1%	7.3%	18.1%	30.7%	32.6%	20.7%	16.3%	6.3%	4.9%	5.8%
Sales	0.8%	2.1%	1.6%	3.4%	2.3%	2.0%	3.1%	2.5%	2.0%	2.3%	3.3%	8.7%
Other	8.3%	15.0%	5.0%	5.7%	7.4%	1.5%	1.9%	2.2%	3.0%	4.9%	7.0%	4.9%

Notes: Investment in oil sector reported on a GDP accounting basis. Distribution of oil investment based on Ministerio de Energía y Minas data definitions that are different from GDP accounting methodology.

Sources: Banco Central de Venezuela, Anuario de Cuentas Nacionales (Caracas, various issues); Ministerio de Minas e Hidrocarburos, Petróleo y Otros Datos Estadísticos (Caracas, various issues).

Petroleum sector investment was largely directed to production fields, refining, and marketing, which was consistent with changes that occurred within the industry. Substantial amounts of investment occurred during a period when petroleum production was actually falling gradually. Investment was necessary despite declining output because of the need to increase known reserves, which by 1973 had fallen to a level equivalent to only 11 years of production. Table 10.5 provides data on petroleum investment. The expansion that occurred in petroleum investment stands in direct contrast to the instability that characterized nonpetroleum fixed investment.

Although petroleum revenues generated large surpluses that represented increasing levels of retained values by this public enterprise, these had little or no discernable impact on gross fixed capital formation. It is important to note, however, that private investment fell substantially midway through this decade and toward the end of the period. It was affected by the external crisis suffered by many Latin American countries from 1983 to 1985.

In conclusion, the contribution of the petroleum industry revenues to the Venezuelan economy during this period was most significant. Despite large increases in petroleum sector investment, it was not sufficient to offset declines in investment in other sectors. Gross fixed capital formation for the economy as a whole fell even while the retained values of the petroleum industry increased. The economy's rate of capital formation declined during this period.

It is important to note that the retained values in the petroleum industry (Table 10.5) were calculated by subtracting from its total receipts the direct costs and depreciation expenses incurred. Revised oil capital formation, as well as implicit taxes resulting from the exchange rate differential tax, were considered when calculating the total retained values of petroleum.

THE CONTRIBUTION TO GROSS NATIONAL PRODUCT OF EXPENDITURES BY THE OIL INDUSTRY

In nominal terms, the value of petroleum production doubled during the period, growing at an annual average rate of 6.28 percent. This was the result of continuous increases in the price of crude oil that took place during nearly the entire period under study. In the years in which the market prices of oil fell, currency devaluations resulted in an increase in the domestic currency value of petroleum production.

Retained values per barrel of petroleum produced quadrupled during the period, growing at a higher rate than total retained values. This results from a gradual decline in the volume of production measured in terms of barrels produced. It is interesting to note that the retained value of expenditures by the petroleum industry represented approximately 90 percent of its total expenditures during most of the period (see Table 10.6). Before the nationalization of the industry, concessionaires were encouraged to increase their domestic expenditures.

Table 10.6.
Retained Value of Oil Sector Expenditures, 1974–1985

	1974	1975	1976	1977	1978	1979	1980	1981	1982	1983	1984	1985
Total Oil Sector Expenditures (Mill. Bs.)	49,923	40,510	40,185	44,889	42,992	66,974	89,830	99,069	88,053	75,868	106,465	102,134
Retained Value of Oil Expenditures (Mill. Bs.)	45,430	36,054	38,979	41,747	38,693	59,607	81,745	90,153	73,084	80,420	107,530	112,347
Ratio of Retained Value to Expenditures	0.91	0.89	0.97	0.93	0.9	0.89	0.91	0.91	0.83	1.06	1.01	1.1
Retained Value per barrel of Oil (Bs.)	41.83	42.12	46.4	51.1	48.98	69.31	103.08	117.23	105.61	122.4	162.92	182.81
Retained Value of Oil Expenditures (Mill. 1957 Bs.)	9,270	7,012	7,209	7,136	7,122	7,462	6,935	7,252	6,500	7,589	6,727	7,080

Notes: Oil sector expenditures include capital expenditures. Retained value of oil expenditures includes revenues from exchange differential and does not include capital expenditures.

Sources: Banco Central de Venezuela, *Anuario de Cuentas Nacionales* (Caracas, various issues); Ministerio de Minas e Hidrocarburos, *Petróleo y Otros Datos Estadísticos* (Caracas, various issues).

After nationalization, there was a clear public policy to channel petroleum revenues to domestic suppliers. Both actions were meant to lift multiplier impacts on the domestic economy. In addition, the exchange rate differential yielded considerable revenues to the government and thus helped to finance the growth of public spending. This policy also had stimulative effects on the domestic economy. The proportion of petroleum GDP to total GDP is given in Table 10.7.

Despite the considerable increase in the petroleum sector's revenues, GDP originating in the petroleum sector declined between 1974 and 1985 owing to the decline in the volume of production. The stimulative effects of increased petroleum sector-related expenditures and public spending were only partially successful in generating GDP growth. Between 1974 and 1985, GDP grew at a rate of 1.5 percent in real terms. GDP in nonpetroleum sectors grew at a rate of 2.2 percent in real terms. The growth performance was indeed disappointing. These figures, however, may be somewhat misleading because very large increases in real output occurred in 1974, and if one uses 1973 as a point of comparison, the growth rates are somewhat higher.

A sector-by-sector examination of GDP presents a somewhat mixed picture. We may note from Table 10.7 that agricultural GDP in real terms grew at an annual average growth rate of 2.53 percent. This result is disappointing for a country with such a high agricultural potential. It appears to be the result of failure to initiate a coherent agricultural policy,

Table 10.7.
Value of Oil Production, GDP Originating in the Oil Sector, and Total GDP by Sector, 1974–1985 (millions of 1957 bolívares)

	1974	1975	1976	1977	1978	1979	1980	1981	1982	1983	1984	1985
Total GDP:	58,236	61,769	67,187	71,704	73,237	74,215	72,739	72,520	73,014	68,913	67,980	68,167
Value of Oil Production	47,871	39,174	38,884	42,473	38,920	60,930	80,845	86,508	71,784	63,769	95,664	91,250
GDP Originating in the Oil Sector	44,636	34,472	36,536	38,537	35,293	55,392	73,677	77,335	64,726	50,257	88,412	85,130
Oil Sector GDP	8,645	6,705	6,757	6,587	6,497	6,935	6,251	6,222	5,758	5,499	5,532	5,365
Oil GDP as a Percent of Total GDP	14.8%	10.9%	10.1%	9.2%	8.9%	9.3%	8.6%	8.6%	7.9%	8.0%	8.1%	7.9%
Other Sector of GDP:	49,537	55,047	60,419	65,115	66,743	67,277	66,494	66,304	67,271	63,427	62,459	62,815
Agriculture	3,795	4,062	3,915	4,222	4,358	4,485	4,569	4,484	4,644	4,663	4,700	4,967
Electricity, Water, Public Utility	1,214	1,422	1,510	1,620	1,606	1,854	1,870	2,163	2,429	2,527	2,526	2,592
Construction	2,975	3,511	4,249	5,284	5,864	5,292	4,420	4,326	3,961	3,436	2,253	2,160
Nonpetroleum Mining	817	790	654	549	557	601	611	602	502	419	484	540
Transportation & Communication	6,675	7,349	8,304	9,208	9,942	9,446	9,402	9,738	10,076	8,707	8,444	8,839
Commerce	6,128	7,061	7,954	8,299	8,299	7,874	6,623	6,448	6,614	6,724	6,370	6,188
All other Services	20,341	23,174	25,526	27,881	28,057	28,920	28,986	30,123	29,336	33,745	29,908	29,893

Note: The value of oil production is in millions of bolívares unadjusted for inflation.

Sources: Banco Central de Venezuela, *Anuario de Cuentas Nacionales* (Caracas, various issues); Ministerio de Minas e Hidrocarburos, *Petróleo y Otros Datos Estadísticos* (Caracas, various issues).

and it is reflected in low productivity within this sector. It is not until the latter part of this period that a satisfactory growth is observed in agricultural output (6 percent in 1985). In this same statistical table we can observe that the production of water and electric services doubled during the period. This sector grew to an annual rate of 7.22 percent, but it represents only a small proportion of total GDP.

When considering the manufacturing sector, one may examine indicators of value added by type of manufacturing industry (Table 10.8). The industries that experienced the most growth during the period were the producers of food, beverages, and paper. Certain industries producing intermediate goods (for example, the basic chemical industry) also grew at an accelerated pace during the period. It should also be noted that traditional industries and those of intermediate goods were more positively affected by the economic stimulus provided by the petroleum sector and public policy that followed, than the rest of the nation's industries.

In Table 10.7, one finds the growth pattern of the construction industry that constituted an important aspect of the development of the rest of the Venezuelan economy. Even though the sector grew at an increasing rate in the first five years, due primarily to the large demand for both public and private infrastructure, this sector was negatively affected in the later period by the credit crunch caused by the private capital flight, and by the national economic recession that began in 1979.

The growth of the mining sector during these years was characteristically negative. The mining GDP excluding petroleum diminished gradually at an annual growth rate of –4.68 percent (Table 10.7).

Finally, the growth rate of the service sector in the economy was positive in real terms. As is evident in Table 10.7, this sector as a whole grew

Table 10.8.
Value Added Index for Manufacturing, 1973–1985 (1968 = 100)

Industry	1973	1974	1975	1976	1977	1978	1979	1980	1981	1982	1983	1984	1985	% Change 1973-1985
Food	110.2	125.7	141.3	158.7	173.7	178.0	189.6	237.7	327.4	365.9	390.1	493.1	611.6	4.6
Beverages	110.1	125.1	144.1	151.5	153.9	164.8	182.8	193.9	442.2	502.2	593.2	559.7	608.1	4.5
Tobacco	100.0	100.9	103.3	103.6	107.2	110.8	143.7	215.7	296.6	313.0	298.2	269.9	335.0	2.4
Textiles	115.4	146.3	159.3	170.5	196.6	217.8	230.0	278.1	217.4	202.5	211.4	324.3	360.1	2.1
Gems	125.9	137.3	151.2	168.7	197.5	207.8	246.7	278.1	194.6	198.8	213.8	301.3	302.2	1.4
Paper	120.3	152.8	165.3	165.4	176.2	210.8	242.7	311.6	438.9	483.2	520.0	714.8	760.1	5.3
Printing	133.5	165.7	193.9	214.2	223.6	245.2	266.5	323.5	338.0	384.3	383.1	489.2	644.3	3.8
Leather	166.1	184.6	186.9	198.4	215.6	233.4	271.2	309.0	339.1	346.1	334.0	469.3	617.0	2.7
Chemicals	106.6	121.2	132.9	142.5	147.4	153.8	171.7	190.5	301.3	303.3	270.3	446.7	522.9	3.9
Lumber	139.8	153.0	168.6	202.9	220.1	230.1	255.6	304.0	246.5	264.2	259.6	301.6	332.8	1.4
Rubber Products	110.8	125.9	128.8	129.3	130.8	133.8	139.3	170.6	239.9	234.0	228.7	234.3	366.3	2.3
Metal Products	130.0	157.4	170.2	175.2	180.1	193.7	221.0	245.2	317.4	344.5	300.2	411.4	495.1	2.8
Basic Metals	115.2	155.2	176.2	169.2	174.1	209.2	218.6	242.3	517.5	611.6	491.4	570.7	550.1	3.8

Source: Banco Central de Venezuela, *Anuario de Cuentas Nacionales* (Caracas, various issues).

by 34.5 percent, which represents an average annual growth rate of 2.75 percent. Of all the activities in the service sector, nontransportation and noncommercial services was the one that experienced the most expansion.

It is evident by analyzing the components of total GDP that the impact of events in the petroleum sector on the rest of the economy was quite positive during the beginning years of the period. This cannot be claimed, however, for the subsequent years. It is important to note that during this period macroeconomic policies did not foster a continuation of the growth performance witnessed in the years immediately following 1973. Nevertheless, the contributions of the petroleum sector permitted Venezuelans to achieve a standard of living, and an accumulation of foreign reserves, that rivaled levels of more industrialized nations.

This period describes the Venezuelan economy initially as one of abundance and subsequently as one of restrictions. The economic boom created by the substantial petroleum revenues, besides raising the standard of living for all Venezuelans, brought about at the same time a change in domestic priorities. Dramatic changes occurred in the pattern of consumption and savings.

The productive capacity in Venezuela was negatively affected, however, by the great dependence on petroleum revenues that occurred during the period. Meanwhile, Venezuelan imports grew at a disproportionate rate, nontraditional exports deteriorated under a growing neglect, as reflected by overvalued exchange rates and diminished non-oil investment rates. At the same time, public outlays grew in such a way that even in abundant periods there existed budget deficits that had to be financed by borrowing, both internally and externally.

The OPEC policies of raising the price of petroleum brought as a consequence the development of alternative sources of energy, and the discovery of new oil resources, which eventually reduced the markets for Venezuelan petroleum. This factor, together with failure to take full advantage of the petroleum sector's contribution, precipitated the worst economic crisis of the 20th century for the country.

The petroleum boom of the mid-1970s brought a restructuring of economic priorities. The economy relied more and more heavily on oil sector revenues to finance public spending and to stimulate demand in other sectors. Macro policies and trade policies led to disincentives to domestic investment in non-oil sectors. These factors left the economy vulnerable to both external and internal pressures that emerged during the mid-1980s.

CHAPTER 11

1986–1990

THE CONTRIBUTION THROUGH THE EXTERNAL SECTOR

During the 1986–1990 period, the share of oil in total petroleum exports declined. This was the result of a formidable expansion of the country's nontraditional exports, mostly produced by state enterprises, counterbalancing declining oil exports. For example, in 1988, to compensate for the large diminution of the export of petroleum products, Venezuela placed in the world markets unusually large quantities of aluminum and nonmonetary gold, the latter for the first time in decades. The low point in terms of oil exports to total exports occurred in 1989, when the share fell to 76.4 percent, again when the exportation of nonpetroleum products practically jumped from their 1988 levels.

These trends abruptly changed in 1990, when the Persian Gulf conflict brought windfall gains to petroleum exporters, raising the share of petroleum in total Venezuelan exports to almost 80 percent. Even then this was below the original levels at the beginning of the period, signaling a subdued contribution of oil to the economic development of Venezuela through the external sector, notwithstanding that from the beginning to the end of the period, in absolute numbers of both exports and foreign exchange earnings, the oil contribution expanded, as Table 11.1 shows. The principal determinant of all these results was the gyration of the prices of petroleum products, which rose to $17.95 per barrel of oil in 1987, then fell to $13.51 in 1988, and went through the roof to $35.50 in 1990, especially at the end of the year.

Table 11.1.
Petroleum Sector Indicators and External Sector Performance, 1986–1990 (millions of dollars)

	1986	1987	1988	1989	1990
Total Exports	9,122	10,576	10,082	12,915	17,278
Oil Exports	7,592	9,054	8,023	9,862	13,780
As Percent of Total	83.2%	85.6%	79.6%	76.4%	79.8%
Foreign Exchange Inflows					
Total	10,552	12,941	13,647	14,792	21,329
Oil	7,625	8,984	7,987	9,625	15,687
As Percent of Total	72.3%	69.4%	58.5%	65.1%	73.5%
Change in the Terms of Trade	-114.68	-633.38	-426.75	-454.89	-120
International Reserves	9,876	9,402	6,607	7,546	11,759

Sources: Banco Central de Venezuela, *Anuario de Cuentas Nacionales* (Caracas, various issues); Ministerio de Minas e Hidrocarburos, *Petróleo y Otros Datos Estadísticos* (various issues).

Resulting from the trends described above, the import capacity and international reserves figures are presented in Table 11.1. The former constantly declined during the period, with the exception of a rebound in 1990, which did not surpass the import availability of the initial years of this phase. Import dependency was crucial to the economy, during both the earlier years, when President Lusinchi's model was traditionally an import substituting one, as well as in the more recent years, when the Carlos Andrez Perez government brought about the "great turnaround" in 1989, opening the economy to foreign competition. This was particularly the case with regard to intermediate and capital goods imports. It is clear that a good part of the foreign exchange generated by the Venezuelan oil industry during this period was used instead to service the nation's international debt, twice restructured during these years.

The imports of consumer goods were greatly aided by the multiple exchange rate system implanted in Venezuela as a result of the debt crisis, which applied the lower (most overvalued) rates to consumer necessities. Many other consumer goods were inappropriately imported at these preferential rates through a scandalous corruption case known as RECADI.[1] Such liberal uses came to an abrupt end early in 1989, when imports were severely constrained and the system of exchange-rate differentials ended. Thus, this year was the lowest point for imports during the whole period, with a strong recovery occurring in 1990 due to the spike in oil prices and volumes brought about by the Persian Gulf situation.

On top of the foreign exchange receipts being used to palliate the foreign debt constraints of the nation and the ceaseless appetite of consumers, a large portion of the international reserves followed suit in similar uses. These declined from $10.5 billion at the beginning of this phase to a trough of $3.1 billion in 1989. The deterioration of the Venezuelan foreign exchange position started early, with a 28 percent drop between 1985 and 1986.[2] This was followed by an almost 39 percent decline in 1987, even though in that year the Central Bank of Venezuela consolidated within its own official foreign exchange reserves those belonging to PDVSA and the Venezuelan Investment Fund. This measure, however, could not control the decline in the international assets of the country, which hit bottom in 1989 at about one-third their 1986 levels, and less than 50 percent of the 1987 stocks. However, helped by the approximately 100 percent devaluation of the bolívar in 1989, allied to the establishment of a unified exchange rate, as well as the resurgence in the value of oil exports in 1990, international reserves more than doubled between early 1989 and late 1990.

The contribution of oil through the external sector can be evaluated partly by the use of Venezuelan reserves of convertible currency, gold, and hard currency claims on other countries, because these had been forthcoming largely as a result of petroleum. These assets to a large extent represent a decision to exchange them for black gold lying under ground in Venezuela. During this period, particularly, these foreign reserves were depleted, so it is instructive to reexamine how they were applied. As mentioned above, the three principal uses were to satisfy increasing consumption, to service the foreign debt, and to finance the overseas expansion of PDVSA. There were also increases in intermediate and capital goods imports by the country's state enterprises to make possible the expansion of nontraditional exports and very important outflows of capital. These usages do not seem to have been very fruitful to the development of the country, perhaps with the exception of the foreign investments of PDVSA. The nation continued to exhibit a knack for consumption, corruption, and indebtedness, and its citizens preferred to have their nest eggs abroad and to occasionally take advantage of the certain speculation against the national currency, even to the extent that the national petroleum company preferred to invest its surpluses abroad rather than at home.

Another way of questioning how well the utilization of the petroleum contribution through the external sector has gone, is through the commodity composition of Venezuelan imports shown in Table 11.2. It should be reiterated at the outset that total imports exploded by about 50 percent in the short space of two years between 1986 and 1988, demonstrating the insatiable appetite of Venezuela for foreign goods.[3] Thereafter, they were reduced by an even greater amount to the end of the period, then being lower than in 1986.

Even though the statistics are probably tainted by the RECADI episode,[4] it is clear that there was an increasing use of the external contribution of petroleum to satisfy the needs of Venezuelan consumers. The other side of the coin shows that the expected industrial restructuring of domestic producers, so as to enable them to confront foreign competitors during the drastic liberalization period introduced in 1989 and eventually

Table 11.2.
Imports F.O.B. by Use of Commodity, 1986–1990 (millions of dollars)

	1986	1987	1988	1989	1990
Capital Goods	1,991	1,982	3,076	1,913	1,622
As Percent of Total	26.0%	22.8%	26.8%	27.2%	24.5%
Intermediate Goods	5,139	6,152	7,694	4,637	4,335
As Percent of Total	67.1%	70.6%	67.0%	66.0%	65.6%
Consumer Goods	532	577	706	479	651
As Percent of Total	6.9%	6.6%	6.2%	6.8%	9.9%
Total	7,662	8,711	11,476	7,029	6,608

Source: Banco Central de Venezuela, *Anuario de Cuentas Nacionales* (Caracas, various issues).

to foster private exports, did not appear to take place. This was probably because of the excess capacity existing in the capital stock of the country, and the depressive effects of the structural adjustment package inaugurated by President Perez. Therefore, the contribution on this account failed to be well utilized during this period.

THE CONTRIBUTION THROUGH THE FISCAL SECTOR

During these years various measures were introduced seeking to enlarge the revenues derived from the oil sector, while increasing the degree to which governmental activities were dependent on its hydrocarbon resources. This was compensated by the fact that most of the contribution coming through the exchange rate differential scheme (through which the foreign exchange obtained from oil exports was purchased at a lower rate than that used for sales to the rest of the economy) fell substantially during the period. This implicit subsidy of oil disappeared, as a large number of transactions within the multiple exchange rate scheme of Venezuela took place at the official rate, and the buying rate of the petroleum dollar was raised. Moreover, in 1989, when a unified scheme was implanted, the oil foreign exchange differential dropped down to zero.

This is reflected in Table 11.3, which displays total government revenues, those derived from the petroleum economy, and the latter's share. It should be underlined that because of what has been written just above, the implicit tax on oil generated by the exchange rate differential, at which the petroleum dollars are bought and sold by the Central Bank, diminished greatly as the official exchange rate of the bolívar was sharply devalued. Furthermore, when the dollar exchange rate was unified in early 1989, the differential tax disappears altogether.[5]

At the beginning of the period, the contribution of oil was less then half of the total taxes and other revenues received by Venezuela. By the end of the period the share of oil in the total had almost doubled (from 42 to 82

Table 11.3.
General Government Revenues from Petroleum and All Sources, 1986–1990
(millions of bolívares)

	1986	1987	1988	1989	1990
Total Revenues	100,958	150,621	160,290	293,860	433,139
Petroleum Revenues	42,873	66,092	91,433	225,471	355,535
Petroleum Revenue as a Percent of Total	42.5%	43.9%	57.0%	76.7%	82.1%

Sources: Banco Central de Venezuela, Anuario de Cuentas Nacionales (various issues);
Ministerio de Minas e Hidrocarburos, *Petróleo y Otros Datos Estadísticos* (Caracas, various
issues).

percent). This highest historical proportion in the total income received by
the public sector occurring in 1990 is only approached by the one obtained
in 1974, when oil prices quadrupled as a result of the Yom Kippur War.
Even though this is tied to the severe devaluation of the bolívar, which
makes oil dollar exports to be worth much more in the local currency, it
constitutes a cap to our examination of the influence of petroleum on the
economy, to find that it reached its peak at the end of the period.

Thus, it is patently clear that the fiscal contribution of oil was of very
notable importance during this period. Notwithstanding the fact that the
policymakers increased taxation through higher sales and payroll taxes,
increases in the prices of public services and increased property taxes and
car registration fees, among others, government income sang to the tune
of the vagaries in oil revenues. The state tried to raise more tax income
from petroleum per dollar of oil exports, but found that the devaluation of
the bolívar was a more expedient way for an enlarged budget, and sometimes to compensate for falling oil prices in the international markets. The
latter was the most important exogenous variable acting upon the oil contribution to public revenues.

How did this egregious contribution end up being used by the Venezuelan economy? In nominal terms, government revenues more than quadrupled, and oil revenues went up close to eight times. However, prices more
than doubled, and the government was facing a large deficit during the
whole period. In Table 11.4, the key data on the characteristics of public
expenditures during these years are cited, showing that this variable rose
by about a multiple of five in the period examined. This is significantly
higher than the corresponding revenue expansion.

But how well did the proactive governments of Lusinchi and Perez utilize such a rapid expansion of public funding and the enlarged oil contribution in bolívares that made it mostly possible? For an answer, it is
necessary to look again at Table 11.4 and the investment part of government expenditures depicted there. If the oil contribution is to bear fruit
and contribute to development, it should be fundamentally seeded into

Table 11.4.
Public Investment, Public Outlays, and Changes in Petroleum Revenues,
1986–1990 (millions of bolívares)

	1986	1987	1988	1989	1990
Public Outlays	147,849	222,605	283,410	455,124	754,557
Public Investment	64,405	83,884	104,813	167,620	262,968
Investment as a Percent of Public Outlays	43.6%	37.7%	37.0%	36.8%	34.9%
Change in Public Investment	-14,972	19,479	20,929	62,807	95,348
Change in Oil Revenues	-19,230	23,219	25,341	134,038	130,064
Ratio of Change in Investment to Change in Oil Revenues	0.7786	0.8389	0.8259	0.4686	0.7331

Notes: Public investment includes financial investments. Change in oil revenues does not include revenues from exchange differential.

Sources: Banco Central de Venezuela, *Anuario de Cuentas Nacionales* (Caracas, various issues).

investment that will allow higher output and improve productivity. It is found that a large proportion of public expenditures have been devoted to capital accumulation, upward of 35 percent in every case, and as high as almost 44 percent in 1986. Yet this investment ratio was constantly declining throughout the whole period, which was a negative trait.

Considering the relationship between the oil contribution through the fiscal sector, in terms of the revenues it generates, and the evolution of investment expenditures by the government on a yearly basis, the old slogan of "sowing the oil" can be tested. In this period the evolution of petroleum revenues in absolute terms, as shown in Table 11.4, is exactly paralleled year after year by the change in public investment. Every year but the first there was an expansion of the former, accompanied in the same direction by the latter. In 1986 both petroleum revenues and public investment expenditures suffered a decline. This perfect record is somewhat marred by the fact that only a fraction of the increase in the petroleum contribution was allocated for increased public investment, especially in 1989 and 1990. However, when oil revenues went the other way, the cut in capital accumulation in the government sector was not as correspondingly large.

Altogether, it can be concluded that the oil contribution through the fiscal sector was very large during this period, and that its utilization was partly good and partly bad, the latter having to do with the large public deficits and the declining appropriation of funds for investment during the two tail years of this phase.

THE CONTRIBUTION OF OIL THROUGH INVESTMENT

Although investment in the oil industry is traditionally seen as a weak contributor to the economy and having lost importance until recently, this form of investment *can* be a catalyst for capital accumulation in the economy as a whole. In Table 11.5 these connections are displayed: the total fixed investment (excluding changes in stocks) of Venezuela discriminated into its petroleum and nonpetroleum components. Also shown are gross domestic product and the overall investment ratio. Finally Table 11.5 depicts the decomposition of fixed petroleum investment into its various parts.

Considering first the share of oil in total investment, it can be seen that it constitutes only a small part of the total. However, when compared with previous periods it depicts a rising influence of this contribution during this period. This is so when taken both in absolute numbers and as a proportion of total investment. In nominal terms petroleum investment grew by a multiple of seven, while inflation only tripled. A good part of this expansion took place from 1988 to 1990, when oil investment quadrupled. However, nonpetroleum investment expanded more rapidly in the early years. To illustrate, total investment enlarged by 48 percent in 1987, while the petroleum sector showed only a 15 percent increase, and this explains why the share of oil in the total dropped to 9.9 percent that year (see Table 11.5). But as pointed out before, just the opposite occurred later in the

Table 11.5.
Gross Fixed Investment in Petroleum and Other Sectors, 1986–1990 (millions of bolívares)

	1986	1987	1988	1989	1990
Gross Fixed Domestic Investment (GFDI):	87,606	129,808	174,929	223,825	281,320
Oil Sector	11,163	12,845	20,270	41,898	81,365
Other Sectors	76,443	116,963	154,659	181,927	199,955
Other Sectors (Mill. 1957 Bs.)	14,291	15,908	17,752	10,995	8,522
Oil Investment as a Percent of GFDI	12.7%	9.9%	11.6%	18.7%	28.9%
GFDI a s a Percent of GDP	20.4%	21.2%	28.8%	16.8%	14.2%
Distribution of Oil Investment:					
Production	9,559	11,486	17,437	31,626	64,595
As a Percent of Total	63.7%	68.7%	71.2%	52.7%	55.9%
Transport	74	53	119	85	1,180
As a Percent of Total	0.5%	0.3%	0.5%	0.1%	1.0%
Refining	1,133	1,973	2,811	7,094	12,009
As Percent of Total	7.6%	11.8%	11.5%	11.8%	10.4%
Sales	1,267	1,592	2,482	3,498	5,883
As Percent of Total	8.4%	9.5%	10.1%	5.8%	5.1%
Other	2,966	1,603	1,640	17,709	31,899
As Percent of Total	19.8%	9.6%	6.7%	29.5%	27.6%
Total	14,999	16,707	24,489	60,012	115,566

Notes: Oil sector investment reported on a GDP accounting basis. Distribution of oil investment based on Ministerio de Energía y Minas data, definitions that are different from GDP accounting methodology.

Sources: Banco Central de Venezuela, *Anuario de Cuentas Nacionales* (Caracas, various issues); Ministerio de Minas e Hidrocarburos, *Petróleo y Otros Datos Estadísticos* (Caracas, various issues).

period, with petroleum's participation in total gross fixed investment almost 29 percent in 1990.

In Table 11.5 it is also shown how the fixed investment of the oil industry was distributed according to its major uses. The lion's share was obtained by investment in the production of petroleum, although it fell measurably in 1989 and 1990 (in relative, not absolute, terms). This category includes surveying, exploration, exploitation, extraction, and production. It not only leads to further production of the hydrocarbons, but to the expansion of proven reserves. The trend in the other categories, which have a much smaller importance during this period in terms of their shares, is comparably stable, although they all enlarge notably in absolute numbers. It is unfortunate that the other category is so amorphous but yet so important, particularly at the end.

Clearly the contribution of the oil sector to Venezuelan investment was quite significant during the period. How was it utilized? The first indication is that the investment ratio, the proportion of total fixed investment to GDP, fell substantially in 1989 and 1990; after rising to almost 29 percent of the gross domestic product in 1987, it was cut in half by the last year of the period.

Another manner of considering how well the petroleum contribution has been used is to focus on the retained value of petroleum expenditures and its relation to nonpetroleum investment. The former represents all the value added by the oil sector of Venezuela that is spent domestically on the Venezuelan economy. The latter is the capital accumulation activities (investment) displayed by the manufacturing, agricultural, mining, construction, and other sectors of the economy, excluding petroleum production and refining. If oil's contribution is well utilized, it should be reflected in an increase in nonpetroleum investment.

Except for one instance, a slight fallback in 1988, the retained value of petroleum expenditures in constant 1957 prices (depicted in Table 11.6), shot up straight as an arrow. If the performance of nonpetroleum fixed investment in 1957 prices is examined in Table 11.5, it increased significantly up to 1988, but then declined abruptly in 1989 and 1990. In the latter year it was still just over half of what it was in 1986. Even if the possibility of a one-year lag in the interaction of the two variables is considered, it only coincides in direction in one case, 1988–1989, but then not in magnitude. Therefore it must be concluded that the investment contribution of oil was not properly used toward the end of this period if the deflated series of retained value of petroleum expenditures and of nonpetroleum investment are matched.

Returning to the investment ratio test performed earlier in this section, it is evident that it is closely connected with the experience described just above. Even though the investment contribution of petroleum was among the most vigorous in the century, it was not well utilized during this

Table 11.6.
Retained Value of Oil Sector Expenditures, 1986–1990 (millions of bolívares)

	1986	1987	1988	1989	1990
Total Oil Sector Expenditures	86,992	148,913	164,140	557,111	1,209,047
Retained Value of Oil Expenditures	67,965	127,151	130,957	483,827	1,069,955
Ratio of Retained Value to Expenditures	0.9151	0.9469	0.9285	0.9499	0.9585
Retained Value per barrel of Oil	113.06	210.66	207.88	758.48	1397.17
Retained Value of Oil Expenditures (Mill. 1957 Bs.)	12,009	16,339	14,209	27,627	43,119

Notes: Oil sector expenditures include capital expenditures and do not include revenues from exchange differential. Retained value of oil expenditures does not include capital expenditures or revenues from exchange differential.

Sources: Banco Central de Venezuela, *Anuario de Cuentas Nacionales* (Caracas, various issues); Ministerio de Minas e Hidrocarburos, *Petróleo y Otros Datos Estadísticos* (Caracas, various issues).

period, because of the large drop in the investment ratio and in nonpetroleum investment during 1989 and 1990.

THE CONTRIBUTION OF OIL THROUGH PRODUCTION AND INCOME

If the contribution of oil through its total product and the income it generates are considered, Table 11.6 shows that petroleum expenditures increased almost 14 times from 1986 to 1990. If inflation is discounted, this figure is still a little over 10 times higher in real terms at the end of the period. The growth was particularly large during 1989 and 1990, although there was considerable growth earlier. Thus, Venezuela clearly enjoyed an economic boom sustained on petroleum expenditures during this period, which directly and indirectly (through demand effects via the multiplier-accelerator process and supply effects through local purchases) constituted one of the largest in history.

In the same table, if attention is placed upon the retained value of current expenditures of the petroleum sector, a similar trend is noticeable. Even the ratio of retained value to total expenditures, not including the tax on exchange rate differentials, has an upward tendency during these years, with the exception of a drop in 1988.[6] The drop from 1985 is entirely explained by the exclusion of the tax on petroleum through exchange rate differentials. Per barrel of oil produced, the retained value portion of petroleum expenditures increased practically with no break, and in 1990 it was 12 times higher than in 1986.

What impact did such a push by the petroleum sector have over the economy as a whole, particularly the non-oil portion? For that purpose the data presented in Table 11.7 should be analyzed. Again the oil sector expansion, from the contraction in the middle of the 1980s, represented a

Table 11.7.

Value of Petroleum Production, GDP Originating in the Petroleum Sector, and Total GDP by Sector, 1986–1990 (millions of 1957 bolívares)

	1986	1987	1988	1989	1990
Value of Oil Production	74,272	134,276	141,043	509,370	1,116,334
GDP Originating in the Petroleum Sector	58,444	97,505	111,095	328,321	636,902
Oil Sector GDP	10,325	12,534	12,052	18,755	25,656
Total GDP	104,636	90,830	96,119	88,108	92,530
Oil as a Percent of GDP	9.9%	13.8%	12.5%	21.3%	27.7%
Total Non-Petroleum Sector GDP:	94,311	78,296	84,067	69,353	66,874
Agriculture	5,818	5,553	6,371	5,334	5,121
Electricity, Water & Public Utility	1,367	1,412	1,416	1,311	1,505
Construction	5,817	5,822	6,850	4,118	4,177
Non-Petroleum Mining	659	850	1,041	768	833
Transportation & Communication	5,477	5,240	5,653	4,204	4,331
Commerce	12,234	12,885	14,918	12,609	12,516
All Other Services	26,239	26,196	26,883	20,830	21,254

Note: Value of oil production and GDP are in millions of bolívares, unadjusted for inflation.

Sources: Banco Central de Venezuela, *Anuario de Cuentas Nacionales* (Caracas, various issues); Ministerio de Minas e Hidrocarburos, *Petróleo y Otros Datos Estadísticos* (Caracas, various issues).

very substantial expansion in the value of petroleum production and sectoral GDP. Even after adjusting to 1957 prices, the oil sector GDP rose by two and a half times between 1986 and 1990, representing a very major contribution to the rest of the economy.

Total gross domestic product of Venezuela, by contrast, declined during the same period when expressed in 1957 prices. As a result, petroleum's importance in the Venezuelan economy increased during this period, reverting to the trend established during the early and middle 1980s. As can be seen in Table 11.7, the share of oil in GDP increased by about 33 percent from 1986 and 1988, and then more than doubled at the end of the period. Correspondingly, nonpetroleum gross domestic product shrank during this period by about 30 percent, as is also depicted in Table 11.7.

Even though 1990 was a booming year for oil in the world markets, the trend toward its increasing influence in total economic activity was made during the whole period, already escalating notably in 1989. This contrasts with the behavior of the rest of the economy, which continually lost momentum and contracted by 17.5 percent in 1989, bringing about an overall decline in the gross domestic product of Venezuela of 8.33 percent. These facets resulted from conditions demanded by Venezuelan lenders during this period to ensure service of its international debts. These conditions required macroeconomic stabilization and structural adjustments that depressed the nonpetroleum sectors of the economy. By 1990 the economy seemed to be rebounding from the trough, as the country's non-petroleum gross domestic product deteriorated by only 3.57 percent, and total GDP expanded.

One complicating factor in the nation has been the unleashing of the most severe inflation in its history. This has been determined by a more than tripling of the exchange rate in two steps, one in 1986 and the other in 1989. The latter did away with the remains of the exchange control system established in 1983, and unified the value of foreign exchange into one rate, from then onward freely determined by the market. The inflationary process arising mainly from such measures, resulting from conditions imposed by the participation of Venezuela in the Baker and Brady debt rescheduling plans,[7] certainly affected the creation of product and generation of income in a country accustomed to parameters of price stability.

To provide a more detailed analysis of the breakdown in the nonpetroleum economy throughout these years, Table 11.7 presents its various sectoral components and their evolution from 1986 to 1990. The agricultural sector in constant 1957 bolívares contracted heavily at the end of the period, after rebounding only in 1988. A very similar behavior is shown by construction, a sector of about the same importance as agriculture. The same could be said for transportation and communications. The evolution of the other services sectors follows those of the three sectors just dealt with but, unlike agriculture, it shows a recuperation in 1990, although, as in the case of the other three sectors, not enough to match the 1986 levels. Given the size of the other services sector, larger than all of the three sectors mentioned combined, its almost 20 percent drop in GDP from 1986 contributed very significantly to the decline of the nonpetroleum economy of Venezuela during the period. Three sectors countered the tendencies described above; however, two of them are rather small: non-petroleum mining, and electricity, water, and public utilities. Buoyed by the export diversification and infrastructure drives from 1986 to 1988, these activities, even though affected by the 1989 depression, ended the period with higher gross domestic products than at the beginning. The same can be said of commerce, yet it should be noted that this category is just second to other services in magnitude within the nonpetroleum portion of the economy.

With respect to manufacturing, its performance can be apprized from an examination of its value added figures, this time at 1968 prices, in Table 11.8. The category is divided into its principal components, the most important being food and metal products. These two manufacturing activities decreased during these years by 17 and 13 percent, respectively. In fact, this pattern characterized the rest of manufacturing, with the exception of the paper industry, which was the second smallest one within manufacturing. Practically all subsectors rose in value added in 1988 and

Table 11.8.
Value Added in Manufacturing, 1986–1990 (1968 = 100)

Industry	1986	1987	1988	1989	1990	% Change 1986-1990
Food	2,669	2,404	2,504	2,143	2,278	-0.172
Beverages	126	121	129	110	119	-0.06
Tobacco	903	721	750	666	469	-0.926
Textiles	117	80	90	69	64	-0.828
Gems	80	70	79	58	53	-0.529
Paper	52	47	53	47	53	0.014
Printing	56	48	50	38	31	-0.81
Leather	131	141	160	109	97	-0.352
Chemicals	100	76	80	64	70	-0.428
Lumber	280	270	310	208	170	-0.648
Rubber Products	351	393	353	303	286	-0.229
Metal Products	1,171	1,110	1,118	1,055	1,036	-0.13
Basic Metals	131	127	131	101	83	-0.589

Source: Banco Central de Venezuela, *Anuario de Cuentas Nacionales* (Caracas, 1984–1989 and 1990).

dropped more sharply in 1989. Half of them recovered in 1990 from the 1989 trough, but the rest continued to decrease. The most affected industries were tobacco, textiles, and printing. In addition to those mentioned earlier, only one other subsector declined by less than 20 percent, namely, beverages.

It is patently clear that the oil contribution to production and income through its value of production and current expenditures was extraordinary during this period. The growth of its value added, a very large part of which remains in Venezuela, was very substantial, and even the retained value portion rose to 96 percent in 1990.[8] The retained value of current oil expenditures, even at constant 1957 prices, resulted in a momentous impetus comparable to the heyday years of petroleum expansion in the country. Unfortunately, there is very little to show for the utilization of this contribution in terms of the expansion of overall Venezuelan production and income. It has been stated that the retained value of total expenditures (current plus investment) is a good proxy of the overall contribution of black gold to the rest of the economy. In the last two sections of this chapter its notable expansion has been documented. If the foreign sector and especially the fiscal contributions are also considered, it is easy to understand how large an opportunity has been missed by Venezuela's policymakers in their application to the development of the nonpetroleum side of the Venezuelan economy.

NOTES

1. RECADI is the acronym for the government program allocating foreign exchange to the various importers.

2. It should be noted that during these years Petróleo de Venezuela (PDVSA) began a program of internationalization of its operations, acquiring refineries, gasoline retailers, and other downstream assets in the United States, Europe, and other world markets.

3. It should be noted that for the first time in the 80 years covered by this book, inflationary expectations contributed to the import boom in the years 1986–1988, as inflation became an important component of the decision-making process of the economic agents in the nation.

4. The RECADI scheme ended at the beginning of 1989.

5. With the exception of the spike introduced in 1983, when the multiple exchange rate system was reintroduced in Venezuela after a little more than 20 years, the added revenues brought by this implicit tax had become a very small percentage of total petroleum revenues, as the latter had vastly expanded. Thus, the measurement of oil's fiscal contribution was practically the same whether including or excluding the foreign exchange tax.

6. It should be repeated once more that at the end of the previous period the government kept a wide margin between the dollar rate for petroleum exports and that used for imports by the rest of the economy. These differentials were substantially reduced in 1986 and disappeared completely in 1989. Therefore these revenues are not considered in the tables in this chapter, neither in the fiscal section nor in this section on expenditures. If these exchange differential proceeds would have been considered, the contribution of oil under those two accounts would have been significantly, but not substantially, larger, particularly in 1986 and 1987.

7. The Baker plan restructured foreign debt and provided additional funding from multilateral banks under conditions of structural adjustment and reform by the debtor nation. The Brady plan restructured foreign debt while reducing its total value, requiring policy reforms that would liberalize, deregulate, stabilize, and privatize the debtor country's economy.

8. At the end of the previous period (see Chapter 10), the retained value portion went over 100 percent because of the exchange rate differential implicit tax on oil. However, from 1986 to 1990 this contribution vanished with the foreign exchange reform. Only during part of 1986 and 1987 did it reach an appreciable magnitude. This would have increased petroleum's contribution to the rest of the economy even more.

CHAPTER 12

1991–2000

OVERVIEW TO THE PRESENT

Since the discovery of oil in Venezuela, initially concentrated in large fields along the eastern shore of Lake Maracaibo, the economic development of Venezuela has been intertwined with the exploitation of this national resource. The best depiction of this interaction is found in the relationship between petroleum exports and GDP from the early 20th century to the year 2000. As seen in Table 12.1, the common thread is evident. It is in this case clear that the causality runs from petroleum to the rest of the economy, because the former is an exogenous event involving the discovery and fostering of vast reserves of these products.

If the data mentioned are examined in detail over the past century, it becomes evident that there are decades in which the expansion of the petroleum sector has not been immediately synchronized with the growth of the Venezuelan economy. The decade of the 1960s constituted a waning period for petroleum in the country, as production slackened and oil prices remained steady until the decade's later years. Yet the country implemented its initial import-substitution drive during this epoch, spurred by a major devaluation of the bolívar and the expansion of the Guayana region. In contrast with this experience, in which the contributions of oil in terms of accumulated international reserves and tax revenues were put to good use, the 1970s saw a monumental enlargement of petroleum sector exports that was not carried over as successfully to the rest of the economy, which could only muster modest growth. This period saw the nationalization of the oil industry.

Table 12.1.
Oil Exports and Venezuela GDP, 1922–2000

	1922	1930	1940	1950	1960	1970	1980	1990	2000
Oil Exports (millions of dollars)	2	159	254	1,124	2,183	2,436	19,279	13,780	31,802
GDP (million of 1957 Bs.)	3,085	4,357	5,748	12,593	27,038	49,437	72,739	92,530	113,011
Share	0.001	0.036	0.044	0.089	0.081	0.049	0.265	0.149	0.281

Sources: Jorge Salazar-Carrillo, *Oil and Development in Venezuela during the Twentieth Century* (Praeger, 1994, several pages); Banco Central de Venezuela, *Anuario de Cuentas Nacionales* (various issues); Ministerio de Minas e Hidrocarburos, *Petróleo y Otros Datos Estadísticos* (various issues).

During the 1980s, petroleum exports suffered a relative collapse. This was partly compensated by an increase in its contribution to the overall economy, because part of its profits did not flow abroad but rather to the state, through Petro Ven S.A. (Petroleos de Venezuela Sociedad Anonima, also known for its Spanish acronym PDVSA). Additionally, the several devaluations of the Venezuelan bolívar during the period meant that petroleum taxes expanded greatly in terms of the national currency, which allowed a large expansion in government expenditures. Furthermore, the foreign exchange drawn from hydrocarbon export was purchased at a low bolívar per dollar rate and sold to the importers of nonessential goods and services at a high rate, with the government pocketing the difference as yet another source of revenue originating from petroleum. All of these measures, plus the large external debt, financed expansion of internal investment in the early part of the decade and brought along a significant growth in the nontradable sectors of the economy, within an unstable and distorted economic climate of import controls and double-digit inflation.

THE INSTITUTIONS

Apart from the already mentioned PDVSA, which is in turn a holding company of four major oil producing subsidiaries, and which also owns several foreign companies (like CITGO in the United States), the other main national actor in the petroleum industry is the Ministry of Energy and Mines. The latter evolved over the years from the Ministry of Development in the early part of this century, in which mines and petroleum was just a dependency, to a self-standing Ministry of Mines, with the later addition of "and Hydrocarbons" at the end of its title. More recently, rightly putting the horse before the cart, the mineral part was relegated to the end, and the term *hydrocarbons* was replaced by the more modern and encompassing term, *energy;* thus, the Ministry of Energy and Mines.

Over the years, the brunt of policy making in the petroleum sector has rested with the Ministry. The battles for assigning concessions to the formerly foreign-owned oil companies; for establishing different types of taxes, from royalties to the profits tax; for dealing with production matters ranging from labor conditions to exemptions from custom duties; and even for determining the basic concepts underpinning the famous "plant or sow the oil" motto of the late 1930s were all fought by public servants in this Institution. Venezuela was fortunate to have had leaders of great caliber, from Gumersindo Torres through Nestor Perez to Juan Pablo Perez Alfonso in this public dependency. The latter was well known for introducing the concept of the 50–50 split with the multinational companies of the net income from the petroleum business, which in practical terms meant half ownership of the concerns. This measure spread to the Arab oil-producing states, and then to all other developing countries where oil and its derivatives were exploited. The dramatic growth of petroleum production in Venezuela, as contrasted with its stagnation in practically every other Latin American country, stands as a monument to the efforts of these and other policy makers.

The creation of the Organization of Petroleum Exporting Countries (OPEC) stemmed in great part from the conception of Juan Pablo Perez Alfonso as Minister of Mines and Hydrocarbons in Venezuela in the late forties. From then on, the successive ministers have been Venezuelan government representatives in this international body. Therefore, it is the Ministry that helps set the world oil policy of OPEC, in the same way that it determines the nationwide energy policy for the country. Nevertheless, well-deserved recognition should be given to PDVSA as the management consortium that has ensured the efficiency of the petroleum conglomerate in Venezuela. It had the foresight to organize its member companies along the lines of those nationalized, using Venezuelan personnel primed over the years in the responsibilities of practically running them for their foreign owners. This was possible in turn because these multinationals had trained native persons well, eventually placing them in top positions in their companies. The Venezuelan oil company has been particularly adept at navigating the political shoals and remaining trim in terms of its payroll, while usually expanding its proven energy reserves. Also, it has not been shy in developing collaborations with foreign petroleum multinationals, which were introduced early after nationalization through the figure of service contracts.

IMPACT OF THE OIL CARTEL

It should not be surprising to find that the countries whose subsoil bear petroleum and its derivatives have banded together to form a world cartel. After many years of receiving a small share of the returns from the oil business, they rightly realized that this exhaustible resource provided an opportunity to maximize its present value through the maximization of its net income over a finite lifetime. This rational formula, which applies to any similar financial problem, would require the imposition of limits to the early use of depleting minerals. This was the logical outcome once the producing nations began to control the business, supplementing the oligopoly exercised by the major oil companies known as the "Seven Sisters." But in order to successfully limit output, OPEC had to transform the international oil industry from an oligopoly into a cartel, bringing in its wake large increases in the prices of oil and its derivatives.

It is well known in economics that a cartel can only control price if it limits the sales of all its members. In order to do the latter, it must behave as a virtual monopoly. This in turn requires controlling the large majority of production, and establishing an output goal that would be honored by the members of the cartel as if they were branches of a single holding company. Although these conditions were present in the heady days of OPEC (from 1973 to 1981) it is well known that, as economic theory predicts, they tended to disappear toward the middle of the 1980s. The rising oil prices attracted expanding petroleum sources that have frequently elected to bring their goods to market outside the cartel (North Sea, Mexico, U.S.S.R.), eroding the market share of the cartel's output. In addition, the members of the cartel began to shirk on their obligations, unloading products in the market over their allowed quotas. Moreover, the higher cost of oil brought on the one hand declines in demand, due to conservation and substitutes as well as price increases on practically every good and service in the world economy, because the product is an input used in almost everything.

By the mid-1980s, OPEC was in shambles. Nominal prices had declined drastically and the relative price of oil in terms of other goods and services (particularly those of the imports from petroleum producing nations) was close to that existing in the early 1970s, before their shocking quadrupling around the end of 1973. The share of sales controlled by the oil cartel declined drastically to about 40 percent of the total, as it tried unsuccessfully to keep prices high by reducing its production (in general contrast with the noncartel member nations). Yet in doing so, its discipline began to be increasingly tested as many members exceeded their allotted sale quotas in the markets.

Those circumstances led to the present day situation, in which the *relative* price of oil has returned to that existing before the oil crisis. OPEC recently opened up its productive spigots even more to recapture market share but then retrenched in the beginning of 1999 as prices dropped precipitously in 1998. It is expected that over the next decade the relative price of oil would rise somewhat, and that the cartel would regain part of its former importance and eventually represent somewhat over 50 percent of world output, given its proven reserves vis-a-vis other producers.[1]

LEADING MARKETS FOR HYDROCARBON PRODUCTS

Given the circumstances depicted above, it would seem that market orientation would be essential for Venezuela, placing an increasing production in the world markets. This already has been a clear gambit for PDVSA, which has emphasized downstream investment with the guise of controlling more and more distribution channels, and in the process has become one of the largest oil companies in the world.

What are the principal regions of demand in the world, and how do they jibe with the present composition of buyers of Venezuelan oil? The United States is the main international market for oil and its derivatives. Coincidentally, Venezuela is one of the principal suppliers of the United States. The same cannot be said about the Asian market, although its participation in Japanese oil imports appears promising.

With regard to the other major world market, which is western Europe, PDVSA has remained in competition with its European presence and has a fair chance to expand its market share. It should be understood that over 60 percent of petroleum products are sold in the markets of the Organization of Economic Cooperation and Development (OECD), which groups the industrialized and rich countries of the world and is heavily dominated by the United States and western Europe. The markets in central and eastern Europe are small, and tend to gravitate toward Russian oil supplies.

Finally, another significant market for Venezuelan petroleum is that of Latin America and the Caribbean. More sales are made to these countries than what is sold in Europe. These markets are expanding the fastest, and in them Venezuela has a privileged position, by being a member of all but one of the integration schemes in the region. Although many of these nations have their markets covered by internal production, and even export varying amounts of crude and refined products, none can match the Venezuelan reserves and all are prime candidates as important future sources of demand for the petroleum offerings of this country. The competitiveness of its position can be attested by the signing in the mid-1970s of the San Jose (Costa Rica) Agreement with the Central American and Caribbean nations. Through this mechanism, oil and its derivatives have been sold by Mexico and Venezuela at discounted world market prices. This means that in order not to upset OPEC and other conventions, the prices quoted are reflections of those ruling in the international markets, but part of the sale proceeds are kept by the buying governments under the guise of loans at below market rates of interest, to be eventually repaid. The loans, usually handled by the corresponding central banks, are to be used for development projects. In essence, however, the two lending countries ensure that the nations of Central America and the Caribbean reserve their petroleum markets for their supplies. Recently, Venezuela has unilaterally expanded its offerings in the region, and for the first time has included Cuba (although Mexico has not).

GLOBAL POSITIONING

But the real important moves are not in the area of trade and markets now or in the future, because the ability to serve them will depend on production, and that will be determined by investment. It is here that Venezuela has not positioned itself preeminently. At the moment this country is not the darling of foreign oil investors that it was back in the latter part of the 1990s, as the economic climate under President Chavez has soured with higher taxes and harsher conditions being imposed. Of course, not all is foreign investment, as PDVSA plans to self-finance most of its new investment projects.

In a petroleum product market that is bound to become more competitive, the ability to deliver will be essential. Those that muster the greatest productive capacity will dominate, and Venezuela may not be among the handful of leaders with ample investment funds. However, it is a relatively low-cost supplier, only at a disadvantage with respect to Saudi Arabia, Kuwait, and a few other Arab oil producers. In the past PDVSA has been successful in attaining greater efficiency and in cutting costs. But partnerships with the major foreign oil companies will be needed to undergird this effort. This may be possible because the original notion of service contracts has now expanded into joint ventures for exploration, oil field reactivation, operations, refining and natural gas, and the resources lie in the relatively untroubled waters of the Americas, as opposed to the tinder boxes along the Middle East, Africa, and western Asia.

FINANCIAL CONSTRAINTS

Venezuela has recovered, but not yet fully, from a banking crisis, not unlike that suffered by many Latin American nations, including golden Chile, in the 1980s and 1990s, and even in advanced countries like the United States, Japan, and France. The turmoil exploded in January 1994, when the Central Bank of Venezuela (BCV) seized the second largest bank in Venezuela, Banco Latino. The government then closed or intervened 18 banks altogether, having had to dedicate well over 10 percent (some say over 15 percent) of its gross domestic product to the rescue operation. Some of the banks that did not fail were still affected as a result of the weakness of their loan portfolios, partly because of the domino effect resulting from the collapse of many of the major financial institutions, and the loss of confidence by the public. Only a handful of banks were exempt from significant problems.

The Central Bank was the key institution in preserving the viability of the payments and financial systems at the moment the insolvency of some major Venezuelan banks was discovered in early 1994. It acted, regardless of the causes, to ensure that the systems would not collapse, and avoided their potential impact over the nation's economic activity.

The Central Bank of Venezuela became the lender of last resort by assisting FOGADE (the Spanish acronym for Fondo de Garantia de Depositos, or Deposit Guarantee Fund in English), which in turn aided the troubled banks. Concurrently, the financially solid banks were given incentives so that their excess reserves would be channeled to the problematic ones, with the purpose of supporting their solvent yet illiquid assets. Some other measures were the reduction in the deposit reserve ratios from 15 percent to 12 percent, and the reopening of the overnight window through the mechanism of agent banks.

In order to combat the inflationary pressures of the above, thus stemming the flight from the bolívar to harder currencies, the Central Bank sold zero-coupon bonds in massive quantities to diminish the supply of money. However, the prevailing uncertainties were stronger, giving rise to pessimistic expectations, which led to a sizeable decline in deposits and national currency, with their counterparts in capital flight, loss of international reserves, and pressure on the exchange rate. This led to the abandonment of the crawling peg system that had been implemented in October 1992, and which had meant progressive mini devaluations of the bolívar. On the other hand the rate of inflation rose substantially resulting from the spread of rising import prices and a contraction of aggregate supply.

By mid-1994, another eight commercial banks were intervened, heightening the uneasiness that was already prevalent in the country. This led, on July 9, 1994, to the establishment of a system of exchange controls that pegged the rate at 170 bolívares per U.S. dollar (the parallel market eventually shot up to 350 bolívares). These measures were extended to include interest rates and other sensitive prices that also became controlled. At this juncture the BCV stopped additional financial support of the rescue operations of the banking system through FOGADE, emphasizing its restrictive position in the monetary markets, in order to safeguard the credibility of its anti-inflationary stance. From then on it was the latter institution that directly took up the handling of the banking debacle, and the threats that had endangered the financial and payments systems of the country eventually passed.

Attention shifted to macroeconomic policy and the performance of the financial system during the rest of 1994 and 1995. After the exchange controls were instituted, the excessive liquidity in the economy became even more apparent, with the escape valve of imports having been partially shut. Because GDP was declining, the demand for credit was slumping, making the gap between the supply of money and the demand for money even larger. As a consequence the rates of interest plummeted, resulting in further incentives to capital flight, and pressures on international reserves and the parallel exchange rate.

Interest rates finally stabilized toward the end of 1994, not only because of the open market operations of the Central Bank, but also because of the floating of central government (Treasury) bonds and FOGADE capitalization bonds, that also helped drain reserves, currency, and other forms of money from the system, while helping to take over from the central bank the financial burden of the bank bailout. During 1995, the zero-coupon instruments were replaced by monetary stabilization issues (going as TEMs, from the Spanish acronym of Titulos de Estabilizacion Monetaria). These bore the brunt of the contractionary policy of the Central Bank in 1995, but still, as it had been in 1994, it ended up absorbing part of the onus of the banking crisis, as it had to purchase FOGADE capitalization bonds in large numbers, in addition to repurchasing its own zero-coupon issues. Thus the net outcome of the BCV operations in 1995 was, as it had been in 1994, that of adding to the monetary aggregates. Therefore, the sterilization of its financing of the banking crisis was incomplete to a major degree even in 1995, although less than in the previous year. Yet, there was an improvement in the second half of the year that was instrumental in raising the interest rates in the Venezuelan capital markets, as the placements of TEMs gained dynamism, helping to significantly drain liquidity and consequently lower the rate of inflation in the last months of the year. Notwithstanding, the economy was still in a contractionary state, with a depleted demand for money and lack of confidence by private investors. With the deposit rates of interest being negative in real terms, and the bolívar declining in the parallel markets, capitalists felt it was more profitable and less risky to have their money abroad. Certainly the banking crisis was a major determinant of this state of affairs, although the large fiscal deficits, the exchange controls, and policy inaction by the central government were other factors contributing to the recession. The emergency law which had been passed as a result of the threat to the financial and payments systems at the beginning of 1994, brought a decline of real GDP in the succeeding two-year period, and for the first time ever the BCV was in the red in its profit and loss statement, which limited the credibility of its monetary policy. Clearly, a change in direction had to be in the offing.

The new economic plan instituted in 1996 was called the Agenda Venezuela by the government. Its central point was to request the cooperation of the International Monetary Fund (IMF) and its sister multilateral financial institutions, the World Bank and the Inter-American Development Bank (IDB), in ensuring an end to the financial crisis and reestablishing of economic growth in per capita income, absent from the nation since the early 1990s. Concurrently, it was considered essential to reduce the burden of the foreign debt, by restructuring that part which had not been affected by the Brady rescheduling of 1989, and the medium-term instruments in that operation, which were to be amortized beginning in 1997. All of the above was to be addressed by macroeconomic stabilization and structural adjustment operations with the IMF.

The Agenda Venezuela included the following measures, which were preceded by a devaluation of the official exchange rate to 290 bolívares per U.S. dollar (a 70 percent drop from its value in December 1995).

1. The reduction of the fiscal deficit over, at most, a three-year span, to reach just 2 percent of GDP.

2. Doing away with exchange controls in 1996.

3. The World Bank and the IDB would help improve the operations of the banking sector and cleanse the nonperforming portfolio, while strengthening bank capital.

4. Implementation of the partial privatization of the social security system, with financial help from multilateral agencies.

5. New and improved safety net programs for the poor sectors of the population, financed by the IDB and the World Bank.

6. Deregulation, privatization, and competition in order to stimulate production, as well as the growth of productivity in agriculture, industry, and the petroleum sector.

7. Correction of disequilibria and distortions in the monetary and foreign exchange markets, beginning with the establishment of a market determined unified exchange rate (expected to eventually hover around 470 bolívares per U.S. dollar), and furthering the attaining of positive real rates of interest after deregulating the money markets of the country. In the short run the objective of monetary policy was to lower inflation to 2 percent a month by the beginning of 1997. International reserves were also expected to increase 1.5 billion U.S. dollars during 1996.

8. Support from the multilateral agencies for strengthening the training programs of the labor force, emphasizing improved skills and youth employment opportunities.

9. The rationalization and decentralization of the public sector, including the privatization of state enterprises.

The implementation of these measures in earnest was brought home by the increase in the domestic price of gasoline (amounting to about 500 percent), which was announced on April 15, 1996. This was accompanied by a subsidy to bus fares. Finally the executive branch was to seek an increase in the sales and luxury taxes from 12.5 percent to 16.5 percent (the IMF argued for 18 percent) from Congress.

On April 22, 1996, the exchange controls on current and capital transactions in the balance of payments were abolished, and the exchange rate policy shifted from the Ministry of Finance to the BCV. Both the foreign exchange rates and the various deposit and lender interest rates were now to be determined freely by market forces.

In July 1996 the Board of Directors of the IMF approved the technical assistance requested by Venezuela, together with the issuing of a Standby Credit for 975.6 million SDRs[2] (Special Drawing Rights), equivalent to 1.4 billion U.S. dollars (the first 350 million arrived in August). This was to be followed by a request for the establishment of an extended facility in April 1997. All of the above would pave the way for loans from the IDB and the World Bank for $1.9 billion.

Of the 39 commercial banks remaining in Venezuela after the crisis, seven were owned by foreigners, which included Citibank (U.S.), ING and ABN-AMRO (Dutch), Banco Ganadero and Banco Tequendama (Colombia), Banco do Brasil (Brazil), and Standard Chartered (England). There were also representative offices of many international bank groups.

Altogether, adding investment banks (25), mortgage banks (8), and leasing companies (21) to the existing commercial banks, there were only 93 financial institutions in the country as of March 1996, compared to the 147 companies that existed before the crisis (the insurance sector not included). These had over 1,500 branches. Given the small deposit base of the country (about 13 billion U.S. dollars), which in addition shrank substantially during the crisis (7.3 percent in real terms), the process of further consolidation continued, especially given the monetary tightness required during the early stages of the IMF stabilization and adjustment. This was a formidable challenge to the financial sector, which had mostly recovered by the beginning of 1996.[3]

In 1993 a new law regulating banks and other financial institutions had been passed. It promulgated that a level playing field be established so that foreign investors would have the same investment opportunities as local investors. This was the principal element goading a number of international banks to enter the Venezuelan market.

Together with FOGADE, the banking industry is regulated by the Banking Controller (Superintendencia de Bancos or SUDEBAN), and the Financial Emergency Board created when the crisis broke loose. These institutions strengthened as a result of the Agreement with the IMF and the actions of its collaborating banks. The inspection and supervision of the banks and of the payments systems was also improved.

The privatization of the Banco de Venezuela, Banco Latino, Banco Consolidado, and Banco Republica all took place early in 1997. The banking assets in the hand of FOGADE, as a result of bank closings or interventions, are being sold off. Finally, the efforts begun in the early 1990s to attain the risk-based capital requirements defined by the Basel Accord for private banks, have resumed, as the rules set by the Bank of International Settlements have spread the world over. All of these developments left foreign banks with a large influence in the finances of the country.

THE PERFORMANCE AND CONTRIBUTION OF THE EXTERNAL SECTOR

From the previous sections it is clear that Venezuela confronted very difficult external economic conditions spanning the middle of the decade through 1997. In addition, the dominance of Venezuela and its OPEC partners began to be challenged by conditions within the international oil market after its recovery in the early 1990s. The latter was yet again the result of another crisis in the Middle East, this time being the invasion of Kuwait by Iraq, and the following defeat of the latter in Operation Desert Storm. These events had a perverse impact on Venezuela's oil shares vis-a-vis total exports and GDP as seen in Table 12.2, where a sharp decline is clearly detected in both.

Fortunately, the rapid expansion of the world economy in 1996 and 1997 helped spark a modest recovery in these shares, particularly with respect to GDP, and had produced beneficial effects on oil prices, even while Venezuela was following a strategy of increasing oil production. These were particularly heady years for Venezuelan oil exports, which helped to attenuate the economic crisis described earlier in the chapter. But these

Table 12.2.
Petroleum Sector Indicators and External Sector Performance, 1991–2000 (millions of dollars)

	1991	1992	1993	1994	1995	1996	1997	1998	1999	2000
GDP	53,615	60,753	60,435	60,882	78,296	73,771	88,811	96,095	103,502	121,285
Total Exports	14,968	13,988	14,586	15,905	18,842	23,414	23,443	17,367	20,581	31,802
Oil Exports	12,119	11,014	10,855	11,351	13,630	18,368	18,041	11,914	16,193	24,742
Oil Exp. As % Total Exp.	81.0%	78.7%	74.4%	71.4%	72.3%	78.4%	77.0%	68.6%	78.7%	77.8%
Oil Exp. As % of GDP	22.6%	18.1%	18.0%	18.6%	17.4%	24.9%	20.3%	12.4%	15.6%	20.4%
Foreign Exchange Inflow										
Total	48,240	52,273	44,459	29,510	19,317	31,582	52,296	55,531	31,584	61,210
Oil	11,943	11,933	9,774	8,704	10,959	14,452	18,323	12,038	12,639	19,738
Oil As Percent of Total	24.8%	22.8%	22.0%	29.5%	56.7%	45.8%	35.0%	21.7%	40.0%	32.2%
Terms of Trade	54.6	51.1	47.5	50	54.8	62.1	57.3	42.1	56.5	85.2
% change in Terms of Trade	-16.5%	-6.4%	-7.0%	5.3%	9.6%	13.3%	-7.7%	-26.5%	34.2%	50.8%
International Reserves	14,105	13,001	12,656	11,507	9,723	15,229	17,818	14,849	15,379	20,471

Sources: OPEC Annual Statistical Bulletin, 2001 (summary tables and basic indicators); Banco Central de Venezuela, Anuario de Cuentas Nacionales (Caracas, various issues); and Ministerio de Minas e Hidrocarburos, Petróleo y Otros Datos Estadísticos (various issues).

conditions became unglued by mid-1997 with the Asian crisis, and hit rock bottom in 1998 when the international economy, additionally affected by the Russian default and the Brazilian financial crisis, became quite soft. This decline in demand, allied with increased petroleum supply, led the nominal prices of black gold to slide to just over $11 a barrel, a level significantly lower than the decade average of almost $16.90.[4] Consequently, the value of oil exports in that year (1998) fell by nearly 34 percent, a situation unprecedented in this decade.

Coinciding with these turns of events was the presidential election in Venezuela that brought Hugo Chavez to power. His nationalistic and socialistic policies slowly began to undermine the confidence of investors, both foreign and domestic. Fortunately, oil prices quickly moved upward in 1999 and 2000, but at the cost of significantly reduced oil production.

International reserve movements during the decade also yield evidence of these events, falling to their lowest level in 1995, and which also coincided with the worst terms of trade, before recovering in 1996 and 1997. Despite the policies of the Chavez administration, however, the end of decade figures show a remarkable improvement in both international reserves and terms of trade as compared to the entire previous decade.

Foreign exchange inflows, which fluctuated widely throughout, showed no clear signs of a positive or negative trend, although the decade average in nominal terms was definitely higher than in all the previous periods examined. This accounts, in part, for the dramatic rise in the dollar value of total imports, as seen in Table 12.3. Several important patterns should be noted here. First, capital imports, which represented about 25 percent of total imports from 1986 through 1994, dropped sharply to 18.2 percent in 1995 and, despite a modest rise in 1996 and 1997, continued to decline to the end of the period. By the year 2000, capital imports stood at a mere 14.9 percent.

In contrast, the share of imported consumer goods soared to as high as 20 and 22 percent. Surprisingly, some of the highest consumer import

Table 12.3.
Imports F.O.B. by Use of Commodity, 1991–2000 (millions of dollars)

	1991	1992	1993	1994	1995	1996	1997	1998	1999	2000
Capital Goods	2,764	3,488	2,909	2,139	2,199	1,925	2,649	2,509	2,147	2,309
As Percent of Total	26.9%	27.1%	25.3%	25.2%	18.2%	19.4%	19.4%	16.6%	16.2%	14.9%
Intermediate Goods	6,589	7,001	6,062	4,703	7,497	6,468	8,960	10,451	8,989	10,468
As Percent of Total	64.2%	54.4%	52.7%	55.3%	62.0%	65.1%	65.5%	69.2%	68.0%	67.6%
Consumer Goods	906	2,391	2,533	1,655	2,394	1,544	2,069	2,145	2,077	2,714
As Percent of Total	8.8%	18.6%	22.0%	19.5%	19.8%	15.5%	15.1%	14.2%	15.7%	17.5%
Total	10,259	12,880	11,504	8,497	12,090	9,937	13,678	15,105	13,213	15,491

Source: Banco Central de Venezuela, *Anuario de Cuentas Nacionales* (Caracas, various issues).

shares of the last quarter century occurred in this period, and judging from the latest figure reported, the country's appetite for imported consumer goods shows no signs of abating.

THE CONTRIBUTION THROUGH THE FISCAL SECTOR

The gains made during the previous decade to enlarge the share of government revenues from the oil sector were all reversed during this period as indicated by the figures in Table 12.4, where total government revenue and the revenue derived from petroleum activities in both current and 1957 bolívares, as well as the latter's share of the total are reported. In the beginning of the period, 1991, oil's contribution was nearly 70 percent of all revenues received by the Venezuelan government. By the end, however, that share had fallen to a mere 37 percent, or nearly half its former size.

The government obviously was having difficulty generating additional revenue from other sectors of the economy to make up for the declining oil shares. This is suggested by the fact that total government revenue, reported in 1957 bolívares, fell sharply at the same time that oil sector shares fell (from 1991 to 1995), despite modest growth in the non-oil sectors of the economy. The only significant increases here were seen in 1997 and 2000, and both were fueled by increases in the oil sector's contribution.

This phenomenon is obscured by the current figures that show government revenues increasing 25-fold. However, it is easily explained by the double and triple digit annual rates of inflation that were accompanying one of their worst economic performances of this century. By our estimates, the highest inflation rate was over 115 percent (between 1995 and 1996) while the lowest rate was just under 21 percent (between 1997 and

Table 12.4.
General Government Revenues from Petroleum and All Sources, 1991–2000 (millions of bolívares)

	1991	1992	1993	1994	1995	1996	1997	1998	1999	2000
Total Revenues	807,983	850,057	1,059,370	1,649,204	2,507,222	6,416,667	10,964,098	10,509,146	13,301,827	20,421,003
Petroleum Revenues	562,483	512,378	545,121	763,845	1,032,269	3,403,983	6,012,195	3,518,881	4,277,928	7,537,739
Total Revenues (in 1957 Bs.)	26,933	22,370	20,772	20,112	20,058	23,854	29,473	23,354	23,255	27,974
Petroleum Revenues (in 1957 Bs.)	18,749	13,484	10,689	9,315	8,258	12,654	16,162	7,820	7,479	10,326
Petroleum as a % of Total	69.6%	60.3%	51.5%	46.3%	41.2%	53.0%	54.8%	33.5%	32.2%	36.9%
% change in Petroleum shares	-15.2%	-13.4%	-14.6%	-10.0%	-11.1%	28.8%	3.4%	-38.9%	-4.0%	14.8%

Note: The 1957 valuations are the authors' estimates.

Source: Banco Central de Venezuela, *Anuario de Cuentas Nacionalies* (various issues); and Ministereo de Energia y Minas, *Petróleo y Otros Datos Estadísticos* (Caracas, various issues)..

1998). Also worth noting is that during 5 of the last 10 years analyzed over this period—GDP (as reported in 1957 bolívares) exhibited near zero or negative growth—with the worst episode occurring in 1999.[5]

Table 12.5 presents the period's data on public expenditures. In current bolívares, we see an increase of 19-fold from the beginning to the end of the period. However, as in the case of government revenues, these figures are grossly misleading. When adjusted for inflation, what emerges is a very slight upward trend (with an estimated annual average increase of about 235.55 million in 1957 bolívares), but statistically speaking, not considered significant. For all intents and purposes, government expenditures were flat.

It is interesting to note what percentage of these government expenditures were used for the acquisition of new capital in the public sector. For this, consider the net capital expenditure figures in Table 12.5. In nominal terms, they suggest there was a 25-fold increase in expenditures allotted for new capital, but the sad truth is—when adjusted for inflation—there was no significant growth in these expenditures at all. The 1957 bolívares figures show only a modest positive trend (with an average annual increase of about 79 million 1957 bolívares), but again, as in the case of public expenditures, this was not statistically significant. Therefore, with no clear pattern of rising public capital expenditures it must be concluded that its share out of total expenditures, though fluctuating from year to year, is representative of the decade average of just under 17 percent. This is much lower than the previous period's average of 38.16 percent.

Table 12.5.
Public Investment, Public Outlays, and Changes in Petroleum Revenues, 1991–2000 (millions of bolívares)

	1991	1992	1993	1994	1995	1996	1997	1998	1999	2000
Total Revenues	807,983	850,057	1,059,370	1,649,204	2,507,222	6,416,667	10,964,098	10,509,146	13,301,827	20,421,003
Petroleum Revenues	562,483	512,378	545,121	763,845	1,032,269	3,403,983	6,012,195	3,518,881	4,277,928	7,537,739
Total Revenues (in 1957 Bs.)	26,933	22,370	20,772	20,112	20,058	23,854	29,473	23,354	23,255	27,974
Petroleum Revenues (in 1957 Bs.)	18,749	13,484	10,689	9,315	8,258	12,654	16,162	7,820	7,479	10,326
Petroleum as a % of Total	69.6%	60.3%	51.5%	46.3%	41.2%	53.0%	54.8%	33.5%	32.2%	36.9%
% change in Petroleum shares	-15.2%	-13.4%	-14.6%	-10.0%	-11.1%	28.8%	3.4%	-38.9%	-4.0%	14.8%

Notes: The figures for current government expenditures and government net capital expenditures were calculated based on the percentages of GDP that they reportedly represented in each year. Current government expenditures include net loans granted, extra budgetary expenditures, and Central Bank losses, which in 1995 amounted to 2.8 percent of GDP. Current government expenditures and government net capital expenditures are not directly comparable to the public outlays and public investment figures in previous chapters. The 1957 valuations are the authors' estimates.

Sources: Economic Survey of Latin America and the Caribbean, 1998–2001, by ECLAC (Economic Commission on Latin America and the Caribbean), on the basis of official figures.

The oil sector's contribution through the fiscal sector, in terms of the revenues it generates and the public investment expenditures that are fueled by these revenues, is seen in the last two rows of Table 12.5. When the percentage changes in capital expenditures are compared to the percentage changes in petroleum revenues, the following relationship emerges. The change in petroleum revenues from year to year explains about 45 percent (on average) of the variation seen in the change in capital expenditures, when lagged one year.

From this analysis, it can be concluded that oil's contribution through the fiscal sector was very large indeed, although perhaps not as large as in previous periods. Theory suggests this may be a sign of a maturing economy diversifying away from its staple, and that would be good news. Unfortunately, since public expenditures on capital appear to be largely fueled by oil revenues, any fall in the latter will have dire consequences for this fragile economy in terms of new capital formation.

THE CONTRIBUTION OF OIL THROUGH INVESTMENT

It was indicated in the previous chapter that oil's contribution through investment has been declining over the years, but that the latest figures, from 1989 and 1990 especially, suggested that pattern was about to end. That now appears to be the case, as evidenced by the data in Table 12.6. This table presents total fixed investment (GFDI), the petroleum and nonpetroleum investment components, the overall investment rate (GFDI/GDP), and the decomposition of fixed petroleum investment into its various categories.

The first to be considered is the share of oil in total investment. These numbers are quite impressive when compared with those of the previous two periods spanning 1974 to 1990. In fact, the current period shares are so large they look more like those seen during the 1949–1957 period, except they are even larger. For example, the average annual share for the 1948–1957 period was 27.1 percent compared with the latest period's average of 32.05 percent. The largest shares of oil investment during the current period occurred between 1995 and 1997, the same years that the overall investment rate hit its lowest level since 1991 and in the midst of an economic contraction. (See GDP in 1957 bolívares.) Even when nominal valuations of oil investments are adjusted for inflation, a sizeable increase is still noticeable during the years 1995 through 1997. However, when one compares oil investment levels for the period, they were higher on average at the beginning of the period than at the end of the period (6,003 versus 5,286 in millions of 1957 bolívares). Investment rates followed a similar pattern, fluctuating throughout the period, with an overall annual average rate of 17.72 percent compared to the 20.28 percent average for the previous period.

Table 12.6.
Gross Fixed Investment in Petroleum and Other Sectors, 1991–2000 (millions of bolívares)

	1991	1992	1993	1994	1995	1996	1997	1998	1999	2000
Gross Fixed Dom. Investment (GFDI):	551,965	886,400	1,091,127	1,528,345	2,255,593	4,645,762	8,123,015	9,991,302	9,850,556	11,719,020
Oil Sector Fixed. Inv.	166,505	233,649	321,881	466,201	898,335	1,981,238	2,870,814	2,720,135	2,936,506	3,417,254
Non-Oil Sector Fixed Inv.	385,460	652,751	769,246	1,062,144	1,357,258	2,664,524	5,252,201	7,271,167	6,914,050	8,301,766
Oil Sec. Fixed Inv. (1957 Bs.)	5,550	6,149	6,311	5,685	7,187	7,365	7,717	6,045	5,134	4,681
Non-Oil Sec. Fixed Invest. (1957 Bs.)	12,849	17,178	15,083	12,953	10,858	9,905	14,119	16,158	12,088	11,372
Oil Investment as a Percent of GFDI	30.2%	26.4%	29.5%	30.5%	39.8%	42.6%	35.3%	27.2%	29.8%	29.2%
GFDI as a Percent of GDP	18.2%	21.5%	20.0%	17.6%	16.5%	15.8%	18.7%	19.0%	15.7%	14.2%
Distribution of Investment:										
Production	296,771	460,420	688,980	1,010,077	1,459,633	2,660,703	4,276,528	5,841,438	7,415,615	9,127,766
As a Percent of Total	43.6%	44.8%	44.8%	43.1%	40.0%	40.6%	45.9%	49.6%	52.3%	56.1%
Transport	39,637	50,415	118,630	232,397	336,900	573,997	811,721	565,219	610,847	894,316
As a Percent of Total	5.8%	4.9%	7.7%	9.9%	9.2%	8.7%	8.7%	4.8%	4.3%	5.5%
Refining	175,696	282,505	444,994	801,983	1,504,398	2,532,961	3,206,875	4,296,234	4,908,804	5,246,595
As Percent of Total	25.8%	27.5%	28.9%	34.2%	41.3%	38.6%	34.4%	36.5%	34.7%	32.2%
Sales	21,477	25,638	43,002	35,106	42,985	97,840	188,490	252,791	396,217	556,458
As Percent of Total	3.2%	2.5%	2.8%	1.5%	1.2%	1.5%	2.0%	2.1%	2.8%	3.4%
Other	147,636	209,692	243,408	266,020	302,772	695,629	828,816	814,339	834,856	446,724
As a Percent of Total	21.7%	20.4%	15.8%	11.3%	8.3%	10.6%	8.9%	6.9%	5.9%	2.7%
Total	681,217	1,028,670	1,539,014	2,345,583	3,646,688	6,561,130	9,312,430	11,770,021	14,166,339	16,271,859

Notes: Oil investment reported on a GDP accounting basis. Distribution based on Ministerio de Minas e Hidrocarburos data, definitions that are different from GDP accounting methodology. The 1957 valuations are the authors' estimates.

Sources: Banco Central de Venezuela, *Anuario de Cuentas Nacionales* (Caracas, various issues); Ministerio de Minas e Hidrocarburos, *Petróleo y Otros Datos Estadísticos* (Caracas, various issues).

Table 12.6 also shows how fixed investment in the oil industry was distributed by major uses. The lion's share of oil sector investment was utilized in the production of petroleum, which increased steadily over this period in all but two years (1995 and 1996), in relative terms. This category also includes surveying, exploration, exploitation, and extraction, as well as production. As mentioned in previous chapters, this type of investment not only leads to further roduction of the hydrocarbons, but to the expansion of reserves. The second major use of oil sector investment was in refining. Here we find the highest shares of investment spending in this category occurred in 1995 and 1996, the same years that the shares of investment in production dropped. Combined investment in these two categories was 69.4 percent at the beginning of the period and climbed steadily to 88.3 percent by the end. This suggests a significant reallocation of investment spending had taken place with emphasis on production and refining. The flip side is that in the "other" category listed, investment shares fell from 21.7 percent in 1991 to just under 3 percent in 2000.

The oil sector's contribution can also be examined through the retained value of oil expenditures that represent the value added or income gener-

Table 12.7.
Retained Value of Oil Sector Expenditures, 1991–2000 (millions of bolívares)

	1991	1992	1993	1994	1995	1996	1997	1998	1999	2000
Total Oil Sector Expenditures	1,436,543	1,718,186	2,271,841	3,850,423	5,537,065	16,657,378	20,979,277	16,663,272	22,716,132	39,878,836
Retained Value of Oil Expenditures	1,196,669	1,412,010	1,880,360	3,247,826	4,467,620	14,633,348	17,675,284	13,626,829	19,700,671	34,222,392
Ratio of Retained Value to Expenditures	83.30%	82.18%	82.77%	84.35%	80.69%	87.85%	84.25%	81.78%	86.73%	88.25%
Retained Value per barrel of Oil	1,372.70	1,614.07	2,081.45	3,399.61	4,373.01	13,439.27	15,324.50	11,214.39	17,641.87	29,721.40
Ret. Value of Oil Exp. (1957 Bs.)	47,545	46,979	50,333	52,684	56,413	60,751	66,460	67,772	62,745	64,723
Ret. Value per barrel (1957 Bs.)	54.54	53.7	55.72	55.15	55.22	55.79	57.62	55.77	56.19	56.21

Notes: Oil sector expenditures include capital expenditures. Retained value of expenditures does not include capital expenditures or revenues from exchange differential. The 1957 valuations are the authors' estimates.

Sources: Banco Central de Venezuela, *Anuario de Cuentas Nacionales* (Caracas, various issues); Ministerio de Minas e Hidrocarburos, *Petróleo y Otros Datos Estadísticos* (Caracas, various issues).

ated in the oil sector that is retained or spent within the economy. These figures are found in Table 12.7. Again, because of inflation over this period, the nominal valuations are misleading. A truer picture is seen in the inflation-adjusted 1957 bolívares figures. Two interesting patterns emerge. First, the average 1957 valuation of the retained value in the oil sector is significantly higher in this period than in any other during this century. Even last period's average of 22,660 is considerably less than this period's average of 57,640 reported in millions of 1957 bolívares. When one considers only the current period, there is a statistically significant positive trend of about 2,411 per year, on average, despite the large decline in 1999.

Second, with reference to the ratio of retained value to total expenditures, the decade average of 0.84 is more than 10 percent lower that the previous period's average of 0.94, indicating that the overall downward trend in this ratio that first appeared after 1985 is still holding. However, because the last two years (1999 and 2000) show ratios that are higher than the decade average, this may be a sign that the downward trend is about to be reversed.

THE CONTRIBUTION OF OIL THROUGH PRODUCTION AND INCOME

The contribution of oil through its total product and the income it generates are considered in Table 12.8. The nominal valuations reported here would seem to show that Venezuela's GDP grew 27-fold and that the oil sector's GDP grew 28-fold. In reality, however, when inflation is accounted for—as seen in the 1957 bolívares valuation—these numbers plummet to 1.1 and 1.4, respectively. Growth in total GDP and oil sector GDP has not

Table 12.8.
Value of Oil Production, GDP Originating in the Petroleum Sector, and Total GDP by Sector, 1991–2000

	1991	1992	1993	1994	1995	1996	1997	1998	1999	2000
Gross Domestic Product (mill bs.)	3,037,492	4,131,483	5,453,903	8,675,172	13,685,686	29,437,682	43,343,669	52,482,466	62,577,039	82,450,674
Value of Oil Production (mill bs.)	665,492	785,647	969,901	1,671,820	2,367,190	7,778,329	8,755,039	6,422,505	9,916,209	18,688,206
				in millions of 1957 bolívares						
Oil Sector GDP	22,731	22,460	24,063	25,187	26,970	29,044	31,773	32,400	29,997	30,943
Total GDP	101,533	107,686	107,983	105,445	109,612	109,395	116,365	116,563	109,469	113,011
% change in GDP	9.7%	5.7%	0.3%	-2.4%	3.8%	-0.2%	6.0%	0.2%	-6.5%	3.1%
Oil as a Percent of GDP	22.4%	20.9%	22.3%	23.9%	24.6%	26.6%	27.3%	27.8%	27.4%	27.4%
Total Non-Petroleum Sector GDP	76,941	82,838	81,799	78,600	80,570	78,548	81,883	81,157	76,780	79,081
Manufacturing	16,827	17,880	17,635	17,029	18,202	17,253	18,011	16,997	15,431	16,029
Agriculture	5,051	5,153	5,309	5,251	5,222	5,325	5,452	5,485	5,368	5,498
Electricity & Water	1,702	1,778	1,834	1,860	1,908	1,932	2,023	2,049	2,072	2,118
General Government	9,132	9,230	8,978	9,011	9,075	8,728	8,429	8,502	8,599	8,879
Construction	5,982	8,048	7,606	6,286	5,972	6,038	7,074	7,053	5,886	5,727
Non-Petroleum Mining	624	730	814	900	975	1,001	1,068	1,020	914	989
Transportation, Storage & Communication	5,116	5,387	5,434	5,250	5,422	5,513	6,012	6,364	6,468	6,995
Financial Institutions	13,866	14,400	14,507	14,208	14,264	13,790	14,209	14,350	13,879	14,187
Commerce	13,799	15,175	14,563	13,399	13,571	12,595	13,105	12,707	11,490	11,945
All Other Services	6,702	7,445	7,240	7,064	8,031	8,178	9,208	9,635	9,364	9,701
Import Rights	1,861	2,388	2,120	1,658	2,073	1,803	2,709	3,005	2,692	2,987

Notes: Years 1999 and 2000 are preliminary figures. All other services include financial, community, social, and personal services.

Sources: Banco Central de Venezuela, *Anuario de Cuentas Nacionales* (Caracas, various issues); Ministerio de Minas e Hidrocarburos, *Petróleo y Otros Datos Estadísticos* (Caracas, various issues).

been as spectacular as in some periods. In fact the 1957 valuations show that there were three contractions in GDP occurring between 1993 and 1994 (–2.350 percent), 1995 and 1996 (–0.225 percent) and 1998 and 1999 (–6.086 percent). Each contraction in total GDP was spurred on by a corresponding contraction in non-oil sector GDP, particularly in its three largest components: manufacturing, financial institutions, and commerce—all of which are highly sensitive to foreign investment flows.

Table 12.9 shows what happened to value added in the manufacturing sector, the largest component of non-oil GDP. Of the 19 subcomponents listed, not one shows a clear pattern of positive growth for the decade. In fact, in the first column of that table, where the percentage changes between the years 1991 and 1999 are listed, only five showed a positive change, and those were in the smallest of the subcomponents. The largest negative percentage changes occurred in textiles, leather, transport equipment, and paper. Even the largest subcomponents like chemicals and pharmaceuticals (–8.92 percent), and iron steel and nonferrous metals (–12.57 percent), experienced significant negative growth.

Fortunately, oil sector GDP continued to grow despite this calamitous economic environment. Perhaps most telling of all is what happened to

Table 12.9.
Value Added in Manufacturing, 1991–1999 (millions of 1957 bolívares)

	% change 1991-1999	1991	1992	1993	1994	1995	1996	1997	1998	1999
Food	-1.72%	2,563	2,729	2,769	2,773	2,668	2,665	2,553	2,621	2,519
Beverages	-15.72%	1,285	1,365	1,430	1,384	1,564	1,417	1,244	1,157	1,083
Tobacco	9.11%	549	617	675	644	695	623	589	658	599
Textiles	-41.17%	1,681	1,676	1,379	1,356	1,460	1,417	1,248	1,119	989
Leather	-33.92%	401	414	354	338	349	318	360	335	265
Wood products and nonmetallic furniture	-0.21%	481	541	517	490	486	439	477	490	480
Paper	-26.43%	420	468	452	438	457	345	368	330	309
Printing	14.58%	336	340	350	386	473	369	429	450	385
Chemicals and pharmaceuticals	-8.92%	2,153	2,342	2,221	2,040	2,229	1,986	1,935	1,884	1,961
Rubber Products	-7.58%	343	324	338	345	343	300	329	306	317
Plastic Products	-18.44%	499	508	484	451	507	554	599	566	407
Clay, glass, and other nonmetallic minerals	9.29%	947	1,008	1,105	1,030	1,150	1,119	1,198	1,284	1,035
Iron, Steel, and nonferrous metals	-12.57%	2,666	2,695	2,655	2,714	2,881	2,887	3,159	2,611	2,331
Metal Products	10.52%	1,036	1,134	1,144	1,133	1,233	1,217	1,241	1,185	1,145
Machinery other than electric	-5.81%	344	401	403	334	315	322	423	385	324
Electrical machinery	15.86%	391	446	469	300	320	375	636	571	453
Transport equipment	27.30%	381	506	513	404	546	479	866	684	485
Other industries	-1.71%	350	367	378	469	526	422	356	359	344
TOTAL	-8.30%	16,827	17,880	17,635	17,029	18,202	17,253	18,011	16,997	15,431

Source: Banco Central de Venezuela. *Anuario de Cuentas Nacionales* (Caracas, various issues).

the share of oil sector GDP out of total GDP. As seen in Table 12.8, these percentages are much larger than in the previous three periods, and resemble the numbers seen during the 1957–1965 period. Different interpretations can be assigned to this phenomenon but the one most applicable is that oil sector activity continues to be the most stable and reliable source of income and production in this economy, despite what appears to have been a weaning of the economy's reliance on oil activity in the past.

This begs the question, why was non-oil sector activity so volatile and unstable over this period? To what extent does the blame rest on the macroeconomic stabilization and structural adjustments imposed by the IMF? Certainly they influenced relative investment levels in favor of the oil sector vis-a-vis the non-oil sector. Recall from Table 12.6 that this decade saw a sizeable increase in the percentage of oil investment to total investment spending, even though total investment levels were flat and/or declining. It is fortunate that PDVSA was capable of self-financing most of its new investment projects because it would have been nearly impossible, given the poisonous economic climate under President Chavez, to have maintained the investment levels seen in this decade if forced to rely on foreign investment flows, as was the case in the non-oil sectors of the economy.

Another contributing factor to the decline in non-oil GDP may also lie in the reallocation of investment spending taking place within the oil sector itself. This decade saw increases that favored oil production and refining activities at the expense of categories like transportation and "other" which may have had intrinsically larger income-multiplier effects than other oil related activities. Whatever the case may be, it is clear that the future of the Venezuelan economy still rests on the fortunes of its oil sector.

NOTES

1. See World Bank, Commodity Markets and the Developing Countries, several issues.

2. These are monetary units used in international official currency transactions, particularly by the IMF, and their value is based on the fluctuating parities of the five strongest currencies in the world.

3. During the continued inflationary years in Venezuela, a novelty of the 1990s, its bankers had found a way to profit from the inflationary float, a condition that disappeared given the diminishing rhythm of price increases in succeeding years.

4. This average does not include the 1998 figure.

5. This can be seen in Table 12.8, under total GDP in millions of 1957 bolívares.

CHAPTER 13

Conclusions

Almost every peripheral country in the not-so-distant past and more recently has had a pattern of trade based on the export of primary products and the importation of industrial goods. The major source of growth in these countries was the export sector or one or a few lines in it. Such sector lines usually constituted a sizeable portion of the product originated in these countries.

If these activities expand satisfactorily over a long period of time (two or three decades), would their influence upon the other sectors be sufficiently strong so as to bring about a parallel expansion of the economy? As has been seen in Chapter 2, there are affirmative and negative views on this question, while others believe there is no general rule. Most periods of expansion in primary export activities in peripheral countries occurred in the past. Hence, history might contribute to settling this debate, even though the expositors of these views also hold contradictory beliefs as to the historical outcomes. Very little effort has been made to resolve the debate in an empirical fashion.

It is our belief that in peripheral countries with the characteristics mentioned above, primary export sectors or lines can transmit their growth to the whole economy. This usually takes place automatically, but in many cases it requires an efficacious manipulation of the impact of the potential leading sector upon the rest of the economy.

FROM 1936 TO 1973

The Venezuelan economy in the 20th century is a test case for these views. Petroleum activities in 1929, when GDP estimates were initiated, represented about 10 percent of economic activity. In terms of retained value of total expenditures, petroleum grew at a 12.3 percent compounded yearly average rate from 1936 to 1973.[1] Even in terms of petroleum GDP, in constant 1957 bolívares, the growth amounted to more than 6.5 percent yearly. It is clear that petroleum fits the definition of a potential leading sector during these years.

In 1936 the Venezuelan economy exported almost exclusively primary products and produced very little of its industrial goods at home. Primary activities dominated the economy and a great portion of the industrial establishment was small scale and of the craft and artisan type.[2] Petroleum was the main source of growth in Venezuela over the next four decades, as shown in preceding chapters.

Exports accounted for 23.7 percent of total GDP in 1936, even though world trade had not recuperated from the jolt of the Depression. By 1940 the participation of exports in total GDP had risen to 31.1 percent. Thus, just before the war Venezuela was in every sense an open-economy, tied to the advanced nations through international markets. It traditionally had depended on the international economy for an important portion of its necessities and requirements, and as a basic source of its economic progress.

In its expansion, the Venezuelan oil industry contributed to the growth of the other sectors. Its main contributions were fourfold: (1) its financing of the public sector and the provision of services of an essentially public character by the industry, while absorbing a minimal portion of the government's budget (see Table 13.1); (2) the foreign exchange earnings it supplied; (3) the increase in economic wealth and productive capacity of the nation taking place through petroleum investment, and the strengthening of the Venezuelan capital goods industry that it brought about; and (4) the income and current expenditures originating in the oil industry and the multiplier-accelerator repercussions they created throughout the economy, leading to an increase in aggregate demand and a larger volume of savings.

With respect to the two latter contributions, special importance must be attached to the retained portions of petroleum investment and current expenditures, which have a more direct and immediate impact on the rest of the economy. In fact, although there are many other contributions, the retained value of total expenditures is an approximate reflection of the combined total. The petroleum industry provided a large share of the total foreign exchange earnings of the economy.

While at the beginning net capital inflows constituted an important part of these earnings, this has not been the case since the late 1950s. Petroleum exports have risen tremendously over time, at an average compounded rate of 6.5 percent (for the dynamic 1936–1973 period) and so have its related effects, such as import availability, and its inflation-combating

Table 13.1.
Share of Energy and Mines on Central Government Expenditures, 1940–1980

Year	Percent
1940	2.4
1945	4.0
1950	6.7
1955	3.1
1960	1.6
1965	1.6
1970	2.0
1975	1.8
1980	0.2

Notes: The information reported for 1940, 1945, and 1950 is for the Development Ministry, which included the Department of Mines and Hydrocarbons at the time. After 1950, the information is directly from the Ministry of Mines and Hydrocarbons, and later, the Ministry of Energy and Mines.

Sources: Banco Central de Venezuela, *La Economía Venezolana en los Ultimos Treinta Años* (Caracas, 1971); Ministerio de Fomento, *Memoria* (various years).

capabilities, that have been referred to as its balance of payments contribution.

Oil has also contributed a large share to government revenues. Taxes derived directly from the oil sector rose at an annual average compounded rate of 15.1 percent during the golden years, with their share in total tax revenues increasing as well. As in the balance of payments contribution, other effects related to oil taxes are part and parcel of its public sector contribution, such as the low tax pressure on other sectors and the possibility of extending public services while averting deficit financing.

The investment contribution of petroleum from 1936 to 1973 was not quite as impressive. In real terms, oil investment only grew at a compounded annual average rate of 4.1 percent. But, if 1958 is taken as the terminal year, that rate is much higher, at about 11.1 percent. Despite the fact that the share of oil in total investment declined through time, the investment contribution of petroleum was still substantial, especially in helping to further the development of the construction and metal industries.

Another important contribution was the exogenous income-expenditure injections of oil into the flow matrix of the Venezuelan economy, which were quite considerable. As petroleum is export oriented, changes in its price do not directly or necessarily affect internal prices in Venezuela. Thus, the income-expenditure injections, expressed in current terms, are the relevant ones. Total current petroleum expenditures rose at an annual average compounded rate of more that 11 percent from 1936 to 1973. The GDP of the petroleum industry in current terms grew at a similar pace. Clearly, the overall expenditure contribution, which embraces other related effects, experienced a formidable increase over this dynamic period.

No other contributions have been examined in detail over this period. But the tremendous increase in the retained value of total expenditures suggests that their growth would have been comparable. Total retained value increased at a 12.3 percent annual average compounded rate of growth. This means that in 1973 the retained value of total expenditures in the oil industry was 74 times larger than in 1936.

Over these years total retained value increased, in absolute terms, more than the total expenditures of the oil industry. Thus, the share of total retained value to total expenditures rose. One of the reasons for this was the influence of government policies at the time. The Venezuelan government was juggling a number of important variables, such as the native wage bill of the industry, its local purchases, and the amount of oil tax it collected to influence this share.[3] Occasionally, however, the share would change as a result of the decisions of the oil companies.

The government was quite successful in enlarging the retained value portion up to 1948. From 1948 to 1957 the pressure was off. When it resumed in 1958, it was concurrent with a confidence crisis in the oil industry with respect to the economic and political future of Venezuela and with misgivings about the status of the companies and the organization of the Venezuelan oil industry in the years ahead. As a result, investment dropped off considerably, and exports stagnated.

For the manipulation of the portion of total expenditures retained in Venezuela, tax policy was mainly used. In previous chapters, the question of the effects of high tax pressure on oil sales has been briefly considered. Up to 1957, the increasing tax pressure on the oil industry did not affect petroleum exports. But as taxes continued to rise from 1958 to 1965, it took its toll on exports (see Table 13.2). Even when decreasing oil prices are taken into account, the growth in oil exports from 1957 onward is much slower, as the figures show, notwithstanding that total world exports of oil continued to expand at a brisk pace during the latter period. Thus, the higher tax pressure from 1958 to 1965 appears to have had a negative impact on oil exports.

This illustrates the fact that there are limits to the juggling of the retained value portion of total expenditures. At a certain point, an increase of, say, 1 percent in the tax rate on oil might actually bring about a decrease in total retained value, or a smaller rise than if no change in taxes had taken place. Thus, the maximization of the absolute size of retained value of total expenditures over the long run, which had to be the central objective of petroleum policy in Venezuela, might have required the sacrifice of immediate gains under certain circumstances.

However, the situation changed considerably in the late 1960s and 1970s. A conservationist policy with respect to petroleum became preva-

Table 13.2.
Tax Pressure on the Oil Industry and Oil Exports, 1936–1973

Year	Tax Pressure (percent)	Exports (mill. US $)	Year	Tax Pressure (percent)	Exports (mill. US $)
1936	10.47	133	1955	30.50	1,791
1937	8.40	167	1956	31.46	2,086
1938	21.13	187	1957	32.58	2,570
1939	18.46	170	1958	38.62	2,299
1940	17.53	262	1959	37.38	2,128
1941	15.83	324	1960	36.58	2,149
1942	19.11	206	1961	38.34	2,213
1943	22.00	254	1962	41.07	2,343
1944	25.48	342	1963	41.97	2,336
1945	31.73	332	1964	45.73	2,341
1946	29.19	485	1965	45.46	2,305
1947	29.34	664	1966	46.17	2,221
1948	30.05	1,069	1967	49.42	2,333
1949	28.05	966	1968	49.12	2,425
1950	28.85	1,124	1969	55.17	2,449
1951	29.68	1,297	1970	54.14	2,496
1952	29.54	1,384	1971	54.43	3,127
1953	27.99	1,428	1972	62.75	3,509
1954	29.43	1.564	1973	66.56	5.294

Note: Tax pressure defined as taxes accrued over value of production.

Sources: Banco Central de Venezuela, *La Economía Venezolana en los Ultimos Treinta Años* (Caracas, 1971); Ministerio de Fomento, *Anuario Estadístico* (Caracas, several years); Ministerio de Minas e Hidrocarburos, unpublished statistics; authors' own calculations.

lent. Venezuela felt that the expansion in the production of oil was not appropriate, given the increasing exhaustion of the reserves of this nonrenewable resource. This was especially true because foreign corporations were then exploiting these reserves. At that juncture the continued pressures to increase the retained value portion out of the total oil expenditures made sense, given the goals of the government. Of course, implied was the discouragement of investment in, and exports of oil, *except* if they were the result of substantially higher oil prices. All this may involve a sacrifice in the *absolute* figures of retained value of oil expenditures.

It is clear that the contribution of the oil industry to the other sectors of the Venezuelan economy has been considerable. To a great extent the policy decisions of the Venezuelan government brought this about. The government was also instrumental in reaping the potential benefits of petroleum's contributions. However, frequently these contributions were inefficiently utilized.

In general, it should be noted that government policies determining the contributions of oil, and directing their use, left ample room for improvement. Seemingly, the government did not have clearly defined policy objectives in relation to the petroleum industry and its influence on the economy, or if it had, it did not consistently follow them.

The economy experienced a considerable expansion from 1936 to 1973. Total GDP, in 1957 prices, grew at a 6.5 percent average annual compounded rate of growth. Nonpetroleum GDP expanded at a 7 percent annual average rate. This is one of the fastest growth rates during a comparable time span in contemporary economic history. Notwithstanding a very high population growth rate, per capita GDP, in constant 1957 bolívares, increased at an approximate compounded average of 3.25 percent yearly.

In the meantime, the Venezuelan economy experienced a strong industrialization process. If oil and mining are excluded, secondary activities were the most dynamic sector in the economy during this interval. The process gained strength from 1942 on, and based itself in an expansion of the market and in the substitution of industrial imports. As a result, by 1973 Venezuela had become a semi-industrialized society. The agricultural sector grew disappointingly during most of these periods, however, while the tertiary sector expanded more of less in consonance with the overall growth of the economy.

Enormous progress took place in the Venezuelan infrastructure from 1936 to 1973. The basic conditions for achieving a takeoff were met by the late 1950s. In the 1960s, a new era dawned in Venezuela, with the economy becoming increasingly resilient and soaring into self-sustained growth.

Even though it slackened considerably during the 1960s, investment in Venezuela, in real terms, increased at an 8.4 percent average compounded annual rate from 1936 to 1973. Even though the rate of capital accumulation accelerated somewhat during the early 1970s, its rate of expansion had been significantly greater prior to 1957. The growth in investment was higher in the nonpetroleum part of the economy. From 1936 to 1973 nonpetroleum gross fixed domestic investment, measured in 1957 bolívares, grew at an average annual compounded rate of 9.4 percent.

From 1936 to 1955 total GDP, in 1957 bolívares, grew at a 9.2 percent rate of growth per year, on average. During this period, the average investment rate, in constant bolívares, was 23.8 percent yearly. From 1955 to 1973 the rate of growth decreased to a yearly average of 5.75 percent. At the same time, the rate of capital formation also decreased to an annual average of 18.6 percent. Although the differences are small, these facts show that increases in capital formation were tied to higher rates of growth over the long run, which is in agreement with Kuznets's findings. It should be noted that this test is more fitting to Kuznets's proposition than those reported in previous chapters, as they cover a longer time span. Kuznets usually used two or three decades in his empirical studies, using 15-year periods only as an exception.

THE DISTRIBUTION OF THE GAINS FROM GROWTH

1936–1973

The absolute increase in retained value of total expenditures of the oil industry from 1936 to 1973 comes to about 5.9 times the total GDP of Venezuela in 1936, if both are expressed in current bolívares. The growth of the Venezuelan economy, resulting to an important degree from the massive influence of oil, was considerable. Yet, the rise in product and income per capita can be impressive and still not affect most of the people, because of an unequal income distribution.

The process of economic development in Venezuela has been marred by such income distribution problems. They relate to the personal distribution of income and also the regional one.

Table 13.3.
Volume of Oil Exports, 1950–1973 (thousands of cubic meters)

Year	Exports	Year	Exports
1950	82,619	1962	175,165
1951	93,566	1963	178,362
1952	99,491	1964	186,935
1953	96,423	1965	188,748
1954	104,118	1966	184,635
1955	117,433	1967	195,061
1956	134,539	1968	196,009
1957	149,498	1969	197,929
1958	141,432	1970	201,343
1959	149,586	1971	191,723
1960	156,238	1972	180,095
1961	160,420	1973	185,616

Source: Ministerio de Minas e Hidrocarburos, *Petróleo y Otros Datos Estadísticos* (Caracas, 1974).

Only very recently has some attention been devoted to the study of the personal distribution of income in Venezuela. Empirical proof of the anomaly in the personal income distribution was first presented by the Commission to Study the Fiscal System of Venezuela, directed by Carl Shoup.[4] Since then, various studies have appeared, based on the national survey of income and expenditures undertaken by CORDIPLAN (the national planning agency of Venezuela) in 1962, and another nationwide data collection effort on housing which included information on income. The latter was jointly carried out by the National Savings and Loan Bank and the National Housing Commission.[5] They tend to confirm what the Shoup Commission found in 1957.

The effects of a highly concentrated distribution of personal income on economic development have been subject to controversy. According to some economists, an unequal income distribution facilitates a high savings rate, which is essential for growth. Others believe that a less-skewed income distribution is tied to the expansion of the middle class, and thus to a more numerous entrepreneurial class, while bringing about larger internal markets.

Various studies have looked at how greater or less equality in the distribution of income affects growth.[6] The general conclusion has been that important changes in the former have relatively weak effects on growth. In the case of Venezuela, it appears that the inequality in its personal income distribution did not hamper the development process noticeably. The high savings rate during these decades is partly the result of its skewed distribution of income. Even though the domestic market would have been larger if greater equality had prevailed, the substantial immigration that took place after World War II, and the elaborate business promotion system of the government, assured a strong economy and a healthy demand for capital.

A worrisome fact, however, is that the personal distribution of income in Venezuela appears to be getting worse. This is the conclusion reported in an article that attempted to compare the various estimates of the pattern of personal income distribution across time, starting with the Shoup study.[7] Furthermore, if the functional distribution of income, represented by the factor shares, is considered, the distribution of income, after becoming generally more equal up to1963, began to move in the opposite direction (see Table 13.4).

As to the regional distribution of income, previous chapters have shown that, up to 1950, growth was highly concentrated in Caracas and in the areas where petroleum operations were taking place. From then on, other territories began to increase their participation in the economic growth of the country (for example, the state of Bolivar in the Guayana region and the Maracay, Valencia, and Barquisimeto areas), but Caracas and its environs still gained the most. It was only from the 1960s onward that centers

Table 13.4.
Share of Labor in National Income, 1936, 1949–1973

Year	Percent	Year	Percent
1936	46	1961	62
1949	61	1962	60
1950	60	1963	61
1951	58	1964	56
1952	55	1965	56
1953	58	1966	57
1954	57	1967	58
1955	56	1968	58
1956	55	1969	58
1957	52	1970	57
1958	54	1971	57
1959	60	1972	56
1960	61	1973	57

Sources: Evelyn M. Baran, *The Economic Development of Venezuela*, Ph.D. dissertation, Redcliffe College, 1950; and Banco Central de Venezuela, *Memoria* (Caracas, 1959); and *Informe Económico* (Caracas, various years).

of economic activity not related to the exploration of oil began to show dynamism comparable to that of Caracas.

Regional disparities in growth rates usually occur while a nation grows. Although such disparities are, to some extent, essential to economic development, a great deal of regional inequality can be eliminated without the rate of development being affected. In fact, sometimes by so doing, the rate of economic growth might even be improved. In this sense, the performance of the Venezuelan economy left much to be desired.

In conclusion, the outstanding record of the Venezuelan economy in terms of economic growth during this period was accompanied by an unjust distribution of income. However, the pace of economic growth and development does not appear to have been significantly affected by such income distribution problems.

Even though the labor share in the national income of Venezuela has had an irregular movement throughout time, it has grown considerably if 1936 is taken as the initial period. Furthermore, various indices of wages, prices, and real wages confirm the gains in real standards of living of the labor force from the mid-1930s to 1973.[8]

Yet there are indications that some labor groups only reaped minimal gains over these years. These are easily recognizable by a comparison of the employment and product-originated shares of the various groups. Improvements in productivity and real income have been especially small for agricultural workers, and quite limited for a large chunk of the workers in the service sector. Furthermore, these golden years of development seem to have left by the wayside increasing numbers of unemployed and underemployed workers. All these conditions define limitations to, and reductions of, the welfare gains derived by many Venezuelans from the growth process described previously.

In 1936 Venezuela, a peripheral country, with its pattern of trade based on primary-type exports, imported most of the industrial goods it required. It specialized in the production of oil for the world markets, with this product providing its main source of growth. The rest of the Venezuelan economy successfully grafted its expansion onto that of petroleum. Although there were unfavorable effects stemming from the petroleum industry during the time interval examined, they were neutralized by public policies and overcome by the contributions of the industry, allowing the Venezuelan economy to expand briskly.

In this context, it should be mentioned that Venezuela grew in spite of the play of some of the adverse factors mentioned by the development economists whose views were examined in Chapter 2. Some of these were as follows: (1) the unfavorable movement of the terms of trade during certain periods; (2) the very high rate of population growth which was partly the result of the openness of the economy; (3) the organization of petroleum operations in units that had enclave-like characteristics (leakages, a monopsony-monopoly position, and so forth); (4) the immigration of foreign labor into the oil industry and the rest of the economy; (5) the factor proportions that stressed the utilization of capital rather than labor in the advanced sector; (6) the fierce competition of imports with native goods; and (7) the absence of the basic preconditions for a takeoff. Other factors that, according to these economists, impede the carry-over of a primary type export expansion never did materialize in the Venezuelan case. For instance, the quite famous demonstration effect did not have a significantly deleterious effect on the rate of savings, and perverse factor movements were generally not important either.

The Venezuelan economy from 1936 to 1973 fits our hypothesis quite well. The petroleum industry acted as a leading sector during most of this time span, bringing about the development of the economy. Government policy had a central role in neutralizing some of the ill effects of the industry, extracting a sizeable contribution from petroleum and determining its effective use. Moreover, the Venezuelan experience underlines the importance of the catalytic role of government policy in bringing about a carry-over of the export expansion into the rest of the economy. In many cases, the eventualities assumed by the classical and neoclassical economists and their followers, by some staple and regional economists, and by some economic historians, does not work in peripheral countries.

The case of petroleum in Venezuela seems to contradict the viewpoint that denies that primary production for exports can bring forth economic growth in the rest of the economy, or which makes this conditional to the presence of certain social and economic factors. Certainly, these preconditions or factors were not present in Venezuela during all or most of the time period covered by this study.

It shows that a potentially leading primary type export sector is capable of bringing about the economic development of a peripheral country with a pattern of trade based on primary product exports. Although a cursory examination of the evidence in many countries for different historical time periods suggests that this experience can be generalized, a greater number of case studies are required before definite conclusions can be reached on this issue. Not only would a wider range of countries be needed, but a greater coverage from the standpoint of products.

Although there are other reasons determining the aversion toward primary type exports, to an important degree it stems from the belief that these products cannot efficiently transmit their expansion to the other sectors of the economy, and that no successful development process can be ignited if they are relied upon. The empirical evidence examined suggests that this is an ill-founded belief. Granted, that testing of these ideas remains incomplete, a reexamination of the economic policies of many peripheral countries is suggested by the conclusions of this study.

It should be emphasized that, even if the results were more general, they would not imply that primary exports should revert to a central role in the economies of peripheral countries.

Our results would recommend the formulation of development policies only after a careful evaluation of all alternatives, *including* those in which primary exports play an important role. The results furthermore suggest that, in scanning for an optimum growth path, the ineffectiveness of primary exports as leading sectors should not be taken for granted.

From 1900 to 1935

Venezuela was one of the poorest countries in Latin America at the turn of the century. Its economy was based on the export of coffee and cocoa, and other minor items like hides. Its trade sector was typically in balance, with exports slightly exceeding imports, in order to allow for repayment of the country's external debt.[9]

However, prospecting Venezuelans followed leads of black substance (petroleum) emerging freely around Maracaibo Lake, and mounted an effort to find exploitable deposits. They lacked the experience and the know-how it took, which was first developed in Pennsylvania in the late 19th century and spread to northern Europe, to accomplish the early commercial finds. As has been described in Chapter 4, the Caribbean Development Corporation, a subsidiary of the Anglo-Dutch Shell Oil Company, finally began the production and sale of oil from 1914 onward.

Because the hypothesis that this research has been trying to test has to do with primary activities as leading sectors in economic development, and that presupposes that the activity in question has attained a certain critical minimum size, it should be noted that the first three decades of oil production did not achieve this threshold. It is true that petroleum sales and value added spurted from 1914 to 1930, but the initial base was very low (zero at the limit), and relative to the total economic activity of Venezuela, the sector was insignificant. When petroleum began to approach the requisite minimum size, the world depression of the 1930s postponed the start of the testing period until 1936. It was then that petroleum revenue, production, and investment began a golden path expansion at a very brisk pace, and from a size relative to the total economy that was relevant to the hypothesis.

After the end of World War I, and particularly since the sensational explosive find of Los Barrosos in 1922, oil activity began to rapidly transform Venezuela from a rural agricultural economy to an increasingly urban one. But in the first third of the century, the oil, mineral, construction, and commercial riches that were to later warp the social economy of the country, had not begun to generate major pockets of poverty or sizable inequalities. The negative effects of oil prospecting, extraction, and transportation had only left in their wake a small sliver of farmers on the eastern side of Lake Maracaibo. The nation was characterized more by the relative equality of poor societies, which growth processes have not yet dented. Economic privilege at the time was that typically generated by land-holding latifundia (although with little prevalence of absenteeism) and by the political corruption of the long dictatorship of Juan Vicente Gómez and his cronies. In fact, the latter's presence made impossible the setting of the preconditions for growth, as he was vehemently opposed to it, as his refusal to establish oil refineries in Venezuela during his mandate makes evidently clear.

The Period from 1974 to 2000

By 1973 Venezuela seemed to have taken off into self-sustained growth. But many developing countries in Latin America, Asia, and central and eastern Europe have shown just how fickle W. W. Rostow's five stages of economic growth can be. There are many examples that show retrogression is not only possible but also plausible within historical contexts, as empire after empire has bitten the dust. Venezuela appears to be a recent case in point.

It is all the more remarkable because the slippage has occurred within a period marked by the highest oil prices in memory, achieved at various surging spells in 1974–1975, 1979–1980, 1989–1990, and 1999–2000.[10] The petroleum sector during this period certainly has had the size to continue to be the leading activity of the Venezuelan economy, but it otherwise lacked the dynamism of the golden growth path of 1936–1973. The rate of expansion was disappointing and uneven. So contrasting with the early 1900–1935 period, it was not the relative mark that petroleum left in the overall economy that was lacking, but the steady growth path that characterized the exploration and exploitation of oil in the initial part of the century. Thus, oil activities do not qualify as a leading sector of economic growth in the latter part of the century in terms of its rate of growth (or rather its lack thereof).

This makes evident one of the dilemmas of primary sector expansion, in terms of ensuring an adequate relay of other lines of production once the maturity of the original line's expansion loses its momentum, because of that or other reasons. This does not seem to happen as frequently if there are multiple leading sectors or if they are composed of industrial products. And even though this problem does not detract from the qualities of leading sectors, through growth paths, as illustrated during 1936 to 1973 in Venezuela, it raises doubts about the resiliency of the development experience when the expansion of the leading sector slackens. Certainly, although not central to the hypothesis tested, this is one of the assertions of development economists mentioned in Chapter 2 that remains valid, at least from the vantage point of Venezuelan experience.

On top of the downers of the growth experience of Venezuela, it appears clear that the distribution of income worsened in the last quarter of the century, both from a regional and personal income viewpoint. This can also be said of the newly measured levels of poverty and indigence.

Looking at the results from household surveys conducted by the Venezuelan Central Statistics and Information Office and the Central Bank's family budget studies on household income and expenditures, it appears that real national income per head, after expanding during the 1970s, retraced its steps and lost ground during the 1980s. This trend continued unabated during the 1990s. Looking at poverty, the number of persons below the poverty line increased except in the countryside (where it happens that the rate is most severe). The same stands for the levels of indigence.[11]

In terms of wage income, a decline of over 30 percent in the real minimum wage of urban workers between 1980 and 1989 was accompanied by an increase in urban unemployment of nearly 50 percent during the same time period. All these certainly suggest that wage incomes were under pressure in this period. The rampant inflation that atypically characterized the Venezuelan economy during the 1990s was generally tied to declining real wages, so a worsening of constant-purchasing-power wages certainly occurred. The crime waves afflicting the urban areas of the country are an indication of the extreme tensions of increasing portions of the population, being pressured by low wages, poverty, and even indigence.

With respect to regional inequalities, the population of Venezuela had become one of the most urbanized in Latin America between 1970 and the late 1980s. The rate of urbanization grew from 61 percent to 80 percent in less than two decades. (Only Argentina and Uruguay are presently more urban.) The population is concentrated in seven or eight mid- to large-sized cities, with Caracas and its environs being a megalopolis. These large urban areas have left the rural countryside in their wake, with increasing disparity between the income levels in these segments of Venezuelan society. Even the gulf between Caracas and the other cities seems to have widened as industries, the service sector, and government are increasingly concentrated there, notwithstanding the continuing encroachment of shantytowns (*ranchos*) along many of the hilly areas of the capital city.

SUMMARY

Using Venezuela as a test case, this book has endeavored to consider whether primary products should be trusted as leading sectors of economic development. Recall that in order to qualify (from Chapters 2 and 3) a sector must have a significantly large specific weight relative to the economy as a whole, and deploy a rapid pace of expansion. Only the period from 1936 to 1973 qualifies for the test of the hypotheses in this country. This is why emphasis has been placed on this period in the concluding chapter.

Even during the solid years of golden growth, it became evident in the analysis that unless the various contributions of the leading sector are put to good use by the government, there might not be a carryover of the expansion in the primary export line to the rest of the economy. Overall the contributions of oil investment, the fiscal side of the economy, its foreign sector, its product, income, backward and forward linkages, multiplier and accelerator effects, and generally its overall contribution through the retained value of its total expenditures, were well utilized by the Venezuelan government, although there was plenty of room for improvement. Thus the Venezuelan economy grew rapidly, although it did not develop as much, beset by income distribution problems and general inequalities.

Yet the leading sector faltered, without leaving the country prepared to move into other expanding lines, during the period from 1974 to 2000.

This lack of resilience on the part of the Venezuelan economy underlines another risk of relying entirely on one, rather than several, export lines, and in successfully facing declines in the export potential of primary products for cyclical or structural reasons. More recently, for example, Chile has been basing its expansion, from the mid-1970s to the present, on an array of primary products, not just one.

In the last quarter of this century, the lack of dynamism in the petroleum industry could not be countenanced even with the multiplying of their prices up to the year 2000. The income terms-of-trade effect was the reverse side of the coin of stagnation in the volumes of oil produced. The latter had deleterious effects over a substantial part of the retained value of total expenditures, particularly in important aspects of production and backward and forward linkage factors. At the same time, the external and fiscal impacts were dissipated through a surge in consumptive imports and unproductive government projects. The spree was not satisfied with the petroleum boom, but necessitated the acquisition of a sizeable foreign debt. Matters only became worse when not only did oil production stagnate and decline further, but also their prices began to recede, on and off, to lower levels. The increasing corruption involved in governmental affairs during the last three decades led to political disarray that eventually buried the traditional political parties (as well as new movements) of Venezuela and generated an aura of uncertainly that persists to this day, pervading the whole socioeconomic fabric of the country.

NOTES

1. This was the "Golden Period" of development through petroleum in Venezuela. Earlier in the century, it was still a smallish part of the economy, while later its influence was restricted to a favorable or unfavorable terms-of-trade effect, without a significant increase in production or investment in the oil industry.

2. See Banco Central de Venezuela, *El Ingreso Nacional de Venezuela* (Caracas, 1949).

3. The government manipulated other variables, such as the price of oil by-products in the local market; the level of skills of the workers in the industry; the use of company roads, schools, and hospitals by the general public; and processing and further use of crude oil and its by-products.

4. See Carl Shoup, *The Fiscal System of Venezuela* (Baltimore, 1954).

5. See CORDIPLAN, *Primera Encuesta Nacional de Ingresos y Gastos Familiares en Venezuela* (Caracas, 1962). Also see Comisión Nacional de la Vivienda and Banco Nacional de Ahorro y Préstamo, *Estudio del Mercado Real de Vivienda* (Caracas, 1970).

6. See, for example, William Cline, *Potential Effects of Income Redistribution on Economic Growth: Latin American Cases* (New York, 1972).

7. See Hector Valecillos, "Consideraciones en torno a la Distribución del Ingreso en Venezuela y Examen de sus Posibles Cambios Recientes," in *Cuadernos de la Sociedad Venezolana de la Planificación,* nos. 108–10. Also consult this essay for tabular information on the patterns of income distribution in Venezuela. It should be noted that during the Perez Jimenez years, the functional distribution of income also seems to have suffered a setback, as Table 13.4 suggests.

8. Wage information is quite scarce in Venezuela, and generally unreliable. However, with data presented in the Memorias of the Banco Central de Venezuela, the following real wage index was constructed, from the mid-1950s:

Year	Index
1946 (first semester)	100.0
1948 (first semester)	132.2
1950 (first semester)	140.2
1952 (first semester)	152.6
1954 (first semester)	180.1
1955 (second semester)	186.0

Unfortunately the Central Bank discontinued the calculation of the series on which this index was based. From 1956 on, the information is less satisfactory, but consult Dirección General de Estadísticas y Censos, *Anuario Estadístico* (Caracas, various years), and *Encuesta Nacional de Hogares por Muestreo* (Caracas, various years).

9. Actually at the beginning of the 20th century, the Western powers, led by Germany and backed by the United States, laid siege to the Port of La Guaira, just north of Caracas, and remained in control until Venezuela agreed to the resumption of its external payments, and established a repayment plan with exports as collateral.

10. Although the latter is questionable once we adjust for price increases in nonpetroleum goods during the last quarter of the century, which left the price of petroleum in real terms at just about the levels attained in the early to mid-1970s.

11. It should be noted that the poverty line in Venezuela stood at $70.60 (in 1988 prices) and the line of indigence at $35.30, both being monthly figures. Certainly an important factor in compressing these levels even further, in real terms, is the increase in the relative price of foodstuffs in Venezuela which rose at the highest clip in Latin America, increasing by 127.7 percent compared to other goods and services included in the consumer price index, from 1970 to 1986. As of this writing, poverty touches 68 percent of Venezuelans according to Moises Naim, "The Venezuelan Story: Revisiting the Conventional Wisdom," *Journal of Democracy,* (April 2000). It had increased the most and the fastest in all of Latin America, save Chile according to Terry Lynn Karl, *The Paradox of Plenty: Oil Boom and Petrostates* (Berkeley, 1997). If the last 20 years are considered, indigence has tripled and poverty has more than doubled. Only Nicaragua, Haiti, and Guayana were worse during the two decades as stated by Naim, *op. cit.* Yet, according to the Inter-American Development Bank (IDB), *Economic and Social Progress in Latin America 2000 Report,* inequality was less than the mean for Latin America. In fact only Costa Rica, Peru, and Uruguay had a more egalitarian distribution of income. However, it suffered one of the worst declines in equality during the 1990s, accord-

ing to Miguel Szekeli and Marianne Hilbert, "The 1990s in Latin America: Another Decade of Persistent Inequality," Working Paper (2000). As to regional concentration of income, it should be noted that urbanization rates in Venezuela reached 87 percent, according to the Lincoln Institute of Land Policy, *Access to Land by the Urban Poor, 2002, Annual Round Table*, (Cambridge, Mass., 2002).

Bibliography

Adams, N. A. "Import Structure and Economic Growth: A Comparison of Cross-Section and Time-Series Data." *Economic Development and Cultural Change,* January 1967.

Auty, R. *Patterns of Development: Resources, Policy and Economic Growth.* London: Edward Arnold, 1995.

Auty, R. M., and A. H. Gelb. "Political Economy of Resource-Abundant States." In *Resource Abundance and Economic Development,* ed. R. M. Auty. New York: Oxford University Press, 2001.

Baldwin, R. E. *Economic Development and Growth.* New York: John Wiley, 1966.

———. "Export Technology and Development from a Subsistence Level." *Economic Journal,* March 1963.

———. "Patterns of Settlement in Newly Settled Regions." *Manchester School of Social and Economic Studies* 24 (1956): 161–79.

Banco Central de Venezuela. *Anuario de Cuentas Nacionales.* Caracas, various years.

———. *El Ingreso Nacional de Venezuela.* Caracas, 1949.

———. *La Economía Venezolana en los Ultimos Treinta Años.* Caracas, 1971, 1972.

———. *La Economía Venezolana en los Ultimos Veinticinco Años.* Caracas, 1966.

———. *Informe Económico.* Caracas, 1965, 1969, 1972, 1973, and various other years, and unpublished data.

———. *El Ingreso Nacional de Venezuela.* Caracas, 1949.

———. *Memoria.* Caracas, 1947, 1949, 1959, and various other years.

Banco Interamericano de Desarrollo. *Datas Básicos y Parámetros Socio-Económicos de Venezuela, 1950–1965.* Washington, D.C., 1967.

Baran, E. M. "The Economic Development of Venezuela." Ph.D. diss., Radcliffe College, 1959.

Baran, P. *The Political Economy of Growth.* New York: Monthly Review Press, 1957.

Bauer, P. "International Economic Developments." *Economic Journal,* March 1959.

Birdsall, N., T. Pinckney., and R. Sabot. "Natural Resources, Human Capital, and Growth." In *Resource Abundance and Economic Development,* ed. R.M. Auty New York: Oxford University Press, 1997.

Bracho Sierra, J.J. *Cincuenta Años de Ingresos Fiscales.* Caracas, 1963.

Bulmer-Thomas, Victor. *The Political Economy of Central America Since 1920.* Cambridge: Cambridge University Press, 1987.

Cairncross, Alec K. "International Trade and Economic Development." *Económica,* August 1961.

Cardosa, Ciro F.S. "The Formation of the Coffee Estate in Nineteenth-Century Costa Rica." In *Land and Labour in Latin America. Essays on the Development of Agrarian Capitalism in the Nineteenth and Twentieth Centuries,* ed. Kenneth Duncan and Ian Rutledge with the collaboration of Colin Hardin. Cambridge: Cambridge University Press, 1977.

Caves, Richard E. "Review" of Gerald Meier's *International Trade and Development. Economic Development and Cultural Change,* October 1964.

———. "Vent-for-Surplus Models of Trade and Growth." In *Trade , Growth, and the Balance of Payments,* ed. R.E. Baldwin et al. Chicago: Rand McNally, 1965.

Caves, Richard E., and Richard H. Holton. *The Canadian Economy: Prospect and Retrospect, Harvard Economic Studies.* Vol. 112. Cambridge, Mass.: Harvard University Press, 1959.

Chambers, E.J., and D.F. Gordon. "Primary Products and Economic Growth: An Empirical Measurement." *Journal of Political Economy* (August, 1966): 315–32.

Cline, W. *Potential Effects of Income Redistribution on Economic Growth: Latin American Cases.* New York: Praeger, 1972.

Comisión Nacional de la Vivienda and Banco Nacional de Ahorro y Préstamo. *Estudio del Mercado Real de Vivienda.* Caracas, 1970.

Corden, W.M. " The Effects of Trade on the Rate of Growth." In *Trade, Balance of Payments and Growth,* ed. J.N. Bhagwati et al. Amsterdam, 1971, pp. 117–43.

Corden, W.M., and J.P. Neary. "Booming Sector and Dutch Disease Economics: A Survey." *Economic Journal* 92 (1982): 64–111.

CORDIPLAN. *Primera Encuesta Nacional de Ingresos y Gastos Familiares en Venezuela.* Caracas, 1962.

Córdova, Armando. "La Estructura Económica Tradicional y el Impacto del Petróleo en Venezuela." *Economía y Ciencias Sociales,* January–March 1963.

Cortés Condé, R.R. "The Export Economy of Argentina 1880–1930." In *The Latin American Economies: Growth and the Export Sector 1880–1990,* ed. R. Cortés Condé and S. Hunt. New York: Macmillan, 1985.

Diaz-Alejandro, C.F. "No Less Than One Hundred Years of Argentine Economic History." In *Comparative Development Perspectives,* ed. G. Ranis et al. Boulder: Westview, 1984.

Dirección General de Estadísticas y Censos. *Anuario Estadístico.* Caracas, 1938, 1951.

———. *Encuesta Nacional de Hogares por Muestreo.* Caracas, various years.

Duncan, R.C. "Agricultural Export Prospects for Sub-Saharan Africa." *Development Policy Review* 11 (1993): 31–45.

Economic Commission for Latin America, United Nations. *Recent Facts and Trends in the Venezuelan Economy.* Mexico, D.F., 1951.

Economic Survey of Latin America and the Caribbean, United Nations Publication, 1998–2001.

Egaña, M. R. *Tres Décadas de Producción Petrolera*. Caracas, 1947.

Evans, D. "Alternative Perspectives on Trade and Development." In *Handbook of Development Economics*, ed. H. Chenery and T. N. Srinivasan. Amsterdam: North Holland, 1989.

Ferran, B. Unpublished estimates presented in lectures on the economic development of Venezuela, delivered at the Universidad Central De Venezuela, Caracas, 1963.

Findlay, R., and M. Lundah. "Natural Resources, "Vent-for-Surplus," and the Staples Theory." In *From Classical Economics to Development Economics*, ed. G. M. Meier. New York: St. Martin's Press, 1994.

Gelb, A. "Adjustment to Windfall Gains." In *Natural Resources and the Macroeconomy*, ed. J. P. Neary and S. Van Wijnbergen. Center for Economic Policy Research: MIT Press, 1986.

Grubel, Herbert. "The Demand for International Reserves: A Critical Review of the Literature." *Journal of Economic Literature*, December 1971.

Gunder Frank, A. *Capitalism and Underdevelopment in Latin America*. New York: Monthly Review Press, 1967.

Haberler, Gottfried. *International Trade and Economic Development*. Cairo: National Bank of Egypt, 1959.

Hirschman, A. *The Strategy of Economic Development*, Yale Studies in Economics, 10. New Haven, Conn.: Yale University Press, 1958.

Informes de Conservación. Caracas, several years.

Innis, H. *The Fur Trade in Canada: An Introduction to Canadian Economic History*. New Haven, Conn.: Yale University Press, 1930.

———. *The Cod Fisheries: The History of an International Economy*. New Haven, Conn.: Yale University Press, 1940.

Inter-American Development Bank (IDB). *Economic and Social Progress in Latin America 2000 Report*, 2000.

Karl, T. L. *The Paradox of Plenty: Oil Boom and Petrostates*. Berkeley: University of California Press, 1997.

Krueger, A. "Trade Policy as an Input to Development." *American Economic Review, Papers and Proceedings* 70, no. 2 (May 1980): 288–92.

Kuznets, Simon. *Six Lectures on Economic Growth*. Glencoe, Ill.: Free Press, 1959.

Lal, D., and H. Myint. *The Political Economy of Poverty, Equity and Growth*. Oxford: Clarendon Press, 1996.

Lewis, W. A. "Economic Development with Unlimited Supplies of Labour," *The Manchester School of Economic and Social Studies*, 1954.

Lieuwein, Edwin. *Petroleum in Venezuela*. Berkeley: University of California Press, 1954.

Lincoln Institute of Land Policy. *Access to Land by the Urban Poor, 2002, Annual Round Table*. Cambridge, Mass.: 2002.

Maza-Zavala, D. F. *Venezuela: Una Economía Dependiente*. Caracas, 1964.

Meier, Gerald E., ed. *From Classical Economics to Development Economics*. New York: St. Martin's Press, 1994.

Meier, Gerald E. "Economic Development and the Transfer Mechanism: Canada 1895–1913." *Canadian Journal of Economics and Political Science*, February 1953.

———. *The International Economics of Development*. New York: Harper & Row, 1968.

———. "Conditions of Export-Led Development Note." In *Leading Issues in Economic Development*, ed. G. E. Meier. Oxford: Oxford University Press, 1984.

Mill, John Stuart. *Principles of Political Economy*, ed. W. J. Ashley. New York: Longmans, Green, 1929.

Ministerio de Fomento. *Anuario Estadístico*. Caracas, 1937, 1938, 1957–1963, and various other years.

———. *Censo de Población*. Caracas, 1950, 1961.

———. *Memoria*. Caracas, several years.

———. *Revista de Fomento*. Caracas, various years.

Ministerio de Fomento, Dirección General de Estadísticas. *Anuario Estadístico*. Caracas, 1938 and various years.

Ministerio de Minas e Hidrocarburos. *Petróleo y Otros Datos Estadísticos*. Caracas, 1964, 1965, 1966, 1969, 1972.

Ministerio de Minas e Hidrocarburos, Oficina Técnica. Unpublished data.

Myint, H. "The 'Classical Theory' of International Trade and the Underdeveloped Countries." *Economic Journal* (June 1958): 317–37.

Myrdal, G. "Trade as a Mechanism of International Inequality." In *Leading Issues in Economic Development*, ed. G. E. Meier. Oxford: Oxford University Press, 1984, pp. 498–503.

Naim, M. "The Venezuelan Story: Revisiting the Conventional Wisdom," *Journal of Democracy*, 12, no. 2 (April 2000).

North, D. C. "Agriculture in Regional Economic Growth" and ensuing "Discussion" by V. W. Ruttan and O. V. Wells, *Journal of Farm Economics* (December 1959).

———. *The Economic Growth of the United States, 1970–1860*. New York: Norton, 1966.

Nurkse, R. *Patterns of Trade and Development*. Wicksell Lectures. Stockholm: Almquist, 1959.

———. "Trade Theory and Development Policy." In *Economic Development for Latin America*, ed. H. S. Ellis. New York: St Martin's Press, 1961, pp. 236–45.

OPEC Annual Statistical Bulletin. Summary Tables and Basic Indicators, 2001.

Perez Castillo, J. P. "Some Aspects of Venezuela's Economic Development during the Post–World War II Period: 1945–1960." Ph.D. diss., Tulane University, 1963.

Prebisch, R. *The Economic Development of Latin America and Its Principle Problems*. Santiago: ECLA/UN, 1950. Reprinted in *Economic Bulletin for Latin America* 4: 277–303.

———. "Commercial Policy in the Underdeveloped Countries." *American Economic Review*, May 1959.

Rabe, S. "The Road to OPEC: United States Relations with Venezuela, 1919–1979." *The Americas*, April 1983.

Robertson, D. H. "The Future of International Trade." In *Readings in the Theory of International Trade*, ed. H. S. Ellis and Lloyd Metzler. Philadelphia, Pa.: Irwin, 1947.

Rodriguez, F., and J. D. Sachs. "Why Do Resource Abundant Economies Grow More Slowly? A new explanation and an application to Venezuela," *Journal of Economic Growth* 4 (1999): 277–303.

Rollins, C. "Raw Materials Development and Economic Growth: A Study of the Bolivian and Venezuelan Experience." Ph.D. diss., Stanford University, 1956.

Salazar-Carillo, J. *Oil and Development in Venezuela during the Twentieth Century.* Westport, Conn.: Praeger, 1994.

Singer, H. W. "The Distribution of Gains between Investing and Borrowing Countries." *American Economic Review, Papers and Proceedings of the Sixty-Second Annual Meeting,* 1949; *American Economic Review* 40 (May 1950).

Shoup, C. *The Fiscal System of Venezuela.* Baltimore: Johns Hopkins Press, 1954.

Smith, A. *An Inquiry into the Nature and Causes of the Wealth of Nations.* London: W. Stratham, 1776; and Cannan edition, New York: Modern Library, 1937.

Szekeli, M., and M. Hilbert. "The 1990s in Latin America: Another Decade of Persistent Inequality." Working Paper. Interdevelopment Bank, 2000.

United Nations. *Statistical Yearbook.* New York, 1954.

United States Tariff Commission. *Economic Controls and Commercial Policy in Venezuela.* Washington, D.C.: U.S. Government Printing Office, 1945.

Valecillos, H. "Consideraciones en torno a la Distribución del Ingreso en Venezuela y Examen de sus Posibles Cambios Recientes." *Cuadernos de la Sociedad Venezolana de la Planificación.* Nos. 108–10.

Veloz, R. *Finances and the Economy of Venezuela from 1830 to 1944.* Caracas, 1945.

Wallich, H. "Monetary Problems of an Export Economy." *Harvard EC Studies.* Vol. 88. Cambridge, Mass.: Harvard University Press, 1950.

Watkins, M. "A Staples Theory of Economic Growth." *Canadian Journal of Economics and Political Sciences* (May 1963): 141–58.

———. "Booming Sector and Dutch Disease Economies: Survey and Consolidation." *Oxford Economic Papers* 36 (1984): 359–80.

World Bank. *Commodity Markets and the Developing Countries.* Several years.

Index

About the Authors

JORGE SALAZAR-CARRILLO is Professor of Economics at Florida International University and Director of FIU's Center of Economic Research. He is also a former non-resident Senior Fellow at the Brookings Institution.

BERNADETTE WEST is a Lecturer in Economics at the University of Miami and Florida International University.